Pictures on front cover:

The pictures on the front cover of this book are an A to Z of black achievers. Some pictures have been chosen because of their names, while others have been included cryptically because of the field they are in, or genre they represent. See if you can work out all the clues.

(Answers on the back cover)

The Ultimate Guide on Black Entertainment Achievement & History

Volume I

BY

Jak Bubeula-Dodd

Nu Jak Media Publishing
London

Nu Jak Media books may be purchased for educational, business, or sales promotional use. For information please write to: Special Markets Department, Nu Jak Media Publishing, 122-126 High Road, London NW6 4HY.

First published in the United Kingdom in 1997 by Edutainment and Leisure Enterprises in association with Pepukayi Book Distribution Services.

SECOND EDITION

Library of Congress Cataloging-in-Publication Data

ISBN 0-9532017-1-6

305. 896
BUB

Preface

...for Qiana and Kaiyin and Xi'ann.

Thanks

Firstly, thanks to Glynis, the yin of my yang, and our three children Qiana, Kaiyin and Xi'ann for the love, understanding and time afforded me to complete this book. Next, I would like to thank all the people who helped to make it possible. Firstly, those in the US, Sandy "Madam Prez" Merid who's Midas touch made anything and everything seem possible, Robert Tate whose initial enthusiasm and inspiration allowed me to dare to dream, to Mel Watkins for his advice and professional guidance, and to Charles Harris former vice president of HarperCollins, whose encouraging words and actions set the ball in motion for this edition.

I would also like to express my sincere gratitude and thanks to Jimmy Lawrence for the time, hours, and resources spent supporting the project – Thanks again Jim; to Pepukayi Book Distribution Services for providing the wherewithal and infrastructure to develop an earlier edition of this book, to Joseph Jules who provided me with what seemed an endless source of research material, to Jacinta Gerald-Gayle for her eternal optimism and love, to Clive Francis and his Silver Graphic Ink Team (particularly for the creative input of Vasco Horta) for their design and flare, to my life long friend Jay Mastin, who was always there and always willing to provide a helping hand, to Blossom Jackson, for her important suggestions early on, to BDJ Ventures in Philadelphia (singling out Darnell K. Daisy) for their belief, commitment and patience, to the comedian Rudi Lickwood for his unique contribution, to Dinah Lartey, for constantly keeping me on my toes and helping me to stick to deadlines, to Sandra Mae Thomas for her proof reading amendments, to Ronald Cushney and Joi "with an eye" Ferguson for their continuing moral support, to Ismail Muhammad for co-ordinating the book's production, and a very very special thank you to Anthony "let's get the job done" Noel, whose involvement served as a catalyst for the completion and availability of this book.

To all of those who gave me the encouragement when I needed it, a heartfelt thanks; you know who you are. It's fair to say I would not have finished this book without you. I would also like to thank the staff of Schomburg Center for Research in Black Culture in New York, London University for the use of the library facilities at the School of African and Oriental Studies, and I extend that to all the libraries I have utilized which are far to numerous to mention. I have to say a big thank you for the photographic contribution to this work given by Europe's largest black newspaper - *The Voice* - with which I had a weekly column for four years, especially the head of photography, Colin Patterson. I would also like to thank the Johnson Publishing Company whose sources were very helpful in compiling this book. Whether it was an *Ebony* article, or an excerpt from *Before the Mayflower*, often their publications were a reliable source of information. At this point a special mention must go to ALL the authors whose research I have included. I truly can appreciate the work pioneers like J. A. Rogers had to go through. In particular I thank and applaud authors like Ivan Van Sertima and Jessie Carney Smith whose material I found invaluable and consistently inspiring. And before I forget, I have to thank all the achievers who came and made their contribution, because without them there would have been nothing for any of us to write about. But above all I thank The Creator for ordaining the positive forces of the universe and destiny to allow this book to come into being.

About the Author

The Author, Jak, as the saying suggests, is a man of many talents and indeed he has mastered many of these. He does, however, regard himself primarily as an artist/producer - the medium most natural to him in expressing his creativity. He was born in London during the 1960s to parents from the Caribbean but was raised by his evangelist grandmother, with a church upbringing in the Pentecostal tradition. It was as leader of his church band, *The Conquerors,* that he had the opportunity to develop his early musical creativity.

Jak recalls that while growing up he was always interested in learning about the achievements of great people regardless of color. 1970s London was, and still is, the most cosmopolitan city in the UK, if not Europe. However, at the time this was not often reflected on the TV or other media. This was certainly true of the educational institutions with its teaching curriculum that had yet to embrace a new multi-cultural dynamism that had become the new reality in the United Kingdom.

Nonetheless, Jak looks back fondly on his school years remembering whenever there was a school general assembly, he was asked to sing and play the piano before the teachers and pupils. Ironically, it was his love affair with music that stimulated his interest in African beats and rhythms as a whole, and African American music in particular. This in turn fuelled his interest in other achievements by people of color, in the United States, and although he couldn't have known at the time, he was laying the foundations for a subject he would later study more meticulously.

From school Jak went to college to study sociology but soon quit to join a newly formed pop band with a publishing deal and spent most of the 1980s playing and recording experimental music. This included a series of music workshops where he taught music to the unemployed. This vocation prompted Jak to return back to his studies-the result of which -led to a new career as a peripatetic social worker.

Whether it was because of his cultural background, or a result of his life experiences, Jak quickly discovered that for him (and for other black men in the social work profession), the bulk of his case loads involved working with young people from the black community at risk of social exclusion. At about this time, Jak also became a part-time model and was used in an international advertising campaign, as the "face of *Interflora*" (the flower people). This single campaign lasted for three and a half years and set a record for a black British male model. It was, however, his experiences as a social worker that inspired him to devise a multi-cultural educational package, which could be played as a game.

Out of this educational package came two prototype board games, one of which was *Nubian Jak*. Initially, the concept involved highlighting achievements that people of color made to the UK and Europe. It became a world first when it was released at London's International Toy & Hobby Fair in January 1995, to rave media and public reviews. Next, a world version was researched and developed resulting in its introduction to the US in February 1996, to an equally enthusiastic reception.

The brand has since been developed into an exciting series of multi-media and edutainment products, some going on to win awards. There is also a Nubian Jak Academy involving educational life coaches working with schools, cultural institutions, youth organizations to facilitate workshops. In the summer of 2003, Jak was headhunted by a TV production company called, Zeal TV, to appear in a groundbreaking Channel 4 television series called *SuperHuman*. Although, Jak had previously received a fair amount of media coverage, when the show was screened in April and May 2004, to several million viewers around the UK, he was no longer Black Britain's biggest secret. A few months later this book would be released...

Jak and the box: Playing Black Jak?

About the book

Without a doubt, completing this book has been the hardest task I have ever had to undertake. It involved years of painstaking research, which became as much a labor of love, as it later became, a difficult and lonely journey. Although it is an expansion of the *Nubian Jak* game concept, none of my experiences with academia could prepare me for what I was trying to do. If one can imagine what it is like to study eight different topics simultaneously at degree level, well at least that's how it felt to me! And to compound this intensity, some of the facts discovered were so incredible I was left with a feeling of ambivalence. First, because I was completely overwhelmed by the information I was uncovering, and second, because I realized how difficult it would be to convince others of these truths. Especially, as some of it challenged the accepted perspective of the status quo. What I was attempting to do, no less, was symbolically piece together the jigsaw of the African experience and its Diaspora, by examining world history and the overall impact made to popular culture. Some mission! I was hoping the end result would be like a hall of fame edutainment book series, comparable to a global black *Guinness Book of Records* and a *Who's Who* of people of African descent. In truth, the enormity of such a task with the resources I had available made it appear beyond me, not to mention the implications and consequences. In fact, there were some questions that were not included because of the controversy and repercussions I knew they would cause. These were sacrificed not due to any cowardliness on my part, but for the overall good of this work. Besides you don't give a baby rare steak to eat. There were also so many other difficulties I faced including; geography, finance, language and stuff I won't mention. Although some things are impossible to achieve, sometimes the impossible is achievable. That is why it's true "The man who removes a mountain begins by removing small stones".

Anyway, I knew from a cultural standpoint, I was qualified to at least attempt the challenge. Being born in London of African Caribbean parentage, and having spent a bit of time in the United States, could only help me. Whether I have failed or succeeded, I will leave for history to determine.

Volume one is divided into two parts with each section consisting of eight chapters covering a specific topic. In part one there are multiple-choice questions to convey information about an event or personality, with the vast majority using no more than twenty-five words. For the record, the longest question in the book uses forty-five words,

while the shortest uses only four. It's also worth mentioning that I chose to adopt the Americanized spelling in this book solely for marketing and distribution reasons.
The second half of the book, part two, provides the answers with references of which there are over four thousand separate sources. Contributions to Africa, the Americas, Asia, Australia, and Europe are examined.

Because *Book of World Facts* is meant as a general account of a collective group experience, some questions may appear much easier than others. For instance, an African American youth is more likely to know about the exploits of Michael Jordan than the fact that Jesse Russell did as much as anybody in helping to kick-start the mobile phone industry. On the other hand, their parents may be well acquainted with many of the names during the civil rights era, but not be familiar with the man who helped in the liberation of the first black republic in the Americas- Toussaint L'Overture of Haiti. What is more relevant is that the questions are posed in such a way that they can be asked in ten or twenty years from now and still be relevant.

All in all, the contents of this book have culminated in it being a versatile reference guide that makes entertaining reading, or fun with family and friends. Yet it can be used in educational establishments such as schools, colleges, and universities.

It has been often said that "never has so many people known so little about so much". Ironically, with all the distractions of modern life, the real challenge facing us is that we may have to unlearn so many things in order for us to be able to learn things new.
Alas, some may find this book leads to even more questions than it can answer. But it is hoped that this will stimulate those individuals to conduct their own research. One could argue that it is these final missing pieces of the jigsaw, that need to be re-connected to the global picture of civilization, before humanity can understand where we are coming from. Only then can we make that successful transition, TOGETHER, in this new millennium.

Further information about *Nubian Jak* can be accessed at the web site:
www.nubianjak.com

Jak (October 2004)

Contents

Part I

Part II

Contents

Part I

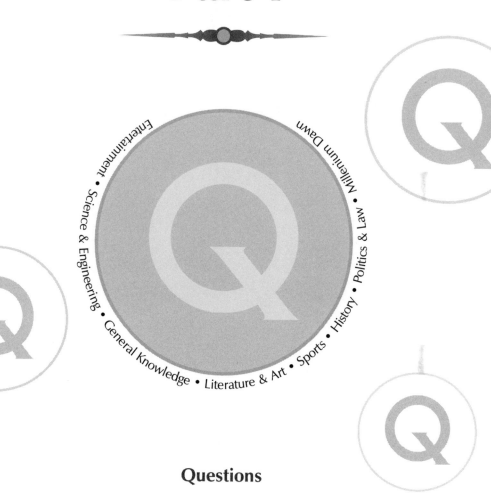

Entertainment • Millennium Dawn • Politics & Law • History • Sports • Literature & Art • General Knowledge • Science & Engineering

Questions

Entertainment

Beethoven (Sketch from life by Letronne)

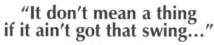

"It don't mean a thing
if it ain't got that swing..."

Duke Ellington

The language of entertainment is usually able to cross cultural divides and communicate universal feelings or emotions. Whether it's actors in silent movies or instrumentalists within a particular musical genre, entertainment enhances our lives and in some cases has been the fabric used to hold on to, or express ones humanity.

Because music is numbered among the seven liberal arts (the others being grammar, logic, rhetoric, maths, geometry, and astronomy), it has been used by virtually every culture in the advancement of their civilization. It is also an ever present in nature. For instance the whistling of the wind, or the sound of rain on hollowed surfaces, not to mention the singing of the birds. There is even a school of thought that believes a culture without music is like a culture without a soul. So if music is a universal language then it can be used to interpret and communicate ideas through the expressions of rhythm, dance, and acting.

Researching this topic was by comparison to other chapters in this book relatively easy. It may also be because of my personal interest in the entertainment industry. Equally, there is compelling evidence available highlighting the impact people of color have made to this field globally. Traditionally this has been a medium in which it has been difficult to suppress black creativity and its influence on mass popular culture.

The following questions in this section map out some of the contributions black artists have made to the entertainment industry. Many of these performers having achieved world-wide acclaim in their particular genre, have gone on to become international role models for a variety of positive causes.

A thorough cross-section of areas are explored, ranging from classical music and hip-hop, to reggae and jazz. Films, theater and dance are also included.

So relax and enjoy yourself through edutainment as you test your wit against your friends, family, or colleagues, in this, the first chapter of Nubian Jak's Book of World Facts.

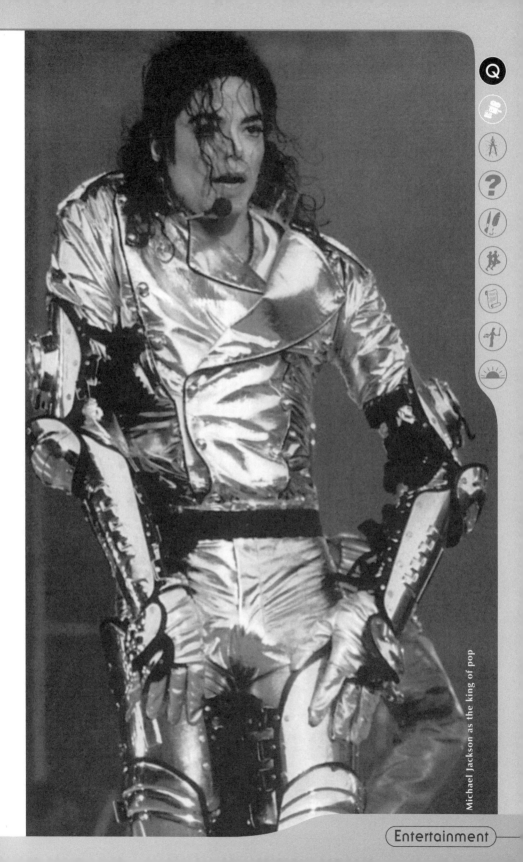

Michael Jackson as the king of pop

Taking five: Lauryn Hill

5.
Two of the following three female artists have both won five Grammies at a single award ceremony. Name the odd one out.
A) MARIAH CAREY
B) LAURYN HILL
C) ALICIA KEYS

6.
Which musical style from Southern Bronx was born out of the expressions of graffiti art, body popping, and rap?
A) GARAGE
B) HIP HOP
C) GANGSTER RAP

1.
For which one of the following films has Denzel Washington *not* won an Oscar?
A) THE PELICAN BRIEF
B) GLORY
C) TRAINING DAY

7.
The Cuban ballet dancer Carlos Acosta is regarded as one of the world's greatest contemporary dancers. But before becoming a ballet star what was his chosen style of dance?
A) TAP DANCING
B) MODERN JAZZ
C) BREAK DANCING

2.
Name the international music corporation that appointed L. A. Reid as its President and CEO in July 2000.
A) ARISTA
B) POLYDOR
C) E.M.I.

8.
In summer of 2003 Sean Paul made pop music history having 2 dancehall songs in the UK top three. Name the odd one out.
A) LIKE GLUE
B) BREATHE
C) GIMME THE LIGHT

3.
Which rap star collaborated with former Spice girl singer Mel B on her first solo international number one *I Want You Back*?
A) BUSTA RHYMES
B) MISSY ELLIOT
C) DR. DRE

9.
For which style of music is Kirk Franklin best known?
A) GOSPEL
B) BLUES
C) DRUM "N" BASS

4.
What is the biggest selling jazz album of all time and who recorded it?
A) HERBIE HANCOCK-MR HANDS
B) GEORGE BENSON-BREEZIN'
C) MILES DAVIS-*KIND OF BLUE*

10.
A Kiss from a Rose earned Seal three Grammy Awards. From which movie was it on the soundtrack?
A) THE LONG KISS GOODNIGHT
B) BATMAN RETURNS
C) BATMAN FOREVER

11.
This legendary artist penned the Eric Clapton
hit *I Shot the Sheriff*. Name him.
A) JIMI HENDRIX
B) BOB MARLEY
C) CURTIS MAYFIELD

12.
Which actor's voice was featured as Darth
Vader in *Stars Wars* and as the father of
Mustafa in *The Lion King*?
A) JAMES EARL JONES
B) ARSENIO HALL
C) GREGORY HINES

13.
Trinidadian musicians blended soul with
calypso to come up with this up-tempo dance
music. Name it.
A) SALSA
B) SOCA
C) CHUTNEY

14.
The song *Someday* by Eternal was the first
recording by a female group used as a
soundtrack for a Disney animation film. Name it.
A) ALADDIN
B) POCAHONTAS
C) THE HUNCH BACK OF NOTRE DAME

15.
Before being presented with the lifetime
achievement award at the 2002 Oscars, which
1960s film earned Sidney Poitier an Academy
Award for best actor?
A) GUESS WHO'S COMING TO DINNER
B) THE DEFIANT ONES
C) LILIES OF THE FIELD

16.
Which singer sang the title track to the James
Bond films *Goldfinger, Diamonds Are Forever*
and *Moonraker*?
A) CARLY SIMON
B) SHIRLEY BASSEY
C) BARBARA STREISAND

17.
Name the music awards founded by Kanya King
in the 1990s that has become the most
prestigious black awards ceremony in the world.
A) SOUL TRAIN AWARDS
B) THE MOBO'S
C) THE EMMA'S

18.
Always On Time, What's Love and what other
song in 2002, made Ashanti the first female
artist to have 3 records in the US top 10 charts?
A) ROCK WIT U
B) FOOLISH
C) RAIN ON

19.
Name the legendary record label founded by
the Jamaican producer, Coxone Dodd.
A) ISLAND
B) STUDIO 1
C) TROJAN

20.
Who is the most nominated Grammy award
artist of all time?
A) QUINCY JONES
B) LOUIS ARMSTRONG
C) ARETHA FRANKLIN

21.
Who has become the most sampled singer in
pop music history?
A) JAMES BROWN
B) GEORGE CLINTON
C) WYCLEF JEAN

Gospel prince: Kirk Franklin

Entertainment

Shooting Star: Bob Marley

27.
Which song by Destiny's Child was used as a soundtrack on the feature film *Charlie's Angels*?
A) INDEPENDENT WOMAN
B) SAY MY NAME
C) SURVIVOR

22.
Including 16 top 10 hits, name the first girl group in pop music history to score 5 consecutive U.S. No. 1s.
A) THE SPICE GIRLS
B) THE SUPREMES
C) THE THREE DEGREES

28.
Manu Dibango fused the Cameroon's traditional rhythms with Western pop, and is regarded as one of the founding pioneers of what musical style?
A) HIGH LIFE
B) WORLD MUSIC
C) SKA

23.
Cedric and Joel Hailey's hits include *All My Life*, *It's Real*, and *Thug N U Thug N Me*, but name their original band?
A) DREW HILL
B) JODECI
C) BOYZ II MEN

29.
Which singer songwriter was known as the "Father of the Blues"?
A) MUDDY WATERS
B) W. C. HANDY
C) B. B. KING

24.
Of the three following Rolling Stones chart toppers, which one was penned by the soul singer Bobby Womack?
A) THE LAST TIME
B) JUMPIN' JACK FLASH
C) I CAN'T GET NO SATISFACTION

30.
Who at the time of her double platinum debut album *Miss Thang* was the youngest person ever to top the U.S. album charts?
A) ROXANNE SHANTÉ
B) AALIYAH
C) MONICA

25.
Former *Brookside* soap star Paul Barber played a lead role in one of the highest grossing British films ever made. Name it.
A) THE FULL MONTY
B) HARRY POTTER
C) NOTTING HILL

31.
Who is generally acknowledged as the "Queen of Gospel Music"?
A) MAHALIA JACKSON
B) SHIRLEY CEASAR
C) YOLANDA ADAMS

26.
Al Jarreau was the first singer to have received Grammy awards in 3 different categories. Jazz, Rhythm and Blues: name the other category?
A) REGGAE
B) POP
C) GOSPEL

32.
What does LL stand for in LL cool J?
A) LYRICAL LORD
B) LIVING LEGEND
C) LADIES LOVE

33.
Which ragga megastar recorded the multi-million selling album *Mr. Lover Man*?
A) ELEPHANT MAN
B) SHAGGY
C) SHABBA RANKS

34.
Which Chubby Checker song is the only same recording to date to twice reached the Number One spot on the U.S. Billboard charts?
A) THE LAMBADA
B) THE LOCOMOTION
C) THE TWIST

35.
The actor Don Cheadle's film credits include *Boogie Nights*, *Oceans 11*, and two of the following three films. Name the odd one out.
A) PHONE BOOTH
B) SWORDFISH
C) TRAFFIC

36.
The rapper and actor, Tupac Shakur, starred in two of the following movies. Name the odd one out.
A) NEW JACK CITY
B) GRIDLOCK'D
C) MENACE II SOCIETY

37.
Whose compositions include *Mood Indigo*, *Sophisticated Lady* and *Satin Doll*?
A) COUNT BASIE
B) DUKE ELLINGTON
C) BILLY STRAYHORN

38.
Which unique musical style was created in Britain with the dominant influence of ragga and dance music?
A) JUNGLE
B) BANGRA
C) ACID HOUSE

39.
Which style of jazz music did Charlie Parker and Dizzy Gillespie help to innovate?
A) BEBOP
B) COOL JAZZ
C) SWING

40.
Which entertainer was born Tracy Marrow?
A) TRACY CHAPMAN
B) MR. T
C) ICE T

41.
Who was the first black screen star to win an Oscar?
A) BILLY DEE WILLIAMS
B) HATTIE McDANIEL
C) DOOLEY WILSON

42.
Which reggae super group penned the dance classic *Now That We Found Love*, the nineties smash *Generation Coming*, and the 2003 hit *Ain't Giving Up*?
A) INNER CIRCLE
B) UB 40
C) THIRD WORLD

43.
Who founded DEF JAM Records?
A) KRS-ONE
B) SUGE KNIGHT
C) RUSSELL SIMMONS

The godfather: James Brown

Entertainment

44.
In Spring 2003 Aisha Tyler became the first black actor to be included as one of the main cast in which multi Emmy winning series?
A) CHEERS
B) FRIENDS
C) ALLY MACBEAL

45.
Which duo scored success with the hits *Murder She Wrote* and *Tease Me*?
A) JIMMY JAM AND TERRY LEWIS
B) OUTKAST
C) SHAKA DEMUS AND PLIERS

46.
Who directed *Daughters of the Dust*, the first internationally acclaimed film by an African American woman?
A) NGOZI ONUWURA
B) DARNELL MARTIN
C) JULIE DASH

47.
Who recorded the first international rap hit *Rapper's Delight*?
A) THE ROCK STEADY CREW
B) ERIK B. AND RAKIM
C) THE SUGAR HILL GANG

48.
Between 2002 and 2003 the UK's most prestigious music prize, the Mercury Music Award, was won by a couple of the following three acts. Name the odd one out.
A) TERRI WALKER
B) MS DYNAMITE
C) DIZZEE RASCAL

49.
Kevin Hooks' filmography includes *Roots-The Gift*, *Strictly Business*, and *Passenger 57* but which one of the following TV shows has he not directed.
A) FAME
B) ST. ELSEWHERE
C) A DIFFERENT WORLD

50.
Which award winning black British director wrote Channel 4s most successful TV comedy series, *Desmonds*, and the critically acclaimed movie *For Queen And Country*?
A) TRIX WORREL
B) TERRY JERVIS
C) ISAAC JULIEN

51.
Which rapper has the nickname "God's Son"?
A) NELLY
B) NAS
C) JA RULE

52.
Who played Lt. Uhura in the cult space age TV series *Star Trek*?
A) NICHELLE NICHOLS
B) DIAHANN CARROLL
C) EARTHA KITT

53.
Whose *Diamond Life* album previously set a record as the biggest selling debut album by a British woman?
A) SADE
B) MICA PARIS
C) BERVERLEY KNIGHT

54.
Who is the only female singer to date to have seven consecutive number 1s in the U.S. pop charts?
A) DIANA ROSS
B) JANET JACKSON
C) WHITNEY HOUSTON

55.
Chuck D led this influential hip-hop outfit that included Professor Griff, Terminator X and Flavor Flav. Name it.
A) PUBLIC ENEMY
B) ARRESTED DEVELOPMENT
C) WU-TANG CLAN

56.
What year did Isaac Hayes win an Oscar for his musical score to the movie *Shaft*?
A) 1971
B) 1974
C) 1976

57.
She was the first black international opera superstar, and received a forty-two minute standing ovation at the Metropolitan Opera House in 1961, for her role as Leonora in *Verdi's Il Travatore*. Name her.
A) JESSYE NORMAN
B) LEONTYNE PRYCE
C) MARIAN ANDERSON

58.
Which popular British comedian and co-host of the annual *Red Nose Day* has helped to raise over $140 million for famine relief worldwide?
A) LENNY HENRY
B) RICHARD BLACKWOOD
C) ALI G

59.
Name the internationally renowned DJ sound system from London that Philip Levi, Tipper Irie, Smiley Culture, and Maxi Priest have all performed with.
A) SAXON
B) MASTERMIND
C) JAH SHAKA

60.
In the summer of 2004 Usher became only the second male solo artist since Elvis Presley to have three top 10 hits in the US charts at the same time. Who was the first?
A) JUSTIN TIMBERLAKE
B) 50 CENT
C) EMINEM

61.
Which guitaring giant penned the Rock Classics *Crazy Joe*, *Foxy Lady* and *Voodoo Child*?
A) LENNY KRAVITZ
B) JIMI HENDRIX
C) BO DIDLEY

62.
It was the first reggae song played on U.S. radio and topped the UK national charts. Name it.
A) THE ISRAELITES
B) UP TOWN TOP RANKING
C) YOU CAN GET IT IF YOU REALLY WANT

63.
Which Hip-hop soul diva has had multiple platinum No.1 albums with *What's the 411*, *My Life* and *No More Drama*?
A) MACEY GRAY
B) MARY J. BLIGE
C) JENNIFER LOPEZ

64.
Who was the founder of Tamla-Motown records?
A) SMOKEY ROBINSON
B) WILSON PICKET
C) BERRY GORDY

65.
In 1995 *This Is How We Do It* became an international dance anthem for which recording star?
A) MC HAMMER
B) MONTELL JORDAN
C) COOLIO

66.
Which 1940s musical starred Cab Calloway, Fats Waller and Lena Horne, the title of which has become Lena Horne's signature tune?
A) STRANGE FRUIT
B) STORMY WEATHER
C) HEARTS IN DIXIE

67.
Beethoven is described on record by his contemporaries as being "brown, dark, swarthy, tawny", even as "red". But how many symphonies did Beethoven write?
A) FIVE
B) NINE
C) TWENTY SEVEN

Entertainment

68.
For which branch of the arts did Katherine Dunham and Alvin Ailey become world-renowned?
A) ACTING
B) DANCE
C) PERFORMANCE POETRY

69.
Which band formerly led by Michael Rose became reggae's first ever Grammy-award winners?
A) STEEL PULSE
B) THE TWINKLE BROTHERS
C) BLACK UHURU

72.
Halle Berry became the first black recipient of the best actress award at the Oscars for her role in which of the following films?
A) FLINTSTONES
B) MONSTER'S BALL
C) X-MEN

73.
Which of the following Jazz artists originally led a nineteen band called the Jazz Warriors?
A) JULIAN JOSEPH
B) RONNY JORDAN
C) COURTNEY PINE

Talent has everything to do with it: Angela Bassett

70.
Which actress won a Golden Globe Award for her portrayal of Tina Turner in *What's Love Got To Do With It*?
A) ANGELA BASSETT
B) THANDIE NEWTON
C) ROBIN GIVENS

71.
Which artist/producer has a recording studio named Paisley Park?
A) JERMAINE DUPRI
B) PRINCE
C) R. KELLY

74.
The Ethiopian filmmaker, Haile Gerima's 1993 international award-winning screenplay, *Sankofa*, was named after which type of animal?
A) BEAR
B) BABOON
C) BIRD

75.
Which reggae artist is known as "The Cool Ruler"?
A) DENNIS BROWN
B) GREGORY ISAACS
C) PETER TOSH

76.
Samuel L. Jackson is in the record books as the actor believed to have made the most films during what decade?
A) 1970s
B) 1980s
C) 1990s

77.
Name the most successful group of contemporary Gospel music.
A) COMMISSIONED
B) SOUNDS OF BLACKNESS
C) THE WINANS

Playing it cool? Dennis Brown

78.
Seven Seconds Away was an international hit for Neneh Cherry and which Senegalese singing sensation?
A) YOUSSOU N'DOUR
B) SALIF KEITA
C) BAABA MAAL

82.
Which actor starred in the motion pictures *Coming to America* and *The Nutty Professor*?
A) MARTIN LAWRENCE
B) CHRIS TUCKER
C) EDDIE MURPHY

79.
Which music pioneer introduced the technique of "Scratching" in Hip Hop and appeared on the cover of *Time* magazine after recording *The Message*.
A) GRANDMASTER FLASH
B) KOOL HERC
C) AFRIKA BAMBAATA

83.
You Send Me, Chain Gang, Only Sixteen, and *Cupid* were all hits for which legendary soul crooner?
A) RAY CHARLES
B) SAM COOK
C) JACKIE WILSON

80.
Which British actress of the theater and TV had a leading role in the multi-Oscar winning film *Cry Freedom*?
A) CARMEN MONROE
B) JOSETTE SIMON
C) CATHY TYSON

84.
With what instrument are the names Lester Young, Coleman Hawkins and Sonny Rollins associated?
A) ALTO SAX
B) TENOR SAX
C) TRUMPET

81.
T Boz, Left Eye and Chilli are names associated with which female super group?
A) TLC
B) SWV
C) MIS-TEEQ

85.
Which of the following songs by the "Queen of soul" Aretha Franklin was her first U.S Number One?
A) RESPECT
B) SAY A LITTLE PRAYER
C) SISTERS ARE DOING IT FOR THEMSELVES

Entertainment

Jazz tenor: Lester's music remains forever young

90.
Which famous record label pioneered 'The Memphis Sound' of the 1960s and 1970s?
A) STAX
B) TAMLA-MOTOWN
C) BLUE NOTE

91.
Name the Blues singer who popularized *Shake, Rattle and Roll* before it was covered by Bill Haley and the Comets.
A) BIG BILL BRONZY
B) BIG JOE TURNER
C) BLIND LEMON JEFFERSON

86.
Which young singing sensation starred in her own TV sit-com called *Moesha*?
A) BRANDY
B) MYA
C) TATIANA ALI

92.
In April 2000 which song made Craig David the youngest British male artist ever to have a UK solo number one?
A) SEVEN DAYS
B) FILL ME IN
C) I'M WALKING AWAY

87.
He wrote and directed the first blaxploitation movie *Sweet Sweetback's Badaass Song*. Name him.
A) GORDON PARKS
B) MARIO VAN PEEBLES
C) MELVIN VAN PEEBLES

93.
Oliver Edward Nelson wrote the film score for two of the following TV series. Name the odd one out.
A) SIX MILLION-DOLLAR MAN
B) STREETS OF SAN FRANCISCO
C) IRONSIDE

88.
Which British group introduced new break beats to dance music in the late 1980s, winning a 1989 Grammy for the single *Back to Life*?
A) ASWAD
B) SOUL II SOUL
C) FIVE STAR

94.
Which one of the following three Grammy-winning songs by Ray Charles earned him two Grammy awards?
A) GEORGIA ON MY MIND
B) HIT THE ROAD JACK
C) I CAN'T STOP LOVING

89.
Which film director owns a production company with the name '40 Acres and a Mule'?
A) DOUG McHENRY
B) SPIKE LEE
C) JOHN SINGLETON

95.
His plays include *Me Yu An Me Taxi*, *We Run Tings* and *Boy Blue*. Name the famous Caribbean comic.
A) OLIVER SAMUELS
B) NORMAN BEATON
C) CURTIS WALKER

96.
Which Janet Jackson album became the first in pop music history, to span seven top five hits on the U.S. Billboard charts?
A) JANET
B) CONTROL
C) RHYTHM NATION

97.
Which soul crooner penned the classic *What's Going On* concept album?
A) TEDDY PENDERGRASS
B) MARVIN GAYE
C) AL GREEN

98.
Which actor had lead roles in the Spike Lee films *Mo' Better Blues* and *Jungle Fever*?
A) WESLEY SNIPES
B) DENZEL WASHINGTON
C) OSSIE DAVIS

99.
Tina Turner had an international hit with *We Don't Need Another Hero* from a film in which she starred. Name it.
A) WHAT'S LOVE GOT TO DO WITH IT
B) TOMMY
C) MAD MAX 3

100.
He has received more Grammies to date than any other pop performer and he is the leading black artist for having top ten hits. Name him.
A) MICHAEL JACKSON
B) STEVIE WONDER
C) JAMES BROWN

101.
One of the most successful producers in modern popular music is Kenneth Edmonds. By what name is he better known?
A) DMX
B) HEAVY D
C) BABYFACE

102.
Forest Whitaker directed two of the following three motion pictures. Name the odd one out.
A) WAITING TO EXHALE
B) STRAPPED
C) BIRD

103.
The legendary Prince Buster was acknowledged as the "King" of which type of music?
A) SKA
B) ZOUK
C) REGGAE

104.
Which successful film sequel starred Danny Glover as the ever-vigilant cop, Roger Murtaugh?
A) LETHAL WEAPON
B) DIE HARD
C) BEVERLY HILLS COP

105.
Name the best-known work by the "Father of Ragtime Music" Scott Joplin.
A) THE STING
B) MAPLE LEAF RAG
C) THE ENTERTAINER

Claiming his 40 Acres: Spike Lee

Entertainment

Filling in his audience: Craig David

109.
Which Michael Jackson recording was the first album ever to enter the U.S. and UK charts at number one?
A) BAD
B) THRILLER
C) DANGEROUS

110.
Name the singing sensation who's musical backing band was called the Love Unlimited Orchestra.
A) LUTHER VANDROSS
B) ALEXANDER O'NEAL
C) BARRY WHITE

111.
Under the Broadwalk, Up On A Hill and *Spanish Harlem*, were all hits for which harmony group?
A) THE NEPTUNES
B) THE O'JAYS
C) THE DRIFTERS

106.
Which actress's credits include *Big Momma's House*, the soap opera *Guiding Light*, the sci-fi drama *Stigmata*, and the romantic comedy *Best Man*?
A) NIA LONG
B) SANAA LATHAN
C) VIVICA FOX

112.
Which reggae artist's 2001 Grammy award-winning album Art and Life included the hits *Who am I* and *Girls Dem Sugar*?
A) BEENIE MAN
B) ZIGGY MARLEY
C) BOUNTY KILLER

107.
Name the greatest influence on the Beatles and the Rolling Stones, who is sometimes acknowledged as the "Godfather of Rock N Roll".
A) LITTLE RICHARD
B) CHUCK BERRY
C) ELVIS PRESLEY

113.
With which legendary band are the names David Ruffin, Eddie Kendriks, Paul Williams and Dennis Edwards associated?
A) THE WHISPERS
B) THE TEMPTATIONS
C) THE FOUR TOPS

108.
For which film is Jamaican singer, Jimmy Cliff, best remembered?
A) SMILE ORANGE
B) THE HARDER THEY COME
C) COUNTRY MAN

114.
For which film in 1997 did Marianne Jean-Baptiste become the first black British screen star to receive an Oscar nomination?
A) TRAIN SPOTTING
B) LOCK STOCK AND TWO SMOKING BARRELS
C) SECRETS AND LIES

115.
Name the group led by George Clinton responsible for producing the dance classic, *One Nation Under A Groove*.
A) CAMEO
B) PARLIAMENT-FUNKADELIC
C) BRASS CONSTRUCTION

116.
Which monster selling rap single was a soundtrack to the successful box office movie *Dangerous Minds*?
A) GANGSTA'S PARADISE
B) DON'T BELIEVE THE HYPE
C) HARD KNOCK LIFE

117.
Name the most successful black sitcom series in the history of modern television.
A) DIFFERENT STROKES
B) FRESH PRINCE OF BEL-AIR
C) THE COSBY SHOW

118.
Which one of the following films was the first work by the actor/director Robert Townsend?
A) METEOR MAN
B) THE FIVE HEARTBEATS
C) HOLLYWOOD SHUFFLE

119.
When Roberta Flack's *First Take* album went to the top of the US album charts in 1972, it was a first for an African American woman. But which of her classics propelled the Fugees, in 1996, to become "the biggest selling act on the planet"?
A) KILLING ME SOFTLY
B) READY OR NOT
C) THE CLOSER I GET TO YOU

120.
Name the rapper who had a lead role in the John Singleton films *Boyz N the Hood*, *Higher Learning* and *Barber Shop*.
A) ICE CUBE
B) ICE T
C) SNOOP DOGG

121.
Lou Bega's *Mambo No. 5 (A Little Bit of Monica)* earned him the Y2K World Music's "biggest selling artist" award for which country?
A) GERMANY
B) HOLLAND
C) SPAIN

122.
Dana Elaine Owens Starred in *Set it Off*, *Chicago* and was the executive producer of *Bring the House Down*, but by what name is she better known?
A) QUEEN LATIFAH
B) LUCY LIU
C) FOXY BROWN

123.
Who was the first African American entertainer to have his own Radio and TV show in the U.S.?
A) NAT KING COLE
B) SAMMY DAVIS JR.
C) BILLY ECKSTINE

124.
Which R. Kelly song during the 1990s became the longest running number 1 in the R&B chart for more than 30 years?
A) YOU REMIND ME OF MY JEEP
B) BUMP AND GRIND
C) I BELIEVE I CAN FLY

125.
Which group is associated with the innovator of "New Jack Swing", Teddy Riley?
A) INTRO
B) SILK
C) BLACKSTREET

126.
Which popular Jamaican DJ and singer had hits with *Walk Like a Champion*, *Untold Stories*, and *Shiloh*?
A) BUJU BANTON
B) SANCHEZ
C) CAPLETON

Entertainment

High flyer? R. Kelly

131.
Name the popular music production team often referred to as the "Rhythm Twins".
A) SLY AND ROBBIE
B) STEELEY AND CLEVIE
C) DJ LUCK AND MC NEAT

132.
This Golden Globe Award-winning actress starred in the Hollywood musicals *Carmen Jones* and *Porgy and Bess*. Name Her.
A) DOROTHY DANDRIDGE
B) LENA HORNE
C) RUBY DEE

127.
Founded by Bob Johnson in 1980 it went on to become the largest black cable TV station in the world. Name it.
A) STAR TV
B) B.E.T.
C) ERBAN T.V.

133.
Which singer took British reggae, also known as 'Lover's Rock', to the top of the charts with *Silly Games*?
A) JANET KAY
B) CAROL THOMPSON
C) LOUISA MARKS

128.
Which highly acclaimed reggae singer is referred to as "The Messenger"?
A) LEE "SCRATCH" PERRY
B) LUCIANO
C) FREDDY McGREGOR

134.
Antonio Fargas starred in Keenan Wayans' blaxploitation spoof, *I'm Gonna Get You Sucka*, but in which TV series did Fargas achieve fame?
A) MASH
B) CAGNEY AND LACEY
C) STARSKY AND HUTCH

129.
She was the first black woman to win a Grammy award, and her hits include *Manhattan* and *Every Time We Say Good-bye*. Name her.
A) ELLA FITZGERALD
B) SARAH VAUGHAN
C) NINA SIMONE

135.
Which of the following "New Skool" of African American actors starred in the films *The Mod Squad*, *Love and Basketball*, and *In Too Deep*?
A) OMAR EPPS
B) MORRIS CHESTNUT
C) LORENZ TATE

130.
In which TV science fiction series did Avery Brookes play the Starfleet commander, Benjamin Sisco?
A) DR. WHO
B) RED DWARF
C) DEEP SPACE NINE

136.
Bill Duke directed two of the following three motion pictures from tinsel town. Name the odd one out.
A) A RAGE IN HARLEM
B) SISTER ACT II
C) BEVERLEY HILLS COP III

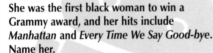

137.
Which Jamaican evergreen wrote the classic reggae song *The Tide is High* that became an international chart topper for punk band Blondie in the 1980s?
A) JOHN HOLT
B) KEN BOOTH
C) BUNNY WAILER

138.
The double acts of Coles and Atkins as well as the Williams brothers are best remembered for what style of dancing?
A) MODERN
B) TAP
C) BALLET

139.
With which 1990 film did Whoopi Goldberg win an Oscar?
A) GHOSTS
B) FATAL BEAUTY
C) SISTER ACT

140.
Creator of the *Scary Movie* sequels, Keenan Ivory Wayans, also developed which pioneering TV comedy series in 1990?
A) HANGING WITH MR. COOPER
B) DEF COMEDY JAM
C) IN LIVING COLOR

141.
Which critically acclaimed film records the conflict between the L. A. gangs, the Bloods and the Crips?
A) JUICE
B) SOUTH CENTRAL
C) COLORS

142.
Her hits include *Breathe Again*, *How Many Ways* and *He Wasn't Man Enough*. Name her.
A) TONI BRAXTON
B) ANITA BAKER
C) DONNA SUMMER

143.
Will Smith played one of the leading roles as a pilot in one of the highest grossing films of all time. Name it.
A) MISSION IMPOSSIBLE
B) MEN IN BLACK
C) INDEPENDENCE DAY

144.
Which legendary record label scored its first number-one hit with the Marvelettes classic *Please Mister Postman*?
A) MOTOWN
B) DECCA
C) BLUE NOTE

145.
In 1992 a Jamaican dancer named Gerald Levy introduced a style of dance that took the world by storm. Name it.
A) SHUFFLE
B) RUB-A-DUB
C) BOGLE

146.
He was the first artist to receive Grammy awards for both Jazz and Classical music. Name him.
A) WYNTON MARSALIS
B) QUINCY JONES
C) DUKE ELLINGTON

On a mission: An independent Will Smith

147.
Which gospel classic written in 1905 by Reverend Charles A. Tindley contains the first documented chord structure for Rock N Roll music?
A) STAND BY ME
B) ABIDE WITH ME
C) ROCK OF AGES

148.
Name the artist of Nu Soul who recorded the albums *Embrya* and *Now* after his classic 1996 debut *Urban Hang Suite*.
A) D'ANGELO
B) MAXWELL
C) JOE

149.
With which rap group did rock band Aerosmith record the international hit *Walk This Way*?
A) SALT-N-PEPA
B) N.W.A.
C) RUN DMC

150.
Which classical composer was often called "the Moor" after being nicknamed the "black-a-moor" in his childhood by his patron, Prince Esterhazy?
A) SAMUEL COLERIDGE TAYLOR
B) LUDWIG VAN BEETHOVEN
C) JOSEPH HAYDN

151.
Which British rock group led by singer Phil Lynot had international hits with *Whisky in a Jar*, *Dancing in the Moonlight* and *The Boys Are Back in Town*?
A) FINE YOUNG CANNIBALS
B) THIN LIZZY
C) HOT CHOCOLATE

152.
Which female group recorded the evergreen R&B dance tracks *Dance Turned into Romance* and *Nights Over Egypt*?
A) THE EMOTIONS
B) EN VOGUE
C) JONES GIRLS

153.
Which legendary South African artist became the first African singer to (twice) have a record go platinum on the day of its release?
A) BRENDA FASSIE
B) HUGH MASEKELA
C) MARIAM MAKEBA

154.
Which film starring Whitney Houston spanned the multiplatinum international smash, *I Will Always Love You*?
A) THE PREACHERS WIFE
B) THE BODYGUARD
C) WAITING TO EXHALE

155.
Born in Tennessee in 1894, she would grow up to become known as the "Empress of the Blues". Name her.
A) MA RAINEY
B) MA BAKER
C) BESSIE SMITH

156.
Name the garage outfit whose members have included Mega Man, Romeo, Harvey and Lisa Maffia?
A) DAMAGE
B) BONE, THUGS AND HARMONY
C) SO SOLID CREW

157.
Dean Dixon and Henry Lewis were two outstanding classical music exponents of the twentieth century. What were they?
A) SOLOISTS
B) CONDUCTORS
C) COMPOSERS

158.
Which of the following jazz legends played and composed on the double bass?
A) COUNT BASIE
B) CHARLES MINGUS
C) THELONIUS MONK

159.
Which producer and actress starred in the films *Scream 2*, *The Nutty Professor*, and *The Matrix: Reloaded*?
A) TISHA CAMPBELL
B) JADA PINKETT
C) GARCELLE BEAUVOIS

160.
In what Stephen Spielberg sci-fi flick did black Irish pop sensation, Samantha Mumba, make her acting debut?
A) E.T.
B) JURASSIC PARK
C) THE TIME MACHINE

161.
Which actor had a lead role in the films *The Shawshank Redemption*, *Seven* and *Deep Impact*?
A) VIN DIESEL
B) MORGAN FREEMAN
C) JAMIE FOX

Caught in time: Samantha Mumba

162.
Martiniquan born, Euzhan Palcy, in 1989 became the first black woman to direct a major U.S. studio film. Name it.
A) A DRY WHITE SEASON
B) SARAFINA
C) BLACK SHACK ALLEY

163.
What station in 1929 became the first licensed black radio station in the world?
A) THE HARLEM BROADCASTING CORPORATION
B) ETHIOPIAN WIRELESS CORPORATION
C) JAMAICA BROADCASTING CORPORATION

164.
Richard Pryor starred in two of the following three movies. Name the odd one out.
A) HARLEM NIGHTS
B) GREASE LIGHTNING
C) TRADING PLACES

165.
Name the successful 1980s cop series in which Philip Michael Thomas starred as Ricardo Tubbs.
A) HILL STREET BLUES
B) MIAMI VICE
C) KOJAK

166.
He starred in *Pulp Fiction*, *The Negotiator* and *Star Wars*, and was the first person to ever receive a best supporting actor award given at the Cannes Film Festival. Name him.
A) BLAIR UNDERWOOD
B) LOUIS GOSSETT JR.
C) SAMUEL L. JACKSON

167.
A year after the classical composer George Walker received this award, Wynton Marsalis, in 1997 received it for his slavery Ontario *Blood On The Fields*. Name the award.
A) EMMY
B) GRAMMY
C) PULITZER

Entertainment

168.
Who sang bass on *Otello*, which won the 1997 Grammy for Best Opera Production?
A) WILLARD WHITE
B) LAURENCE FISHBURNE
C) LUCIANO PAVAROTTI

169.
How many versions of Wayne Smith's 1985 release *Under Mi Sleng Teng*, were covered in that same year?
A) 239
B) 129
C) 59

170.
Which Motown legend led a band called The Miracles?
A) STEVIE WONDER
B) SMOKEY ROBINSON
C) MARVIN GAYE

171.
Who in 1959 wrote *A Raisin In The Sun*, the first black stage production on Broadway?
A) AUGUST WILSON
B) DOUGLAS TURNER
C) LORRAINE HANSBERRY

172.
Life magazine photographer, Gordon Parks, filmed only three screenplays for this classic movie sequel. Name it.
A) THE MACK
B) SHAFT
C) SUPERFLY

173.
Which British songstress penned the UNESCO song *Little Child* and whose hits include *You Gotta Be* and *Life*?
A) DES'REE
B) JAMELIA
C) GABRIELLE

174.
Name the musical that became in the mid 1990s the longest running off-Broadway play in the history of African-American theater.
A) PORGY AND BESS
B) FIVE GUYS NAMED MO
C) MAMA I WANNA SING

175.
In what category did Cuba Gooding Jr. win the 1997 Oscar for his involvement in the film *Jerry Maguire*?
A) BEST SUPPORTING ACTOR
B) BEST ACTOR
C) BEST DIRECTOR

176.
Which hip-hop icon penned the multi-platinum rap albums *Ready To Die*, *Born Again* and *Life After Death*?
A) TUPAC SHAKUR
B) NOTORIOUS B.I.G.
C) JAY-Z

177.
Name the internationally renowned African musician who was the innovator of Afro-Beat.
A) FELA KUTI
B) KING SUNNY ADE
C) MORY KANTE

178.
Which dub poet's hits include *Every Time I Hear the Sound* and *People Court*?
A) MUTABARUKA
B) GIL SCOTT HERON
C) DANA BRYANT

179.
Tamara Dobson starred in both sequels of this classic 1970s blaxpoitation film. Name it.
A) CLEOPATRA JONES
B) SHEBA BABY
C) CAR WASH

180.
For which form of music is Charley Pride best known?
A) ROCK
B) COUNTRY AND WESTERN
C) DISCO

181.
In what profession did Ira Aldridge become a stage phenomenon in Europe during the nineteenth century?
A) SINGING
B) BALLET
C) ACTING

182.
Who in 1984 took black British soul to the top of the American R&B chart for the first time with *Caribbean Queen*?
A) JUNIOR GISCOMBE
B) BILLY OCEAN
C) EDDIE GRANT

183.
What does the MG in Booker T. and the MGs stand for?
A) MY GANG
B) MUSICAL GIANTS
C) MEMPHIS GROUP

184.
The names Dr. Dre, Easy-E and Ice Cube are associated with which pioneering rap outfit?
A) N.W.A.
B) PUBLIC ENEMY
C) CYPRESS HILL

185.
Which of the following was a 1972 Hollywood produced cross-cultural animation flick?
A) FELIX THE CAT
B) FRITZ THE CAT
C) TOPCAT

186.
What do the initials B.B. in B.B. King stand for?
A) BIG BROTHER
B) BLUES BOY
C) BLACK BEAUTY

187.
Michael, Jackie, Tito and Jermaine were four of the original Jackson 5. Name the fifth member.
A) RANDY
B) MARLON
C) JANET

188.
For what style of music is the famed jazz pianist, Jimmy Yancy, best known?
A) SWING
B) RAGTIME
C) BOOGIE WOOGIE

189.
How many consecutive Emmys did Bill Cosby win for his pioneering role in the 1960s TV detective series *I Spy*?
A) TWO
B) THREE
C) FIVE

190.
Blaxploitation movie queen, Pam Grier, starred in two of the following three films. Name the odd one out.
A) JACKIE BROWN
B) COFFY
C) LET'S DO IT AGAIN

191.
Which blues song originally recorded by "Big Mama" Willy Mae Thorton became a multi-million selling single for Elvis Presley?
A) HOUND DOG
B) JAILHOUSE ROCK
C) HEARTBREAK HOTEL

Entertainment

192.
She was one of the I Threes, had internationally success with *Feel like Jumping* and *Electric Boogie*, and is often referred to as "The Queen of Reggae". Name her.
A) JUDY MOWAT
B) MARCIA GRIFFITHS
C) RITA MARLEY

193.
The Broadway play *Kiss of the Spider Woman*, the song *Save the Best for Last* and the film *Erasure*. Who starred in all three?
A) BEYONCÉ KNOWLES
B) VANESSA WILLIAMS
C) QUEEN LATIFAH

194.
How many Grammy awards did Michael Jackson receive in 1984 for *Thriller*, the most successful album in pop music history?
A) SIX
B) EIGHT
C) TEN

195.
Name the multitalented British singer and producer, who penned the soul ballad masterpiece *There's Nothing Like This*, and had a hit with the William De Vaughan classic *Be Thankful for What You Got*.
A) OMAR
B) LEMAR
C) GOLDIE

196.
In which one of the following films did actor Laurence Fishburne play the part of a young soldier in Vietnam?
A) APOCALYPSE NOW
B) THE KILLING FIELDS
C) GOOD MORNING VIETNAM

197.
Name the party classic penned by the Caribbean calypso singer, Arrow.
A) NANNY WINE
B) FEELING HOT HOT HOT
C) SUGAR BOOM SUGAR BOOM

198.
Who starred in the first all black talking movie, *Harlem Is Heaven*?
A) AL JOLSON
B) PAUL ROBESON
C) BILL "BOJANGLES" ROBINSON

199.
Name the composer born in London in 1875, whose works include *Hiawatha's Wedding Feast, A Tale of Old Japan* and *An African Suite*.
A) GEORGE BRIDGETOWER
B) EDWARD ELGAR
C) SAMUEL COLERIDGE TAYLOR

200.
Who recorded the first ever posthumous, number one song in American pop music history?
A) OTIS REDDING
B) JACKIE WILSON
C) BROOK BENTON

201.
Who is generally acknowledged as the "King of Calypso Music"?
A) THE MIGHTY SPARROW
B) SUPER BLUE
C) LORD KITCHENER

There's nothing like his music: Omar

202.
In what role did Josephine Baker appear in the *Follies Bergeres* when she became the toast of Paris during the 1920s?
A) MADAME BUTTERFLY
B) LA BUTTERFLY
C) LIMBO EXOCTICA

203.
In which country was the international singer Neneh Cherry born?
A) FRANCE
B) SWEDEN
C) U.S.A.

204.
Name the US and UK number one smash hit and act, whose Grammy winning single has become the biggest ever selling rap release to date?
A) I'LL BE MISSING YOU-PUFF DADDY
B) WHERE IS THE LOVE-BLACK EYE PEAS
C) YOU CAN'T TOUCH THIS-MC HAMMER

205.
The Dells are the longest-recording R&B group of all time. Name the year that *Oh What a Night* became their first hit.
A) 1956
B) 1960
C) 1962

206.
Before it was bought by Capital radio in 2004 it was the oldest black commercial radio station in continuous existence in Britain. Name it.
A) DREAD BROADCASTING CORPORATION
B) KISS FM
C) CHOICE FM

207.
Rudolph Dunbar conducted the London and Berlin Philharmonic Orchestras in the 1940s before writing a world-renowned book for which musical instrument?
A) CELLO
B) CLAVICHORD
C) CLARINET

208.
Three Times a Lady, *Say You Say Me*, and *Hello* were all hits for ballad specialist Lionel Ritchie. Name his original band.
A) MAZE
B) COMMODORES
C) EARTH, WIND AND FIRE

209.
Name the black actor of silent films who was known as "The black Valentino" during the 1920s.
A) GEORGE REED
B) SAM LUCAS
C) LORENZO TUCKER

210.
Which pianist and singer wrote the Rock 'n' Roll standard, *Blueberry Hill*?
A) FATS WALLER
B) FATS DOMINO
C) FAT LARRY

211.
His hits include the international smash *I Can See Clearly Now* and *Tears On My Pillow*. Name him.
A) JOHNNY MATHIS
B) JOHNNY NASH
C) JOHN LEE HOOKER

212.
Louis Gossett Jr. won an Oscar for his portrayal as a strict serviceman in this film. Name it.
A) IRON EAGLE 2
B) AN OFFICER AND A GENTLEMAN
C) COURAGE UNDER FIRE

213.
What was the first international hit for dancehall music's most successful singer and DJ, Shaggy?
A) OH CAROLINA
B) BOOMBASTIC
C) IT WASN'T ME

Entertainment

Midknight traveller: Was Gladys *That Lady?*

214.
This talented family collaborated on the jazz soul classic *Every Generation*, and includes Herbie, Ronnie and Debbie. What is their surname?
A) MARSALIS
B) LAWS
C) ISLEY

215.
Name the avant-garde jazz group formed by saxophonist Wayne Shorter.
A) RETURN TO FOREVER
B) JAZZ MESSENGERS
C) WEATHER REPORT

216.
With what percussion instrument are the names Baby Dodds, Art Blakey and Max Roach associated?
A) DRUMS
B) PIANO
C) TIMPANI

217.
Which songwriting team has been credited with creating the 1970s 'Sound of Philadelphia'?
A) KENNY GAMBLE AND LEON HUFF
B) HOLLAND-DOZIER-HOLLAND
C) WOMACK AND WOMACK

218.
Which production duo was responsible for the success of the disco acts, Chic and Sister Sledge?
A) ASHFORD AND SIMPSON
B) ROGERS AND EDWARDS
C) McFADDEN AND WHITEHEAD

219.
In 1969 and 1987 James Earl Jones received the Tony award for best actor, so did John Kani and Winston Ntshona in 1975. But who in 2004 became the Tony Award's first black female recipient for best actress?
A) PHYLICIA RASHAD
B) PATRICIA ROUTLEDGE
C) MARY ALICE

220.
Which group penned the pop classics *That Lady*, *You Walk Your Way* and *For the Love of You*?
A) GLADYS KNIGHT AND THE PIPS
B) THE ISLEY BROTHERS
C) KOOL AND THE GANG

221.
What profession did Robert Tuduwali undertake during the 1950s when he became Australia's first Aboriginal superstar?
A) POP SINGER
B) MOVIE STAR
C) TV PRESENTER

222.
Who exploded onto the music scene in 1997 debuting with *On and On* and the Grammy winning hip-hop collaboration *You Got Me*?
A) LIL' KIM
B) FAITH EVANS
C) ERYKAH BADU

223.
Ain't Nobody, *I'm Every Woman* and *I Feel For You* were all hits for this former lead singer of Rufus. Name her.
A) DIONNE WARWICK
B) PATTI LABELLE
C) CHAKA KHAN

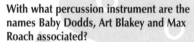

224.
The first international million-selling single for Island Records was this classic 1964 Ska hit by Millie Small. Name it.

A) KINGSTON TOWN
B) MY BOY LOLLIPOP
C) BROWN GIRL IN THE RING

Oh Shaggy: Dance Hall Star

Entertainment

Science & Engineering

George Carruthers with Ultra-Violet Spectrograph

**"Our deepest fear is not that
we are inadequate. Our deepest fear is that
we are powerful beyond measure…"**
Nelson Mandela

Ironically, although chapter two may be the shortest of the eight chapters in this book, it is the one with the longest introduction. The reason for this is that the input people of African descent have made to scientific innovation, is the least known. Not only is there a great deal of ignorance among the wider community as a whole but most people of color, are themselves, unaware of the many significant contributions or improvements. Often the consequence for this lack of knowledge during our socialization is a low level of expectancy both internally and externally. It's difficult to relate to a particular subject when there is an apparent absence of role models. This is why it is important to feed a young mind with the truth. El Hajj Malik El-Shabazz aka Malcolm X once referred to this by saying "Educate a man and you educate an individual, educate a woman and you educate and liberate a nation..." Fortunately, more and more students are considering entering the science & engineering professions, excited by the challenges the future holds in these fields.

Some people have tried to justify the apparent lack of representation by arguing it is because of physiological/craniological differences. Fortunately, this myth is being shattered daily because of the attention given to some of the more recent accomplishments of black innovators in technology.

For example, it is a fact that the man who drew up the plans for Alexander Bell's telephone was an African American named Lewis Latimer. Likewise, it was two other African Americans, Lee Burridge with help from Newham Marsham, who brought to us the design patent for the modern typewriter. More recently Dr. Mark E. Dean spearheaded the team that gave the world the home personal computer. Dr. Dean still owns three of the original nine

patents that all PCs are based on. What he, and the two cited earlier examples could not have known, was that, they were providing the basic foundation for the later phenomenal concept of the Internet to take place. Access to information would never be limited again. Speaking of which, a friend sent me a little story by email that I have borrowed and adapted. The first part of it really happened.

It relates to a thirteen-year-old boy named NJ.

...One Sunday he and some friends were out trying to sneak into a West London cinema without paying. The plan was for one of them to act as a foil, while the others got in through a rear entrance. The foil would then come round to the back and join up with his friends to see the movie. This plan had worked on so many occasions previously, that perhaps the boys had understandably become a little complacent. Or possibly the foil strategy had become familiar to a suspicious cinema attendant. Whatever the reason, while they were attempting to sneak in they were discovered by the attendant. As they ran off laughing the attendant gave chase after NJ, blurting out the usual color prejudicial remarks while in pursuit but one line stuck out "you couldn't even event the wheel"...

Although the boy had never given this much thought before, he couldn't recall learning anything about scientific achievements in relation to black people in any of his lessons at school. On his return back home to the high rise flats where he lived with his grandmother; the words of the cinema attendant were still ringing in his ears. Before he went to bed that night he prayed to The Creator, asking for all the things that black people had invented to be revealed to him. But The Creator, knowing how long that would take, promised instead to show NJ what it would be like if just a few of the things that black people invented over the last 100 years or so, had not been. With this assurance the boy fell asleep.

The next day he woke and began to prepare for school as usual. After freshening up he went to put on his school uniform but found the clothes were still wet. The Creator had decreed that George Sampson, a black man, had not invented the clothes dryer. Not to be denied, the boy began looking for the spare set he had folded away in his draw. But when he went to iron them, he noticed he couldn't find the ironing board, because a black woman named Sarah Boone had not invented it.
His grandmother, who was a P/T Seamstress, had already left for work, and now in a slight state of panic with no school uniform to wear, NJ thought he would put on his one of his Sunday best outfits, the one that closest matched his school uniform. After doing this he looked to put on his shoes, but was dismayed to find there was only an old disheveled pair. The reason for this was the mass production of shoes had not happened, because another black man, Jan Matzelinger, had not invented the shoe lasting machine.

To NJ, it seemed like his grandmother had played one of her pranks on him. She had a sense of humor much younger than her fifty-something in years. Going over to the refrigerator to get his breakfast he was surprise to see its contents including, the dairy products and frozen foods, all laying on the floor...surely not the fridge? Yes! It was an African American named John Standard who had invented the refrigerator. By now most of the food had gone off and had to be thrown away. But when NJ went to reach for the dustpan to sweep up the rest of the rubbish he couldn't find it, because The Creator had seen to it that Lloyd P. Ray had not invented the dustpan. And it was no better when he turned to get the mop because Thomas W. Steward, another black

man, had not filed his invention and patent for this cleaning instrument. Because of the smell caused by the spoilt food, the room had to be aired. So NJ went over to the air-conditioning unit but found that, not only was there no switch to turn it on, it had not even been installed. Why? Because another black man named Frederick Mckinley Jones, had not invented this device.

It was like living in a different house, a different world, and yet the boy had not yet quite grasped what was happening. He decided to see if any mail had arrived but there were none for two reasons. First, William Barry had not invented the post marking and canceling machine, and second, Phillip Downing had not invented the letterbox drop, both black men. NJ knew that despite the bazaar events around him, he could not stay to find out how they were caused otherwise he would be late for school.
He went to collect his school satchel but on checking inside it, he found his textbooks missing. Apparently, W. A. Lavette's revolutionary improvement of the printing press had not yet been unleashed on the world. Did this mean no schoolwork? NJ pondered that perhaps this cloud had a silver lining, until he noticed his pencil had a broken tip that could not be sharpened. You see without John Love there was no pencil sharpener and because another black named William Purvis had not invented the fountain pen, there was nothing to write with.

Things were now well beyond a joke. With his satchel more-or-less empty, NJ picked it up and left for school immediately. However, when he got outside he realized there was no lift to take down to the ground floor. That's because a black man named Alexander Miles had not yet filed the patent for the invention of the elevator. When NJ peered over the balcony of his high-rise apartment block, all he could see was traffic in chaos. Cars were being driven erratically because two black

Science & Engineering

men, Robert Spikes and Joseph Gammel had not yet invented the automatic gear shift or the supercharge system for internal combustion engines respectively. There were no buses on the road to take him to school either, because another black inventor, Elbert T. Robinson had, not designed its precursor the electric trolley. Anyway it would not have been safe to ride regardless, because Garret Morgan's Traffic light, arguably the best-known invention by an African American, was nowhere to be seen on the roads.

The shock of it all was becoming too much for NJ and he began to feel faint. That's when he heard a voice informing him that collapsing with a heart attack at this point was not a good idea. He was soon to learn that in this strange new world they had yet to successfully perform open heart surgery, because the African American physician, Daniel Hale Williams, had not set the precedent in 1893. A Transplant was also out of the question because Dr. Hamilton Nakia had not been involved in this historic procedure. And if that weren't daunting enough, if there were a need for a blood transfusion, this too would simply not be possible. The explanation was clear. Charles Drew, another black man, had not yet found a way to preserve and store blood. When he did, it would lead to him starting the world's first ever blood bank.

At this point, the boy remembered what he had asked The Creator to show him the night before. Then, and only then, did he begin to understand what it would be like in a world without any black inventors.

Like the wheel, we often forget that the science of mathematics, as with all the major sciences, has its origins in Africa. Pyramid building was first practiced in Africa, south of Egypt, and the earliest stone pyramids are in fact found in what is now present day Uganda. Another fact seemingly overlooked by academia, is the archaeological, botanical, linguistic, and metallurgical evidence of African presence in South America before Christ. Even the Pyramids of Mexico are modeled along the same lines as the step pyramids in North East Africa. Why this connection is not often discussed in institutions of learning worldwide is a constant source of speculation and conjecture to the few who know.

The information in this section attempts to shed light on some of the unique inventions and innovative creations made by black inventors, from Lewis Latimer's carbon filament, which gave us Bell's light bulb to Imhotep's step Pyramid at Saqqara. Many of the inventions included are in fact improvements. For instance, before the red, amber and green automatic stop light, there was a cruder traffic light, which can be seen in earlier silent movies. It simply had a sign with the words 'Stop' and 'Go'. It's worth pointing out that because of the historical inaccuracies of omitting black genius, some have inadvertently overstated the impact of some inventions. This is unfortunate because there is so much truth out there waiting to be brought to the fore, it makes the exercise of "overstating" totally unnecessary and even more counterproductive. An example of this misconception among some black folk, is that Henry Thomas Sampson helped cellular phone technology with his invention of the 'Gamma Electric Cell'. There are now a few gathering sources which point to this misconception and I, like many, believed it to be true. However, it is an error. Mr. Sampson's invention is based on finding radiation in the ground. How this myth became propagated is fascinating, but it has been exploded on the page of this book and must not be retold. If anyone comes across that notion again please make sure it is corrected, or direct the source to the Black Inventor's Museum in Canada. The Museum is the largest gatherer of

Black achievement in the field of science world-wide. The museum also has records of patents (currently in use) owned by the renowned African American telecommunications engineer named Jesse Russell, who has seriously figured in cellular phone technology.

Unlike the previous section there is less emphasis on trivia; however, the presentation remains light-hearted in order to keep the reader entertained and the information accessible. As the questions may prove to be awe inspiring and the answers enlightening, it is hoped that an important dimension in evaluating our world will be encouraged, particularly by educationalists who have a responsibility to inform accurately - as well as to be accurately informed.

All of the sources in part two, pertaining to the questions on science and engineering, can be found on the Internet. The books can also usually be ordered over the Net, using one of the popular search engines.

Imhotep as the Greek god of medicine: Aesculapius

**Endeavouring to reach for the stars:
Dr. Mae Jemison**

225.
In 1987 Neurosurgeon, Dr. Ben Carson, led the world's first successful operation to separate Siamese twins, joined at what part of the body?
A) FRONT OF THE CHEST
B) SIDE OF THE HIP
C) BACK OF THE HEAD

226.
In 1989 Dr. Philip Emeagwali performed the world's fastest ever computer calculation, a process that revolutionize Internet technology efficiency. How fast was it?
A) 3.1 BILLION CALCULATIONS PER SECOND
B) 31 MILLION CALCULATIONS PER SECOND
C) 31 TRILLION CALCULATIONS PER SECOND

227.
Vice president of IBM Dr. Mark Dean led the team that developed the *ISA Systems* for home PCs, and holds how many of the 9 original computer patents that all PCs are based on?
A) 3
B) 6
C) 9

228.
On which spacecraft was George Carruthers's *Ultra-Violet Spectrograph* used as the first camera to take a picture of Earth from the moon?
A) SPUTNIK
B) APOLLO 1
C) APOLLO 16

229.
Which East African country is host to the world's oldest known astronomical observatory?
A) KENYA
B) ERITREA
C) SUDAN

230.
What type of eye surgery was revolutionized in 1986 with the invention of the *Laserphoto Probe* by the ophthalmologist Dr. Patricia Bath?
A) COLOR BLINDNESS
B) CATARACTS
C) DIABETIC RETINOPATHY

231.
In 1969 Dr. Khalil Messiha discovered an ancient Egyptian model for a form of transport dated between 300b.c. and 400b.c. Name it.
A) CAR
B) GLIDER
C) BOAT

232.
Seven years after he invented the Hand Stamp, William B. Purvis designed and patented which writing instrument in 1890?
A) FOUNTAIN PEN
B) LEAD PENCIL
C) FELT TIP PEN

233.
In 1992 after obtaining a British patent, Professor Charles Ssali released Marian-dina, a treatment said to have an "80% success rate" with which disease?
A) COMMON COLD
B) TB
C) HIV/AIDS

234.
Name the electrical apparatus with the registration number 371,207 that was patented by Alexander Miles in October 1887.
A) ELEVATOR
B) ESCALATOR
C) REVOLVING DOORS

235.
Name the space shuttle on which Dr. Mae Jemison was an astronaut, when in September 1992 she became the first black woman in space.
A) STAR SHIP ENTERPRISE
B) CHALLENGER
C) ENDEAVOR

236.
What profession did Apartheid South Africa attribute to Dr. Hamilton Naki after he assisted Christiaan Barnard in performing the world's first heart transplant in 1967?
A) NURSE
B) GARDENER
C) ROAD SWEEPER

237.
Name the home security system spearheaded and pioneered by the African American electrical scientist Louis Alexander.
A) BARBED WIRE FENCING
B) VIDEO INTERCOM
C) BURGLER ALARM

238.
What visual aid was designed and perfected by the Moors of Spain?
A) BINOCULARS
B) MAGNIFYING GLASS
C) EYE GLASSES

239.
The *Ishango Bone* is the oldest source on this topic known to man. What area of science does it related to?
A) MATHEMATICS
B) MEDICINE
C) MUSIC

240.
What space project did Major Isaac Gillam IV direct at NASA's Dryden Center from its draft stages to its launch off?
A) THE FIRST U.S. SPACE SHUTTLE
B) THE FIRST SATELLITE ON MARS
C) STAR WARS

241.
What type of building is the *Praca De Toirus*, the oldest remaining representation of African architecture in Portugal?
A) MOSQUE
B) BULL RING
C) UNDERGROUND TUNNEL

242.
In which of the following countries was a metal producing mine carbon dated to be 43,000 years old, discovered in 1970?
A) SWAZILAND
B) RWANDA
C) BURUNDI

243.
Which one of the following did African American Doctor, Clilian Powell, help to refine as a form of diagnostic treatment?
A) LASER TREATMENT
B) X RAY
C) ARTIFICIAL INSEMINATION

244.
What branch of science was pioneered in Europe before World War II, by the zoologist, Ernest Just?
A) HUMAN BIOLOGY
B) MARINE BIOLOGY
C) BRAIN SURGERY

Pioneer: Dr. Ernest Just

Science & Engineering

Bugs Life: Charles Turner

249.
What year did Dr. Daniel Hale Williams become the first person to successfully perform open-heart surgery?
A) 1893
B) 1940
C) 1966

250.
Which of the following inventions by Elijah McCoy gave rise to the phrase, 'The Real McCoy'?
A) LAWN SPRINKLER
B) LUBRICATION FLUID
C) STEAM DOME

245.
Name the operation performed by the Banyoro doctors of Uganda, recorded in the *Edinburgh Medical Journal* in 1884?
A) APPENDIX REMOVAL
B) PLASTIC SURGERY
C) CAESAREAN SECTION

251.
The Gas Mask inventor, Garrett Morgan, designed what popular mechanism used to aid traffic?
A) BRAKES
B) FOG LIGHTS
C) TRAFFIC LIGHT

246.
The best-known invention by the engineer Robert Shurney, are tyres designed for what?
A) CONCORD
B) NASA'S MOON BUGGY
C) JEEP

252.
Name the star known for centuries to the Dogon people of West Africa, which was recently discovered by the *Einstein* orbiting satellite.
A) SIRIUS B
B) ALPHA CENTURA
C) THE SUN

247.
What term used by Nubian scholars described the hypotenuse, two thousand years before Pythagoras was born?
A) SINGLE MATRIX
B) TRIPLE SALKO
C) DOUBLE REMEN

253.
In 1883 Jan Matzelinger received a patent for designing the first machine that could mass-produce what?
A) SHOES
B) HATS
C) WIGS

248.
In 1899 the prolific inventor, Granville T. Woods, patented this amusement apparatus, which has become a popular fairground attraction. Name it.
A) ROLLER COASTER
B) BUMPER CARS
C) BIG DIPPER

254.
Norbert Rillieux invented a machine that could extract and refine a product from which raw material?
A) FLOUR FROM WHEAT
B) SUGAR FROM SUGAR CANE
C) OIL FROM COCONUTS

255.
At what university in 1959 did Davidson Nicol discover for diabetics, the chemical structure of human insulin?
A) OXFORD
B) LONDON
C) CAMBRIDGE

256.
Apart from the air-conditioning unit, Frederick McKinley Jones has received patents for two of the following three inventions. Name the odd one out.
A) PORTABLE REFRIGERATOR
B) TICKET DISPENSING MACHINE
C) UNDERWATER CLOCK

257.
At 12:09 on February 9, 1995, who became the first black astronaut to walk in space?
A) BERNARD HARRIS
B) GUION BLUFORD
C) RON McNAIR

258.
The black entomologist Charles Turner of St. Louis, Missouri, was the first to prove that insects can do what?
A) HEAR
B) SEE
C) SMELL

259.
On June 7th 1892 George Sampson received patent number 476,416 for which utility appliance?
A) CLOTHES DRYER
B) WASHING MACHINE
C) DISH WASHER

260.
Name the popular beauty treatment invented by Christina Jenkins in the U.S. during the 1950s?
A) FINGER NAIL EXTENSIONS
B) SKIN WAXING
C) THE HAIR WEAVE

261.
In 1821 Thomas Jennings became the first African American to receive a government recognized protection patent. Name his invention.
A) DRY-CLEANING SOLVENT
B) WASHING POWDER
C) FURNITURE POLISH

262.
Which food was used by Percy Julian to produce the substitute steroid *Cortisone*?
A) KIDNEY BEAN
B) BAKED BEANS
C) SOYBEAN

263.
Dr. Leonidas H. Berry pioneered this instrument, which detects diseases of the stomach and intestine. Name it.
A) STETHOSCOPE
B) FIBER OPTIC ENDOSCOPE
C) LITMUS TEST

264.
For which type of transport has U.S. Sergeant Adolphus Samms, developed an Airframe Center Support?
A) HELICOPTER
B) ROCKET
C) AIRPLANE

265.
Which scientist has the distinction of being the very first person to successfully transform electric current into sustained light?
A) LEWIS LATIMER
B) OLIVER BULB
B) ALEXANDER BELL

266.
Why was the illiterate Jededia Buxton, heavily featured in the popular English paper, *The Gentlemen's Magazine*, in 1788?
A) HE SPOKE 5 LANGUAGES
B) HE WAS A MATHEMATICS GENIUS
C) HE INVENTED SHOE POLISH

Science & Engineering

Nurse with a crime of passion: Mary Seacole

272.
For which mode of transport did I. R. Johnson invent a frame, J. M. Certain, the parcel carrier; and David Boker, the inner tube?
A) BICYCLE
B) CAR
C) MOTOR BIKE

267.
Name the English landmark that some archeologist suggest was built by the *Damnonii* people or "black Druids", aka ancestors of the English 'Silures', in the third millennia BC.
A) HADRIANS WALL
B) STONEHENGE
C) CANTERBURY RUINS

273.
What blood disorder is known as 'Cold Season Rheumatism'?
A) ARTHRITIS
B) SARCOIDOSIS
C) SICKLE CELL

268.
Which Amino acid was Dr. Harold D. West the first to synthesize in a laboratory?
A) GLUTAMINE
B) THEONINE
C) TYROSINE

274.
Which doctor first pioneered blood transfusion and the preservation of plasma?
A) CHARLES DREW
B) DANIEL HALE WILLIAMS
C) ROLAND SCOTT

269.
For which disease did an African slave named Oneissimus develop an antidote in 1706?
A) CHICKEN POX
B) MEASLES
C) SMALLPOX

275.
How many industrial products did George Washington Carver create from the peanut?
A) 105
B) 215
C) 325

270.
Which African "Father of Medicine" lived circa 2980b.c. and was later revered as the god Aesculapius in Greece?
A) AKHNATEN
B) OSIRIS
C) IMHOTEP

276.
In what year did Cuba's Arnaldo Tamayo Mendez become the first black cosmonaut in space?
A) 1976
B) 1980
C) 1982

271.
Which historical nurse died in London in 1881 after saving many British soldiers during the Crimean War of 1855?
A) FLORENCE NIGHTINGALE
B) MARY SEACOLE
C) SUSIE KING TAYLOR

277.
Hypatia, the last great African woman physicist of antiquity, is best remembered for which branch of mathematics?
A) GEOMETRY
B) FRACTIONS
C) ALGEBRA

278.
According to Scottish folklore, a tall African tribe erected the 'Standing Stones of Callenish'. On what Scottish Island are these stones?
A) ISLE OF LEWIS
B) ISLE OF CALLY
C) SHETLAND ISLAND

279.
What development in human civilization was first undertaken in the Nile Valley some 18,000 years ago?
A) LANGUAGE
B) FARMING
C) CATTLE HERDING

280.
Dr. Louis Wright and his daughter Jane Wright are on record as being among the first pioneers, of what form of cancer treatment?
A) RADIOTHERAPY
B) CHEMOTHERAPY
C) HORMONE REPLACEMENT THERAPY

281.
In 1892 Ms Sarah Boon received a patent for her invention of which household appliance?
A) IRONING BOARD
B) VACUUM CLEANER
C) WASHING MACHINE

Bridging the gap between genius and nut:
George Washington Carver

282.
Meredith Gourdine designed and patented a generator for power stations, which could cheaply convert which natural substance into energy?
A) WATER INTO STEAM
B) COAL IN NUCLEAR ENERGY
C) GAS INTO ELECTRICITY

283.
In 1965 Robert Powell published some of the first research material for which branch of photography?
A) HOLOGRAMS
B) PHOTOCOPYING
C) STILL LIFE

284.
Approximately how far is the earth from the sun?
A) 100 MILLION MILES
B) 97 MILLION MILES
C) 93 MILLION MILES

285.
The chilled groove wheel and the third line used by subway trains are designs by which African American inventor?
A) ELBERT ROBERTSON
B) DR. LLOYD HALL
C) GRANVILLE T. WOODS

286.
Name the year Sarah E. Goode became the first black woman to obtain U.S. Patents for her folding cabinet bed.
A) 1885
B) 1905
C) 1925

287.
Salix Capensis is a traditional remedy by the Bantu speaking people of Africa, but it is better known to the world as what?
A) ASPIRIN
B) VASELINE
C) TOOTHPASTE

Science & Engineering

288.
An African American housewife named Henrietta Bradberry designed and patented this devise just after World War 2. Name it.
A) ANSWER MACHINE
B) SUBMARINE TORPEDO DISCHARGER
C) FURNITURE POLISH

289.
For what fuel type did cricket legend Ron Headley develop the cleaner-aired emission system the *ECOCHARGER*?
A) GAS
B) PETROL
C) DIESEL

Flagging traffic: Garrett Morgan's red, yellow and green operatus

290.
Weather planet engineer Raymond Coleman helped to design and test the power converters for *Nimbus A*. What is *Nimbus A*?
A) FIRST GLOBAL SATELLITE
B) FIRST PASSENGER SPACE ROCKET
C) FIRST SPACE LABORATORY

291.
What letter found on doctors prescriptions represents the Egyptian god of medicine?
A) H
B) R
C) X

292.
What popular flavor was first mass-produced in the 19th century after Edmund Albius discovered how to artificially pollinate its plant?
A) STRAWBERRY
B) CHOCOLATE
C) VANILLA

293.
John Albert Burr achieved fame and fortune for his design of which gardening tool in 1899?
A) SHOVEL
B) LAWN MOWER
C) GARDEN HOSE

294.
Dr. Samuel Kountz pioneered the technique for the transplantation of which human organ?
A) LIVER
B) KIDNEY
C) BRAIN

295.
The Nubian Stella calendar was based upon the study of which astrological cycle?
A) THE MOON
B) THE STARS
C) THE SUN

296.
For which branch of mathematics in 1919, did Dr. Elmer S. Imes become the first theorist to discover rational states of molecules?
A) QUANTUM PHYSICS
B) THEORY OF RELATIVITY
C) ELECTRO MAGNETISM

297.
On September 17, 1878 Mr. W. A. Lavalette received a patent for producing two types of what?
A) CARBON PAPER
B) TRACING PAPER
C) PRINTING PRESS

298.
Which Jamaican naturalist was honored with having several animals, including 2 fish and a species of bird, named after him?
A) SIR PAUL ROBINS
B) LORD FINCH
C) RICHARD HILL

299.
The Ghanaian scientist Dr. Raphael Armattoe was the runner up for the Nobel Prize in physiology in 1948. What water borne disease did he find a cure for?
A) TYPHOID
B) RINGWORM
C) GUINEA-WORM DISEASE

300.
What car engine component was did Edmond Berger help to pioneer in the 19th century and was later improved upon with the design of Charles Banks?
A) RADIATOR
B) SPARK PLUG
C) OIL FILTER

301.
Apart from an electric device in all guided missiles and IBM computers, name Otis Boykin's best-known invention to date.
A) HEARING AID
B) CONTROL UNIT FOR PACEMAKERS
C) VOICE BOX

302.
The enzymologist, Dr. Robert Ratcliff, was the first scientist to develop the technique of gluing together what?
A) GENES
B) BONES
C) SKIN

303.
Name the household appliance patented by John Standard on July 14, 1891.
A) MICROWAVE
B) OVEN
C) REFRIGERATOR

304.
By what name is the document of a 16th century B.C. Egyptian priest known, generally accepted as the oldest medical treatise in existence?
A) THE ALEXANDER RHIND PAPYRUS
B) THE EBERS PAPYRUS
C) THE EDWIN SMITH PAPYRUS

305.
What is the nearest star to the earth?
A) ALPHA CENTAURI
B) PROXIMA CENTAURI
C) SIRIUS

306.
For which type of transport did the African American inventors, J. F. Pickering, W. G. Madison, and J. E. Whooter receive patents?
A) AIRSHIP
B) YATCH
C) MOTORBIKE

307.
What is the name of the protein prevalent in African hair that gives it unique texture?
A) MELANIN
B) KERATIN
C) VITAMIN E

308.
Name the African American woman whose immortal *HeLa Cells* have been described as the twentieth Century "Most Important Tool in Biomedical Research".
A) HENRIETTA LACKS
B) HELEN LAKER
C) DR. ANGELA FERGUSON

309.
Patented by G. Tolliver in 1891, this propeller design was in common use twenty-nine years later, on what?
A) POLICE HELICOPTERS
B) JUMBO JETS
C) SHIPS FOR THE U.S. NAVY

310.
In 1834 Henry Blair became only the second African American to be awarded a U.S. protective patent. Name his invention.
A) SEED PLANTER
B) CORN HARVESTER
C) TRACTOR

Science & Engineering

Passed his induction: Granville T. Woods

311.
Give the name of the train security system patented by R. A. Butler in 1897.
A) TRAIN ALARM
B) TRAIN HORN
C) EMERGENCY BRAKES

312.
Hero's Fountain, designed and built by a first century Egyptian physicist, is thought to be the world's first ever what?
A) DRINKING TAP
B) STEAM ENGINE
C) PUBLIC BATHS

313.
Written by an ancient Nubian scribe, name the document, and the city where it is kept, known as the world's oldest document on advanced mathematics.
A) PAPYRUS OF ZURICH
B) PAPYRUS OF ATHENS
C) PAPYRUS OF MOSCOW

314.
On what subject was the black medic and most honored physician in Portuguese history, Jose de Sousa Martins, the world's leading authority?
A) AMPUTATION
B) QUARANTINE AND SANITATION
C) MEDITATION

315.
The first black private medical college celebrated its 129th anniversary in 2005. Name it.
A) TOUGALOO COLLEGE
B) MOREHOUSE COLLEGE
C) MEHARRY MEDICAL COLLEGE

316.
Which one of the following monuments built by Africans in Europe is not in Spain?
A) THE ROUND TOWER OF ABERNATHY
B) THE GENERALIFE
C) THE ALHAMBRA

317.
The black London GP, John Alcindor, wrote papers on Influenza, Cancer and Tuberculosis before assisting which medical organization during World War I?
A) INTERNATIONAL RED CROSS
B) ST. JOHNS AMBULANCE BRIGADE
C) COMMONWEALTH MEDICAL SERVICES

318.
How much did a New York railroad company pay Andrew J. Beard for his *Train Coupler* invention in 1897?
A) $10,000
B) $50,000
C) $100,000

319.
Founded in Atlanta by African American doctors, this U.S. medical institution celebrated its centenary in 1995. Name it.
A) NATIONAL MEDICAL ASSOCIATION
B) AMERICAN MEDICAL ASSOCIATION
C) NATIONAL DENTAL ASSOCIATION

320.
The bacteriologist William A. Hinton developed the standard test for which sexually transmitted disease?
A) GONORRHOEA
B) HERPES
C) SYPHILIS

321.
Among his inventions, Charles V. Richey patented this device for registering caller identification when using which communication gadget?
A) CB RADIO
B) TELEPHONE
C) PAGER

322.
Dr. Lloyd Hall, the world's leading authority on food preservation, had approximately how many patents on food chemistry?
A) 5
B) 55
C) 105

323.
What invention did G. E. Becket, P. B. Downing and F. Shrewcraft all patent before 1900?
A) LETTER BOX
B) LETTER SEAL
C) LETTER HOLDER

324.
What animal bones discovered by black cowboy, George McJunkin, in the first half of the 20th century, led to the scientific realization that America was inhabited for 10,000 years and not 4000 years as originaly thought?
A) BEAR
B) BISON
C) BUFFALO

325.
With his patent number 1,889,814, Richard B. Spikes in 1932 made driving a car easier. Name his invention.
A) AUTOMATIC GEAR SHIFT
B) CAR HORN
C) INDICATOR LIGHTS

326.
Thought to be his most significant invention, Granville T. Woods received international recognition after patenting this electrical device in 1887. Name it.
A) AUTOMATIC AIR BRAKE
B) TELEPHONE TRANSMITTER
C) INDUCTION RAILWAY TELEGRAPH

327.
Which was the first African country to set up its own independent Space Agency?
A) SOUTH AFRICA
B) NIGERIA
C) LIBYA

328.
Percy Julian's synthesis of the drug *Physostigmine* in 1933 helped to treat Glaucoma. It also improved the memory of patients suffering with which disease?
A) PARKINGSON'S
B) AMNESIA
C) ALZHEIMER'S

Generating ideas: Meredith Gourdine

329.
On November 23rd, 1897, John L. Love patented this useful writing accessory. Name it.
A) INVISIBLE INK
B) PENCIL SHARPENER
C) WRITING PAD

330.
What type of equipment used in space did the African American scientist, Wilbert Dyer, develop for NASA during the 1970s?
A) SATELLITE TRACKER
B) UFO TRACKER
C) RADIOWAVE MONITOR

331.
Mr. C. B. Brookes pioneered this revolutionary piece of cleaning machinery, then it was later improved upon by Hallstead and Page. Name it.
A) DOG POOPER SCOOPER
B) STREET SWEEPER
C) ELECTRIC MOP

332.
The mathematician and astronomer Benjamin Banneker built the first one of these in North America. Name it.
A) TELESCOPE
B) CLOCK
C) COMPASS

Great time keeper: Benjamin Banneker

General Knowledge

Revellers at the Notting Hill Carnival

'Be not arrogant because of your knowledge.
Take counsel with the ignorant as well as with the
wise. For the limits of knowledge in any field have
never been set and no one has ever reached them...'

The Husia

No question and answer book would be complete without a general knowledge section. One could be forgiven for thinking that general knowledge with an African centered perspective, would be something that only those with specialist knowledge would be able to answer.

Those initial reservations would not be as prevalent if one was asked to review general knowledge questions from a western viewpoint. And yet, because of the increasing use of cable and satellite technology, there are a number of media conglomerates with the ability, resources, and infrastructure to disseminate information to vast audiences over the globe. It's fair to say the majority of these are western owned. Therefore, knowledge from a western perspective has become the global norm. However, on closer inspection, it may come as a surprise to learn that there is very little to distinguish between black general knowledge and common knowledge.

Speculation on why this is so, may lead us to believe that most of what there is to know about people of color is already in the public domain, or understood by the masses - consciously or subconsciously. Alternatively, it could be because of our prior familiarization with a particular piece of information but unaware of its origin. Whatever the explanation, consequently what follows is a potpourri of questions involving different time periods throughout history and covering areas including; big business, culture and traditions, cuisine, ethnology, fashion, and geography.

The goddess Isis suckling her son Horus

Nubian Jak board game:
Originally Egyptian?

Model citizen: Iman

333.
What do the initials *FUBU* of the popular international clothing brand stand for?
A) FOR U BY US
B) FOR US BY US
C) FOR UNIVERSAL BEAUTY & UNDERSTANDING

334.
Who was the first black model to appear on the international cover of *Vogue* magazine?
A) NAOMI CAMPBELL
B) IMAN
C) BEVERLY JOHNSON

335.
On what date is *Martin Luther King Day* a national holiday in the United States?
A) THIRD MONDAY IN JANUARY
B) JULY 4TH
C) APRIL 4TH

336.
What word best describes the work and activities of the showman David Blaine?
A) IMPERSONATOR
B) ILLUSIONIST
C) MAGICIAN

337.
What delicacy first sold in Philadelphia by Augustus Jackson, decades later had another African-American named Alfred Cralle patent its serving utensil in 1897?
A) POPCORN
B) CANDYFLOSS
C) ICE CREAM

338.
Suzette Charles, Debbie Turner, Marjorie Vincent and Kimberly Aiken have been winners of which beauty pageant?
A) MISS U.S.A.
B) MISS AMERICA
C) MISS UNIVERSE

339.
By what name was the 727-ton vessel the *SS Yarmouth* later called the Frederick Douglas, better known?
A) THE JESUS CHRIST
B) THE Q.E.2
C) BLACK STAR SHIPPING LINE

340.
Which style of clothing did street-style guru, Karl Kani, introduce to mainstream fashion?
A) STRING VESTS
B) BAGGY CLOTHES
C) TRACK SUITS

341.
Which flower native to tropical countries is drank all around the world as an herbal drink?
A) HIBISCUS
B) CAMOMILE
C) GINSENG

342.
The African American inventor Benjamin Banneker designed the final layout of which famous American city?
A) ATLANTA
B) WASHINGTON, D.C.
C) MIAMI

343.
What significance did the ancient Egyptians attach to the scarab insect, otherwise known as the dung beetle?
A) FERTILITY AND PRODUCTIVITY
B) RESURRECTION AND IMMORTALITY
C) A GOOD HARVEST

344.
Africa, America, Asia, Australia, and Europe are represented in which internationally recognized symbol?
A) THE UNITED NATIONS FLAG
B) THE WHITE DOVE
C) THE OLYMPIC RINGS

345.
Throughout the African continent the calabash is used as a bowl or a dish in which to serve food. What exactly is a calabash?
A) PLANT
B) STONE
C) SEA SHELL

346.
What is the largest city in South Africa?
A) CAPETOWN
B) JOHANNESBURG
C) PRETORIA

347.
What type of instrument is a Mbira?
A) THUMB PIANO
B) STEEL DRUM
C) PIANO

348.
A black Pequot Indian tribe owns the most profitable casino in the world. Name it.
A) FOXWOODS RESORT
B) MGM GRAND, LAS VEGAS
C) TAJ MAHAL, ATLANTIC CITY

349.
Which is the only religion, other than Christianity, to recognize Jesus in its religious scriptures?
A) HINDUISM
B) JUDAISM
C) ISLAM

350.
Which board game introduced to Europe by the Moors had its origins discovered on ancient Egyptian sculptures?
A) NUBIAN JAK
B) DRAUGHTS
C) CHESS

351.
What world-renown venue first opened in Harlem in 1934?
A) THE COTTON CLUB
B) APOLLO THEATER
C) CARNEGIE HALL

352.
Who was the first African American to appear on a U.S. stamp?
A) BOOKER T. WASHINGTON
B) LOUIS ARMSTRONG
C) MARTIN LUTHER KING

353.
At the beginning of 2003 Radhouane Charbib of Tunisia, and Hussain Bisad of Somalia, were numbered 1& 2 in the world, as what?
A) TALLEST PEOPLE
B) FATTEST PEOPLE
C) OLDEST PEOPLE

354.
In which country is the famous Toetihuacan sun pyramid?
A) MEXICO
B) EGYPT
C) GREECE

General Knowledge

One of the first African American self-made millionairess: Madame C. J. Walker

355.
Which animation series features the characters Thurgood, Mrs Avery and Murial Stubbs?
A) SOUTH PARK
B) THE PJS
C) FAMILY GUY

356.
Name the traditional British dance brought to Europe by the invading Moors of eighth century Spain.
A) FLAMINGO
B) MORRIS DANCING
C) JUMPING THE BROOM

357.
Paul Du Chaillu was the explorer who introduced this animal to the western world. Name it.
A) GORILLA
B) RHINO
C) GIRAFFE

358.
What ocean divides America from Africa?
A) PACIFIC OCEAN
B) ATLANTIC OCEAN
C) AFRICAN OCEAN

359.
Who in 1987 bought the multinational food enterprise, *The Beatrice Group*, which was at that time valued at 2.5 billion dollars?
A) JOSEPH JETT
B) REGINALD LEWIS
C) JOHN H. JOHNSON

360.
Of the following symbols, which one was originally used in parts of Africa and Asia for special religious ceremonies?
A) HAMMER AND SICKLE
B) THE CROSS
C) SWASTIKA

361.
In what business did Madame C. J. Walker and Annie Turnbo Malone specialize, before becoming the first African American women self-made millionaires?
A) COSMETICS
B) COTTON
C) FOOD

362.
This fashion designer's specialty is ladies wear, and his clients included Diana, Princess of Wales. Name him.
A) JOE HASELY-CAYFORD
B) BRUCE OLDFIELD
C) OSWALD BOATENG

363.
What is the more familiar name of the African 'River Horse'?
A) HIPPOPOTAMUS
B) RHINOSAURUS
C) WILDEBEEST

364.
Spelman is the female wing or sister of which American educational institution?
A) MALCOLM X ACADEMY
B) MOREHOUSE COLLEGE
C) HOWARD UNIVERSITY

365.
Which Caribbean island has produced Nobel Prize winners for both economics and literature?
A) ST. VINCENT AND THE GRENADINES
B) ST. LUCIA
C) BARBADOS

366.
Along with English what is the most common language spoken in Africa?
A) SWAHILI
B) FRENCH
C) ARABIC

367.
Which fortune 500 company with over $600 billion in assets, did Franklin Raines in the summer of 1998, become the first African American to head?
A) AMERICAN EXPRESS
B) RANK XEROX
C) FANNIE MAE

368.
What pioneering hairstyle helped the "Godfather of British Dance Music" Jazzie B, to received an NAACP image award in 1989?
A) AFRO
B) WET-LOOK PERM
C) FUNKI DREADS

369.
Name the legendary Wild West hero who in 1971 became the first black cowboy elected to the Cowboy Hall of Fame.
A) NAT HOOPER
B) BILL PICKETT
C) BUFFALO BILL

370.
Which toy brand introduced the African American dolls *Christi* and *Moja*, and the Hispanic doll *Teresa*?
A) BARBIE
B) CINDY
C) IMAANI

371.
What popular snack did Hyram S. Thomas introduce to the world in 1850?
A) POTATO CHIP CRISPS
B) TOFFEE APPLE
C) POPCORN

372.
Which plant is reported to have grown on King Solomon's grave?
A) MISTLETOE
B) ORCHIDS
C) MARIJUANA

373.
Where in North Africa would you find the famous town of Casablanca?
A) MOROCCO
B) EGYPT
C) ALGERIA

374.
According to folklore, which people are alleged to have descended from an Egyptian princess name Scotia, via her marriage to a Greek man?
A) CROATIANS
B) SCOTTISH
C) SCANDINAVIANS

375.
Across the Atlantic, name the closest country to the African continent.
A) MADAGASCAR
B) BRAZIL
C) GUYANA

376.
In 1971 this firm became the first black company listed on the American stock exchange. Name it.
A) DANIELS AND BELL
B) TLC BEATRICE INTERNATIONAL
C) JOHNSON PRODUCTS

General Knowledge

In Vogue: Sean Jean "P Diddy" Combs

381.
Name the center for excellence and learning founded by Booker T. Washington in 1881.
A) HAMPTON INSTITUTE
B) TUSKEGEE INSTITUTE
C) LINCOLN UNIVERSITY

382.
The *Cullinan Stone* in the English Crown Jewels is one of the largest of its type ever found. What is it?
A) DIAMOND
B) RUBY
C) SAPPHIRE

377.
This popular tourist attraction in the state of Milwaukee is a history museum founded by the civil rights veteran James Cameron. Name it.
A) BLACK INVENTORS MUSEUM
B) BLACK HOLOCAUST MUSEUM
C) AFRICAN AMERICAN MUSEUM

383.
Until recent discoveries this name was used to describe the oldest human ancestor known to man. What is it?
A) NEANDERTHAL
B) HOMO ERECTUS
C) LUCY

378.
Which desert runs through Botswana, Namibia, and South Africa?
A) SAHARA
B) CHALBI
C) KALAHARI

384.
What animal was used to portray Horus, the Egyptian god of the sky?
A) FALCON
B) COBRA
C) BULL

379.
What name is given to the American city founded by Haitian immigrant Henri Jean Baptiste Point Dusable in 1772?
A) CHICAGO
B) LAS VEGAS
C) BOSTON

385.
Which fruit with a yellow flesh is part of the national dish of Jamaica?
A) LEMON
B) ACKEE
C) GUAVA

380.
'Diana of the Ephesians' was a black deity in southern Europe who later became known by what title?
A) VENUS OF LOVE
B) GODDESS OF CHASTITY
C) GODDESS OF FERTILITY

386.
Two of the following three disciplines are an integral part of carnival celebrations. Name the odd one out.
A) LIMBO
B) MASQUERADE
C) CALYPSO

387.
What does the Ghanaian name 'Kwesi' mean?
A) BORN TO LEAD
B) BORN ON A WEDNESDAY
C) BORN ON A SUNDAY

388.
Before it was bought by *L'oreal* in 1998, this company was the largest African American owned producer of black beauty and hair care products. Name it.
A) TCB
B) LUSTRE
C) SOFT SHEEN

389.
Which fashion guru was the first black male to appear on the cover of *Vogue*?
A) SEAN JEAN COMBS
B) TYSON BECKFORD
C) RUPAUL

390.
At 4160 miles in length what is the longest river in the world?
A) AMAZON
B) NILE
C) MISSISSIPPI

391.
What word introduced into the English language is a tribute to the black pirate, Amir-Al-Bahr?
A) ADMIRAL
B) ADMIRABLE
C) ADMIRE

392.
What began officially in 1965 and has become the largest street festival in Europe?
A) MONTREUX JAZZ FESTIVAL
B) CANNES FILM FESTIVAL
C) NOTTING HILL CARNIVAL

393.
Born in Turkey and laid to rest in Palestine, the third-century black saint known as George of Lydda is depicted on the national flag of which country?
A) IRAQ
B) GREECE
C) ENGLAND

394.
After becoming president of *Time Warner* in 1995 what position did Richard Parsons take in 2000 for the amalgamated media group AOL-Time Warner?
A) CO-CHIEF OPERATIONS DIRECTOR
B) DEPUTY VICE-CHAIR
C) MARKETING PRESIDENT

395.
Give the name of the Caribbean Island known as the Emerald Island.
A) MONTSERRAT
B) ANTIGUA
C) NEVIS

396.
Which African country was the source and origin of freemasonry?
A) SENEGAL
B) EGYPT
C) MOROCCO

397.
Name the princess in mythology who was the daughter of Agenor, the black king of Tyre, and whose name was given to a continent.
A) ASTRAL
B) AMERICANA
C) EUROPA

398.
Known as the 'Traveling Romanies', this group claims descent from ancient Egypt. Who are they?
A) PICTS
B) CELTS
C) GYPSIES

General Knowledge

Billionaire: Oprah Winfrey

403.
Which country's national flag includes the colors, red, yellow, and green and a black star?
A) ETHIOPIA
B) GHANA
C) JAMAICA

404.
How does history remember Adelaide Smith, one of the most pioneering women activists of nineteenth century Europe?
A) ABOLITIONIST
B) MISSIONARY
C) AFRICAN FEMINIST

399.
The term "Amen" used to end prayer was originally the name of a deity in which region?
A) UPPER EGYPT
B) LOWER EGYPT
C) RIVER EUPHRATES

405.
Which goddess is the most honored and revered of all time?
A) HATHOR
B) ISIS
C) SHEBA

400.
What yellow or white starchy tuber is eaten like a potato?
A) DASHEEN
B) YAM
C) BREAD FRUIT

406.
Which black Pope of Rome introduced the *Feast of Purification* into the Catholic religion?
A) GALASIUS
B) ST. PETER
C) MILITIADES

401.
What country has the largest population of people of African descent outside of Africa?
A) PAPUA NEW GUINEA
B) BRAZIL
C) U.S.A.

407.
It has many names but is best known as Oware. What is Oware?
A) AFRICAN DANCE
B) AFRICAN CUISINE
C) AFRICAN BOARD GAME

402.
What is the capital city of Nigeria?
A) ABUJA
B) LAGOS
C) ACCRA

408.
The Wolof people are the main ethnic group of which African country?
A) SENEGAL
B) GAMBIA
C) SOMALIA

409.
Name the famous spear created by the Zulu king, Shaka.
A) EXCALLIBAR
B) ASSEGAI
C) MIOLNIR

410.
Which Island has on its coat-of-arms the words 'Out of Many One People'?
A) CUBA
B) JAMAICA
C) SEYCHELLES

411.
Until recently which capital city had as many as thirteen North East African obelisks also known Cleopatra's Needles?
A) ROME
B) WASHINGTON DC
C) LONDON

412.
Which city in the U.S. is home to the African American Museum?
A) DETROIT
B) ATLANTA
C) DALLAS

413.
Name the only country with one color on its national flag.
A) KUWAIT
B) LIBYA
C) SENEGAL

414.
What is the collective name for the group of islands that includes Martinique and Guadeloupe?
A) THE SEYCHELLES
B) THE CAYMAN ISLANDS
C) THE WINDWARD ISLANDS

415.
In which country can the city of Timbuktu be found?
A) MALI
B) MALAWI
C) MOROCCO

416.
What name is given to the instrument brought to the north of Britain by the migrating black settlers of the Iberian Peninsular?
A) BUGLE
B) SPANISH GUITAR
C) BAGPIPES

417.
Formally known as 'Lake Nyanza' it is the second largest in the world and largest lake in Africa. Name it.
A) LAKE CHAD
B) LAKE VICTORIA
C) LAKE TANGANYIKA

418.
Name the cover girl who won a contract for an exclusive international campaign by *Revlon* during the mid 1990s.
A) IMAN
B) TYRA BANKS
C) VERONICA WEBB

419.
In the Biblical book of *Genesis*, Asenath, the Egyptian wife of Joseph, bore him two sons. Name them.
A) JACOB AND ESAU
B) MANASSEH AND EPHRAIM
C) CAIN AND ABEL

420.
Which talk show host owns the highly successful TV and film studios, *HARPO Productions*?
A) MONTEL WILLIAMS
B) ROLANDA WATTS
C) OPRAH WINFREY

General Knowledge

421.
Into which river does the Victoria Falls flow?
A) ZAMBEZI RIVER
B) RIVER ORANGE
C) BLUE NILE

422.
'Lady's Fingers' is a nickname used around the world to describe which African vegetable?
A) CHILLI PEPPERS
B) OKRA
C) GREEN BANANA

423.
Easter Island is off the continent of South America. But in what part of the world is Christmas Island?
A) AUSTRAL ASIA
B) ANTARTICA
C) CARIBBEAN

424.
In which British country was the goddess 'Nigra Dea' worshipped, better known in France as the celebrated 'Virgin of Chartres'?
A) SCOTLAND
B) ENGLAND
C) WALES

425.
Dunns River Falls is a famous tourist attraction in which country?
A) KENYA
B) UGANDA
C) JAMAICA

426.
Name Africa's largest country.
A) ALGERIA
B) SUDAN
C) CONGO

427.
Name the Gospel Standard and well-known hymn composed by the Reverend Thomas Dorsey.
A) PRECIOUS MEMORIES
B) TAKE MY HAND PRECIOUS LORD
C) OH HAPPY DAY

428.
Name the world's most populous Muslim country.
A) INDONESIA
B) ALGERIA
C) SAUDI ARABIA

429.
What do the words Sierra Leon mean?
A) MOUNTAIN IN THE SEA
B) LION MOUNTAIN
C) SEA LION

430.
What type of instrument is an Amadinda also known as Akadinda?
A) XYLOPHONE
B) GUITAR
C) VIOLIN

431.
From which country in the *Bible* was Moses' wife, Hanna?
A) ETHIOPIA
B) LEBANON
C) EGYPT

432.
In 1996 Denny Mendez became the first black beauty queen to win which beauty pageant?
A) MISS ITALY
B) MISS AUSTRALIA
C) MISS RUSSIA

433.
With which news program is the highly rated journalist, Ed Bradley, associated?
A) CNN NEWS
B) TODAY SHOW
C) 60 MINUTES

434.
In Greek mythology, Leto by Zeus is the mother of which deity?
A) THOR
B) MARS
C) APOLLO

435.
In April 1787 Richard Allen and Absalom Jones founded the *African Free Society*. Later they helped to establish America's first independent church. Name it.
A) AFRICAN METHODIST EPISCOPAL CHURCH
B) ABYSSINIAN BAPTIST CHURCH
C) ETHIOPIAN ORTHODOX CHURCH

436.
How many *Declarations of Innocence* were recited in the 'Egyptian Mystery System' before they became known as the *Ten Commandments*?
A) ELEVEN
B) FORTY-TWO
C) ONE HUNDRED

437.
Running Wild was the black musical that introduced which American dance craze?
A) THE CHARLESTON
B) THE MOONWALK
C) THE JITTERBUG

438.
In which African country would you expect to find the Dinka, Shilluk, and Nuba peoples?
A) ETHIOPIA
B) SUDAN
C) KENYA

439.
Until the beginning of 2001 how many directorships involving the 500 richest U.S. companies were held by the corporate lawyer, Vernon E. Jordan?
A) TWENTY
B) FIFTEEN
C) TEN

440.
What is the biblical term for the original inhabitants of Persia?
A) ELAMITES
B) HITTITES
C) KUSHITES

441.
When Anita St. Hill won this beauty pageant in 1996, she emulated Melanie Abdounn's achievement two years prior as the first black *Miss United Kingdom*. What crown did Ms St. Hill win?
A) MISS ENGLAND
B) MISS REPUBLIC OF IRELAND
C) MISS GREAT BRITAIN

442.
Which one of the following was named after Cyprian, the martyred African saint, who is commemorated by Catholics and Protestants every September?
A) SISTINE CHAPEL IN ROME
B) REPUBLIC OF CYPRUS
C) CINNAMON

443.
How many Islands in the Atlantic Ocean make up the Canary Islands?
A) 7
B) 10
C) 15

444.
What year did the international celebration known as *African Liberation Day* begin?
A) 1958
B) 1963
C) 1965

General Knowledge

445.
What type of instrument is a Gangan or a Dundun?
A) FLUTE
B) BONGOS
C) TALKING DRUM

446.
Jazz, Night Shade, Saracen, and Sabre were famous British and American TV personalities. As what did they achieve fame?
A) WRESTLERS
B) GLADIATORS
C) DANCERS

447.
Since 1989 the *Peters Projection* has been replacing the *Mercator's Projection* as the most accurate design to date, of what?
A) COMPUTER SCREEN
B) WEATHER SATELLITE
C) WORLD ATLAS

448.
Which of the following written by the poet James Weldon Johnson has come to be regarded as the African American national anthem?
A) LIFT EVERY VOICE AND SING
B) OL' MAN RIVER
C) WE SHALL OVERCOME

449.
What is the capital of Trinidad?
A) PORT-AU-PRINCE
B) PORT OF SPAIN
C) SPANISH TOWN

450.
Which West African country did Agbani Darego represent when she became *Miss World* in 2001?
A) GHANA
B) GAMBIA
C) NIGERIA

451.
In 1663 a new English coin was struck, made from West African gold. What did it become known as?
A) THE KRUGERRAND
B) THE GUINEA
C) THE STERLING

452.
The Chaga, Gogo, Nayasa, and Sambaa people are just some of the ethnic groups that make up this country. Name it.
A) GHANA
B) TANZANIA
C) RWANDA

453.
Which famous personality had the nickname "Satchmo"?
A) SATCHEL PAIGE
B) LOUIS ARMSTRONG
C) NAT KING COLE

454.
What is the correct term to describe the group of people from Central Africa known as Pygmies?
A) TWA
B) BUSHONGO
C) WATUSI

455.
In which African kingdom is the 'Oba' the ruling monarch?
A) ZANZIBAR
B) BENIN
C) NIGER

456.
Which desert divides North Africa from the Middle East?
A) NUBIAN
B) SAHARA
C) NEGEV

457.
They are depicted on Cretan remains and were known as Amazons in the story of *Helen of Troy*. Who were the Amazons?
A) ETHIOPIAN JEWS
B) SUDANESE PRINCESSES
C) AFRICAN WOMEN SOLDIERS

458.
Which African country's coastline includes the Atlantic Ocean and the Mediterranean Sea?
A) MOROCCO
B) ALGERIA
C) TUNISIA

459.
At 19,340 feet what is the highest mountain in Africa?
A) ATLAS MOUNTAINS
B) MOUNT KILIMANJARO
C) MOUNT KENYA

460.
To what ethnic group in North Africa do the Tuareg people belong?
A) KIKUYA
B) ARAB
C) BERBER

461.
Saint Maurice, "The Moor," is the German Patron Saint for two of the following industries. Which is the odd one out?
A) CLOTHES MAKERS
B) SWORD SMITHS
C) IRON SMITHS

462.
The Kora is a harp-like lute that is used mainly in which region of continental Africa?
A) WEST AFRICA
B) EAST AFRICA
C) NORTH AFRICA

463.
What nickname was given to the black cowboy Nat Love because of his phenomenal shooting accuracy?
A) DEAD EYE DICK
B) DEADWOOD DICK
C) MIDNIGHT RIDER

464.
The French-based African Rumba Rock musician, Papa Wemba, became known as the "King of the Sapeurs". Who or what are the "Sapeurs"?
A) FASHION DESIGNERS MOVEMENT
B) CONTEMPORARY DANCE MOVEMENT
C) RAVE ORGANIZERS

465.
For which East African country is Asmara the capital?
A) ERITREA
B) SOMALIA
C) ETHIOPIA

466.
Name the restaurant franchise founded by Naomi Campbell, Elle Macpherson, and Christy Turlington.
A) HARD ROCK CAFE
B) FASHION CAFE
C) PLANET HOLLYWOOD

467.
Benedict, "The Moor," considered to be the most humble and sacrificing of the Christian saints, was born on which Mediterranean Island?
A) SICILY
B) PHOENICIA
C) CORSICA

468.
What position was given to Abraham Hannibal by royal appointment, because of loyalty to his close friend Peter "The Great"?
A) ROYAL PATRON
B) HEAD OF THE RUSSIAN PARLIAMENT
C) COMMANDER IN CHIEF OF THE RUSSIAN ARMY

General Knowledge

Party time: Kente cloth and Kwanzaa celebration

473.
What country did Janelle Penning Commissiony represent when she became the first black *Miss Universe* in 1977?
A) TRINIDAD AND TOBAGO
B) JAMAICA
C) U.S.A.

474.
Which African capital city lies closest to the equator?
A) KAMPALA
B) ADDIS ABABA
C) KHARTOUM

469.
For which country is Nairobi the capital?
A) KENYA
B) NIGER
C) ANGOLA

475.
Dounne Alexander Moore's herbal food line known as *Grammas* is sold throughout Europe in major chains. What type of food is it?
A) BISCUITS
B) CEREALS
C) SAUCES

470.
Chevalier De St. Georges, "The black Prince Charming" in eighteenth century France, led which republican army during the French revolution?
A) LA LOYALISTS
B) LA LEGION FOREIGN
C) LA LEGION NOIRE

476.
What did the symbol of the *Ankh* represent in Ancient Ethiopia and Egypt?
A) LIFE
B) WISDOM
C) THE CREATOR

471.
Name the Egyptian deity who was often represented as the head of a Jackal.
A) OSIRIS
B) ANUBIS
C) SET

477.
From which African country does the fabric known as Kente cloth originate?
A) BOTSWANA
B) KENYA
C) GHANA

472.
Born in Bermuda in 1788, she later became the first black woman to have her memoirs published after escaping slavery. Name her.
A) SOJOURNER TRUTH
B) MARY PRINCE
C) HARRIET TUBMAN

478.
In which year did Jennifer Josephine Hosten of Grenada become the first black woman to win the *Miss World* crown?
A) 1968
B) 1970
C) 1974

479.
What is the largest and heaviest bird on planet earth?
A) PENGUIN
B) PEACOCK
C) OSTRICH

480.
In what year was the black Dominican lay brother, Martin de Porres, canonized as a saint of the Roman Catholic Church?
A) 1639
B) 1662
C) 1962

481.
What is the official language of Zambia and Zimbabwe?
A) ENGLISH
B) SHONA
C) XHOSA

482.
More people have died from this disease than any other in human history. Name it.
A) CANCER
B) MALARIA
C) CHOLERA

483.
What is the unit of currency used in Nigeria?
A) DOLLAR
B) CEDI
C) NAIRA

484.
In African culture, what is a Griot?
A) AN ORAL HISTORIAN
B) A MEDICINE MAN
C) A HIGH PRIEST

485.
What is the official language of Ethiopia?
A) SWAHILI
B) AMHARIC
C) ARABIC

486.
What is the capital city of Zimbabwe?
A) MONROVIA
B) HARARE
C) DAKAR

487.
What musical festival began in Jamaica's Montego Bay in 1978?
A) REGGAE SUNSPLASH
B) CARIBBEAN JAZZ FESTIVAL
C) CALYPSOFEST

488.
What is the smallest country in the western hemisphere?
A) GRENADA
B) BELIZE
C) BERMUDA

489.
In 1857 the naval captain, William Hall, became the first black person to be awarded this decoration. Name it.
A) THE VICTORIA CROSS
B) COMMANDER OF THE BRITISH EMPIRE
C) KNIGHTHOOD

490.
Name Africa's most populous nation.
A) EGYPT
B) NIGERIA
C) ETHIOPIA

General Knowledge

491.
Arguably the most popular beverage in ancient Egypt was a drink called Zythus. What type of drink was it?
A) WINE
B) BEER
C) SPIRITS

492.
Europe's leading culturist of the ninth century was an African Moor named Zaryab. Which one of the following contributions was *not* his?
A) INTRODUCING ASPARAGUS TO EUROPE
B) IMPROVING THE LUTE INSTRUMENT
C) DESIGNING THE HARPSICHORD

493.
The 'Paps of Anu' named after Danu, the most revered of the black Irish deities, is what type of geological formation in Ireland?
A) MOUNTAINS
B) CLIFFS
C) CAVES

494.
Name Britain's most popular broadcaster who since 1992 has been the International Television News's anchorperson for *News At Ten*?
A) MOIRA STEWART
B) RAGEH OMAAR
C) TREVOR McDONALD

495.
From which country in 1921 did the woman aviation pioneer, Bessie Coleman, become the first black woman to gain a pilot's license?
A) U.S.A.
B) FRANCE
C) GERMANY

Literature & Art

Egyptian Hieroglyphs

"Nothing can dim the light that shines from within"

Maya Angelou

Literature and Art are two of the most pervasive mediums in conveying the thoughts and aspirations of the human spirit. Whether it be a contemporary work of fiction, or a historical artifact, the contributions made by black writers and artists to this field of human endeavor, is just beginning to receive the credit and status it deserves. After all, some of the oldest paintings ever discovered, including the Lascaux cave paintings in France, leave unmistakable fingerprints of the black artists who drew them. The oldest representation of a human body is the Grimaldi figurine known as 'The Venus of Willendorf'. Even the earliest forms of paleography preceding and influencing the Egyptian hieroglyphs, have yet to be deciphered and understood. As for the African influence on religious art, it is evident from the earliest pictures of the Madonna and child in Europe, including France's 'Vierge Noire' or 'Our Lady of Puy', Russia's 'Notre Dame of Kazan', Spain's 'Queen of the Pyrenees', Poland's 'Lady of Czestochowa', Italy's 'Santa Maria di Siponto', and the painting of Christ inside the Franciscan Order in Rome - All of these images are depicted as black.

Then there is the book of the *Old Testament* in the *Bible*. A lot of its initial subject matter and personalities have either been removed or re-authored. Now I understand that to many people this is of no significance, because it is indeed the content of the *Bible* that is relevant, not who wrote it, i.e. it is God's word. But if we accept God represents truth, then we should also accept the truth about those who wrote "the truth". It reminds me of when I was growing up and I used to have...er...differences of opinions with my grandmother. If ever I was winning an argument she would often try to shut me up by saying "you know too much for your own good". In other words "shut up!". My weakness back then was that I found it difficult to shut up if I felt I was in the right. Perhaps this weakness is now my strength. An example of what I mean is, there is so much evidence now available which proves that as wise as he was, Solomon could not have written the book of *Proverbs* as alleged. The continuation of such an assertion is nothing short of embarrassing. Nowadays modern Christians tend to look no further than the *King James* edition to provide them with the "Gospel Truth". The early revision and editing of these religious texts by Latin and Greek scholars has resulted in confusion for those who try to use the *Bible* as a historical source. At this point, it is worth reminding ourselves that the oldest book in Western civilization, Homer's *Odyssey*, was written apparently in the 9th Century B.C. This is, at the very least, 3000 years after the formulation of the Egyptian Hieroglyphs.

When analyzing some of the historical works by people of African descent made to literature, one does not have to actually look much further than Greek literature. Not only are many of the early characters in Greek mythology black, the Greek scholars themselves paid homage to their teachers, with a few exceptions, notably Aristotle. He, on sacking the Egyptian library at Alexandria, mysteriously became credited with authorship of over 200 of its books. In sub-Saharan Africa there are records in Islamic literature, of many of the revered schools of learning, including the library of Timbuktu, which was twice razed to the ground. The real tragedy is that most of the books destroyed were single-issue copies. When a book was destroyed, a generation of knowledge went with it.

The following questions attempt to provide a backdrop to some of these influential writers and the impact of their work through the ages. It also offers a contemporary account of some of the popular figures in the fields of literature and art today.

Rosetta, it is written in the stone

Exhaling: Terry McMillan

500.
What famous sculpture on view at the Museum of the City of New York was originally designed as a woman of color breaking free from chains?
A) SPHINX
B) VENUS DE MILO
C) STATUE OF LIBERTY

501.
The author Robert Beck is better known by which name?
A) ICEBERG SLIM
B) THE MACK DADDY
C) THE DON DADA

496.
In 2001 Stephen L. Carter received the largest advance from a publisher for a first-time work of fiction. Name his debut novel.
A) DAUGHTER: A NOVEL
B) EMPEROR OF OCEAN PARK
C) SNAKESKIN

502.
What written language did the black writer, Alexander Pushkin, help to create?
A) GERMAN
B) FRENCH
C) RUSSIAN

497.
Which literary heavyweight wrote the novels *Mama*, *Disappearing Acts* and *Waiting To Exhale*?
A) BELL HOOKS
B) BEBE MOORE-CAMPBELL
C) TERRY McMILLAN

503.
Whose autobiography was entitled *The Long Walk To Freedom*?
A) SUGE KNIGHT
B) MIKE TYSON
C) NELSON MANDELA

498.
Which of the following novels by contemporary British writer, Zadie Smith, was a bestseller before being turned into a mini TV series in the UK?
A) THE AUTOGRAPH MAN
B) WHITE TEETH
C) DIENTES BLANCOS

504.
Name the black British newspaper that was founded by Rupert Murdoch's Ghanaian son-in-law in 1995.
A) THE VOICE
B) THE NEW NATION
C) THE WEEKLY JOURNAL

499.
What is the oldest form of writing known to man?
A) GREEK ALPHABET
B) HIEROGLYPHS
C) BRAILLE

505.
Which of the following books by Walter Mosley introduced Easy Rawlins to the world in 1990?
A) A LITTLE YELLOW DOG
B) WHITE BUTTERFLY
C) DEVIL IN A BLUE DRESS

506.
Which American coin featuring F. D. Roosevelt was designed in 1943 by the African American sculpture, Selma Hortense Burke?
A) NICKEL
B) DIME
C) SILVER BUCK

507.
What famous novel by Ernest J. Gains became a successful TV movie starring Cicely Tyson?
A) THE WOMEN OF BREWSTER PLACE
B) THE AUTOBIOGRAPHY OF MISS JANE PITTMAN
C) DRIVING MISS DAISY

508.
The legendary James TOP, New York's 'Fab Five Freddy', and the Haitian American Jean-Michel Basquiat, are best remembered for which type of art?
A) GRAFFITI
B) MODERN ART
C) POTTERY

509.
Which one of the following magazines is part of the Quincy Jones Entertainment group?
A) INSPIRED
B) PRIDE
C) VIBE

510.
Name the famous poem by Claude McKay that was adopted by Winston Churchill during World War II?
A) FLANDERS FIELDS
B) IF WE MUST DIE
C) SHAPE OF KINGS TO COME

511.
Name the NBA great whose best-seller autobiography was published in two volumes, *Bad as I Wanna Be* and *Walk on the Wild Side*?
A) DENNIS RODMAN
B) CHARLES BARCLAY
C) SHAQUILLE O'NEAL

512.
Which increasingly popular Kemetic word was symbolized as a boat in antiquity, and represented the principles of karma or natural law?
A) GEB
B) MAAT
C) KISMET

513.
Which supermodel wrote the best selling novel *Swan*?
A) TYRA BANKS
B) ALEK WEK
C) NAOMI CAMPBELL

514.
For what style of writing was, Sappho, the most successful female lyricist of ancient Greece?
A) COMEDY
B) POETRY
C) GREEK TRAGEDY

515.
Of the following works by Bebe Moore Campbell, give the name of her first published novel.
A) YOUR BLUES AIN'T LIKE MINE
B) SWEET SUMMER
C) BROTHERS AND SISTERS

Black Russian: Alexander Pushkin

Beloved by many: Toni Morrison

516.
Name the classic book of daily meditation written by the internationally renowned author, Iyanla Vanzant.
A) ACTS OF FAITH
B) HUSIA
C) TAPPING THE POWER WITHIN

517.
What is the name of the weekly newspaper distributed internationally by the Nation of Islam?
A) FREEDOM'S JOURNAL
B) THE ALARM
C) THE FINAL CALL

518.
With which book did Toni Morrison, the 1993 Nobel Prize winning novelist, win the Pulitzer Prize in 1988?
A) TAR BABY
B) BELOVED
C) SONG OF SOLOMON

519.
Name one of Africa's most prolific female writer's whose works include *In the Ditch*, *Second Class Citizen*, and *The Joys of Motherhood*.
A) GRACE AGOT
B) BUCHI EMECHETA
C) NTOZAKE SHANGE

520.
She was the most influential female writer during the Harlem Renaissance, and later published the literary masterpiece *Their Eyes Were Watching God*. Name her.
A) ZORA NEALE HURSTON
B) JESSIE REDMON FAUSET
C) NELLA LARSEN

521.
Which country has controversially been the trustee of the priceless Benin Bronzes since 1897?
A) BRITAIN
B) FRANCE
C) HOLLAND

522.
In classical Greek literature, two black women founded *The Oracle of Dodona*. In which form do the women appear?
A) CATS
B) DOVES
C) DRAGONS

523.
Give the other name for one of the most adored paintings in Russian history, *The Virgin of Vladimir*.
A) QUEEN OF THE PYRENEES
B) OUR LADY OF ST. PETERSBURG
C) NOTRE DAME OF KAZAN

524.
Which award-winning American literary classic was the first novel published by Ralph Ellison?
A) THE FOXES OF HARROW
B) THE FIRE NEXT TIME
C) INVISIBLE MAN

525.
Originally known as Djhuiti, by what other name was the ancient Kemetic god of writing known?
A) THOTH
B) PAPYRI
C) PTAH

526.
Name the black European painter whose portrait fetched over $3.5 million dollars, a world record, when it was auctioned at Christies of London in 1970?
A) ROBERT DUNCANSON
B) JUAN DE PAREJA
C) RON MOODY

527.
This writer's work includes the play *Amen Corner* and the novels *Go Tell It On The Mountain*, and *Giovanni's Room*. Name him.
A) JAMES BALDWIN
B) AUGUST WILSON
C) LANGSTONE HUGHES

528.
Which one of the following books did the French writer, Alexander Dumas Pere, *not* write?
A) THE 3 MUSKETEERS
B) THE 4 MUSKETEERS
C) THE COUNT OF MONTE CRISTO

529.
What is the most successful work to date by the best-selling novelist, Alice Walker?
A) SINGLE BLACK FEMALE
B) THE COLOR PURPLE
C) TEMPLE OF MY FAMILIAR

530.
In West African and Caribbean folk tales, what kind of creature is *Anansie*?
A) SPIDER
B) SNAKE
C) FOX

531.
The *Golden Stool* is the most sacred emblem of which West African people?
A) MANDINKA
B) IGBO
C) ASHANTI

532.
He was Islam's first Muezzin and helped to write the *Quran*. Who was he?
A) MOHAMMED
B) BILAL
C) ALI

533.
Name America's first black newspaper, published in 1827 by its first black graduate, John Russwurm.
A) FREEDOM'S JOURNAL
B) THE AFRO-AMERICAN
C) WATCHMAN

534.
Which African American newspaper is the oldest continually published non-religious newspaper in the United States?
A) PITTSBURGH COURIER
B) PHILADELPHIA TRIBUNE
C) AMSTERDAM NEWS

535.
Name Victor Headley's cult classic novel, which was first published by the X Press in 1991.
A) ICED
B) YARDIE
C) BABY FATHER

Prolific: Buchi Emecheta

Masking emotions: Benin Art

539.
Name the Trinidadian intellectual who in 1936 wrote the first internationally acclaimed Caribbean novel, *Minty Alley*, and later the literary masterpiece, *The Black Jacobeans*?
A) C. L. R. JAMES
B) UNA MARSONS
C) GEORGE PADMORE

540.
What was the name of the debut book published by the comedian Chris Rock in 1997?
A) ROCK THIS
B) ROCK MY WORLD
C) DON'T ROCK THE BOAT

541.
Which author was the first to translate the Jamaican dialect into a concise written language?
A) MUTABARUKKA
B) MIKEY SMITH
C) LOUISE BENNETT

536.
Name the black woman said to be Shakespeare's mistress, and of whom he allegedly wrote *Dark Lady of the Sonnets*.
A) LUCY MORGAN
B) LISA MORTON
C) LETISHA MORANN

542.
In Greek mythology, which daughter of the Ethiopian Monarch, Capheus, did Perseus marry?
A) MEDUSA
B) APHRODITE
C) ANDROMEDA

537.
In which Pulitzer prize-winning book by Alex Haley does the character Kizzy appear?
A) THE NEXT GENERATION
B) THE AUTOBIOGRAPHY OF MALCOLM X
C) ROOTS

543.
Who became the first black writer to win the Pulitzer Prize for literature, with the poetry collection *Annie Allen* in 1950?
A) STERLIN A. BROWN
B) GWENDOLINE BROOKS
C) FRANK YERBY

538.
Best-known for his novels *Dopefiend*, *Never Die Alone*, and *Daddy Cool*, how many novels did the former pimp, drug addict and arm robber turned writer, Donald Goines, pen during his short 5 year writing career?
A) 12
B) 16
C) 25

544.
Which ancient book records the love affair between King Solomon and Queen Makeda of Sheba?
A) THE SONG OF SOLOMON
B) THE VEDAS
C) THE KEBRA NEGAST

545.
In which decade did the Harlem Renaissance begin?
A) 1920s
B) 1940s
C) 1960s

546.
What literary prize was founded in 1994 by the author and actress Marsha Hunt?
A) THE ORANGE LITERARY PRIZE
B) THE BOOKER PRIZE
C) THE SAGA PRIZE

547.
Detroit has the *Wall of Dignity*, but which other U.S. city exhibits a famous African American mural called *Wall of Respect*?
A) CHICAGO
B) LOS ANGELES
C) ATLANTA

548.
'I am a man and nothing human is alien to me', was immortalized by the stylist, Terence Afer, in what language?
A) GREEK
B) LATIN
C) SPANISH

549.
This Liberian is regarded as being one of the most important black political writer's of the nineteenth century. Name him.
A) FREDERICK DOUGLASS
B) EDWARD WILMOT BLYDEN
C) GLADSTONE WILBERFORCE

550.
What does the word 'Krishna' mean in the ancient Hindu language?
A) BLACK
B) GOD PHARAOH
C) THE ENLIGHTENED ONE

551.
Which English poet of Jamaican descent wrote the masterpiece *The Ring and the Book* in 1869?
A) WILLIAM BLAKE
B) WALT WHITMAN
C) ROBERT BROWNING

552.
Who became Britain's first dub poet after publishing *Voices of the Living and the Dead*, in 1974?
A) JEAN "BINTA" BREEZE
B) BENJAMIN ZEPHANIAH
C) LINTON KWESI JOHNSON

553.
Whose autobiography was entitled *Lady Sings the Blues*?
A) ETHEL WATERS
B) BILLIE HOLIDAY
C) DIANA ROSS

554.
Plato, Socrates, Shakespeare and La Fontaine are just a few western writers profoundly influenced by which great African writer of the sixth century B.C.?
A) JOB
B) AESOP
C) AKHNATON

Free spirit: Maya Angelou

Literature & Art

Taking an Odyssey: Derek Walcott

559.
How many languages are written on the
Rosetta Stone?
A) THREE
B) FOUR
C) FIVE

560.
In Homer's, *The Iliad*, who are described as
either "The Worthy" or "Favorites of the Gods"?
A) PHOENICIANS
B) EGYPTIANS
C) ETHIOPIANS

555.
Which famous author wrote the autobiographical
I Know Why The Cage Bird Sings?
A) ROSA GUY
B) TONI MORRISON
C) MAYA ANGELOU

561.
Which book in the *Bible* records the victories
of the Ethiopian monarch, Taharqa, in Asia?
A) EXODUS
B) KINGS
C) CHRONICLES

556.
How many black people did the early
periodical, *The Gentlemen's Magazine*,
estimate in 1764, to be living in London at
that time?
A) 20,000
B) 10,000
C) 5,000

562.
In the ancient Kemetic story of Set slaying his
brother Osiris, how many pieces did Isis
gather to reassemble Osiris's body?
A) SEVEN
B) FOURTEEN
C) TWENTY-ONE

557.
Henry Ossawa Tanner, the famous black
nineteenth century religious artist, painted
two of the following three masterpieces.
Name the odd one out.
A) LAND OF THE LOTUS EATER
B) DANIEL IN THE LION'S DEN
C) BANJO LESSON

563.
Which of the following journalists became the
New York Times first black managing editor in
September 2001?
A) JAYSON BLAIR
B) LLOYD M. GARRISON
C) GERALD BOYD

558.
Which award-winning novel by Chinua
Achebe became the first internationally
recognized work of African fiction in English?
A) MAN OF THE PEOPLE
B) THINGS FALL APART
C) GIRLS AT WAR

564.
In Greek mythology, what was the other name
for Zeus, also known as 'The Father of the
Gods'?
A) EGYPTOS
B) IONA
C) ETHIOPS

565.
With works including *Omeros* and *The Star-Apple Kingdom*, in what year did the St. Lucian writer, Derek Walcott, awarded the Nobel Prize for literature?
A) 1992
B) 1996
C) 1999

566.
What was the reward offered for the capture David Walker, following his publishing of *Walker's Appeal* in 1829?
A) $5,000
B) $10,000
C) $20,000

567.
What was unusual about the way Ntozake Shange first wrote her 1982 novel *Sassafrass, Indigo and Cyprus*?
A) IT WAS WRITTEN IN DIALECT
B) IT WAS WRITTEN IN CAPITALS
C) IT CONTAINED NO PUNCTUATION

568.
What is the best-known work by the Nubian saint, Augustine?
A) THE CONFESSIONS
B) THE CITY OF GOD
C) THE KAMA SUTRA

569.
Because of this pioneering author, *African Heritage Month* (black history month) has become a celebrated festival throughout the Western Hemisphere. Name Him.
A) CARTER G. WOODSON
B) GEORGE W. WILLIAMS
C) J. A. ROGERS

570.
According to the Japanese proverb who must have some "African Blood in order to be brave"?
A) SAMURAI WARRIOR
B) SUMO WRESTLER
C) BUDDHIST MONK

571.
What 'Sura' or chapter in the *Quran*, is named after the celebrated Ethiopian sage Lokman?
A) FIRST
B) THIRTY-FIRST
C) FIFTY-FIRST

572.
In 1773, twelve years after she was taken from Cameroon, Phillis Wheatley became the first Diaspora based African woman to do what?
A) PAINT A MASTERPIECE
B) OWN A NEWSPAPER
C) PUBLISH A BOOK

573.
Which *Old Testament* book has its origins in the earlier writings of Pharaoh Amen-em-ope?
A) GENESIS
B) PROVERBS
C) PSALMS

Perfect figurine: Venus of Willendorf

Scholar: Henry Louis Gates, Jr.

578.
What Alice Randall novel, given publication permission by the Atlanta Appeals Court in October 2001, parodies the American classic, *Gone With the Wind*?
A) GONE TO LUNCH
B) INHERIT THE WIND
C) THE WIND DONE GONE

579.
Which religious work of art has been attributed to Ishmael, son of Abraham in the *Bible* and *Torah*?
A) ARK OF THE COVENANT
B) THE KA'ABA
C) DEAD SEA SCROLLS

574.
How old is the Grimaldi carving known as *The Venus of Willendorf*?
A) 10,000 YEARS
B) 15,000 YEARS
C) 25,000 YEARS

580.
Its first edition was printed in 1834 and today it is recognized as the oldest black newspaper in existence. Name it.
A) (HAITI'S) LE NOUVEAU MONDE
B) THE JAMAICA GLEANER
C) THE AFRICAN TIMES

575.
The black Madonna in the painting known as *Our Lady of Czestochowa*, is the most sacred emblem of which country?
A) AUSTRIA
B) CZECHOSLOVAKIA
C) POLAND

581.
Which former Pulitzer Prize winner was appointed Poet Laureate for the United States between 1993 and 1995?
A) RITA DOVE
B) NIKKI GIOVANNI
C) MAYA ANGELOU

576.
What is the name for the Egyptian sun god?
A) AMON
B) SET
C) RA

582.
Why did Turner Prize winner, Chris Ofili's, *Virgin Mary* painting, threaten the closure of New York's Brooklyn Museum after an exhibition in 1998?
A) HE USED BULL DUNG
B) HE USED ELEPHANT DUNG
C) HE USED HORSE MANURE

577.
Name the magazine first published in 1945 and owned by the Johnson Publishing Company.
A) EBONY
B) JET
C) BLACK ENTERPRISE

583.
The author of *Lessons in Living*, Susan L. Taylor, was the former editor-in-chief of which magazine?
A) ESSENCE
B) UPSCALE
C) SISTER 2 SISTER

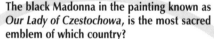

584.
A black Roman writer named Tiro, born circa 103A.D. is on record as being the first to develop which form of writing?
A) JOINED UP WRITING
B) SHORTHAND WRITING
C) CAPITAL LETTERS

585.
What academic term is often used to describe the spoken or written slang of "black English"?
A) PATIOS
B) EBONICS
C) CREOLE

586.
Which famous book by Harper Lee, was about a black farmer named Tom Robinson, falsely accused of rape?
A) THE ADVENTURES OF HUCKLEBERRY FINN
B) UNCLE TOM'S CABIN
C) TO KILL A MOCKINGBIRD

587.
Who wrote the award-winning children novel, *Hacker*, and *Pig Heart Boy*, the film version of which won a BAFTA for best children's drama?
A) CARYL PHILLIPS
B) VENESSA WALTERS
C) MALORIE BLACKMAN

588.
Which book in the *New Testament* traces the paternal genealogy of Jesus back to the black king Solomon?
A) ST. MATTHEW
B) ST. JOHN
C) REVELATION

589.
In 1996, Calixthe Beyala, won the French academy's prestigious *Grand Prix* award for literature. Name the novel.
A) BATULA
B) LES HONNEURS PERDUS
C) NOIRE UN BLANC

590.
For which institution of learning is the writer and scholar, Henry Louis Gates, Jr., a director of education?
A) MOORHOUSE
B) YALE
C) HARVARD

591.
What was the name of the black knight that the beautiful, Queen Isolde, falls in love with, in the *Legend of King Arthur*?
A) SIR PALAMEDES
B) SIR LANCELOT
C) SIR GALAHAD

592.
Who, in 1986, became the first African to receive the Nobel Prize for literature?
A) PATRICK CHAMOISÉAU
B) WOLE SOYINKA
C) AIMÉ CÉSAIRE

593.
This former Howard University professor's work include, *Cry the Beloved Country*, which was made into a film. Name the American painter.
A) LOIS MAILOU JONES
B) LEROY CAMPBELL
C) BRENDA JOYSMITH

594.
Which of the following books by South African writer Peter Abrahams was arguably the most powerful novel involved in the dismantling of apartheid?
A) TONGUES OF FIRE
B) A WREATH FOR NDOMO
C) MINE BOY

595.
What monumental book did the "Father of Trinidadian Politics," Eric Williams, leave as his political legacy?
A) CRIME AND PUNISHMENT
B) RACE AND CLASS
C) CAPITALISM AND SLAVERY

Literature & Art

596.
His house at 219 North Summit Street, Dayton, Ohio, is a national shrine. He was America's first renowned black poet. Name him.
A) WILLIAM WELLS BROWN
B) PAUL LAURENCE DUNBAR
C) CLAUDE McKAY

597.
Whose autobiography was entitled *Off the Court* and whose memoirs, *Days of Grace*, was published after his untimely death in 1993?
A) ARTHUR ASHE
B) THURGOOD MARSHALL
C) SUN RA

598.
The prolific twentieth century Caribbean writer, Wilson Harris, author of *Palace of the Peacock* and *The Waiting Room*, was a native of which country?
A) GUYANA
B) TRINIDAD
C) BELIZE

599.
For what literary style is the award-winning writer, Nikki Giovanni, best remembered?
A) SCIENCE FICTION
B) POETRY
C) CHILDREN'S BOOKS

600.
Which world-renowned abolitionist started a newspaper called the *North Star*?
A) FREDERICK DOUGLASS
B) BOOKER T. WASHINGTON
C) DAVID WALKER

601.
This famous institution at Ipet Isut in ancient Kemet, was the first known of its kind anywhere in the ancient world. What was it?
A) A HOSPITAL
B) A LIBRARY
C) A MUSEUM

602.
Name the literary giant whose works include *The Weary Blues*, *The Big Sea*, and the long-running Broadway hit *Mulatto*.
A) LANGSTON HUGHES
B) IMAMU AMIRI BARAKA
C) LEROI JONES

603.
The second century African writer, Lucius Apulius, is still recognized as one of the all-time great exponents of this particular writing genre. Name it.
A) ROMANCE
B) DRAMA
C) SATIRE

604.
Which recently discovered Rembrandt masterpiece depicts the anointing of an Ethiopian man by the apostle Philip?
A) THE BAPTISM OF THE EUNUCH
B) TWO ABYSSINIANS
C) THE CALLING OF ST. MATTHEW

605.
Which play attributed to William Shakespeare is about the love affair between, Tamora, the Queen of Goths, and Aaron, the black-a-moor?
A) MACBETH
B) OTHELLO
C) TITUS ANDRONICUS

606.
In March 1997, Ekow Eshun, became the youngest ever and the first black editor, for a British glossy international magazine. Name it.
A) GQ
B) ARENA
C) VANITY FAIR

607.
Richard Wright wrote two of the following novels. Both were American Book-of-the-Month Club selections. Name the odd one out.
A) BLACK BOY
B) NATIVE SON
C) THE BLUEST EYE

608.
Athasan Mohammed's book, History and *Description of Africa*, was for three centuries the most authoritative in Europe-on what subject?
A) AFRICAN GEOGRAPHY
B) AFRICAN ART
C) AFRICAN RELIGION

609.
Which British author wrote *The Unbelonging* in 1985, *A Kindness to the Children* in 1992, and *Waiting in the Twilight* in 1998?
A) JOAN RILEY
B) CRYSTAL ROSE
C) JESSICA HUNTLEY

610.
The great eighteenth century Arabic translator, Job Ben Solomon, is said to have written from memory which well-known book?
A) THE BIBLE
B) THE QURAN
C) THE ENGLISH DICTIONARY

611.
In what year was the writer, Ben Okri, awarded the prestigious Booker Prize for his novel, *The Famished Road*?
A) 1989
B) 1991
C) 1993

612.
In the *New Testament* book of *St. Mark*, a North African helped Jesus to carry the cross. Name him.
A) SIMON OF CYRENE
B) STRANGER OF GALILEE
C) PAUL OF TARSUS

613.
Which New York institute houses the largest collection of black literature in the world?
A) NEW YORK LIBRARY
B) SCHOMBURG CENTER FOR RESEARCH IN BLACK CULTURE
C) MALCOLM X LIBRARY

Literature & Art

Sport

Super Bowl legend, Jerry Rice

"Some things are impossible to achieve,
but that doesn't mean the impossible
isn't sometimes achievable"

Jak

Like entertainment, black success in the arenas of sport is unquestionable. The reason for this is sporting prowess is measured by ability not color. Records, goals, and achievements have more to do with an individual's own desire and commitment, than they do with having to overcome insurmountable hurdles. Therefore, the information in this section more than in any other chapter of this book, identifies what can be achieved when (pardon the pun) one is allowed to compete on a "level playing field".

Because human potential is unlimited and our spirit infinite, there is no achievement made by one person being that cannot be surpass by another. The saying "records are there to be broken" is never more appropriate than when applied to sporting endeavor. However, as was explained in the introduction, the way the questions are phrased means that they can be asked in ten or twenty years from now and still be relevant. For instance, if in 2012 the question is asked *How many home runs did Barry Bonds hit in 2001 when establishing a new season's best in baseball?* The question is like a historical snapshot. It does not imply the record will not be broken, on the contrary it was the all-time record at the time of the book's publication. The record may well stand in ten years time but as remarkable as it is, it will eventually be surpassed. The evidence to support this assumption is based upon the fact that the score was achieved with the most number of walks i.e. pitchers choosing not to throw the ball properly at the person batting, but instead sacrificing a free "walk" unopposed, to first base.

Put simply, this goes to underline that when given circumstances of parity and opportunity, it is only natural that people of color distinguish themselves. From sport to academia, the example is the same. And fortunately for a significant number, athletic excellence has become a route to better education through sponsorships, scholarships and bursaries. The flip side to this is the unfortunate contention where certain students are actively encouraged to concentrate on a particular sport rather than on their academic pursuits. Still, its worth mentioning that aside from the financial rewards of a successful athlete, there is something primeval in our acknowledgement of the fastest male or female person on two legs, or the best pound for pound boxer in the world.

The following questions with their answers in section two provide a backdrop to a cross section of sporting activities around the world. This includes track and field, American football, boxing, swimming, baseball, rugby, basketball, golf, cricket, soccer, tennis and many more.

The answers in part two provide easy access to sporting institutions and authorities, on all the mentioned sports above and many more.

Seeing the woods for the trees

614.
Who was the first boxer to become heavyweight-boxing champion of the world four times?
A) EVANDER HOLYFIELD
B) MIKE TYSON
C) MUHAMMAD ALI

615.
She was the first black woman tennis player to win the U.S. Open since Althea Gibson. Name her.
A) LORI McNEAL
B) VENUS WILLIAMS
C) SERENA WILLIAMS

618.
For what team did Barry Bonds play when becoming baseball's season home run king in October 2001, hitting 73 runs in a single season?
A) L. A. DODGERS
B) ATLANTA BRAVES
C) SAN FRANCISCO GIANTS

619.
What sport involving a Jamaican Olympic team was featured in the film *Cool Runnings*?
A) SPRINT RELAY
B) BOBSLEIGH
C) JUDO

Double exposure: Venus and Serena Williams

616.
Name the NFL legend whose world record of 16,726 yards was surpassed by Emmitt Smith in 2003.
A) O J SIMPSON
B) JIM BROWN
C) WALTER PAYTON

617.
With 1281 goals to his tally, by what other name is the popular South American soccer player, Edson do Nascimente, better known?
A) PELE
B) MARADONNA
C) RENALDO

620.
Wilt Chamberlain, the only person to score 100 points in a professional basketball match, was one of the very first players ever to use this basketball action. Name it.
A) SKY HOOK
B) FINGER ROLL
C) SLAM DUNK

621.
On August 24, 1981, Charles Chapman became the first black swimmer to swim across this geographical water region. Name it.
A) ATLANTIC OCEAN
B) MEDITERRANEAN SEA
C) ENGLISH CHANNEL

622.
To celebrate the anniversary of Tenzing Norgay and Edmond Hilary's ascent, Sibusiso Vilane of South Africa became, in May 2003, the first African born climber to reach the peak of which mountain?
A) MOUNT SINAI
B) MOUNT EVEREST
C) MOUNT KILAMANJARO

623.
Although Anthony Ervin tied for the 50 meter freestyle gold at the Sydney Olympics, in what event during the 1988 Olympic games did Anthony Nesty of Surinam become the first black swimmer to win Olympic Gold?
A) 100 METER BACKSTROKE
B) 100 METER FREESTYLE
C) 100 METER BUTTERFLY

624.
Lady Gwendolyn Ashborough, organizer of the *Concordia Cup* competition, runs Allegria Para Siempre, who are one of the world's most successful teams in this sport. Name it.
A) BOWLING
B) POLO
C) FENCING

625.
In what position did Doug Williams of the Washington Redskins play, in his record-setting performance at Super Bowl XXII?
A) WIDE RECEIVER
B) QUARTERBACK
C) CENTER

626.
Former Holland captain, Ruud Gullit, also captained which soccer team, when dedicating his 1988 European Footballer of the Year award to Nelson Mandela?
A) AC MILAN
B) SAMPDORIA
C) CHELSEA

627.
By what record-breaking margin did Tiger Woods win the U.S. Masters golf tournament in 1997?
A) 18 STROKES
B) 12 STROKES
C) 9 STROKES

628.
Which player became the first black captain of the West Indian cricket team in 1960?
A) CLIVE LLOYD
B) LEARY CONSTANTINE
C) FRANK WORRELL

629.
In 1992 Ron Simmons became the first black heavyweight world champion for what sport?
A) WRESTLING
B) SUMO WRESTLING
C) ARM WRESTLING

630.
In what English sports league did Uriah Rennie become the first black referee in 1997?
A) SOCCER PREMIER LEAGUE
B) RUGBY SUPER LEAGUE
C) COUNTY CRICKET LEAGUE

631.
The black jockey, Isaac Murphy, was the first three-time winner of which horseracing classic?
A) THE KENTUCKY DERBY
B) THE ENGLISH DERBY
C) THE MELBOURNE CUP

632.
Name the sprint queen whose performances at the 1988 Olympic Games produced two world records and four medals.
A) EVELYN ASHFORD
B) FLORENCE GRIFFITH-JOYNER
C) VALERIE BRISCO-HOOKS

633.
France's former *Davis Cup* captain and French open winner, Yannick Noah, won how many titles throughout his tennis career?
A) THIRTY-SEVEN
B) TWENTY-THREE
C) NINETEEN

Sport

Batting not average: Hank Aaron

637.
In between leading the Chicago bulls to Six NBA championships during the 1990s, Michael Jordan played for which Major League baseball team?
A) CHICAGO CUBS
B) CHICAGO WHITESOX
C) CHICAGO BEARS

638.
Dubbed "the black Pearl," he has scored more international goals for Portugal than any other soccer player. Name him.
A) RIVELINO
B) EUSEBIO
C) SUBBUTEO

639.
By what name is the wrestler and box office draw, Dwayne Johnson, better known?
A) THE ROCK
B) BOOKER T
C) EDDIE LADD

634.
In what event was the twice Olympic gold medallist, Ed Moses, unbeaten for nine years?
A) 200 METERS
B) 400 METERS
C) 400 METER HURDLES

640.
Hank Aaron notched up 755 of these setting an all-time major lead record before his retirement in 1976. Name his achievement.
A) MOST NUMBER OF CATCHES
B) MOST HOME RUNS
C) MOST STRIKE OUTS

635.
He has stolen more bases than any other player in the history of baseball. Name the all-time great.
A) WILLIE MAYS
B) RICKY HENDERSON
C) SAMMY SOUSA

641.
His historic world record of 400 Test runs against England in April 2004 is thought to be among the best innings of all time. But what other world record score by Brian Lara is to date, still the highest achieved in first-class cricket?
A) 1001
B) 701
C) 501

636.
The legendary New Zealand international rugby player, Jonah Lomu, was best known for playing in which position?
A) WINGER
B) FLY HALF
C) PENALTY KICKER

642.
In which tennis grand slam competition has the 1970s Aboriginal player, Evonne Goolagong Cawley, won two Championship titles?
A) THE U.S. OPEN
B) THE FRENCH OPEN
C) WIMBLEDON

643.
George Weah, the first player to be named World, African, and European soccer player of the year, represented which country in international football?
A) GHANA
B) LIBERIA
C) NIGERIA

644.
By what name is the South African rugby team known?
A) THE SPRINGBOKS
B) THE ALL BLACKS
C) THE ELEPHANTS

645.
What world record time established for the 200 meters by Michael Johnson was set at the 1996 Atlanta Olympics?
A) 18.99 SECONDS
B) 19.32 SECONDS
C) 19.66 SECONDS

646.
On 30 September 2002, Chris McAlister of the Baltimore Ravens recorded the longest play in NFL history, by returning the ball for a touchdown after running how many yards?
A) 99 YARDS
B) 107 YARDS
C) 150 YARDS

647.
Name the track and field star who broke Bob Beamon's twenty-five year record for the long jump.
A) CARL LEWIS
B) WILLY BANKS
C) MIKE POWELL

648.
He is considered the greatest long distance runner ever, and set numerous world records for 5000 and 10,000 meters. Name him.
A) HICHAM EL GUERROUJ
B) HAILE GEBRSELASSIE
C) HENRY RHONO

649.
From which African region are the 'Super Eagles' and the 'Indomitable Lions', both winners of the gold medal for soccer at 1996 and 2000 Olympics respectively?
A) SOUTH AFRICA
B) EAST AFRICA
C) WEST AFRICA

650.
In 1972 Milwaukee Bucks' Wayne Embry became the first black general manager of a major league sports team. Name the sport.
A) HOCKEY
B) SOCCER
C) BASKETBALL

651.
Name the Dutch international midfield player, who in May, 2003, became the first soccer player to win the champions league with three different clubs.
A) CLARENCE SEEDORF
B) FRANK RIJKARD
C) EDGAR DAVIDS

652.
Name the former European *Golden Boot* winner who in 1998 became the all-time leading goal scorer for London's most successful premier league soccer club, Arsenal.
A) THIERRY HENRY
B) IAN WRIGHT
C) PATRICK VIERA

Cricketing phenomenon: Brian Lara

Sport

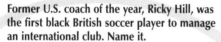

Boxed in: Mike Tyson

657.
In what sport did sprinting phenomenon Marion Jones excel, before claiming 5 medals at the 2000 Olympics in Sydney?
A) SOCCER
B) LONG JUMP
C) BASKETBALL

658.
Which Javelin thrower at the 1980 Moscow games became the first black athlete to win a throwing event at the Olympics?
A) FATIMA WHITBREAD
B) MARIA CARIDAD COLON
C) TESSA SANDERSON

653.
Name the first black professional basketball team to win a basketball championship.
A) HARLEM GLOBE TROTTERS
B) NEW YORK RENAISSANCE FIVE
C) UTAH JAZZ

659.
Who was the first British boxer to become world champion at three different weights?
A) DUKE McKENZIE
B) CHRIS EUBANKS
C) NIGEL BENN

654.
Former U.S. coach of the year, Ricky Hill, was the first black British soccer player to manage an international club. Name it.
A) NEW YORK COSMOS
B) TAMPA BAY ROWDIES
C) D.C. UNITED

660.
Which boxing legend fought Muhammad Ali three times and starred in the "Thrilla in Manila"?
A) GEORGE FOREMAN
B) JOE FRAZIER
C) KEN NORTON

655.
How old was Mike Tyson when he defeated Trevor Berbick to become the youngest world heavyweight champion in boxing history?
A) NINETEEN
B) TWENTY
C) TWENTY-ONE

661.
In 1968 Gary Sobers, still considered to be the greatest all rounder in cricket history, became the first player to do what with a cricket ball?
A) HIT THIRTY-SIX RUNS OFF A SIX BALL OVER
B) TAKE SIX CONSECUTIVE WICKETS
C) BOWL THE BALL AT 100 MILES PER HOUR

656.
Who was the first black tennis player to win a singles title at Wimbledon?
A) ARTHUR ASHE
B) ALTHEA GIBSON
C) JAMES BLAKE

662.
At what age did the 1960 triple Olympic sprint gold medallist, Wilma Rudolph, learn to walk?
A) FIVE
B) EIGHT
C) TEN

663.
Who became the first general secretary of the Professional Boxing Authority in 1993, before going on to manage the Sydney Olympics super heavyweight champion, Audley Harrison?
A) DON KING
B) HOWARD EASTMAN
C) COLIN McMILLAN

664.
Javier Sotomayor of Cuba, is still affectionately known as "Superman" for his 1993 world record jump of 2.45 meters. Name his event.
A) HIGH BOARD DIVING
B) HIGH JUMP
C) TRIPLE JUMP

665.
How many touchdowns did Emmitt Smith make for the Dallas Cowboys in 1995 when establishing the NFL record for touchdowns in a single season?
A) TWENTY-FIVE
B) THIRTY
C) THIRTY-FIVE

666.
Who won the *Heisman Trophy* in 1985, was baseball's all-star game MVP in 1989, and played American Football with the L.A. Raiders?
A) BO JACKSON
B) DEION SANDERS
C) ANTHONY YOUNG

667.
With which team is the *Super Bowl* legend and to date the NFL's highest scoring wide receiver, Jerry Rice, mainly associated?
A) DENVER BRONCOS
B) SAN FRANSICO 49ERS
C) MINNESOTA VIKINGS

668.
Who set a world record for hitting the most number of Sixes (84) in international Test cricket, and the most number of Test runs (1710) in a single year?
A) BRIAN LARA
B) SIR GARFIELD SOBERS
C) VIV RICHARDS

669.
Which heptathlete took gold at the 2000 Sydney Olympics to claim the title "the world's greatest all round female athlete"?
A) MARION JONES
B) DENISE LEWIS
C) JACKIE JOYNER-KERSEE

670.
With which NHL world championship team did Grant Fuhr in 1981 become the first drafted black hockey player?
A) BUFFALO SABRES
B) EDMONTON OILERS
C) WINNIPEG JETS

671.
Who in Athens in 2004 became only the third woman in Olympic history to win both the middle distance events of 800 metres and 1500 metres?
A) MESERET DEFAR OF ETHIOPIA
B) KELLY HOLMES OF GREAT BRITAIN
C) HASNA BENHASSI OF MOROCCO

Showing her power: Marion Jones

Sport

Don King and Howard Eastman:
Was either of them the first general secretary
of the Professional Boxing Authority?

675.
Which governing body made Thomas Hearns'
1995 victory over world cruiserweight
champion, Lenny Lapaglia, the first boxer to
win belts at six different weights?
A) IBF - (INTERNATIONAL BOXING
  FEDERATION)
B) WBO - (WORLD BOXING
  ORGANISATION)
C) WBU - (WORLD BOXING UNION)

676.
Give the nickname of five times world karate
champion, and co-star of several Bruce Lee
films, Ron Van Clief.
A) BLACK TIGER
B) BLACK LION
C) BLACK DRAGON

677.
In what weight category did the African
American marine, Emmanuel Yarbrough,
become the first black World Sumo
Champion in 1995?
A) OPEN
B) HEAVYWEIGHT
C) LIGHTWEIGHT

672.
In 1991 at the World Championships in
Munich, French skater, Surya Bonaly, became
the first woman skater to achieve what jump?
A) BACK SOMERSAULT
B) QUADRUPLE
C) TRIPLE AXIS WITH TOE LOOP

673.
With which team in 1989 did Arthur Shell Jr.
become the NFL's first black head coach in
the modern era?
A) L. A. RAIDERS
B) GREENBAY PACKERS
C) SAN DIEGO CHARGERS

674.
On July 19, 1997, in Belgium, Daniel Komen
of Kenya became the first man to run under 8
minutes, for which distance?
A) 2 MILES
B) 3 MILES
C) 5,000 METERS

678.
In which sport did former U.S. champion,
Dominique Dawes, win an Olympic gold
medal with team USA at the 1996 Atlanta
games?
A) SYNCHRONIZED SWIMMING
B) SPRINT RELAY
C) GYMNASTICS

679.
Which club did Ken Griffey Jr. represent for
11 history-making years, before signing for
the Cincinnati Reds in the year 2000?
A) TEXAS RANGERS
B) SEATTLE MARINERS
C) NEW YORK JETS

680.
For which NBA team is the number 33
associated with the legendary Patrick Ewing?
A) SAN DIEGO CLIPPERS
B) NEW YORK NICKS
C) SEATTLE SUPERSONICS

681.
In 1999 Lamine Diac became president of the IAAF. What premier sports competition does the IAAF organize?
A) WORLD CUP FOOTBALL
B) WORLD CHAMPIONSHIP ATHLETICS
C) BASEBALL WORLD SERIES

682.
Which country's soccer team did the 3 time African footballer of the year, Roger Milla, captain in the 1990 and 1994 World Cup?
A) CAMEROON
B) NIGERIA
C) GHANA

683.
Who, on Boxing Day 1908, became the first black heavyweight champion of the world?
A) JOE LOUIS
B) SONNY LISTON
C) JACK JOHNSON

684.
Which team did Nigeria's Hakeem Olajuwon represent when he was twice voted the NBA's Most Valuable Player?
A) HOUSTON ROCKETS
B) BOSTON CELTICS
C) ORLANDO MAGIC

685.
How many Olympic gold medals has the track and field star, Carl Lewis, won?
A) TEN
B) NINE
C) EIGHT

686.
Who did Lennox Lewis defeat when he became only the third boxer to become a three-time heavyweight champion of the world?
A) MIKE TYSON
B) HASIM RAHMAN
C) EVANDER HOLYFIELD

Among the greatest: Frazier, Foreman and Ali

Sport

687.
Who was the first black cricketer to represent England?
A) ROLAND BUTCHER
B) PHILIP DEFRAITAS
C) DEVON MALCOLM

Knocking spots off the competition:
Linford Christie

688.
Which former boxing champ still holds the record for successfully defending his world heavy weight title twenty-seven times?
A) JOE LOUIS
B) ROCKY MARCIANO
C) MUHAMMAD ALI

689.
Who, at the 1996 Atlanta Games, became only the second woman ever to defend her Olympic 100 meter sprint title?
A) GWEN TORRENCE
B) MERLENE OTTEY
C) GAIL DEVERS

690.
With a record breaking 11 English championships, name the sport associated with the former European champion, Desmond Douglas.
A) WEIGHTLIFTING
B) TABLE TENNIS
C) BADMINTON

691.
Tiger Woods was the first player to consecutively win how many U.S. amateur golf championships?
A) THREE
B) FOUR
C) FIVE

692.
The French track and field star, Marie José Peréc, is to date, the only female athlete in Olympic history to successfully defend which event?
A) 200 METERS
B) 400 METERS
C) 1500 METERS

693.
Which basketball team did Earvin "Magic" Johnson lead to five NBA Championships?
A) L.A. LAKERS
B) WASHINGTON BULLETS
C) NEW YORK NICKS

694.
Known as 'The Governor', who was the first black soccer player to captain the senior English squad?
A) VIV ANDERSON
B) PAUL INCE
C) JOHN BARNES

695.
In what position is the former Professional Footballer of the Year, Paul McGrath, the most honored Irish international soccer player ever?
A) STRIKER
B) DEFENDER
C) GOAL KEEPER

696.
After masterminding Monaco's 1997 French championship, Jean Tigana, managed which London soccer club owned by *Harrods'*, Muhammad Al Fayed, to promotion into English football's Premier League?
A) QUEENS PARK RANGERS
B) CHELSEA
C) FULHAM

697.
Which soccer club made Laurie Cunningham Britain's first million pound black player in 1981 and in 2001 signed France's Zinedine Zidane for $73 million?
A) REAL MADRID
B) BARCELONA
C) JUVENTUS

698.
Who at nineteen years and 5 months replaced Magic Johnson as the youngest player in NBA history to feature in an all-star game?
A) TIM HARDAWAY
B) GRANT HILL
C) KOBE BRYANT

699.
In 1992 Martin Stephan and Art Prince became the first black sailors to compete in which maritime competition?
A) AROUND THE WORLD YACHT RACE
B) COWES WEEK REGATTA
C) THE AMERICAS CUP

700.
Give the nickname of baseball great, Reggie Jackson, who jointly holds the record for most home runs in a *World Series* game.
A) MR. SPRING
B) MR. JULY
C) MR. OCTOBER

701.
Bill White became its first African American president in 1989, succeeded in 1994 by its second, Len Coleman. Name the U.S. sporting body.
A) UNITED STATES OLYMPIC COMMITEE
B) BASEBALL'S NATIONAL LEAGUE
C) MAJOR LEAGUE SOCCER

Figuring things out: Debi Thomas

702.
From whom did George Foreman regain the heavyweight crown in 1995, to become the oldest heavyweight boxing champion in history?
A) MICHAEL MOORER
B) JAMES "BUSTA" DOUGLAS
C) RIDDICK BOWE

703.
How many times did Sugar Ray Robinson win the world middleweight boxing crown?
A) FIVE
B) FOUR
C) THREE

Six of the best: Michael Jordan

704.
In what event did Daley Thompson, the former British, European, Commonwealth, World, and Olympic champion compete?
A) HEPTATHLON
B) DECATHLON
C) PENTATHLON

705.
Jackie Joyner-Kersee, often regarded as the greatest all round female athlete ever, was the first consecutive Olympic gold medal winner in which event?
A) PENTATHLON
B) DECATHLON
C) HEPTATHLON

706.
Excluding the Chicago Bulls, which other team in the NBA did Dennis Rodman won the NBA Championship with?
A) DETROIT PISTONS
B) PHILADELPHIA 76ERS
C) SAN DIEGO SPURS

707.
Which baseball team did former Detroit great, Cecil Fielder, help to win the *World Series* in 1996?
A) FLORIDA MARLINS
B) NEW YORK METS
C) NEW YORK YANKEES

708.
Sir Clyde Walcott became the first black Chair of what governing sports body, in the summer of 1993?
A) INTERNATIONAL CRICKET COUNCIL
B) INTERNATIONAL FOOTBALL FEDERATION
C) INTERNATIONAL OLYMPIC COMMITTEE

709.
While helping his country to win the rugby world cup in 1995, Chester Williams became the first South African to score 4 tries in an international match. Who was it against?
A) SAMOA
B) AUSTRALIA
C) NEW ZEALAND

710.
For which sport was Cuba's Pablo Lara a three time world champion, world record holder, and Olympic champion?
A) FENCING
B) JAVELIN
C) WEIGHT LIFTING

711.
In 1948, Alice Coachman, became the first American woman to win an Olympic gold medal for track and field. Name her event.
A) 100 METER HURDLES
B) 400 METER HURDLES
C) HIGH JUMP

712.
Who to date is the only sports star to have played in the *SuperBowl* and *World Series*?
A) BO JACKSON
B) DEION SANDERS
C) JACKIE ROBINSON

713.
Which *Formula One* Grand Prix racing team did Nigerian, Prince Malik Ado Ibrahim, pay $120 million to become the owner in 1999?
A) JORDON
B) ARROWS
C) FERRARI

714.
Who won the blue riband event of the hundred meters sprint at the 2004 Olympics in Athens?
A) BERNARD WILLIAMS
B) JUSTIN GATLIN
C) SHAWN CRAWFORD

715.
Teofilo Stephenson and Felix Savon are to date the only two fighters in Olympic history to win 3 Gold medals in this event. Name it.
A) JUDO MIDDLEWEIGHT DIVISION
B) MIDDLEWEIGHT BOXING
C) HEAVYWEIGHT BOXING

716.
For what event did Deon Hemmings become Jamaica's first woman Olympic gold medallist, and the Caribbean's only female winner at the Atlanta games?
A) 400 METER HURDLES
B) 800 METER HURDLES
C) 800 METERS

717.
The black French Aristocrat, Julius Soubise, taught horse riding and which other subject at England's Eton college during the eighteenth century?
A) ARCHERY
B) FENCING
C) BOXING

718.
In 1888 Arthur Wharton became the first black soccer player in the English football league. What club did he represent?
A) TOTTENHAM HOTSPUR
B) PRESTON NORTH END
C) LIVERPOOL

719.
In which international sports competition did the British speed skater, Wilf O'Rielly, win gold in the winter of 1991?
A) COMMONWEALTH GAMES
B) WORLD CHAMPIONSHIPS
C) X GAMES

720.
He is the only NBA player to be named MVP six times, and is the highest scoring player in professional basketball history. Name him.
A) JULIUS "DR. J" ERVING
B) KAREEM ABDUL-JUBBAR
C) MICHAEL JORDAN

721.
Between 1897 and 1901 Major Taylor was the fastest athlete on earth, setting numerous world records. What was his sport?
A) CYCLING
B) ROWING
C) SPRINTING

722.
In what event did, Josiah Thugwane, become in 1996, the first black South African to win Olympic gold?
A) 15 KILOMETER WALK
B) POLEVAULT
C) MARATHON

723.
Who was the first male track and field athlete to win the 200 and 400 meters track events at a major Championship?
A) JESSE OWENS
B) HERB McKINLEY
C) MICHAEL JOHNSON

724.
Name the former world record holder, who is the most successful fast bowler in international cricket history with 519 wickets in 132 Test matches.
A) MALCOLM MARSHALL
B) COURTNEY WALSH
C) LANCE GIBBS

725.
Who was the first boxer to regain the Heavyweight Championship of the world?
A) JACK JOHNSON
B) FLOYD PATTERSON
C) JOE FRAZIER

Sport

726.
He is one of the highest capped rugby captains of the 'British Lions', and was appointed coach of the national side in 1994. Name him.
A) JEREMY GUSCOTT
B) JASON ROBINSON
C) ELERY HANLEY

727.
With 25 major championship medals, who in 1999 he became the first hurdler to regain a World Championships title, and whose 110 meter hurdles world record of 12.91 seconds has stood since 1993?
A) COLIN JACKSON
B) ALLEN JOHNSON
C) GREG FOSTER

728.
Linford Christie won every major title for the 100 meters. How many times was he sprint champion of Europe?
A) TEN
B) EIGHT
C) SIX

729.
Before her Sydney 2000 Olympic gold medal, Cathy Freeman first flew the Aboriginal flag after her double gold winning performance, at which Games?
A) AUSTRALIAN CHAMPIONSHIPS 1998
B) GOODWILL GAMES 1996
C) COMMONWEALTH GAMES 1994

730.
Martin Offiah, the first British post-war rugby player to surpass 500 tries, established a British record for tries in a single rugby league match. How many?
A) THIRTEEN
B) TEN
C) NINE

731.
Which British boxer became the middleweight boxing champion of the world, after inflicting the first defeat on Sugar Ray Robinson?
A) LLOYD HONEYGHAN
B) JOHN CONTEH
C) RANDOLPH TURPIN

732.
In what year did Jackie Robinson become the first black player in baseball's National League?
A) 1947
B) 1945
C) 1940

733.
Which team managed by Cito Gaston became the first non-American team to win the *World Series* in 1992, 1993, and 1994?
A) TOKYO YORIMURI GIANTS
B) TORONTO BLUE JAYS
C) MONTREAL EXPOS

734.
Arguably the greatest 800 meters runner in track and field history, Wilson Kipketer, represented for most of his career which country in international sport?
A) ETHIOPIA
B) KENYA
C) DENMARK

735.
Who did Frank Bruno defeat in November 1995, to become the WBC Heavyweight boxing champion of the world?
A) DONOVAN "RAZOR" RUDDOCK
B) OLIVER McCALL
C) LENNOX LEWIS

736.
In which sport is the *African Nations Cup* competed?
A) GOLF
B) SOCCER
C) YACHT RACING

737.
He has run under 10 seconds for 100 meters more than any other sprinter in athletics history, and establish a world record for the distance by shaving off the biggest margin since the introduction of the electronic timing. Name him.
A) LEROY BURRELL
B) BEN JOHNSON
C) MAURICE GREEN

738.
Who was the first American football player to rush for more than 2,000 yards in a single season?
A) O. J. SIMPSON
B) BARRY SANDERS
C) WILLIE ANDERSON

739.
How many times has the Javelinist, Tessa Sanderson, represented Great Britain in Olympic competition?
A) FOUR
B) SIX
C) SEVEN

740.
For which basketball team did Shaquille O'Neal play before later leading L.A. Lakers to triple world championships in 2000, 2001 and 2002?
A) ORLANDO MAGIC
B) DETROIT PISTONS
C) CHICAGO BULLS

741.
Name the only boxer to simultaneously hold three world championship titles at different weights.
A) OSCAR DE LA HOYA
B) HENRY ARMSTRONG
C) SUGAR RAY LEONARD

742.
In the Summer of 2004 Tonique Williams-Darling become the first athlete from the Bahamas to win a track and field Olympic gold medal. Name her event.
A) 100 METERS
B) 200 METERS
C) 400 METERS

743.
Name the only baseball player to win MVP awards in both US. leagues, and who in 1974 became baseball's first black manager.
A) FRANK ROBINSON
B) BOB GIBSON
C) ROY CAMPANELLA

744.
Between 1984 and 2002 Brendan Batson was the deputy chief executive for which English sports body?
A) PROFESSIONAL FOOTBALL ASSOCIATION
B) PROFESSIONAL BOXERS ASSOCIATION
C) SPORTS COUNCIL

745.
Jesse Owens's four gold medals at the 1936 Olympics include the 100 and 200 meters, 100 meter relay and which other event?
A) 110 METER HURDLES
B) 400 METERS
C) LONG JUMP

746.
Name the NCAA's top career scorer for women, who in 1985 became the first woman to play basketball for the Harlem Globetrotters.
A) LYNETTE WOODWARD
B) CHERYL MILLER
C) PAM McGEE

747.
With which sport is hall-of-famer Satchel Paige associated?
A) BASEBALL
B) ICE HOCKEY
C) AMERICAN FOOTBALL

748.
In what role did Emmet Ashford become Major League Baseball's first African American, on April 23rd, 1966?
A) PITCHER
B) MANAGER
C) EMPIRE

749.
He was the first black PGA member, and first black golfer to win a major professional tournament. Name him.
A) CHARLIE SIFFORD
B) VEJAY SINGH
C) LEE ELDER

Sport

750.
With which club did soccer great, Ruud Gullit, become the first black manager to win the world's most famous domestic soccer trophy, *The FA Cup*?
A) MANCHESTER UNITED
B) NEWCASTLE UNITED
C) CHELSEA

751.
In what sports league did Chuck Cooper and Nathan "Sweetwater" Clifton become the first black players in 1950?
A) INTERNATIONAL BASKETBALL ASSOCIATION
B) NATIONAL FOOTBALL LEAGUE
C) NATIONAL HOCKEY LEAGUE

752.
In 1875 Oliver Lewis rode to victory in the first ever *Kentucky Derby*. Name his horse.
A) ARISTIDES
B) ARISTOTLE
C) THE ARISTOCRAT

753.
What additional belt in Sugar Ray Leonard's 1988 super middleweight victory over Lenny Lapaglia, gave him his fifth boxing title at different weights?
A) SUPER MIDDLEWEIGHT
B) LIGHT HEAVYWEIGHT
C) CRUISERWEIGHT

754.
With which sport was, Donna Cheek, of the U.S.A. and the British Rastafarian, Oliver Skeet, associated?
A) FLAT RACING
B) SHOW JUMPING
C) STEEPLE CHASING

755.
Whose bronze in the women's singles, and gold in the women's doubles, at the Seoul Olympics, made her become the first black Olympic tennis champion?
A) VENUS WILLIAMS
B) LORI McNEIL
C) ZINA GARRISON

756.
Who won the *European Cup* with Ajax, and via Milan, Barcelona went on to become Holland's all-time leading soccer goal scorer?
A) JIMMY FLOYD-HASSLEBAINK
B) EDGAR DAVIDS
C) PATRICK KLUIVERT

757.
Who set an NFL world record in 1991 for completing 404 passes, and was the first quarterback to throw 5,000 yards in a season?
A) JAMES HARRIS
B) WARREN MOON
C) RANDALL CUNNINGHAM

758.
By what name was the former world Heavyweight boxing champion, Arnold P. Cream, better known?
A) SONNY LISTON
B) JERSEY JOE WALCOTT
C) THE BROWN BOMBER

759.
Chicago's Washington Park, July 19, 1891, Monk Smith becomes one of horse riding's all-time greats by jockeying how many victories in one day?
A) SIX
B) EIGHT
C) TEN

760.
Which hall-of-famer integrated the New York Giants, and later went on to become the NFL's first black coach?
A) TONY DUNGY
B) EMLEN TUNNEL
C) RAY RHODES

761.
Former world champion Debi Thomas and 5 times European champion Surya Bonaly are names associated with which sport?
A) BODY BUILDING
B) FIGURE SKATING
C) SURF BOARDING

762.
Who did former world middleweight, super middleweight and light-heavy weight boxing champ, Roy Jones, defeat in 2003 to become WBA heavyweight champion of the world?
A) JOHN RUIZ
B) DAVID TUA
C) CHRIS BYRD

763.
How many touchdowns did Gayle Sayers make when setting his historic NFL punt return record with the Chicago Bears in 1965?
A) FIVE
B) SIX
C) EIGHT

764.
The black jockey, Willy Simms, had twice won the *Kentucky Derby* before becoming the first American to win which English horse race?
A) THE ENGLISH SWEEPSTAKES
B) THE ST. LEDGER
C) THE OAKS

765.
Who did Muhammad Ali defeat in the fall of 1978 to become the first boxer to become heavyweight champion of the world three times?
A) LARRY HOLMES
B) LEON SPINKS
B) MICHAEL SPINKS

766.
George Gregan, the highest capped scrum half in the history of international rugby, captained which country through to the 2003 Rugby World Cup final?
A) AUSTRALIA
B) ENGLAND
C) FRANCE

767.
In what sport during the nineteenth century did, Tom Molineaux, become American champion?
A) BOXING
B) WRESTLING
C) ROWING

768.
Former Orlando Magic star, John Amaechi, was the first Brit inducted into the NBA hall of fame. He also played for two of the following teams. Name the odd one out.
A) NEW YORK NICKS
B) DALLAS MAVERICKS
C) UTAH JAZZ

769.
Known as the godfather of Kenyan athletics, whose gold medals at the 1968 and 1972 Olympics started Kenya's dominance at world middle distance running?
A) MOSES KIPTANUI
B) KIP KEINO
C) CHARLES KIMANTHI

770.
Which legendary middleweight world-boxing champion was nicknamed "Marvellous", and had the word pre-fixed before his name?
A) FELIX TRINIDAD JR.
B) MIKE McCALLUM
C) MARVIN HAGLER

771.
Maria Mutola of Mozambique, the first athlete to win gold at six different world championships, was the first woman to run which event in under two minutes?
A) 1000 METERS
B) 1500 METERS
C) THE MILE

772.
In what year did Charles Sampson of Los Angeles become the first black rodeo world champion?
A) 1952
B) 1972
C) 1982

773.
Name the piece of sporting equipment invented by George F. Grant in 1899?
A) GOLF TEE
B) SNOOKER CUE
C) TENNIS BALL

Sport

History

The Sphinx

"I am Nature, the universal Mother,
Mistress of all the elements
Primordial child of time..."

Isis

So much of what is now called black history has remained hidden and shrouded in mystery. It is the aim of this section to shed a little more light on the subject. Significant events and their chronological dating are included, while formidable personalities, who until now have scarcely been heard of, are also introduced. I have tried to include as many important names, events, and dates as possible, but inevitably some will be left out. Nevertheless, like preceding chapters, I have attempted in the answers sections to provide a complete, comprehensive, and accessible bibliography.

If one were to enquire about the Second World War from an English, American or Japanese war veteran, or indeed from a German or Russian historian, more than likely each would interpret the outcome from their own national perspective. Inevitably, each account would differ from the others, but that does not mean that any particular version should be dismissed. On the contrary, each account would provide an important chapter in the establishment of an overall unbiased consensus of the truth. The same is to be said of the African experience on the mother continent and in the Diaspora. As Marcus Garvey once said "A person without a knowledge of their history is like a tree without roots..."

Africa has yet to recant its relationship with non-Africans, there on the continental landmass at the center of the world. Africans by nature are warm, welcoming and trusting people. How did a place that was once seen as a fertile paradise, source of farming - architecture and medicine - the home of the gods, become a haven for exploitation and underdevelopment? It's fair to say that although this downward spiral began thousands of years ago, collusion and indifference from the continent's indigenous people and leaders has not helped things. There is an African proverb that says, "An army of sheep led by a lion, will defeat an army of lions led by a sheep".

It is generally accepted that Africa is the birthplace of humankind. Anthropological evidence has made this fact irrefutable. Equally, it should not be forgotten that Africa was the cradle of civilization, language, and high culture. That is not to say that other groups did not subsequently innovate their own concepts...they did. I am simply identifying the source.

Today, wherever you may go, it is difficult to escape the fact that travelers from the African continent, had at some time in antiquity visited that part of the world - some remaining as settlers after having migrated permanently. As civilization progressed it was natural for each generation to learn from the previous one, just as it is natural for a child to learn from its mother.

Is it a coincidence that on the South American continent there are gigantic stone heads of prehistoric African travelers who conducted trade with the indigenous Americans? There is evidence that Africans were resident in China at the foundation of the first Chinese dynasty. The Scottish historian, David MacRitchie, demonstrated in his four-volume work, *Ancient and Modern Britons*, that black settlers had migrated to the British Isles before the arrival of the Celts. Even the *Rig Veda* (Indian Holy Book) is clear on who the original inhabitants of India (the Dravidians) were.

Indeed, the further we go back, the clearer the origin of humanity, civilization and high culture becomes.

Zulu King Shaka with Assegai Spear

Didn't have tunnel vision: Sojourner Truth

774.
How is Saint Victor, I who died in 199A.D. best remembered in history?
A) HIS IMAGE IS ON THE SHROUD OF TURIN
B) HE WAS THE FIRST AFRICAN POPE
C) HE WAS THE FIRST CHRISTIAN MARTYR

775.
What relation was the black Queen, Charlotte Sophia, to Queen Victoria of England?
A) GREAT GRANDMOTHER
B) GRANDMOTHER
C) GRAND AUNT

776.
With seventy-thousand elephants and one hundred-thousand men, Hannibal of Carthage crossed which mountainous region in 218b.c.?
A) THE ALPS
B) THE BLUE MOUNTAINS
C) THE TIBETAN MOUNTAINS

777.
Where, specifically, in the ancient world was the kingdom of Kush?
A) ETHIOPIA
B) NUBIA
C) MEROE

778.
Where in America was there a concentration of Africans before the arrival of the Pilgrim Fathers in 1620?
A) JAMESTOWN, VIRGINIA
B) PEARL HARBOR, HAWAII
C) ST. THOMAS, U.S. VIRGIN ISLANDS

779.
A mythical Christian king named Prestor John was thought to have ruled this country in the fifteenth century. Name it.
A) JORDAN
B) ETHIOPIA
C) SUDAN

780.
Known as the 'Eternal City', what was the first capital of Egypt after its unification in the fourth millennium b.c.?
A) MEMPHIS
B) THEBES
C) CAIRO

781.
Which black Irish ruler assisted the Anglo Saxons in the sixth century, by crushing an anti-Saxon rebellion?
A) GERALD
B) GODFREY
C) GORMUND

782.
Which African American in 1770 became the first martyr in the War of Independence?
A) CRISPUS ATTUCKS
B) THOMAS CABIN
C) JAMES CROW

783.
Name the famous queen who was the wife of the 'Heretic King', Pharaoh Akhnaton.
A) CANDACE
B) NEFETARI
C) NEFERTITI

784.
By what more common name did the fifty-fourth Massachusetts Regiment become known?
A) ROUGH RIDERS
B) STORM TROOPERS
C) BUFFALO SOLDIERS

785.
What was the naval rank of Pietro Olonzo Nino, the Moor who sailed Columbus's flagship to America in 1492?
A) CAPTAIN
B) COMMANDER-IN-CHIEF
C) HEAD COOK

786.
How many Candace Queens ruled in the great East African empire of Meroe?
A) THREE
B) FIVE
C) NINE

787.
The African American entrepreneur, Edward James Roye, became the president of which country in 1870?
A) DOMINICAN REPUBLIC
B) BELIZE
C) LIBERIA

788.
Who was the leader of the Underground Railroad in America during slavery?
A) SOJOURNER TRUTH
B) JOHN BROWN
C) HARRIET TUBMAN

789.
What year was the Arabian invasion of Egypt?
A) 6 A.D.
B) 640 A.D.
C) 1066 A.D.

790.
Said to be Ghana's greatest ever ruler, in which century did the formidable emperor-general, Tenkhamenin, reign?
A) 7th
B) 11th
C) 17th

Going Underground: Harriet Tubman

791.
Alessandro De Medeci, the famous black Italian, was the son of a maidservant named Anna. Who was his father?
A) POPE PETER I
B) POPE JEAN PAUL III
C) POPE CLEMENT VII

792.
On which continent are there large stone sculptures featuring a pre-historic African civilization know as the Olmec?
A) ASIA
B) SOUTH AMERICA
C) AUSTRALIA

History

Big headed: Olmec stone

793.
Who was the Zulu King when the 1867 Zulu War broke out?
A) CETEWAYO
B) SHAKA
C) BAMBAATA

794.
It is the only survivor of the original Seven Wonders of the World, but for which fourth dynasty pharaoh was the great Gizah pyramid built?
A) KHUFU
B) KHAFRA
C) MENKARA

795.
The coastline of which continental landmass was partly explored by Norsemen in the tenth century including a famous black Viking named Thorhall?
A) ANTARCTICA
B) NORTH AFRICA
C) NORTH AMERICA

796.
Which one of the following was named after General Tarik, the commander who led the Moorish invasion of Europe in 711A.D.?
A) THE TARIFF TAX
B) THE TAURUS MOUNTAINS
C) THE ROCK OF GIBRALTAR

797.
By what other name were Africa's first foreign rulers, 'The Shepherd Kings' of the thirteenth to seventeenth Egyptian dynasties, better known?
A) HYKSOS
B) BABYLONIANS
C) BERBERS

798.
By what other name is Niger Val Dub, the black Scottish King of the Picts between 997 and 1004A.D., better known?
A) KING KENNETH
B) KING VALENTINE
C) NIGEL THE BRAVE

799.
Which group refers to the beginning of the world as 'The Dreamtime'?
A) MAORIS
B) ABORIGINES
C) INNUITS

800.
Born of Ethiopian origin, Akbar "The Great" was a distinguished Muslim ruler in which country?
A) ARABIA
B) TURKEY
C) INDIA

801.
Which empire did Queen Yaa Asantewa fight against when becoming the last African woman to lead a major war in Africa?
A) BRITAIN
B) BELGIUM
C) FRANCE

802.
Two of the following three Roman Emperors were black. Name the odd one out.
A) FLAMANIUS
B) FIRMUS
C) MACRINUS

803.
Which country did the Sea-Rover, Leo "The African," invade with 54 ships and approximately 11,000 men in 904A.D.?
A) ITALY
B) GREECE
C) CYPRUS

804.
What name is used to describe the oldest Jewish civilization on record?
A) ASHKENAZIM
B) FALASHA
C) KOSHER

805.
On March 29, 1809, the black sovereign, Gustavus IV, abdicated from the throne of which country?
A) AUSTRIA
B) ICELAND
C) SWEDEN

806.
Arguably the greatest female ruler in history, Queen Hatshepsut ruled over Egypt in what dynasty?
A) EIGHTEENTH
B) NINETEENTH
C) TWENTIETH

807.
In which country can the descendants of the ancient Colchian people, still be found, living in a place called Colchi today?
A) CHILE
B) MALTA
C) RUSSIA

808.
Who became the first Emperor of Haiti in 1791?
A) CHRISTOPHE I
B) JAQUES DESSALINES
C) TOUSSAINT L'OVERTURE

809.
Which US president had several children with a slave girl named Sally Hemings?
A) THOMAS JEFFERSON
B) ABRAHAM LINCOLN
C) GEORGE WASHINGTON

810.
Although he declined Pope Vitalian's offer to be Archbishop of Canterbury, which seventh century African bishop built the Monastery of St. Augustine in England?
A) AUGUSTINE
B) HADRIAN
C) JOSEPHUS

The only survivor of the original Seven Wonders of the World: Great Gizah Pyramid

History

811.
Give the area of animal study taught to a young Charles Darwin, by Scottish based black South American, John Edmonston, during the late 1820s?
A) ANTHROPOLOGY
B) GENEALOGY
C) TAXIDERMY

812.
Which African Roman Emperor died in York, England, in the third century?
A) SEPTIMUS SEVERUS
B) CARIGULA
C) LUSIUS QUIETUS

The greatest female ruler of all time:
Hatshepsut

813.
Narma Mena (or Menes) was the first Pharaoh of which Egyptian dynasty?
A) FIRST
B) FOURTH
C) THIRTEENTH

814.
What group, according to Irish history, inhabited Ireland before the arrival of the Celts?
A) IBERIANS
B) MOORS
C) FIRBOLG

815.
How many countries in South America did, Simon Bolivar "The Liberator," help to independence?
A) THREE
B) FIVE
C) SIX

816.
Who did the Roman historian, Tacitus, in 80a.d, refer to as the "Silures", and also as the main inhabitants of western Britain?
A) AFRO SAXONS
B) BLACK PICTS
C) BLACK CELTS

817.
In which country was Queen Phillippa of Hanailt born, before becoming England's first black queen in 1330A.D.?
A) GUINEA
B) BELGIUM
C) FRANCE

818.
Which original Buddhist people of the Indus Valley are thought to have been the first to practice Yoga in the third millennium BC?
A) HARAPPA
B) MOHENJO-DARO
C) BRAHMIN

819.
What name is used to describe the African group living in Western Europe between 15,000 and 25,000 years ago?
A) THE NEANDERTHAL
B) THE GRIMALDI
C) THE OLMEC

820.
What alias did Queen Phillippa of Hanailt's oldest son, Edward, receive in his youth, which stayed with him for life?
A) THE CONFESSOR
B) THE BLACK PRINCE
C) THE BLACK KNIGHT

821.
Which city did the Romans build upon the ruins of a temple to the goddess Isis?
A) ROME
B) ALEXANDRIA
C) PARIS

822.
Which Northern country was inhabited by the Twa African tribe between approximately 1000-1632A.D.?
A) GREENLAND
B) FINLAND
C) NEWFOUNDLAND

823.
Which ruling monarch is a descendent of, Martin Afonso Chicorro, born in 1249 to Portugal's fifth king, and the Moorish princess, Madalena Gil?
A) QUEEN ELIZABETH II OF ENGLAND
B) KING JUAN CARLOS OF SPAIN
C) PRINCE ALBERT OF MONACO

824.
In what year did King Ferdinand and Queen Isabella begin the expulsion of the Moors from Spain?
A) 1472
B) 1492
C) 1502

825.
What was the title of the nineteenth century Sudanese General, Mohammed Ahmed?
A) PRINCE
B) AMIR
C) AL MAHDI

826.
In which century did the most famous of all the black European pirates, Allan Mac Ruari, live?
A) FIFTEENTH
B) SEVENTEETH
C) EIGHTEENTH

827.
What was the subject of 1884-85 Berlin Conference?
A) GERMAN COLONIES IN AFRICA
B) INVESTMENT IN AFRICAN INDUSTRY
C) EUROPE'S CARVING UP OF AFRICA

828.
By what other name was Anna de Medici, formally the mistress of Pope Clement VII, known?
A) THE FRENCH EVE
B) THE ITALIAN CLEOPATRA
C) THE SUN PRINCESS

829.
Known as "Halfdan The black," this king has the distinction of being the first person to unify which northern European country?
A) NORWAY
B) DENMARK
C) SWEDEN

Nefertiti:
Mirror, mirror, who's the cutest of them all?

830.
Which group defeated the Spanish and the British in Jamaica, and succeeded in winning autonomy for themselves?
A) CARIBS
B) ARAWAKS
C) MAROONS

831.
What was the name of the three wars between Rome and Carthage that decided who would control the Mediterranean?
A) PELOPONNESIAN WARS
B) PUNIC WARS
C) WAR OF THE CRUSADES

832.
The Emperors Sonni Ali and Askia "The Great" are names connected with which great African empire?
A) MONOMOTAPA
B) SONGHAI
C) NUBIA

833.
According to Biblical chronology, which Pharaoh had a dispute with Moses over the Hebrews in Egypt?
A) PIANKHY
B) RAMSES II
C) PTOLEMY I

834.
Where did Paul Bogle lead the 1865 October rebellion against British autocracy in Jamaica?
A) MORANT BAY
B) MONTEGO BAY
C) KINGSTON HARBOUR

835.
King Shango, the ancient Kushite and Yoruba king, is nowadays referred to as the god of what?
A) RAINBOW
B) FIRE
C) THUNDER

836.
With which one of the following Roman Emperors did Cleopatra VII not have a child?
A) JULIUS CAESAR
B) AUGUSTUS CAESAR
C) MARK ANTHONY

837.
Which country has a sacred river named after, General Ganges of Ethiopia, whose empire stretched as far as this region at around 5,000b.c.?
A) IRAN
B) INDIA
C) MONGOLIA

838.
Which one of the following countries was not under the dominion of the powerful black Byzantine Emperor, Nicephorus Phocas?
A) BULGARIA
B) POLAND
C) GERMANY

839.
Name the Seminole chief whose scalping of four American soldiers after his African wife had been captured, brought about the Florida War in America.
A) SEQUOYAH
B) GERONIMO
C) OSCEOLA

Human cargo packed liked sardines: Transatlantic slave ship

Statesman: Toussaint L'Overture

843.
Approximately how many black soldiers fought in the Union Army during the American Civil War?
A) 10,000
B) 50,000
C) 185,000

844.
According to official Christian records, three African Women, Falicitus, Perpetua and Nymphano were Christianity's first female martyrs. Give the year.
A) 1 B.C.
B) 1 A.D.
C) 189 A.D.

845.
Which nation was founded in 1695 by King Osei Tutu when he unified all the Akan states of West Africa?
A) MANDIKA
B) ASHANTI
C) ZULU

840.
Which empire was defeated in South America by the military genius of the Brazilian ex-slave, Henrique Dias?
A) HOLLAND
B) SPAIN
C) BRITAIN

846.
The Dubghail were a black tribe who occupied parts of northern Britain until 877A.D. Which Scandinavian country did they come from?
A) DENMARK
B) ICELAND
C) NORWAY

841.
In which Italian city was the black royal, Alessandro de Medeci, the first reigning Duke?
A) FLORENCE
B) NAPLES
C) MILAN

847.
Revered for her military stand against Roman and Arab imperialism, what religion did the seventh century Warrior Queen, Kahina of Mauritania, practice?
A) JUDAISM
B) CHRISTIANITY
C) ISLAM

842.
How long did Queen Nzinga of Angola wage war against Portuguese expansion into her kingdom?
A) TWENTY YEARS
B) THIRTY YEARS
C) FORTY YEARS

848.
One of the greatest conquerors in human history, Pharaoh Tuthmosis III is said to have subdued how many nations and cities during his reign?
A) 428
B) 528
C) 628

History

Sheba: Too wise for Solomon?

852.
The black Queen, Lydia Lili Uokalani, was this country's last monarch before it became a United States overseas territory in 1900. Name it.
A) HAWAII
B) BAHAMAS
C) TAHITI

853.
What name was used by the indigenous people of Northeast Africa to refer to that region before it was renamed Egyptos by the Greeks?
A) HELIOPOLIS
B) NAPATA
C) KEMET

854.
After Africans were offloaded in America during the period of the Trans-Atlantic slave trade, what was the main cargo transported to Europe?
A) SUGAR
B) COTTON
C) TOBACCO

849.
Which West African empire reached its zenith under the rulership of Emperor Mansa Musa?
A) GHANA
B) MALI
C) SONGHAI

855.
Which Egyptian queen, royal mother, and trendsetter, reigned in Egypt for sixty-two years establishing one of the longest reigns by a female monarch?
A) QUEEN TIYE
B) QUEEN CLEOPATRA
C) QUEEN NEFERTITI

850.
How long did the dynasty of the Falasha Queen, Judith, last in Ethiopia after she attacked and conquered Axum in 937A.D.?
A) 100 YEARS
B) 200 YEARS
C) 300 YEARS

856.
A servant named Nabo was the father of Louise-Maria, also known as 'The black Nun of Moret'. Who was her mother?
A) MARIE ANTOINETTE OF FRANCE
B) CATHERINE THE GREAT OF RUSSIA
C) QUEEN MARIE-THERESA OF AUSTRIA

851.
Which southern African country was historically known as Monomotapa?
A) MALAWI
B) ZIMBABWE
C) NAMIBIA

857.
Name the city in Australia which was once occupied exclusively by the Aboriginal ethnic group, the Kulin People?
A) SYDNEY
B) ADELAIDE
C) MELBOURNE

858.
The Carthaginian general, Hamilcar Barca, is credited with founding this European city in the third century b.c. Name it.
A) ATHENS
B) MILAN
C) BARCELONA

859.
Who was executed on November 11, 1831, after leading the largest revolt against slavery in America during the nineteenth century?
A) GABRIEL PROSSER
B) NAT TURNER
C) DENMARK VESEY

860.
Which king of France was married to a Creole woman named Josephine who was born in Martinique, West Indies?
A) NAPOLEON I
B) NAPOLEON II
C) NAPOLEON III

861.
What name was given to the African pirates who captured and sold Europeans into slavery?
A) SKULL SEEKERS
B) SEA ROVERS
C) NIGHT RAIDERS

862.
Give the year when Ethiopia defeated Italy to preserve its independence at the 'Battle of Adwa'.
A) 1897
B) 1936
C) 1941

863.
During what period in world history did a fertile green oasis gradually become the Sahara Desert?
A) NEOLITHIC AGE
B) BRONZE AGE
C) IRON AGE

864.
Which famous world heritage site is said to feature the face of an African Pharaoh named Khafra?
A) EASTER ISLAND CARVINGS
B) THE PHAROS OF ALEXANDRIA
C) SPHINX

865.
How long did Egypt's sixth dynasty ruler, Pepi II occupy the throne, to become the longest documented reign of any monarch?
A) 74 YEARS
B) 84 YEARS
C) 94 YEARS

866.
Which Egyptian dynasty included the military giants Piankhy, Shabaka, and Taharqa?
A) THE GLORIOUS 18TH
B) THE 25TH
C) THE 30TH

867.
Which empire, under the direction of general Cambyses, seized control of Egypt in 525b.c.?
A) ASSYRIA
B) PERSIA
C) MOROCCO

868.
In what year was the economics giant, Shayaam "The Great", enthroned as the renaissance king for the Bakuba kingdom in southern Central Africa?
A) 1430
B) 1530
C) 1630

869.
Which empire in 332b.c. followed the Persian conquest of Egypt?
A) GREEKS
B) ROMANS
C) ASSYRIA

History

870.
Joseph Cinque was the hero of the 1839 *Amistad Affair*, which resulted in a sensational trial at Hartford, Connecticut. What was it?
A) AN INTERRACIAL ROMANCE
B) A POLITICAL SCANDAL
C) A SLAVE REVOLT

871.
Which of the following nations was the first to practice Christianity?
A) EGYPT
B) ETHIOPIA
C) ROME

Making a mole hill out of a moutain:
Hannibal of Carthage

872.
Name the legendary Aboriginal fighter executed in 1833 after leading the resistance to European invaders in Australia.
A) YAGAN
B) TRUGANINI
C) BURNUM BURNUM

873.
The word "slave" and "slavic" was originally applied to which group of people?
A) NORTH AFRICANS
B) SOUTH AMERICANS
C) EAST EUROPEANS

874.
Name the former foreign slaves of Egypt, whose revolt in 1250A.D. gave them control of Egypt until the early sixteenth century.
A) OTTOMAN TURKS
B) KURDS
C) MAMELUKES

875.
Which part of America in the sixteenth century was the Moroccan explorer, Estevanico, the first non-native American to visit?
A) ARIZONA
B) NEVADA
C) CALIFORNIA

876.
Which outstanding African leader rose from child slavery to later found one of the most important trading states in nineteenth century Africa?
A) KING JAJA OF OPOBO
B) KING OSEI BONSU OF BENIN
C) KING PEPPLE OF BONNY

877.
Africans were present in the founding of the first Chinese civilization on record. Name it.
A) TANG DYNASTY
B) SHANG DYNASTY
C) MAO DYNASTY

878.
Which pope in 1452 endorsed chattel slavery by granting King Alphonso papal blessing to enslave Africans?
A) POPE INNOCENT VII
B) POPE NICHOLAS V
C) POPE PIUS III

879.
How many Dutch settlers came with Jan Van Riebeek to South Africa in 1652 - later becoming the ancestors of the Boer nation?
A) NINETY
B) SIXTY
C) THIRTY

880.
Name the elephant ridden by the East African Christian emperor, Abraha Al-Ashram, which instead of attacking Mecca knelt before the city in 569A.D.?
A) MALIK THE WISE
B) MAHMOUD THE PRAISEWORTHY
C) ABDUL THE HUMBLE

881.
Which Germanic group conquered and settled in Carthage, North Africa, in 429A.D.?
A) VANDALS
B) TEUTONS
C) GOTHS

882.
For how long was Toussaint L'Overture imprisoned in solitary confinement in France, until his death in 1803?
A) NINE DAYS
B) NINE WEEKS
C) NINE MONTHS

883.
What was the relationship of the black Duchess of Alafoes, to John VI of Portugal?
A) WIFE
B) MOTHER
C) AUNT

Black English: Queen Charlotte Sophia

Politics & Law

Reverend Jesse Jackson and Baroness Patricia Scotland

**"Injustice anywhere is a threat
to justice everywhere"**
Martin Luther King

The questions in chapter seven are dedicated to highlighting the black politic. Emphasis has been placed on events in the Diaspora. Yet, there is no denying that traditionally, Africans had a political and legal system comparable to any successfully administered legal system on planet earth. Granted that there were often marginal differences from region to region, invariably the law was interpreted by the chief, high priest or elders of a group.

With the era of colonialism came the erosion of indigenous political institutions in Africa. However, it is one thing when an alien law is being applied to you when you are in your own country, but when you are being governed in an unfamiliar place where you are the minority, it's completely different.
As there is plenty of evidence to suggest Africans in America have faced some of the greatest obstacles in terms of institutionalized racism, it's hardly surprising that a great deal of this chapter is dedicated to chronicling some of the systematic efforts they took to combat and dismantle these barriers. This involved the reassertion of mechanisms essential in maintaining their self-esteem. All-the-same, it must be said that the experiences of Africans in America over the last four centuries are not dissimilar to those experienced by people of African descent world-wide. Particularly, wherever the institution of racism has reared its ugly head. That is why it is somewhat surprising and ironic that Africans have had to face prejudice and religious bigotry from other peoples of color (see also history section), as well as encountering inter-ethnic prejudices among themselves. Although we cannot overlook the consequences of racial divide and rule, perhaps it has become all too convenient - from the streets of Washington D.C. to the streets of Rwanda - to apportion blame for the disregard of life among certain individuals within various black communities. Yes it is true that the systematic underdevelopment of African high culture was important in the subjugation of its people and their continent. But to be aware of this and still fall victim to its processes, says as much about the powerful effects of racism and tribalism, as it does about the weakness in the psyche of those who continue to use it as an excuse.

In the final analysis the challenge has forced the painful compromise between trying to dissect the disease of racism while still maintaining and preserving self-love, as well as the parental love for humanity. Amazingly enough, that love has not yet diminished.

It is important in a world where we are all increasingly interdependent on one another, that this love is not lost. If it dies, most of humanity dies with it. This is why it is essential for our global civilization to realize where we are coming from in terms of historical accuracy, in order for us to determine where we should go in the immediate future. Collectively, we may be ignorant, but we are far from stupid. Because as the saying goes, "You can fool some of the people all of the time, you can even fool all the people some of the time, but you can't fool all of the people all of the time".

Founding father of black British politics, Olaudah Equiano

Uniting nations: Kofi Annan

884.
To what organization was Kofi Annan appointed Secretary General in 1996?
A) UNITED NATIONS
B) AFRICAN NATIONAL CONGRESS
C) EUROPEAN SUMMIT

885.
Who in 1989 became the last chair of the Organization for African Unity until it became the African Union in 2001?
A) BOUTROS BOUTROS-GHALI
B) SALIM SALIM
C) GERRY RAWLINS

886.
Two of the following three former cabinet ministers, have served as Surgeon General to the United States government. Name the odd one out.
A) DR. AUDREY MANLEY
B) DR. LOUIS SULLIVAN
C) DR. JOYCELYN ELDERS

887.
Who was the lead defense lawyer in the O. J. Simpson "Trial of the Century"?
A) CHRISTOPHER DARDEN
B) ROBERT SHAPIRO
C) JOHNNIE COCHRANE

888.
After her cabinet position as International Development Secretary, Baroness Valerie Amos became in October 2003, the first black leader of which British political institution?
A) HOUSE OF COMMONS
B) HOUSE OF LORDS
C) HOUSE OF FRAZIER

889.
Azie Taylor Morton was the thirty-sixth treasurer of the United States between 1977-1981. Where has her signature been featured?
A) TRAVELERS CHECKS
B) U.S. DOLLAR BILLS
C) WHO'S WHO OF AUTOGRAPHS

890.
Between 1994 and 1999 Cote, D Ivory statesman, Ivory Dr. Alassane Quattara, was the Deputy Managing Director of which international institution?
A) AFRICAN DEVELOPMENT BANK
B) WORLD BANK
C) INTERNATIONAL MONETARY FUND

891.
In 1980, Mary Eugenia Charles, became the first woman to become prime minister of a Caribbean State. Name the Island.
A) DOMINICA
B) ST. KITTS
C) BELIZE

892.
Between 1990 and 2003 Bill Morris was head of Britain's largest trade union for industry and the private sector. Name it.
A) UNISON
B) TRANSPORT AND GENERAL WORKERS UNION
C) GMB

893.
In Spring 2001, Condoleeza Rice, became one of the world's most powerful women when she was appointed to head which U.S. government department?
A) SOCIAL SECURITY
B) NATIONAL SECURITY
C) ENVIRONMENTAL HEALTH

894.
To which country in the spring of 1997, was Sidney Poitier, appointed Bahamas Ambassador?
A) JAPAN
B) AMERICA
C) FRANCE

895.
Before he was deposed, which president was challenged in 1997, by Africa's first woman leader of a major political party, Ellen Johnson Sirleaf?
A) CHARLES TAYLOR OF LIBERIA
B) HISSSENE HABRE OF SENEGAL
C) IDI AMIN OF UGANDA

Leading the defence: Johnnie Cochrane

896.
For what area of London did John Archer become Britain's first black mayor in 1913?
A) CAMDEN
B) BRIXTON
C) BATTERSEA

900.
Name the political organization founded by Huey Newton and Bobby Seale in 1966.
A) FIVE PERCENT NATION
B) TRANSAFRICA
C) BLACK PANTHER PARTY

897.
What year did Sharon Pratt-Kelly become the first female mayor of Washington D.C.?
A) 1970
B) 1980
C) 1990

901.
In Autumn 2004, who became the first black QC to be appointed as a judge for the British High Courts of Justice?
A) JOHN ROBERTS
B) COURTNEY GRIFFITHS
C) LINDA DOBBS

898.
In 1992 Pierre Sane became the first African head of which British based organization?
A) EUROPEAN COMMISSION
B) GREENPEACE
C) AMNESTY INTERNATIONAL

902.
Which political ideology did the German aristocrat, Ferdinand Lassalle, help to define in the nineteenth Century?
A) CAPITALISM
B) FUNCTIONALISM
C) SOCIALISM

899.
William Davidson was one of the leaders of the 1820 'Cato Street Conspiracy'. What did this plot involve?
A) OVERTHROWING THE BRITISH GOVERNMENT
B) BLOWING UP THE HOUSE OF LORDS
C) STEALING THE CROWN JEWELS

903.
Name the political umbrella led by the former democratic presidential nominee Jesse Jackson.
A) RAINBOW PEOPLE
B) RAINBOW COALITION
C) RAINBOW WARRIORS

Politics & Law

First woman prime minister of a Caribbean
State: Mary Eugenia Charles

904.
The first private prosecution for Homicide in
Britain followed the racist murder of which
teenager?
A) ROLAND ADAMS
B) STEPHEN LAWRENCE
C) DAMILOLA TAYLOR

905.
Who was the U.S. agricultural secretary
during the first eighteen months of the
Clinton administration?
A) MIKE ESPY
B) HAROLD EUGENE FORD
C) BOBBY SCOTT

906.
Who, in 1994, became Britain's first black
member of the European Parliament?
A) LINDA BELLOS
B) PETER HERBERT
C) MARK HENDRIK

907.
What post was given to Colin Powell when he
became part of President George W. Bush's
administration in 2001?
A) SECRETARY OF INTERNATIONAL
   AFFAIRS
B) SECRETARY OF DEFENCE
C) SECRETARY OF STATE

908.
For which international body has Chief Emeka
Anyaoku been head, since his appointment as
secretary general in 1990?
A) COMMISSION FOR NUCLEAR
   DISARMAMENT
B) COMMONWEALTH OF NATIONS
C) WORLD HEALTH ORGANIZATION

909.
Give the year slavery was officially abolished
in the state of Mississippi.
A) 1775
B) 1885
C) 1995

910.
After playing Division one soccer for the
English soccer Club, Everton, Charles Perkins
went on to become Australia's first Aboriginal
university graduate. What year?
A) 1965
B) 1975
C) 1985

911.
On February 12, 1989, Barbara C. Harris
became the first ever woman bishop for
which Christian church?
A) GREEK ORTHODOX
B) ANGLICAN
C) ETHIOPIAN COPTIC

912.
Neville Bonner was the first Aboriginal MP to
sit in Australia's upper House. But in what
year did the Democratic Party deputy leader,
Senator Aden Ridgeway, became only the
second Aboriginal politician to do so?
A) 1999
B) 1989
C) 1979

913.
Patricia Harris, America's first Black woman
ambassador became its first Black woman
cabinet minister, in whose government?
A) JIMMY CARTER
B) RONALD REAGAN
C) GERALD FORD

914.
What right is stated for all U.S. citizens in the fifteenth Amendment?
A) EDUCATION
B) VOTING
C) WELFARE

915.
British civil rights pioneer, Dr. Harold Moody, led two of the following organizations before World War II. Name the odd one out.
A) LONDON MISSIONARY SOCIETY
B) COLORED MEN'S INSTITUTE
C) LEAGUE OF COLORED PEOPLES

916.
Who in 1981 became the first woman governor-general of an independent Caribbean country?
A) DAME MINITA GORDON OF BELIZE
B) DAME EUGENIA CHARLES OF DOMINICA
C) DAME NITA BARROW OF BARBADOS

917.
What was the real name of Gustavus Vassa, sometimes referred to as the "founding father of black British politics"?
A) IGNATIUS SANCHO
B) OTTOBAH CUGOANO
C) OLAUDAH EQUIANO

918.
Give the year Thomas Rainey became the first African American to preside over the U.S. House of Representatives.
A) 1874
B) 1924
C) 1974

919.
Who was the first African American to serve in the U.S. Senate since Reconstruction?
A) OSCAR DE PRIEST
B) ANDREW YOUNG
C) EDWARD BROOKE

920.
In which country, with Yoweri Museveni as president, did Mrs. Specioze Wandira Kazibwe become Africa's first woman vice president in 1994?
A) UGANDA
B) GAMBIA
C) CENTRAL AFRICAN REPUBLIC

921.
With which state in 1960 did Blanche Preston McSmith become America's first black state legislator?
A) ALASKA
B) NEBRASKA
C) DELAWARE

922.
Which British police force did, Norwell Roberts, integrate in 1967, Ron Hope become its first black chief inspector, in 1994 and superintendent in 1996?
A) SOUTH YORKSHIRE POLICE
B) GREATER MANCHESTER POLICE
C) METROPOLITAN POLICE

923.
Which colony in America, in the year 1641, was the first to legalize slavery?
A) VIRGINIA
B) MASSACHUSETTS
C) NEW MEXICO

Condoleeza Rice:
One of the world's most powerful women?

Politics & Law

Public enquiry: Neville and Doreen Lawrence

924.
In what year did Britain first pass an act officially outlawing the institution of slavery?
A) 1772
B) 1833
C) 1838

925.
Give the year Britain's Labour Party national executive member, Diane Abbott, became the first black woman elected to Parliament.
A) 1987
B) 1988
C) 1992

926.
Name the city where, in 1994, Beverley J. Harvard, became the first African American woman chief of police.
A) NEW ORLEANS
B) ATLANTA
C) MEMPHIS

927.
Which church ordained Reverend Eva Pitts as its first black woman priest, after appointing Wilfred Wood as its first senior black bishop in 1985?
A) SEVENTH DAY ADVENTIST
B) DUTCH REFORM CHURCH
C) CHURCH OF ENGLAND

928.
It took this country until 28th July 1868, to declare people of African descent as full citizens. Name it.
A) UNITED STATES
B) CANADA
C) FRANCE

929.
Which Marian Wright Edelman founded organization uses the phrase *Dear Lord be good to me, the sea is so wide and my boat is so small*?
A) AMERICAN MARITIME FUND
B) CHILDREN'S DEFENCE FUND
C) UNITED NEGRO COLLEGE FUND

930.
Which one of the following would be the best definition of democracy?
A) POWER TO THE PEOPLE
B) FREEDOM AND PEACE FOR ALL
C) FREEDOM AND JUSTICE FOR ALL

931.
For which U.S. State, in 1873 did P. B. S. Pinchback become America's first black governor?
A) LOUISIANA
B) TENNESSEE
C) ALABAMA

932.
Name the adviser to four U.S. presidents who also founded the National Council of Colored Women.
A) MARY McCLOUD BETHUNE
B) MARY CHURCH TERRELL
C) QUEEN MOTHER MOORE

933.
For which area of London was Lord David Pitt given the Peership in the late 1980s?
A) GREENWICH
B) HAMPSTEAD
C) FINCHLEY

934.
William Hastie was the first black governor of the Virgin Islands after becoming the first African American federal judge in 1949. Name the court.
A) HIGH COURT
B) MARSUPIAL COURT
C) COURT OF APPEALS

935.
W. E. B. Du Bois became the NAACP's first black president, but in what year was America's oldest and largest civil rights movement founded?
A) 1909
B) 1945
C) 1963

936.
Which former British Labour Party spokesperson on legal affairs became Britain's first black cabinet minister, when he was elected to the treasury in 2002?
A) LEE JASPER
B) KEITH VAZ
C) PAUL BOATENG

937.
Who, in 1968, became the first African American woman to win a seat in Congress?
A) BARBARA JORDAN
B) SHIRLEY CHISHOLM
C) YVONNE BRAITHWAITE BURKE

938.
In 1992 Jocelyn Barrow set a precedent by becoming Britain's first black what?
A) DAME
B) COUNTESS
C) LADY-IN-WAITING

939.
The late Bernie Grant MP was the elected honorary life president of which political organization?
A) THE STANDING CONFERENCE ON RACIAL EQUALITY IN EUROPE
B) ONE NATION FORUM
C) OPERATION BLACK VOTE

940.
What amendment to the U.S. constitution outlawed slavery in America?
A) FIRST AMENDMENT
B) FIFTH AMENDMENT
C) THIRTEENTH AMENDMENT

941.
After one of the greatest comebacks in U.S. political history, which city re-elected Marion Barry as its mayor in 1994?
A) KANSAS CITY
B) WASHINGTON, D.C.
C) SAN FRANCISCO

Stating his case: Colin Powell

Africa's first woman Vice President:
Specioze Wandira Kazibwe

942.
In June 2001, Hyacinth Bennett was elected head of the National Democratic Party becoming this country's first woman party leader. Name it.
A) JAMAICA
B) GUYANA
C) WALES

943.
Which vibrant town in North Carolina was constructed by the law graduate Floyd McKissick, and the U.S. government in 1972?
A) WAKE COUNTY
B) NU JAK CITY
C) SOUL CITY

944.
What was the original profession of William Cuffay, one of the leaders of the nineteenth century London Chartist Movement?
A) TINKER
B) TAILOR
C) SPY

945.
Which former chair of the Democratic Party was appointed U.S. Secretary of Commerce in 1993?
A) RON BROWN
B) WILLIAM H. GRAY III
C) WILLIAM COLEMAN

946.
Before her appointment as Baroness in 1997, Patricia Scotland became the first black British woman to become what in 1991?
A) JUSTICE OF THE PEACE
B) QUEEN'S COUNSEL
C) MAGISTRATE

947.
In what century did Portugal begin its 300-year association with the transatlantic slave trade?
A) FIFTEENTH
B) SIXTEENTH
C) SEVENTEENTH

948.
What office did the black barrister, Gaston Monnerville, hold in France for over ten years?
A) ATTORNEY GENERAL
B) MINISTER OF CULTURE
C) VICE PRESIDENT

949.
What year was the Civil Rights Act passed in the U.S.?
A) 1958
B) 1964
C) 1968

950.
Which famous comedian ran for the American presidency in 1968 with the Freedom and Peace Party?
A) REDD FOXX
B) RICHARD PRYOR
C) DICK GREGORY

951.
After the 1992 U.S. elections how many African Americans held seats in Congress?
A) 30
B) 40
C) 50

952.
What year was the National Urban League founded in America?
A) 1910
B) 1920
C) 1930

953.
What year was flamboyant politician, Adam Clayton Powell, elected to represent New York in Congress?
A) 1944
B) 1955
C) 1966

954.
Where was the nineteenth century black English working-class hero and antislavery lobbyist, Robert Wedderburn, born?
A) RUSSIA
B) AMERICA
C) JAMAICA

955.
Who received a title of rank in 1997, four years after becoming the chairperson of Europe's largest race watchdog, the Commission for Racial Equality?
A) BARONESS ROS HOWELLS
B) LORD HERMAN OUSELEY
C) RAF AIR COMMODORE DAVID CASE

956.
James Benton Parsons was the first African American federal judge elected for life, to which U.S. court?
A) CORONERS COURT
B) COUNTY COURT
C) DISTRICT COURT

957.
After becoming the first black US Congresswoman, in what year did Constance Baker Motley become the first African American woman federal judge?
A) 1946
B) 1956
C) 1966

958.
In 2002 Jamaican premier, P. J. Patterson was elected to his fourth consecutive term in office. Name his political party.
A) PEOPLE'S NATIONAL PARTY
B) JAMAICA LABOUR PARTY
C) NATIONAL DEMOCRATIC PARTY

959.
Name the largest "ethnic" populated borough in Britain for which Merle Amory became Britain's first black woman council leader in 1986.
A) BRENT
B) TOXTETH
C) MOSS-SIDE

960.
During the first administration of President Clinton, Hazel O'Leary became the first ever woman to hold which U.S. cabinet position?
A) SECRETARY OF STATE
B) SECRETARY OF ENERGY
C) PERSONAL SECRETARY

961.
Barbara Jordan became the first black woman president of a U.S. legislative assembly and also entered the U.S. House of Representatives. Name the year.
A) 1972
B) 1982
C) 1992

Attending Premier: P. J. Patterson

Politics & Law

Three of a kind: Bernie Grant, Oona King and Diane Abbott

962.
In 1989 for the London Borough of Hackney, Gus John became Britain's first black director of a local authority. What department did he head?
A) FINANCE
B) EDUCATION
C) WELFARE

963.
The 1954 the Brown v. Board of Education case overturned a famous 1896 American law ruling referred to as "Separate But Equal". Name the case.
A) MURRY v. MARYLAND
B) PLESSY v. FERGUSON
C) DRED SCOTT v. SANFORD

964.
In the spring of 1997 Rodney Slater was appointed U.S. Transportation Secretary, but what cabinet post was appointed to Alexis M. Herman?
A) SECRETARY OF THE ARTS
B) HEALTH SECRETARY
C) LABOR SECRETARY

965.
Which U.S. political party temporarily appointed an African American politician, J. R. Lynch, as its chair in 1884?
A) FREEDOM PARTY
B) PROGRESSIVE PARTY
C) REPUBLICAN PARTY

966.
For which American city have Andrew Young, Maynard Jackson, and Bill Campbell been mayors?
A) ATLANTA
B) ST. LOUIS
C) PHOENIX

967.
Which U.S. state in 1777 became the first to abolish slavery?
A) KENTUCKY
B) VERMONT
C) NEW MEXICO

968.
In 1989 Dacia Valent, later Princess of Katanga, became the first black member of the European Parliament in Brussels. What Italian party did she represent?
A) COMMUNIST PARTY
B) LIBERAL DEMOCRATIC PARTY
C) NATIONAL ALLIANCE PARTY

969.
What government policy was practiced in South Africa from 1948 to 1990?
A) COMMUNISM
B) DEMOCRACY
C) APARTHEID

970.
In 1979 Andrew Young resigned as a UN Ambassador after an unauthorized meeting with which Middle East political group?
A) ISRAEL'S ZIONIST MOVEMENT
B) PALESTINIAN LIBERATION ORGANIZATION
C) IRAQ'S REVOLUTIONARY COMMAND COUNCIL

971.
In 1992 Willie Williams became the first black head of which American Police Department?
A) LOS ANGELES
B) BOSTON
C) HOLLYWOOD

972.
For which London constituency in May of 1997, did Oona King, become Britain's second black female Member of Parliament?
A) BETHNAL GREEN AND BOW
B) BRIXTON
C) HARLESDEN

973.
For which U.S. State in 1990 did Douglas Wilder become the first African American Governor in the twentieth century?
A) GEORGIA
B) OHIO
C) VIRGINIA

974.
In the autumn of 1996 John Taylor of Warwick became the first black Tory elected to which British institution?
A) HOUSES OF PARLIAMENT
B) HOUSE OF LORDS
C) CROWN PROSECUTION SERVICE

975.
Bernice Gaines Hughes was the first African American female Lieutenant Colonel. But name the armed services division where, in June 1995, Marcelite J. Harris became the first African American woman Major General.
A) U.S. COAST GUARD
B) U.S. ARMY
C) U.S. AIR FORCE

976.
In November 1992 in Fulton County - Georgia, Jacquelyn Barrett became the first African American woman to become what?
A) SHERIFF
B) MAYOR
C) MARSHALL

977.
Before becoming head of the Commission for Racial Equality in 2003, political commentator and broadcaster, Trevor Phillips was chairman of the London mayor's governing body. Name it.
A) GREATER LONDON COUNCIL
B) GREATER LONDON ASSOCIATION
C) GREATER LONDON ASSEMBLY

History maker: Carol Moseley Braun

Politics & Law

Lord of the manor: David Pitt of Hampstead

978.
In 1872 Charlotte E. Ray became only the third woman ever in America to qualify for which profession?
A) LAWYER
B) DOCTOR
C) ACCOUNTANT

979.
Who was the first person in Britain to be imprisoned under the 1965 Race Relations Act, for making an inflammatory speech?
A) ENOCH POWELL
B) DARCUS HOWE
C) MICHAEL X

980.
To which department in 1990 was the Connecticut state representative, Gary Franks, the first black republican to be elected in 60 years?
A) THE WHITE HOUSE
B) CONGRESS
C) STATE ASSEMBLY

981.
In November 1992, the Illinois lawyer Carol Moseley-Braun became the first black Democrat to enter which U.S. political institution?
A) HOUSE OF REPRESENTATIVES
B) SENATE
C) PUBLIC HEALTH SERVICE

982.
What year was the Trinidadian civil rights campaigner, Leary Constantine, made a life Peer in the British House of Lords?
A) 1959
B) 1969
C) 1979

983.
In which court in 1939 was Jane Mathilda Bolin appointed the first black woman judge in the U.S?
A) COURT OF DOMESTIC RELATIONS
B) U.S. COURT OF LAW
C) AMERICAN COURT OF JUSTICE

984.
Benedita da Silva helped to found the PT Workers Party, before being elected as this country's first black president in 2002. Name it.
A) BRAZIL
B) PARAGUAY
C) URUGUAY

985.
Name the area of the United Kingdom where Mike Farrell became head of police, after he was appointed Britain's first black Chief Constable September 2003.
A) WINDSOR
B) SURREY
C) KENT

986.
For which South African political party has the leadership of Chief Mangosuthu Buthelezi been associated?
A) AFRIKANER PARTY
B) THE ZULU PARTY
C) THE INKATHA FREEDOM PARTY

987.
During the 1990s while the English actor, T. Robinson, was playing the role of Robin Hood's nemesis sheriff, how many times was black councilor, Tony Robinson, appointed Sheriff of Nottingham?
A) TWO
B) THREE
C) FOUR

988.
In 1968 Dame Hilda Bynoe became the first woman governor for a British Commonwealth country. Name it.
A) GUYANA
B) GRENADA
C) MADAGASCAR

989.
The British conservative party campaigner, Joyce Sampson, was the former vice chair of which women's group during the 1990s?
A) EUROPEAN UNION OF WOMEN
B) FEMINIST MOVEMENT
C) NATIONAL FEDERATION OF BLACK WOMEN BUSINESS OWNERS

990.
In 1991 Bishop Vinton R. Anderson became the first elected black president of which religious organization?
A) SALVATION ARMY
B) WORLD COUNCIL OF CHURCHES
C) CHRISTIAN CHURCH OF SCIENTOLOGY

991.
Name the year Blanche K. Bruce presided over the U.S. Senate, before becoming the longest serving black senator of the nineteenth century.
A) 1878
B) 1888
C) 1898

992.
To which country in 1869 did Ebenezer Bassett become the first African American diplomat?
A) LIBERIA
B) HAITI
C) BOLIVIA

993.
In which U.S. state in 1952 did Mrs. Cora M. Brown become the first African American woman senator?
A) MICHIGAN
B) MINNESOTA
C) MISSOURI

994.
For which country's parliament in 1952, did the writer, Mabel Dove Danquah, become the first African woman elected to an African legislative assembly?
A) ETHIOPIA
B) CHAD
C) GHANA

995.
Name America's first black solicitor general, who in 1967 became the first black judge appointed to the U.S. Supreme Court.
A) CLARENCE THOMAS
B) THURGOOD MARSHALL
C) JAMES B. PARSONS

996.
In 1993 Jesse Brown became the first African American politician to hold this cabinet post in the U.S. Name it
A) VETERANS' AFFAIRS
B) AGRICULTURE
C) THE ARTS

997.
In what year did Elaine Brown become the first and only woman to date to head the Black Panther Party?
A) 1965
B) 1974
C) 1983

998.
France was the first European country to pass a law against slavery. What year was this act passed?
A) 1772
B) 1793
C) 1830

Politics & Law

999.
In 1991 while still incarcerated, prisoner Winston Silcott was elected honorary president of this students union. Name the academic institution.
A) GLASGOW UNIVERSITY
B) OXFORD UNIVERSITY
C) LONDON SCHOOL OF ECONOMICS

1000.
Which American state passed a ruling in 1970 that any person with 1/32 "black blood" was African American?
A) LOUISIANA
B) MAINE
C) ILLINOIS

1001.
How old was Harvard's first black British graduate, David Lammy, when his bi-election victory in June 2000 made him Britain's youngest serving MP?
A) 21
B) 28
C) 35

1002.
In 1969 Melvin H. Evans was appointed governor of this state, before becoming its first ever elected governor a year later. Name the state.
A) CANARY ISLANDS
B) VIRGIN ISLANDS
C) RHODE ISLAND

1003.
Name America's first black cabinet minister, who between 1955 and 1961 was administrator for special projects at the White House.
A) ROBERT WEAVER
B) FREDERICK MORROW
C) CHARLOTTE HUBBARD

1004.
Name the U.S. lobby group founded in 1970, and later led by Kweisi Mfume, before his appointment as president of the NAACP in 1996?
A) SOUTHERN CHRISTIAN LEADERSHIP CONFERENCE
B) 100 BLACK MEN
C) CONGRESSIONAL BLACK CAUCUS

1005.
Name the year that Carl Stokes of Cleveland, Ohio, became the first African American mayor for a major U.S. city.
A) 1947
B) 1957
C) 1967

1006.
Which French king passed an act in 1670 trying to ban mixed marriages in France?
A) LOUIS I
B) LOUIS XIV
C) NAPOLEON BONAPARTE

1007.
For which London borough did Heather Rabbats become the first black British chief executive in April 1994?
A) WANDSWORTH
B) LAMBETH
C) KENSINGTON AND CHELSEA

1008.
In what year did Macon B. Allen become the first black lawyer admitted to the Bar Association of America?
A) 1945
B) 1935
C) 1925

1009.
Before being elected leader of the British House of Lords, Baroness Valerie Amos, became the first black chief executive with which independent organization?
A) HUMAN RIGHTS COMMISSION
B) THE EQUAL OPPORTUNITIES COMMISSION
C) LAW COMMISSION

1010.
The trial of Tawana Brawley brought this civil rights advocate to international prominence. Name him.
A) AL SHARPTON
B) BEN CHAVIS
C) DAVID DINKINS

1011.
In what year did Blaise Diagne become the first African-born politician to enter the French Parliament?
A) 1914
B) 1939
C) 1974

1012.
What first for Britain in 1969 was the Guyanese barrister, Rudy Narayan, instrumental in establishing?
A) LEGAL AID CHARTER
B) PHOTO FIT DIRECTORY
C) LAW ADVICE CENTER

1013.
In which German city did William Amo, an ex-slave, become the state counselor during the eighteenth century?
A) BERLIN
B) BONN
C) HAMBURG

1014.
For what London borough in April 1985 did Bernie Grant become Britain's first black council leader?
A) HACKNEY
B) HARINGEY
C) LAMBETH

1015.
Which Christian body did Donald M. Payne head before becoming the first African American congressman in the state of New Jersey in 1988?
A) THE MOONIES
B) THE MORMONS
C) THE YMCA

1016.
In 1870 Hiram Revels became the first black politician in the U.S. to receive which appointment?
A) SENATOR
B) MAYOR
C) GOVERNOR

1017.
In ancient Egypt, what was the state responsibility given to the Pharaoh's Vizier?
A) STATE ARCHITECT
B) HEAD OF THE NAVY
C) PRIME MINISTER

1018.
What animal found in Africa and parts of India is the imperial symbol of France and Britain?
A) ELEPHANT
B) LION
C) UNICORN

1019.
In 2004 soccer legend, Willington Ortiz, joined black congressmen Luiz Alberto of Brazil and Rafael Erazo of Ecuador, by his election to Parliament, for which South American country?
A) PANAMA
B) COLOMBIA
C) PERU

Politics & Law

Millennium Dawn

Marcus Mossiah Garvey

"Even the future's not what it used to be..."
Unknown

In light of the transition humanity is making into the Age of Aquarius (2000a.d. – 4155a.d.), and will continue to make - more than ever, it is essential that we understand how we are interconnected with all life on earth, and within our solar system. Our planet is but a microcosm, or grain of sand on a cosmic beach that is the universe. Yet, earth is no less (or more) important than any other planet within this universal creation. That said, the constant theme throughout this book has been the quest for truth - if not enlightenment. The question is does this new age we have entered offer any clues towards what lies in store for us?

Those who have an interest in astronomy will know the dominant constellation in earth's ecliptic path for the next two thousand years and beyond will be Aquarius. Since ancient times this sign has been symbolized as the water carrier and enforcer of truth. Aquarius is also thought to represent the most advanced sign of the zodiac, and during this epoch we are likely to see unimaginable technological leaps forward, greater spiritual development, not to mention the distribution and availability of information (truth) en mass. Ignorance is no longer bliss. The importance of this cannot be overstated because at the close of the twentieth century religious bigotry and messianic fatalism abounded. Certainly too many were (and still are) convinced that we had reached the point of no return. The misunderstanding of genetically modified foods, the ever increasing surveillance of people, increasing international conflicts, the threat of military and biological warfare, new super-bugs like Staphylococcus Aureus and MRSA as well as diseases like AIDS, coupled with older diseases like Malaria (still

the developing world's greatest claimant of lives) and the mutated Ebola, its not hard to see why some people have given credence to the apocalyptical notion allegedly awaiting humanity.

The darkest part of the night is just before dawn, and at the dawn of the new millennium over a quarter of earth's population face starvation, while wealthier nations continue to destroy their food surplus. Many people in these wealthier countries suffer from obesity while constantly being fed misinformation about an overpopulated earth. Is the earth really overpopulated when for instance one country in Africa with a population of approximately 50 million people is larger than all of Western Europe? The latter has a population of approximately 300 million people. Or is the African continent itself becoming depopulated? If it were then one would have to ask why? Especially as it is home to the world's largest resource of natural deposits and minerals like plutonium, uranium, gold, diamonds, etc.

It is true that when we take into account the equation of global warming, this could explain why certain parts of the developing world are experiencing more droughts and famines. The dichotomy is that while this is unfolding, other parts of our planet bear witness to more floods. Ironically, again it is the developing world who are most under threat by these floods because of the devastation caused to crops. Forgive the cynicism, but it seems only when certain cities with major international investment value are faced with this threat, will we then be jolted into taking collective action. But by then it may be too late to stem the tide. Perhaps this is consistent with the

Aquarian age, a metaphor for Mother Nature cleansing itself. I, for one, hope that we act now upon what we know, because there is still enough time to avoid such a scenario.

As human beings, we owe it to our ancestors to salvage the future for our children. Maybe we are fortunate that one of the key ingredients essential to human progression is inquisition. Through enquiry comes discovery, and through discovery, order. The old maxim: "You only get out what you put in" is never more true than here. As we only get answers to the questions that we ask, the more questions we ask, the more answers we are likely to get. This motivates us to become better informed so that we are equipped to make informed judgments. Not just theory, but practical knowledge based on experience and evidence. Only when

this is done can we begin to look at taking that magic leap from earth to star.

The final chapter in the first half of this book highlights events that have unfolded within the last hundred years. They too are no less challenging than those mentioned in the previous chapters. In compiling this book it was my dearest wish to make some small contribution to humanity. If it has helped to open the eyes of someone somewhere who will later play a more significant role than I ever could, then I would have fulfilled my reason for being. Equally, I hope readers will have been both entertained and educated. As mentioned in the preface, if this work succeeds in any small measure, it will have inspired the reader into conducting his or her own research.

Winnie Mandela as the South African mother of the nation

Great Xpectations:
El Hajj Malik El-Shabazz (Malcolm X)

1024.
What did Anwar Sadat of Egypt declare himself as after becoming the country's head of state in 1970?
A) PHARAOH
B) PRESIDENT
C) EMPEROR

1025.
In which city did the Nation of Islam leader, Louis Farrakhan, lead the Million Man March in October 1995?
A) NEW YORK
B) NEW JERSEY
C) WASHINGTON, D.C.

1020.
For what war was Colin Powell Chairman of the Joint-Chiefs-of-Staff?
A) WAR IN AFGHANISTAN
B) GULF WAR
C) BOSNIAN-SERB WAR

1026.
After WW2 Dr. Ralph J. Bunche, the U.S. black ambassador to the United Nations, led the mediation for the establishment of which State?
A) ISRAEL
B) ALASKA
C) PALESTINE

1021.
What action by Rosa Parks in Montgomery, Alabama, in 1955 fuelled the modern Civil Rights Movement in the U.S.?
A) REFUSED TO GIVE UP HER SEAT
B) REFUSED TO GET ON THE BUS
C) REFUSED TO PAY ON THE BUS

1027.
Name the concentration camp where suspected terrorists were detained following their capture in Afghanistan, during the American led "War on Terrorism".
A) SAN FRANCISCO BAY
B) GUANTANAMO BAY
C) BAHIA DE COCHINOS

1022.
On April 6, 1909, the African American explorer, Matthew Henson, became the first human to reach the pinnacle of this site. Name it.
A) ATLANTIS
B) SOUTH POLE
C) NORTH POLE

1028.
In what year did President Idi Amin order the expulsion of fifty thousand Asians from Uganda?
A) 1972
B) 1974
C) 1979

1023.
What year was Haile Selassie crowned King of Kings and Emperor of Ethiopia?
A) 1930
B) 1936
C) 1940

1029.
Between 1904 and 1906, the Warrior Queen Kaipkire led the Herero women of Namibia in guerrilla warfare against which country?
A) ANGOLA
B) SOUTH AFRICA
C) GERMANY

1030.
At which Olympics did Tommy Smith and John Carlos hold up clenched fists, in a 'Black Power' salute on the victory rostrum?
A) MUNICH 1972
B) MEXICO 1968
C) BERLIN 1936

1031.
During the second half of the 20th century the Duvalier family, led by the dictators Papa Doc and Baby Doc, became a political dynasty in which country?
A) HAITI
B) NICARAGUA
C) CENTRAL AFRICAN REPUBLIC

1032.
For what issue is the Amazonian martyr Chico Mendes best remembered?
A) STOPPING ACID RAIN
B) PROTECTING THE RAIN FOREST
C) PROTECTING THE OZONE

1033.
What position did the African American, John Gordon, have in the Red Army during the 1917 Russian revolution?
A) CAPTAIN
B) SERGEANT
C) GENERAL

20th century giant: Nelson Mandela

1034.
In what year was Tutankhamen's tomb discovered and opened?
A) 1909
B) 1912
C) 1922

1035.
Which country achieved independence in 1966 and is the only English-speaking country in South America?
A) COLUMBIA
B) GUYANA
C) PANAMA

1036.
Who was assassinated on February 21, 1965?
A) JOHN F. KENNEDY
B) MARTIN LUTHER KING
C) MALCOLM X

1037.
On August 7th 1998, two U.S. embassies in East Africa countries were bombed killing 224 and injuring over 4000, mostly indigenous people. Name the odd one out.
A) KENYA
B) SUDAN
C) TANZANIA

1038.
In which country did the Biafran War take place?
A) NIGERIA
B) GAMBIA
C) LIBERIA

1039.
What was the occupation of the historian and Egyptologist, Cheik Anta Diop?
A) SCIENTIST
B) PUBLISHER
C) ARCHITECT

African star: Kwame Nkrumah

1040.
Kwame Ture, formerly known as Stokely Carmichael, was the first person to popularize which phrase?
A) I AM SOMEBODY
B) NO JUSTICE, NO PEACE
C) BLACK POWER

1041.
In 1984 Jesse Jackson helped free an American Pilot hostage from Syria, and negotiated the release of twenty-two hostages from which country?
A) LEBANON
B) CUBA
C) LIBYA

1042.
Dr. Lloyd Quarterman and Dr. Ralph Gardner were two of six black scientists who worked in secret on the 'Manhattan Project'. What was it?
A) THE BREAKING OF THE "ENIGMA" CODE
B) THE MAKING OF SURFACE TO AIR MISSILES
C) THE CREATION OF THE ATOM BOMB

1043.
To which cultural group did the presidents of Rwanda and Burundi belong before both were killed in an aeroplane crash on April 6, 1994?
A) TUTSI
B) HUTU
C) BANTU

1044.
Following intimidation from Janjiweed Arab militia, name the country ruled by the National Islamic Front, which faced a humanitarian disaster in 2004 with over 1 million of its inhabitants displaced.
A) SOMALIA
B) SUDAN
C) EGYPT

1045.
Who, aged 35, became the youngest person ever to win the Nobel Peace Prize?
A) MAHATMA GANDHI
B) MARTIN LUTHER KING
C) MOTHER THERESA

1046.
In what year did the beating of Rodney King spark the L.A. Riots?
A) 1992
B) 1993
C) 1994

1047.
In which part of the world were the first recorded cases of the disease A.I.D.S discovered?
A) KENYA
B) CALIFORNIA
C) THE FAR EAST

1048.
Which country known historically as Azania became an independent republic in 1960?
A) PAPUA NEW GUINEA
B) NEW ZEALAND
C) SOUTH AFRICA

1049.
Name the ship that arrived in Southampton Harbor in 1948, carrying 492 first-generation post-war Caribbean settlers to Britain.
A) QUEEN MARY II
B) EMPIRE WINDRUSH
C) SS MAYFLOWER

1050.
Name the cult headquarters and the year in which Reverend Jim Jones led the largest mass suicide in history.
A) WACO, TEXAS, 1993
B) THE PEOPLE'S TEMPLE, JONESTOWN, 1978
C) HEAVEN'S GATE, CALIFORNIA, 1997

1051.
Who became the first president of the first West African country to regain its independence in the twentieth century?
A) KWAME NKRUMAH
B) KENNETH KAUNDA
C) LEOPOLD SENGHOR

1052.
Which former U.S. colony became a semi-independent commonwealth state in 1952?
A) PUERTO RICO
B) COSTA RICA
C) HAWAII

1053.
Name the athlete, singer, actor and activist who became a hero for the working class throughout Europe during the 1930s.
A) HARRY BELAFONTE
B) PAUL ROBESON
C) JESSE OWENS

1054.
Who was born Malcolm Ivan Meredith Nurse and later developed the prototype blueprint for Pan-Africanism?
A) MALCOLM X
B) FRANTZ FANON
C) GEORGE PADMORE

1055.
The honorable Marcus Garvey, one of the greatest visionaries of the twentieth century received a symbolic title given to him by his followers. Name it.
A) KING OF KINGS
B) FIRST PRESIDENT OF AFRICA
C) SON OF THE SUN

1056.
In which country did India's nationalist leader and champion of non-violence, Mahatma Gandhi, begin his political career?
A) SOUTH AFRICA
B) ENGLAND
C) TRINIDAD

1057.
A Mohamed Amin videograph inspired this 1985 charity in London and Philadelphia, which raised $76 million for African Famine Relief. Name it.
A) BAND AID
B) LIVE AID
C) COMIC RELIEF

1058.
What happened as a result of the Pan African conference held in Manchester, England, in 1945?
A) CREATION OF A BLACK ECONOMY
B) DECOLONIZATION OF AFRICA
C) REPARATIONS CHARTER

1059.
What was the original occupation of Winnie Mandela, formally known as "The Mother of the Nation" in South Africa?
A) BARRISTER
B) SOCIAL WORKER
C) TEACHER

1060.
Who founded the Nation of Islam in America in the early 1930s?
A) AGHA KHAN
B) ELIJAH MUHAMMAD
C) W. D. FARD

Bowing before the king: Haile Salessie

Millenium Down

1061.
Which country, famous for its ancient stone wonders, achieved republican status on April 18, 1980?
A) ZIMBABWE
B) CHINA
C) MAURITANIA

1062.
Name the two little girls dubbed the "Internet twins" who in early 2001 became the center of an international custody dispute involving four families?
A) TRANDER AND MALISSA
B) BELINDA AND KIMBERLEY
C) JUDITH AND VICKY

1063.
He was known as 'The Lion of Judah' and his achievements include helping to found the Organization for African Unity. Name him.
A) MARCUS GARVEY
B) MENELIK II
C) HAILE SELASSIE

1064.
She campaigned against racism and sexism worldwide and founded Britain's first black weekly newspaper. Name her.
A) ANGELA DAVIES
B) CLAUDIA JONES
C) LUCETTE MICHAUX

1065.
Who received the Nobel Peace Prize in 1984 for his work against apartheid?
A) WALTER SISULU
B) OLIVER TAMBO
C) DESMOND TUTU

1066.
His quick and effective response during this assault made Dorie Miller the first American World War II hero. Name the assault.
A) THE BOMBING OF PEARL HARBOUR
B) THE LIBERATION OF FRANCE
C) THE DROPPING OF THE HIROSHIMA BOMB

1067.
In what year did the great migration of African Americans from the South to Northern cities begin?
A) 1915
B) 1934
C) 1945

1068.
Before his death in prison, this Nigerian entrepreneur and politician helped to found the International Reparations Group in the late 1980s. Name him.
A) CHIEF ABIOLA
B) FELA KUTI
C) GENERAL ABACHA

1069.
Which South American country was mainly ruled by the Netherlands from 1667 until its independence in 1975?
A) EL SALVADOR
B) URUGUAY
C) SURINAM

1070.
Who was Africa's longest serving president?
A) BANDA HASTINGS OF MALAWI
B) IDI AMIN OF UGANDA
C) MOBUTU SESE SEKO OF ZAIRE

1071.
What political office did Patrice Lumumba hold after leading the Congo to independence in 1960?
A) PRIME MINISTER
B) FOREIGN SECRETARY
C) PRESIDENT

1072.
General Nasser of Egypt nationalized this Northeast African resource, leading to the 1967 Arab-Israeli war. Name the resource.
A) SUEZ CANNEL
B) ASWAN DAM
C) THE NILE

1073.
What African 'first fruits' festival was introduced to the USA by Dr. Maulana Karenga, and is celebrated globally every Christmas?
A) ALL SOULS DAY
B) KWANZAA
C) NYABINGI

1074.
In what year did Colonel Muammar Quadafi come to power in Libya?
A) 1960
B) 1969
C) 1981

1075.
Formed in Liberia on August 24, 1990, what is the function of the African organization known as ECOMOG?
A) ECONOMIC TRADE
B) ENVIRONMENTAL PROTECTION GROUP
C) PEACE KEEPING FORCE

1076.
What were nine African Americans proceeding to do on 25 September, 1957 when historically the U.S. government deployed federal troops to defend their rights?
A) ORDERING FOOD AT A WOOLWORTHS STORE IN GREENSBORO, NORTH CAROLINA
B) ENROLLING AT A HIGH SCHOOL IN LITTLE ROCK, ARKANSAS
C) TAKING A FRONT SEAT ON A BUS IN MONTGOMERY, ALABAMA

1077.
Tanganyika and Zanzibar became unified as one independent state in 1964. Name it.
A) TANZANIA
B) TUNISIA
C) SWAZILAND

1078.
What was the nickname of the first President of Kenya, Jomo Kenyatta?
A) FATHER MAU MAU
B) SPIRIT OF THE NATION
C) BURNING SPEAR

1079.
What year did Bruce Williams make the historic discovery of the Nubian kingdom of Ta Seti?
A) 1979
B) 1966
C) 1922

1080.
Give the occupation of the imprisoned human rights activist, Mumia Abu Jamal.
A) DISC JOCKEY
B) DOCTOR
C) JOURNALIST

1081.
How many years of foreign rule in Egypt was ended by its first president, Mohammed Naguib, after he deposed King Farouk I in 1952?
A) 2300 YEARS
B) 3300 YEARS
C) 4300 YEARS

1082.
The international statesman Félix Eboué helped to shape the outcome of World War II by doing what?
A) DISCOVERING ITALIAN MILITARY SECRETS
B) POISONING HITLER
C) ENGAGING THE FASCIST BLOC IN NORTH AFRICA

1083.
Which nationalist leader called for an independent African American state in 1960?
A) FRED HAMPTON
B) ELIJAH MUHAMMAD
C) GEORGE JACKSON

1084.
Which Martinique born writer wrote the critically acclaimed *The Wretched of The Earth*, and joined the Algerians in their struggle for independence?
A) FRANTZ FANON
B) EUZHAN PALCY
C) CHIEK ANTA DIOP

Millenium Down

Dreaming of a better future:
Martin Luther King

1085.
How old was Elián González of Cuba when he was discovered clinging to an inner tube off the Florida coast in 1999?
A) SIX
B) NINE
C) ELEVEN

1086.
What political initiative passed in 1941, encouraged the decolonization of Africa?
A) THE ATLANTIC CHARTER
B) APPEAL TO THE LEAGUE OF NATIONS
C) UNITED NATIONS CHARTER

1087.
One of the most formidable combat units of World War II was the all African American ninety-ninth Pursuits Squadron. What were they?
A) TANK OPERATORS
B) FIGHTER AIRCRAFT PILOTS
C) SPIES

1088.
To which group in Nigeria did the martyred environmental activist, Ken Saro-wiwa belong?
A) YORUBA
B) HAUSA
C) OGONI

1089.
Name the group led by Osama bin Laden, linked to the September 11th 2001 attacks on the U.S.
A) HAMAS
B) AL QAEDA
C) THE TALIBAN

1090.
What was the code-name given to the rescue mission which airlifted fourteen thousand Ethiopian Jews to Israel during May 1991?
A) OPERATION DAVID
B) OPERATION SOLOMON
C) OPERATION MOSES

1091.
On which Japanese city on August 8, 1945, was a 64-detonator plutonium bomb dropped?
A) HIROSHIMA
B) NAGASAKI
C) TOKYO

1092.
In which country during the 1990s did, President Robert Mugabe, dictate a land reform act which encouraged a redistribution of farmland back to the indigenous people?
A) ZIMBABWE
B) ZAMBIA
C) MOZAMBIQUE

1093.
Name the guerrilla army led by the late Jonas Savimbi who, between 1976 and 1996, waged an war against the government of Angola.
A) UNITA
B) RENAMO
C) SWAPO

1094.
Which famous scholar and feminist icon was a former American 'public enemy number one' and had a song dedicated to her by Yoko Ono?
A) BETTY SHABAZZ
B) NINA SIMONE
C) ANGELA DAVIS

1095.
What was the name of the Marxist government that ruled Ethiopia between 1974 and 1987?
A) THE DERG
B) THE JUNTA
C) THE RED ARMY

1096.
Between 1932 and 1972 what was injected as a "medical experiment" on 623 unsuspecting African American men from Tuskegee, Alabama?
A) VITAMIN E
B) PENICILLIN
C) SYPHILIS

1097.
Senegal's first president, Leopold Senghor, helped to write the new French Constitution and assisted in developing which famous concept?
A) P.O.W.E.R.
B) NEGRITUDE
C) UHURU

1098.
Amilcar Cabral was the famous revolutionary who led struggles in Guinea-Bissau and Angola. What year did Cabral become a martyr?
A) 1966
B) 1969
C) 1975

1099.
El Hajj Malik El-Shabazz is better known by what name?
A) LOUIS FARRAKHAN
B) ELIJAH MUHAMMAD
C) MALCOLM X

1100.
In which American state during the 1930s did the famous trial of the nine Scottsboro boys take place?
A) KENTUCKY
B) ALABAMA
C) TENNESSEE

1101.
Which country became an independent commonwealth state in 1960, and a full republic in 1963 with Nnamdi Azikiwe as its first president?
A) GAMBIA
B) NIGERIA
C) NIGER

1102.
John Chilembwe formed the 'Africa for Africans' movement to combat colonialism in Africa during World War I. What was Chilembwe's occupation?
A) REVEREND
B) FISHERMAN
C) FARMER

1103.
In which famous church did Corretta Scott King became the first woman ever to give a sermon in 1968?
A) ST. PAUL'S CATHEDRAL
B) KENSINGTON TEMPLE
C) WESTMINSTER ABBEY

1104.
Rastafari ambassador and reggae legend Bob Marley was the son of an army captain whose family came from which country?
A) ENGLAND
B) WALES
C) SCOTLAND

1105.
What year did the New Cross Fire, which claimed fourteen young lives, lead to one of the biggest civil rights marches in Britain?
A) 1980
B) 1981
C) 1983

1106.
Name the first Caribbean island to achieve political independence from Britain in 1962.
A) JAMAICA
B) TRINIDAD AND TOBAGO
C) BARBADOS

1107.
Throughout the 1970s his was the most recognizable face on the planet. Name him.
A) LOUIS ARMSTRONG
B) MUHAMMAD ALI
C) MICHAEL JACKSON

Millenium Down

1108.
Where was Nelson Mandela detained for a quarter of a century before becoming the first democratically elected president of South Africa in May 1994?
A) CAPE SECURITY PRISON
B) ROBBEN ISLAND
C) RHODE ISLAND

1109.
Before his murder on June 12, 1963, Medgar Evers represented which state as the field secretary for the NAACP?
A) TENNESSEE
B) NEW YORK
C) MISSISSIPPI

1110.
Name the section of the British war effort operated exclusively by Caribbean women throughout World War 2.
A) WOMEN'S ARMY AUXIALIARY CORPS.
B) BRITISH WEST INDIES REGIMENT
C) WEST INDIAN SERVICEMEN AND WOMEN'S ASSOCIATION

1111.
How many black South African demonstrators were shot dead at the Sharpville Massacre on March 21, 1960?
A) FIFTY-SEVEN
B) SIXTY-SEVEN
C) SEVENTY-SEVEN

1112.
Name the West African country dominated and ruled by France from the fifteenth century until 11 August, 1960?
A) GOLD COAST
B) IVORY COAST
C) CAMEROON

1113.
What position in Nigeria's civil government did Umaru Dikko hold before he was accused of embezzling six billion dollars in 1983?
A) SPORTS MINISTER
B) TRANSPORT MINISTER
C) PRIME MINISTER

1114.
Where in South Africa was Desmond Tutu enthroned as an Anglican Archbishop in 1986?
A) TRANSVAAL
B) KWAZULU
C) CAPETOWN

1115.
Which country had its first Asian prime-minister held captive with forty-three other politicians, in May 2000, by businessman turned politician, George Speight?
A) FIJI
B) UGANDA
C) EAST TIMOR

1116.
Until he was deposed in 2003, for how long did Saddam Hussein rule in Iraq?
A) THIRTY FIVE YEARS
B) TWENTY FIVE YEARS
C) TWENTY YEARS

1117.
The biggest uprising in South African history was the Soweto Uprising. When did it take place?
A) 1956
B) 1966
C) 1976

1118.
What year did councilor Henry Sylvester Williams organize the world's first Pan-Africanist conference in London?
A) 1900
B) 1910
C) 1925

1119.
Which Asian group are fighting to establish an independence state called Eelam?
A) INDIAN SIKHS
B) KHMER ROUGE
C) TAMIL TIGERS

1120.
In which former country did Christian Serbs begin a war of ethnic cleansing against Bosnian Muslims and Croats, in 1992?
A) CZECHOSLOVAKIA
B) YUGOSLAVIA
C) SCANDINAVIA

1121.
In 1984 this Indian town became the scene of the world's worst chemical disaster. Name it.
A) BOMBAY
B) BHOPAL
C) PATNA

1122.
Against who did Samora Machel lead Mozambique to independence in 1975?
A) PORTUGAL
B) BELGIUM
C) FRANCE

1123.
Which organization was John Edgar Hoover the head of when he engineered the notorious Counter-Intelligence Programme?
A) CIA
B) FBI
C) A-APRP

1124.
Which award did Ahmed Sekou Ture receive for helping in the 1958 liberation of Guinea?
A) NOBEL PEACE PRIZE
B) LENIN PEACE PRIZE
C) FRENCH LEGION OF HONOUR

1125.
Up until his assassination in 1983, Maurice Bishop was the head of state for which Caribbean island?
A) GRENADA
B) DOMINICAN REPUBLIC
C) ST. VINCENT

1126.
What is the occupation of the groundbreaking scholar and American female academic Dr. Frances Cress Welsing?
A) PSYCHIATRIST
B) ART COLLECTOR
C) ASTRO PHYSICIST

1127.
Which Argentinean revolutionary and Latin American hero was a former confidant of Fidel Castro?
A) EVA PERON
B) AUGUSTUS SANDINO
C) CHE GUAVARA

1128.
Which South African leader was featured in the award-winning motion picture *Cry Freedom*?
A) CHRIS HANI
B) THABO MBEKI
C) STEVE BIKO

1129.
What was the last remaining colony in Africa to achieve independence in 1990?
A) NAMIBIA
B) BURKINA FASO
C) SOUTH AFRICA

1130.
Who shared the Nobel Peace Prize in its centenary year for their work towards "a better organized and more peaceful world"?
A) NELSON MANDELA AND P. W. BOTHA
B) KOFI ANNAN AND THE UNITED NATIONS
C) ANWAR SADAT AND MENACHEM BEGIN

Part II

Entertainment • Millennium Dawn • Science & Engineering • Politics & Law • General Knowledge • Literature & Art • Sports • History

Answers

Entertainment

Answers and Sources

1.

A) THE PELICAN BRIEF

☞ The Evening Standard, Associated Newspaper Group; London, March 25, 2002, p.1.

Additional Information:

☞ Ebony, Johnson Publishing; Chicago, March 1994, pp.110-14.

☞ The Academy Awards Handbook, Pinnacle Books, Windsor Publishing Corp.; USA, 1995.

☞ Ebony, Johnson Publishing; Chicago, December, 1992, pp.124-30.

2.

A) ARISTA

☞ Ebony, Johnson Publishing; Chicago, June 2003, pp.116-124.

Additional Information:

☞ Ebony, Johnson Publishing; Chicago, May 2001, pp.32-33.

☞ Ebony, Johnson Publishing; Chicago, November 2000, p.36.

☞ Arista Records, 6 West 57th Street, New York, NY, 10019, USA.

3.

B) MISSY ELLIOTT

☞ Pride, London, May 1997, pp.52-55.

Additional Information:

☞ Hit Singles: Top 20 Charts from 1954 to the Present Day, Dave McAleer, Carlton; 2001.

☞ The News of the World, London, March 23, 1997, p.3.

☞ Ebony, Johnson Publishing; Chicago, August 2001, pp.68-74.

4.

C) MILES DAVIS – KIND OF BLUE

☞ Miles: The Autobiography, Miles Davis and Quincy Troupe, Simon & Schuster; New York, 1989.

Additional Information:

☞ Icons of Black Music: A History in Photographs 1900-2000, Charlotte Greig, Brown Partworks Ltd.; UK, 1999, pp.36-37.

☞ The 101 Best Jazz Records: A History of Jazz on Records, Len Lyons, Morrow; New York, 1980.

☞ Dancing in Your Head: Jazz, Blues, Rock and Beyond, Gene Santoro, Oxford University Press; New York and Oxford, 1994.

5.

A) MARIAH CAREY

☞ The Recording Academy, 5402 Pico Blvd, Santa Monica, California, USA, 90405.

Additional Information:

☞ Ebony, Johnson Publishing; Chicago, November, 2002, p.68.

☞ Hip-Hop Divas, Vibe Magazine, (ed.), Three Rivers Press; USA, 2001.

☞ Ebony, Johnson Publishing; Chicago, December, 2000, p.138.

6.

B) HIP HOP

☞ Hip Hop: The Illustrated History of Break Dancing, Rap Music and Graffiti, Steven Hager, St.Martin's Press; New York, 1984.

Additional Information:

☞ Vibe History of Hip Hop, Alan Light, (ed.), Vibe Magazine, Three Rivers Press; USA, 1998.

☞ Rap Attack 2: African Rap to New York Hip Hop, David Toop, Serpents Tail; 1991.

☞ The New Beats: Exploring the Music Culture and Attitudes of Hip-Hop, S. H. Fernando, Jr., Doubleday; New York, 1994.

7.

C) BREAK DANCING

☞ Ballet.co Magazine, July, 2003.

Additional Information:

☞ The Sunday Telegraph, (Review Section 'The Arts'), London, 4th January 2001.

☞ The Black Dance Body: A Geography from Coon to Cool, Brenda Dixon Gottschild, Palgrave Macmillan; US, 2003.

☞ The Observer, London, 6 July 2003.

8.

C) GIMME THE LIGHT

☞ The New Nation, Ethnic Media Group; London, 5 May, 2003, p.22.

Additional Information:

☞ The Voice, The Voice Group Ltd.; London, 21 & 30 December, 2002, p.44.

☞ Roots Rock Reggae: An Oral History of Reggae Music from Ska to Dancehall, Chuck Foster, Billboard Books; 1999.

☞ Atlantic Records (Distribution

A

Department), 9229 Sunset Blvd., 9th Floor, Los Angeles, 90069, CA.

9.
A) GOSPEL
☞ Vibe, Quincy Jones and David Salzman Entertainment, Time Publishing Inc.; January, 1998, p.53.
Additional Information:
☞ Ebony, Johnson Publishing; Chicago, November, 2002, p.85.
☞ Serials Review, Volume 20, No. 4. "From Spirituals to Gospel Rap", Timothy Dodge, Gospel Music Periodicals, 1994, pp.67-78.
☞ The Voice, The Voice Group Ltd.; London, July 7, 1997, pp.20-21.

10.
C) BATMAN FOREVER
☞ The Voice, The Voice Group Ltd.; London, March 5, 1996, p.3.
Additional Information:
☞ The New Nation, Western Hemisphere; London, January 6, 1997, p.23.
☞ The Recording Academy, 5402 Pico Blvd, Santa Monica, California, USA, 90405.
☞ Hit Singles: Top 20 Charts from 1954 to the Present Day, Dave McAleer, Carlton; 2001.

11.
B) BOB MARLEY
☞ Bob Marley: An Intimate Portrait by His Mother. Cedella Booker and Anthony Winkler, UK, 1996.
Additional Information:
☞ Bob Marley: Spirit Dancer, Bruce W. Talamon, W. W. Norton & Co.; 1994.
☞ This is Reggae Music, The Story of Jamaica's Music, Lloyd Bradley, Grove Press; 2001.
☞ Bob Marley: Conquering Lion of Reggae, Stephen Davis, Plexus; London, 1990.

12.
A) JAMES EARL JONES
☞ Ebony, Johnson Publishing; Chicago, July, 1995, p.69.
Additional Information:
☞ The New York Times Guide to the Best 1000 Movies Ever Made by Vincent Canby, Times Books; 1999.

☞ Roger Ebert's Movie Yearbook 2000 (Roger Eberts Movie Yearbook, 2000) by Roger Ebert, Andrews McMeel Publishing; 1999.
☞ Halliwell's Film Guide. Leslie Halliwell, 11th Edition, HarperCollins; 1995, p.550.

13.
B) SOCA
☞ The Steel Band Movement: The Forging of a National Art in Trinidad and Tobago. Stephen Stuempfle, Pennsylvania University Press; 1995.
Additional Information:
☞ Caribbean Times, No. 694, Hansib Publishing; London, August 29, 1994.
☞ The Guardian, Guardian Newspapers; London, August 26, 1996.
☞ The Voice, The Voice Group Limited; August 26, 1996.

14.
C) HUNCH BACK OF NOTRE DAME
☞ The Walt Disney Company; Guest Communications, P.O. Box 10040, Beuna Vista, Florida, 32840, USA.
Additional Information:
☞ The Voice, The Voice Group Ltd.; London, September 3, 1996, p.27.
☞ Hit Singles: Top 20 Charts from 1954 to the Present Day, Dave McAleer, Carlton; 2001.
☞ Halliwell's Film Guide 2002. Leslie Halliwell, HarperCollins; London, 2001.

15.
C) LILIES OF THE FIELD
☞ The Measure of a Man; A Memoire. Sidney Poitier, HarperCollins; US, 2001.
Additional Information:
☞ 1999 Facts About Blacks: A Sourcebook of African American Accomplishment. Raymond M. Corbin, Beckham House Publishers; USA, 1st Edition, 1986, p.157.
☞ Black Hollywood: The Black Performer in Motion Pictures, Gary Null, Citadel Press Books, Carol Publishing; USA, 1990.
☞ Encyclopedia of Black America, W. A. Low and Virgil A. Clift, (eds.), Mcgraw-Hill; New York, 1981.

16.

B) SHIRLEY BASSEY

☞ 1999 Facts About Blacks: A Sourcebook of African American Accomplishment. Raymond M. Corbin, Beckham House Publishers; USA, 1st Edition, 1986, p.143.

Additional Information:

☞ The Weekly Journal, Voice Communications; London, February 17, 1994, p.10.

☞ 1994 Radio Times, Film and Video Guide, Derek Winnert, Hodder & Stoughton; 1993.

☞ The Warner Guide to UK & US Hit Singles, Compiled by Dave McAleer, A Carlton/Little, Brown Book; UK, 1994.

17.

B) THE MOBO'S

☞ The New Nation, Ethnic Media Group; London, May 5, 2003, p.5.

Additional Information:

☞ Representing Black Britain: Black and Asian Images on Television, Sarita Malik, Sage Publications; 1st edition, 2001, p.150.

☞ The New Nation, Western Hemisphere; London, 25 November, 1996, p.13.

☞ Gb Craig David, Hannah Mander, Michael O'Mara Books Ltd.; 2001, p.10.

18.

B) FOOLISH

☞ Ebony, Johnson Publishing; Chicago, March 2003, pp.170-174.

Additional Information:

☞ The Recording Academy, 5402 Pico Blvd, Santa Monica, California, USA, 90405.

☞ Ebony, Johnson Publishing; Chicago, May, 2003, p.160.

☞ National Academy of Recording Arts and Sciences, 6255 Sunset Blvd, Suite 1023, Hollywood, 90028.

19.

B) STUDIO 1

☞ Rap Attack 2: African Rap to New York Hip Hop, David Toop, Serpents Tail; 1991, p.39.

Additional Information:

☞ The New Nation, Ethnic Media Group; London, May 5, 2003, p.13.

☞ The Rough Guide to Reggae, 2nd Edition, Peter Dalton and Orla Duane (eds.), Rough Guide Books; 2001.

☞ Roots Rock Reggae: An Oral History of Reggae Music from Ska to Dancehall, Chuck Foster, Billboard Books; 1999.

20.

A) QUINCY JONES

☞ Q: The Autobiography of Quincy Jones, Quincy Jones, Doubleday; New York, 2001.

Additional Information:

☞ The Recording Academy, 5402 Pico Blvd, Santa Monica, California, USA, 90405.

☞ Who's Who of Black Achievers, John Hughes, (ed.), Ethnic Media Group; UK, 1999, p.60.

☞ The Academy Awards Handbook, Pinnacle Books, Windsor Publishing Corp.; USA, 1995.

21.

A) JAMES BROWN

☞ Rap Attack 2: African Rap to New York Hip Hop, David Toop, Serpents Tail; 1991, pp.153-54, 191-93.

Additional Information:

☞ Vibe History of Hip Hop, Alan Light, (ed.), Vibe Magazine, Three Rivers Press; USA, 1998.

☞ Icons of Black Music: A History in Photographs 1900-2000, Charlotte Greig, Brown Partworks Ltd.; UK, 1999, pp.18-19.

☞ The New Beats: Exploring the Music Culture and Attitudes of Hip-Hop, S. H. Fernando, Jr., Doubleday; New York, 1994.

22.

B) THE SUPREMES

☞ Girl Groups: The Story of a Sound, Alan Betrock, Delilah; New York, 1982.

Additional Information:

☞ The Story of Motown, Peter Benjaminson, Grove Press; New York, 1979.

☞ Call Her Miss Ross: The Unauthorised Biography of Diana Ross, J. Randy Taraborrelli, Sidgwick & Jackson; London, 1989.

☞ Ebony Pictorial History of Black America: Volume 3. Civil Rights Movement to

Black Revolution, Johnson Publishing
Company; 1974, pp.241, 265, 300.

23.
B) JODECI
☞ Upscale, Upscale Communications Inc.;
November 1995, pp.80-81.
Additional Information:
☞ Time, Time Inc.; USA, August 21, 1995,
p.48.
☞ The Voice, The Voice Group Ltd.;
London, April 16, 2001, p.39.
☞ Vibe, Quincy Jones and David Salzman
Entertainment, Time Publishing Inc.;
February, 1996, p.61.

24.
C) I CAN'T GET NO SATISFACTION
☞ Who's Who in Rock, Revised Edition
Compiled and Edited by William York,
Arthur Barker Ltd.; 1982.
Additional Information:
☞ Icons of Black Music: A History in
Photographs 1900-2000, Charlotte
Greig, Brown Partworks Ltd.; UK, 1999,
pp.170-71.
☞ New Musical Express Who's Who in
Rock & Roll, Edited by John Tobler,
Hamlyn; 1991.
☞ Hit Singles: Top 20 Charts from 1954 to
the Present Day, Dave McAleer,
Carlton; 2001.

25.
A) THE FULL MONTY
☞ Who's Who of Black Achievers, John
Hughes, (ed.), Ethnic Media Group; UK,
1999, p.26.
Additional Information:
☞ The Voice, The Voice Group Ltd.;
London, September 17, 2001, p.50.
☞ Halliwell's Film Guide 2002. Leslie
Halliwell, HarperCollins; London, 2001.
☞ Television and Society, Nicholas
Abercrombie, Blackwell Publishers;
Cambridge, 1996.

26.
B) POP
☞ The Best of Al Jarreau, Music Dispatch
Publishing; USA, 1990.
Additional Information:
☞ The Recording Academy, 5402 Pico
Blvd, Santa Monica, California, USA,
90405.

☞ The Grammys: For the Record, Penguin
Books; 1993.
☞ Tony, Grammy, Emmy, Country: A
Broadway, Television and Records
Award, Reference. Compiled by Don
Franks, USA.

27.
A) INDEPENDENT WOMAN
☞ Ebony, Johnson Publishing; Chicago,
September, 2001, pp.90-96.
Additional Information:
☞ Ebony, Johnson Publishing; Chicago,
May, 2003, p.164.
☞ Ebony, Johnson Publishing; Chicago,
December, 2000, p.128.
☞ The New Nation, Ethnic Media Group;
London, July 19, 1999, pp.28-29.

28.
B) WORLD MUSIC
☞ Rap Attack 2: African Rap to New York
Hip Hop, David Toop, Serpents Tail;
1991, pp.114, 148.
Additional Information:
☞ Sterns Guide to Contemporary
African Music, Ronnie Graham,
Pluto Press; UK, 1989, pp.21, 29,
261-62.
☞ The Rough Guide to World Music,
Volume 1, 2nd Edition, Simon
Broughton (ed.), Rough Guides
Publishing; 2000.
☞ The Sounds of Music: WOMAD, Frank
Drage, Philip Sweeney and Peter
Gabriel, Virgin; London, 1990.

29.
B) W. C. HANDY
☞ Father of the Blues: An Autobiography,
W. C. Handy, Collier; New York, 1970.
Additional Information:
☞ The Devil's Music: A History of the
Blues. Giles Oakley, Taplinger, New
York, 1977.
☞ The Roots of the Blues: An African
Search. Samuel Charters, Marion
Boyars, Boston, 1981.
☞ The Black American Reference Book.
Mabel M. Smyth, (ed.), Prentice-Hall
Inc.; USA, 1976, p.805.

30.
C) MONICA
☞ Ebony, Johnson Publishing; Chicago,
August, 2000, pp.52-56.

Entertainment

Additional Information:
- ☞ Upscale, Upscale Communications Inc.; November 1995, p.84.
- ☞ Hype Hair, No. 4, Volume 1, No. 1, Word Up!, Video Productions Inc.; USA, November 1995, p.56.
- ☞ Hit Singles: Top 20 Charts from 1954 to the Present Day, Dave McAleer, Carlton; 2001.

31.
A) MAHALIA JACKSON
- ☞ Mahalia Jackson: Movin' On Up, Mahalia Jackson and Evan McLeod Whylie, Hawthorne Books; NY, 1966.

Additional Information:
- ☞ Sweet Soul Music: Rhythm and Blues and the Southern Dream of Freedom, Paul Garolnick, Virgin Books; UK, 1986, pp.338, 348.
- ☞ How Sweet the Sound: The Golden Age of Gospel, Horace Clarence Boyer, Elliot & Clark Publishing; Washington, D.C., 1995.
- ☞ Encyclopedia of Black America, W. A. Low and Virgil A. Clift, (eds.), Mcgraw-Hill; New York, 1981, p.467.

32.
C) LADIES LOVE
- ☞ I Make My Own Rules, LL Cool J. and Karen Hunter, St. Martin's Mass Market Paper; USA, 1998.

Additional Information:
- ☞ Vibe History of Hip Hop, Alan Light, (ed.), Vibe Magazine, Three Rivers Press; USA, 1998.
- ☞ Ebony, Johnson Publishing; Chicago, January, 2003, pp.116-120.
- ☞ The New Beats: Exploring the Music, Culture and Attitudes of Hip Hop. S. H. Fernando, Jr., Doubleday; New York, 1994.

33.
C) SHABBA RANKS
- ☞ Words Like Fire: Dancehall Reggae and Ragga Muffin, Stascha Bader, Central Books; London, 1993.

Additional Information:
- ☞ Roots Rock Reggae: An Oral History of Reggae Music from Ska to Dancehall, Chuck Foster, Billboard Books; 1999.
- ☞ The Weekly Journal, Voice Communications; London, February 3, 1994, p.6.
- ☞ Pride, London, May/June 1994, p.55.

34.
C) THE TWIST
- ☞ The Twist: The Story of the Song and Dance That Changed the World, Jim Dawson, Faber & Faber; Boston, MA., 1995.

Additional Information:
- ☞ Black Firsts: 2000 Years of Extraordinary Achievement. Jessie Carney Smith, Caspar L. Jordan and Robert L. Johns, Visible Ink Press; USA, 1994, p.24.
- ☞ The Weekly Journal, Voice Communications; London, February 3, 1994, p.14.
- ☞ Big Beat Heat: Alan Freed and the Early Years of Rock and Roll. John A. Jackson, Schirmer Books; New York, 1991.

35.
A) PHONE BOOTH
- ☞ The Voice, The Voice Group Ltd.; London, 10 February 2003, p.22.

Additional Information:
- ☞ Halliwell's Film Guide 2002. Leslie Halliwell, HarperCollins; London, 2001.
- ☞ The New York Times Guide to the Best 1000 Movies Ever Made by Vincent Canby, Times Books; 1999
- ☞ Roger Ebert's Movie Yearbook 2000 (Roger Eberts Movie Yearbook, 2000) by Roger Ebert Andrews McMeel Publishing; 1999.

36.
A) NEW JACK CITY
- ☞ Tupac Amaru Shakur 1971-1996, Quincy Jones, Editors of Vibe Magazine (ed.), Three Rivers Press; USA, 1998.

Additional Information:
- ☞ Vibe, Quincy Jones and David Salzman Entertainment, Time Publishing Inc.; April, 1996, (cover).
- ☞ Icons of Black Music: A History in Photographs 1900-2000, Charlotte Greig, Brown Partworks Ltd.; UK, 1999, pp.142-43.
- ☞ Vibe, Quincy Jones and David Salzman Entertainment, Time Publishing Inc.; February, 1996, pp.44-50.

37.
B) DUKE ELLINGTON
- ☞ Duke Ellington, Jazz Masters Series, Peter Gammond, Apollo Press Ltd.; UK, 1987.

Additional Information:
☞ The Music of Black Americans; A History. 2nd Edition, Eileen Southern, W. W. Norton & Co.; 1983.
☞ Biographical Dictionary of American Music, Charles E. Claghorn, Parker Publishing Company; West Nayack, New York, 1973.
☞ The 101 Best Jazz Records: A History of Jazz on Records, Len Lyons, Morrow; New York, 1980.

38.
A) JUNGLE
☞ The Voice, The Voice Group Ltd.; London, January 8, 2001, p.55.
Additional Information:
☞ Black Noise: Rap Music and Black Culture in Contemporary America, Tricia Rose. Westeyan University Press; 1994.
☞ The Voice, The Voice Group Ltd.; London, December 13, 1994, p.6. (24 Hour Section pp.3, 6-7,)
☞ Reggae Island: Jamaican Music in the Digital Age, Tom Weber, Kingston Publications; Kingston, JA., 1992.

39.
A) BEBOP
☞ Swing to Bebop: An Oral History of the Transition in Jazz in the 1940s. Ira Gitler, Oxford University Press; New York, 1985.
Additional Information:
☞ The Music of Black Americans; A History. 2nd Edition, Eileen Southern, W. W. Norton & Co.; 1983.
☞ The Black American Reference Book. Mabel M. Smyth, (ed.), Prentice-Hall Inc.; USA, 1976. pp.816-817.
☞ An Autobiography of Black Jazz. Dempsey J. Travis, The Urban Research Center; Chicago, 1983.

40.
C) ICE T
☞ The Ice Opinion, Pan Books; London, 1994.
Additional Information:
☞ Black Noise: Rap Music and Black Culture in Contemporary America, Tricia Rose. Westeyan University Press; 1994.
☞ The Weekly Journal, Voice Communications; London, January 12, 1995, p.10.
☞ Rap Attack 2: African Rap to New York Hip Hop, David Toop, Serpents Tail; 1991, p.204.

41.
B) HATTIE McDANIEL
☞ Black Hollywood: The Negro in Motion Pictures. Gary Null, Lyle Stuart Press; USA, 1975.
Additional Information:
☞ Ebony, Johnson Publishing; Chicago, March, 1994, p.48.
☞ On the Real Side: A History of African American Comedy. Mel Watkins, Lawrence Hill; USA, 1999, pp.196-97, 283-85.
☞ The Black Heritage Book of Trivia, Morgan White Jr., Quinlan Press; Boston, 1985, p.147.

42.
C) THIRD WORLD
☞ Ebony, Johnson Publishing; Chicago, June, 2003, p.32.
Additional Information:
☞ Moon Handbooks: Jamaica, Karl Luntta, Avalon Travel Publishing; 4th edition, 1999, p.167.
☞ Hit Singles: Top 20 Charts from 1954 to the Present Day, Dave McAleer, Carlton; 2001.
☞ Roots Rock Reggae: An Oral History of Reggae Music from Ska to Dancehall, Chuck Foster, Billboard Books; 1999.

43.
C) RUSSELL SIMMONS
☞ Ebony, Johnson Publishing; Chicago, January, 2001, pp.116-22.
Additional Information:
☞ Rap Attack 2: African Rap to New York Hip Hop, David Toop, Serpents Tail; 1991, pp.158, 173-75.
☞ Vibe History of Hip Hop, Alan Light, (ed.), Vibe Magazine, Three Rivers Press; USA, 1998.
☞ Ebony, Johnson Publishing; Chicago, June, 1995, p.120.

44.
B) FRIENDS
☞ Swerve: A Guide to the Sweet Life for Postmodern Girls, Aisha Tyler, Dutton Books; 2004

Entertainment

Additional Information:
- ☞ The Voice, The Voice Group Ltd.; London, 10 March, 2003, p.3.
- ☞ Joke Stew 1,349: More Hilarious Servings by Judy Brown Andrews McMeel Publishing; (August 15, 2000)
- ☞ That's Anarchy! The Story of the Revolution in the World of TV Comedy, Chrissie Macdonald, Sid Harta Publishers; 2003.

45.
C) SHAKA DEMUS AND PLIERS
- ☞ Hit Singles: Top 20 Charts from 1954 to the Present Day, Dave McAleer, Carlton; 2001.

Additional Information:
- ☞ The Weekly Journal, Voice Communications; London, July 14, 1994, p.16.
- ☞ The Voice, The Voice Group Ltd.; London, December 2, 1996 p.26.
- ☞ Roots Rock Reggae: An Oral History of Reggae Music from Ska to Dancehall, Chuck Foster, Billboard Books; 1999.

46.
C) JULIE DASH
- ☞ Daughters of the Dust, Julie Dash, Dutton; USA, 1997.

Additional Information:
- ☞ Ebony, Johnson Publishing; Chicago, March, 1994, p.114.
- ☞ Essence, February, 1992, p.38.
- ☞ The Weekly Journal, Voice Communications; London, September 23, 1993, p.10.

47.
C) THE SUGAR HILL GANG
- ☞ Rap Attack 2: African Rap to New York Hip Hop, David Toop, Serpents Tail; 1991, pp.16-17, 78-79, 105-6.

Additional Information:
- ☞ Black Noise: Rap Music and Black Culture in Contemporary America, Tricia Rose. Westeyan University Press; 1994, pp.195-96.
- ☞ The Warner Guide to UK & US Hit Singles, Compiled by Dave McAleer, A Carlton/Little, Brown Book; UK, 1994.
- ☞ Black Firsts: 2000 Years of Extraordinary Achievement. Jessie Carney Smith, Caspar L. Jordan and Robert L. Johns, Visible Ink Press; USA, 1994, p.27.

48.
A) TERRI WALKER
- ☞ The Evening Standard, Associated Newspaper Group; London, 10 September, 2003.

Additional Information:
- ☞ The Guardian, Guardian Newspapers; London, 18 September, 2002.
- ☞ The Voice, The Voice Group Ltd.; London, 28 July, 2003, p.10.
- ☞ The Evening Standard, Associated Newspaper Group; London, 18 September, 2002.

49.
C) A DIFFERENT WORLD
- ☞ Today's Black Hollywood, James Robert Parish, Pinnacle Books, Windsor Publishing Corp.; USA, 1995, p.18.

Additional Information:
- ☞ Halliwell's Film Guide. Leslie Halliwell, 11th Edition, HarperCollins; 1995.
- ☞ Black Hollywood: From 1970 to Today, Gary Null, Citadel Press Books; 1993.
- ☞ Variety Movie Guide 96, Edited by Derek Ellery, Hamlyn Books; UK, 1995.

50.
A) TRIX WORREL
- ☞ Encyclopedia of Television, (3 Vols.), Horace Newcomb, Cary O'Dell and Noelle Watson, (eds.), Fitzroy Dearborn Publishers; 1997.

Additional Information:
- ☞ The New Nation, Ethnic Media Group; London, May 5, 2003, p.16.
- ☞ Halliwell's Film Guide. Leslie Halliwell, 11th Edition, HarperCollins; 1995.
- ☞ Television and Society, Nicholas Abercrombie, Blackwell Publishers; Cambridge, 1996.

51.
B) NAS
- ☞ Open Mike: Reflections on Philosophy, Race, Sex, Culture and Religion by Michael Eric Dyson, BasicCivitas Books; 2002, pp. 31, 260-261, 299

Additional Information:
- ☞ The Voice, The Voice Group Ltd.; London, 21 January, 2002, p.44.

- Vibe History of Hip Hop, Alan Light, (ed.), Vibe Magazine, Three Rivers Press; USA, 1998.
- The Voice, The Voice Group Ltd.; London, 21 & 30 December, 2002, p.44.

52.
A) NICHELLE NICHOLS
- Beyond Uhura: Star Trek and Other Memories, Nichelle Nicholls, Bextree; 1995, UK.

Additional Information:
- Ebony, Johnson Publishing; Chicago, December, 1992, p.122.
- Ebony Pictorial History of Black America: Volume 3. Civil Rights Movement to Black Revolution, Johnson Publishing Company; 1974, p.293.
- Facts on File Encyclopedia of Black Women in America: Theatre Arts and Entertainment (Volume 9), Darlene Clark Hine and Kathleen Thompson, (eds.), Facts of File, Inc.; USA, 1997.

53.
A) SADE
- The Best of Sade, Hal Leonard Publishing Corporation; 1994.

Additional Information:
- The Warner Guide to UK & US Hit Singles, Compiled by Dave McAteer, A Carlton/Little, Brown Book; UK, 1994.
- Vibe, Quincy Jones and David Salzman Entertainment, Time Publishing Inc.; September, 1995.
- The Weekly Journal, Voice Communications; London, November 5, 1992, p.9.

54.
C) WHITNEY HOUSTON
- Diva: The Totally Unauthorised Biography of Whitney Houston. Jeffrey Bowman, Headline; UK, 1994.

Recommended Further Reading
- New Musical Express Who's Who in Rock & Roll, Edited by John Tobler, Hamlyn; 1991, pp.151-52.
- Ebony, Johnson Publishing; Chicago, November, 2000, p.47.
- The Billboard Book of Number One Hits, Fred Bronson, Billboard Publications; New York, 1992.

55.
A) PUBLIC ENEMY
- Fight the Power: Rap, Race and Reality. Chuck D. with Yusuf Jah, Delacorte, USA, 1997.

Additional Information:
- Icons of Black Music: A History in Photographs 1900-2000, Charlotte Greig, Brown Partworks Ltd.; UK, 1999, pp.128-29.
- The New Beats: Exploring the Music, Culture and Attitudes of Hip Hop. S. H. Fernando, Jr., Doubleday; New York, 1994.
- Vibe History of Hip Hop, Alan Light, (ed.), Vibe Magazine, Three Rivers Press; USA, 1998.

56.
A) 1971
- The Academy Awards Handbook, Pinnacle Books, Windsor Publishing Corp.; USA, 1995.

Additional Information:
- Icons of Black Music: A History in Photographs 1900-2000, Charlotte Greig, Brown Partworks Ltd.; UK, 1999, pp.66-67.
- Black Americana. Richard A. Long, Admiral; UK, 1985.
- The Warner Guide to UK & US Hit Singles, Compiled by Dave McAleer, A Carlton/Little, Brown Book; UK, 1994.

57.
B) LEONTYNE PRYCE
- 1999 Facts About Blacks: A Sourcebook of African American Accomplishment. Raymond M. Corbin, Beckham House Publishers; USA, 1st Edition, 1986, p.164.

Additional Information:
- The Black American Reference Book. Mabel M. Smyth, (ed.), Prentice-Hall Inc.; USA, 1976.
- The Black Heritage Book of Trivia, Morgan White Jr., Quinlan Press; Boston, 1985, pp.48, 147.
- Ebony Pictorial History of Black America: Volume 3. Civil Rights Movement to Black Revolution, Johnson Publishing Company; 1974.

58.
A) LENNY HENRY
- Who's Who of Black Achievers, John

Hughes, (ed.), Ethnic Media Group; UK, 1999, p.53.

Additional Information:
☞ Black and British, David Bygott, Oxford University Press; 1992, p.74.
☞ Pride, Voice Communications; September/October Edition 1994.
☞ Crucial Films, Public Relations Department, 20 Notting Hill Gate, London, W11 3JE.

59.
A) SAXON
☞ There Ain't No Black in the Union Jack, Paul Gilroy, Hutchingson; UK, 1987, p.179.

Additional Information:
☞ Words Like Fire: Dancehall Reggae and Ragga Muffin, Stascha Bader, Central Books; London, 1993.
☞ The Voice, The Voice Group Ltd.; London, June 4, 2001, p.53.
☞ Reggae Island: Jamaican Music in the Digital Age, Tom Weber, Kingston Publications; Kingston, JA., 1992.

60.
B) 50 CENT
☞ The New Nation, Ethnic Media Group; London, 7 June, 2004, p.20.

Additional Information:
☞ So You Wanna Be a Hip Hop Star - Your Complete Guide: Featuring Nelly, Eminem, Eve, 50 Cent and Other Great Rappers, Kelly Kenyatta and William H Kelly, US, 2004
☞ From Pieces to Weight: Once Upon a Time in Southside, Queens, 50 Cent and Kris Ex, MTV; 2004.
☞ Billboard's Hottest Hot 100 Hits, Updated and Expanded 3rd Edition, Fred Bronson, Watson-Guptill Publications; 3rd edition, 2002, P95

61.
B) JIMI HENDRIX
☞ Hendrix: Setting the Record Strait. John McDermott with Eddie Kramer, Warner Books, Inc.; 1992, USA.

Additional Information:
☞ The Jimi Hendrix Experience, Jerry Hopkins, Plexus; London, 1996.
☞ Jimi Hendrix: Electric Gypsy, Harry Shapiro and Caesar Glesbeek, Manderin; 1995.

☞ New Musical Express Who's Who in Rock & Roll, Edited by John Tobler, Hamlyn; 1991, p.15.

62.
A) THE ISRAELITES
☞ Black and British, David Bygott, Oxford University Press; 1992, p.15.

Additional Information:
☞ The Warner Guide to UK & US Hit Singles, Compiled by Dave McAleer, A Carlton/Little, Brown Book; UK, 1994.
☞ The Voice, The Voice Group Ltd.; July 14, 1997, pp.20-21.
☞ Roots Rock Reggae: An Oral History of Reggae Music from Ska to Dancehall, Chuck Foster, Billboard Books; 1999.

63.
B) MARY J. BLIGE
☞ Ebony, Johnson Publishing; Chicago, August, 2002, pp.94-98.

Additional Information:
☞ Vibe, Quincy Jones and David Salzman Entertainment, Time Publishing Inc.; February, 1996.
☞ Ebony, Johnson Publishing; Chicago, October, 1995, pp.116-18.
☞ Ebony Man, Johnson Publishing; March, 1993, p.49.

64.
C) BERRY GORDY
☞ To Be loved, Berry Gordy, Headline Book Publishing; New York, London, 1994.

Additional Information:
☞ The Motown Story, Don Waller, Scribner; New York, 1985.
☞ The Music of Black Americans. A History, 2nd Edition, Eileen Southern, W. W. Norton & Co.; 1983, p.500.
☞ Motown: The History, Sharon Davis, Guinness Publications; Enfield, 1988.

65.
B) MONTELL JORDAN
☞ Hit Singles: Top 20 Charts from 1954 to the Present Day, Dave McAleer, Carlton; 2001.

Additional Information:
☞ Caribbean Times, Hansib Publishing; London, May 27, 1997, p.15.
☞ Vibe History of Hip Hop, Alan Light, (ed.), Vibe Magazine, Three Rivers Press; USA, 1998.

The Voice, The Voice Group Limited; May 16, 1995, pp.28-29.

66.
B) STORMY WEATHER
☞ Black Hollywood: The Negro in Motion Pictures, Gary Null, Lyle Stuart Press; USA, 1975.
Additional Information:
☞ Ebony, Johnson Publishing; Chicago, August, 1995, p.115.
☞ Encyclopedia of the Musical Film, Stanley Green, Oxford University Press; New York and Oxford, 1981.
☞ The Weekly Journal, Voice Communications; April 28, 1994, p.5.

67.
B) NINE
☞ Beethoven: Impressions of His Contemporaries, Arranged by Oscar Sonneck, 1926, pp.26, 77, 154, 166, 180.
Additional Information:
☞ The New York Times, July 1, 1940, USA.
☞ An Unrequited Love; An Episode in the Life of Beethoven, (Diary of Fanny Giannarastio) by Fanny Giannarastio Del Rio, 1876, p.60.
☞ Sex and Race, Volume 3, J. A. Rogers, 5th Edition, H. M. Rogers Publishers; USA, 1972, pp.306-9.

68.
B) DANCE
☞ Black Dance, Edward Thorpe, Chatto & Windus; London, 1989.
Additional Information:
☞ Revelations: The Autobiography of Alvin Ailey, Alvin Ailey and Peter A. Ailey, Replica Books; USA, 2000.
☞ African Rhythm. American Dance: A Biography of Katherine Dunham, Terry Harnan, Alfred Knopf; New York, 1974.
☞ The Music of Black Americans. A History, 2nd Edition, Eileen Southern, W. W. Norton & Co.; 1983.

69.
C) BLACK UHURU
☞ This is Reggae Music, The Story of Jamaica's Music, Lloyd Bradley, Grove Press; 2001.

Additional Information:
☞ The Rough Guide to Reggae, 2nd Edition, Peter Dalton and Orla Duane (eds.), Rough Guide Books; 2001.
☞ The Weekly Journal, Voice Communications; London, February 17, 1994, p.11.
☞ The Recording Academy, 5402 Pico Blvd, Santa Monica, California, USA, 90405.

70.
A) ANGELA BASSETT
☞ The Voice, The Voice Group Ltd.; London, March 1, 1994, p.5.
Additional Information:
☞ Halliwell's Film Guide. Leslie Halliwell, 11th Edition, HarperCollins; 1995.
☞ Ebony, Johnson Publishing; Chicago, November, 2002, p.72.
☞ Ebony, Johnson Publishing; Chicago, December, 2000, p.124.

71.
B) PRINCE
☞ Prince: Imp of the Perverse, Barny Hoskyns, Virgin Books; London, 1988.
Additional Information:
☞ Ebony, Johnson Publishing; Chicago, January, 1997, pp.128-32.
☞ New Musical Express Who's Who in Rock & Roll, Edited by John Tobler, Hamlyn; 1991, p.249.
☞ Icons of Black Music: A History in Photographs 1900-2000, Charlotte Greig, Brown Partworks Ltd.; UK, 1999, pp.126-27.

72.
B) MONSTER'S BALL
☞ The New York Times, March 25, 2002, USA.
Additional Information:
☞ The Evening Standard, Associated Newspaper Group; London, March 25, 2002, p.1.
☞ Ebony, Johnson Publishing; Chicago, November 2002, pp.186-190.
☞ Halliwell's Film Guide 2002. Leslie Halliwell, HarperCollins; London, 2001.

73.
C) COURTNEY PINE
☞ Vibe, Quincy Jones and David Salzman Entertainment, Time Publishing Inc.; February, 1996, p.98.

Entertainment

Additional Information:
- ☞ Black Music in Britain, Edited by Paul Oliver, Open University Press; 1990.
- ☞ The Voice, The Voice Group Ltd.; London, 12 March 2001 p.46.
- ☞ The New Nation, Western Hemisphere; London, 8 September 1997, p.13.

74.

C) BIRD
- ☞ The New Nation, Western Hemisphere; London, 17 February 1997, p.22.

Additional Information:
- ☞ The Weekly Journal, Voice Communications; London, 26 May 1994, p.3.
- ☞ The Voice, The Voice Group Ltd.; London, 3 May 1994, p.14.
- ☞ The Weekly Journal, Voice Communications; London, December 22, 1994, p.17.

75.

B) GREGORY ISAACS
- ☞ Reggae: Deep Roots Music, Howard Johnson and Jim Pine, Proteus; London and New York, 1982.

Additional Information:
- ☞ The New Nation, Ethnic Media Group; London, 25 August 2003, p.4.
- ☞ Roots Rock Reggae: An Oral History of Reggae Music from Ska to Dancehall, Chuck Foster, Billboard Books; 1999.
- ☞ Pride, London, September 1997, pp.117.

76.

C) 1990s
- ☞ Ebony, Johnson Publishing; Chicago, August, 2003, pp.170-175.

Additional Information:
- ☞ Ebony, Johnson Publishing; Chicago, January, 1997, pp.32-34.
- ☞ The Evening Standard, Associated Newspaper Group; London, August 14, 1998, p.30.
- ☞ Ebony, Johnson Publishing; Chicago, November, 2000, p.70.

77.

B) SOUNDS OF BLACKNESS
- ☞ The Weekly Journal, Voice Communications; London, November 19, 1992, p.11.

Additional Information:
- ☞ The Weekly Journal, Voice Communications; London, December 22, 1994, p.18.
- ☞ Too Close to Heaven, The Illustrated History of Gospel Music, Viv Broughton, British Broadcasting Corporation; 1995.
- ☞ The Voice, The Voice Group Ltd.; December 4, 2000, p.42.

78.

A) YOUSSOU N'DOUR
- ☞ Icons of Black Music: A History in Photographs 1900-2000, Charlotte Greig, Brown Partworks Ltd.; UK, 1999, pp.116-17.

Additional Information:
- ☞ Independent on Sunday, London, 8 December 1996, Real Life Section p.2.
- ☞ The Rough Guide to World Music, Volume 1, 2nd Edition, Simon Broughton (ed.), Rough Guides Publishing; 2000.
- ☞ Sterns Guide to Contemporary African Music, Ronnie Graham, Pluto Press; UK, 1989.

79.

A) GRANDMASTER FLASH
- ☞ Icons of Black Music: A History in Photographs 1900-2000, Charlotte Greig, Brown Partworks Ltd.; UK, 1999, pp.58-59.

Additional Information:
- ☞ Signifying Rappers: Rap and Race in the Urban Present, Mark Costello and David Foster Wallace, Ecco Press; New York, 1990.
- ☞ Vibe History of Hip Hop, Alan Light, (ed.), Vibe Magazine, Three Rivers Press; USA, 1998.
- ☞ Hit Singles: Top 20 Charts from 1954 to the Present Day, Dave McAleer, Carlton; 2001.

80.

B) JOSETTE SIMON
- ☞ Halliwell's Film Guide 2002. Leslie Halliwell, HarperCollins; London, 2001.

Additional Information:
- ☞ The Voice, The Voice Group Ltd.; 5 January 1993, p.14.
- ☞ The Weekly Journal, Voice Communications; London, 25 August 1994, p.9.

Blake Seven, British Broadcasting Corporation, Library Archives, White City, London, W12.

81.
A) TLC
☞ Ebony, Johnson Publishing; Chicago, August, 2002, pp.132-137.
Additional Information:
☞ Hip-Hop Divas, Vibe Magazine, (ed.), Three Rivers Press; USA, 2001.
☞ The New Nation, Ethnic Media Group; London, 7 June 1999, pp.24-25.
☞ Black Noise: Rap Music and Black Culture in Contemporary America, Tricia Rose. Westeyan University Press; 1994, pp.170, 173.

82.
C) EDDIE MURPHY
☞ On the Real Side, Mel Watkins, Lawrence Hill Books; USA, 1999, pp. 563-65.
Additional Information:
☞ Untold, Peter Akinti Publ.; London, August/September, 1998, p.30.
☞ Today's Black Hollywood, James Robert Parish, Pinnacle Books, Windsor Publishing Corp.; USA, 1995.
☞ Ebony, Johnson Publishing; Chicago, January, 1997.

83
B) SAM COOK
☞ Ebony, Johnson Publishing; Chicago, June, 2003, p.89.
Additional Information:
☞ Icons of Black Music: A History in Photographs 1900-2000, Charlotte Greig, Brown Partworks Ltd.; UK, 1999, p.34.
☞ Stars of Soul and Rhythm & Blues: Top Recording Artists and Showstopping Performers, from Memphis and Motown to Now. Lee Hildebrand, Billboard Books; New York, 1994.
☞ The Enclopaedia of Pop, Rock and Soul, Revised Edition, Irwin Stambler, St Martin's Press; New York, 1989.

84.
B) TENOR SAX
☞ The Illustrated Autobiography of Jazz, Brian Case, Stan Britt and Chrissie Murray, Revised Edition, Salamander Books; London, 1987.

Additional Information:
☞ The Encyclopedia of Jazz in the Sixties, New York, Horizon Press; 1966.
☞ Jazz in its Time, Martin Williams, Oxford University Press; New York, Oxford, 1989.
☞ The Story of Jazz: From New Orleans to Rock Jazz, Joachim-Ernst Berendt, (ed.), Barrie & Jenkins; London, 1978.

85
A) RESPECT
☞ Aretha Franklin, Lady Soul, (An Impact Biography), Leslie Gourse, Franklin Watts Incorporated; USA, 1995.
Additional Information:
☞ Ebony Pictorial History of Black America: Volume 3. Civil Rights Movement to Black Revolution, Johnson Publishing Company; 1974.
☞ Icons of Black Music: A History in Photographs 1900-2000, Charlotte Greig, Brown Partworks Ltd.; UK, 1999, pp.50-51.
☞ Hit Singles: Top 20 Charts from 1954 to the Present Day, Dave McAleer, Carlton; 2001.

86.
A) BRANDY
☞ Vibe, Quincy Jones and David Salzman Entertainment, Time Publishing Inc.; May, 1986.
Additional Information:
☞ The New Nation, Ethnic Media Group; London, May 24, 1999, pp.28-29.
☞ Ebony, Johnson Publishing; Chicago, December, 2000, p.128.
☞ The Voice, The Voice Group Ltd.; London, February 26, 2001, p.46.

87.
C) MELVIN VAN PEEBLES
☞ That's Blaxploitation: Roots of the Baadasssss 'Tude (Rated X by an All'Whyte Jury), Darius James, St.Martin's Press; 1995.
Additional Information:
☞ To Find an Image: Black Films from Uncle Tom to Superfly. Bobbs-Merrill, New York, 1974.
☞ Ebony, Johnson Publishing; Chicago, August, 1995, p.40.
☞ Famous Black Entertainers of Today, Raoul Abdul, NY, 1974.

88.

B) SOUL II SOUL

☞ The Recording Academy, 5402 Pico Blvd, Santa Monica, California, USA, 90405.

Additional Information:

☞ Black Noise: Rap Music and Black Culture in Contemporary America, Tricia Rose. Westeyan University Press; 1994.

☞ The Warner Guide to UK & US Hit Singles, Compiled by Dave McAleer, A Carlton/Little, Brown Book; UK, 1994.

☞ Who's Who of Black Achievers, John Hughes, (ed.), Ethnic Media Group; UK, 1999, p.32.

89.

B) SPIKE LEE

☞ Spike Lee: On His Own Terms, Melissa McDaniel, Franklin Watts Incorporated; USA, 1998.

Additional Information:

☞ Ebony, Johnson Publishing; Chicago, May, 1994, pp.28-32.

☞ The New York Times Guide to the Best 1000 Movies Ever Made by Vincent Canby, Times Books; 1999

☞ Ebony, Johnson Publishing; Chicago, June, 1995, p.110.

90.

A) STAX

☞ The Music of Black Americans. A History, 2nd Edition, Eileen Southern, W. W. Norton & Co.; 1983.

Additional Information:

☞ The Enclopaedia of Pop, Rock and Soul, Revised Edition, Irwin Stambler, St Martin's Press; New York, 1989.

☞ Sweet Soul Music: Rhythm and Blues and the Southern Dream of Freedom, Paul Garolnick, Virgin Books; 1986.

☞ Ebony, Johnson Publishing; Chicago, June, 1995, p.112.

91.

B) BIG JOE TURNER

☞ Blues People: Negro Music in White America. Leroi Jones (Amiri Baraka), William Morrow; New York, 1963.

Additional Information:

☞ 1999 Facts About Blacks: A Sourcebook of African American Accomplishment. Raymond M. Corbin, Beckham House

Publishers; USA, 1st Edition, 1986.

☞ Nothing But the Blues: The Music and its Musicians, Lawrence Cohn (ed.), Abbeville Press; New York, 1993.

☞ Urban Blues, Charles Keil, University of Chicago Press; Chicago, 1966.

92.

B) FILL ME IN

☞ GB Craig David, Hannah Mander, Michael O'Mara Books Ltd.; 2001.

Additional Information:

☞ Hit Singles: Top 20 Charts from 1954 to the Present Day, Dave McAleer, Carlton; 2001, p.380.

☞ Ebony, Johnson Publishing; Chicago, July, 2001, p.16.

☞ Wildstar Records Ltd.; 107 Mortlake High Street, London, SW14, 8HQ

93.

B) STREETS OF SAN FRANCISCO

☞ The Black Composer Speaks, Edited by David N. Baker, Et Al, The Scarecrow Press, Inc.; Metachen, New Jersey and London, 1978, p.233.

Additional Information:

☞ 1999 Facts About Blacks: A Sourcebook of African American Accomplishment. Raymond M. Corbin, Beckham House Publishers; USA, 1st Edition, 1986.

☞ Television Theme Recordings: An Illustrated Discography, 1951-1991, Steve Gelfand, Popular Culture Ink; Ann Arbour, MI., 1993.

☞ A Comprehensive Bibliography of Music for Film and Television, Steven D. Westcott, Information Co-ordinators, Detroit, MI., 1985.

94.

A) GEORGIA ON MY MIND

☞ The Recording Academy, 5402 Pico Blvd, Santa Monica, California, USA, 90405.

Additional Information:

☞ Brother Ray: Ray Charles' Own Story. Ray Charles and David Ritz, Dial Press; New York, 1978.

☞ Ebony, Johnson Publishing; Chicago, June, 2003, p.94.

☞ Icons of Black Music: A History in Photographs 1900-2000, Charlotte Greig, Brown Partworks Ltd.; UK, 1999, pp.22-23.

95.
A) OLIVER SAMUELS
☞ The Voice, The Voice Group Ltd.;
   London, May 16, 1995, pp.30-31
Additional Information:
☞ The Weekly Journal, Voice
   Communications; London, April 21,
   1994, p.11.
☞ Toronto Sun, March 24, 1995.
☞ The Jamaica Daily Gleaner, August 31,
   2000.

96.
C) RHYTHM NATION
☞ Out of the Madness: The Strictly
   Unauthorised Biography of Janet
   Jackson, Bart Andrews, Edited by J.
   Randy Taraborrelli, Headline; UK,
   1994.
Additional Information:
☞ Ebony, Johnson Publishing; Chicago,
   November, 2000, pp.180-84.
☞ Hit Singles: Top 20 Charts from 1954 to
   the Present Day, Dave McAleer,
   Carlton; 2001.
☞ Ebony, Johnson Publishing; Chicago,
   January, 1995, pp.94-98.

97.
B) MARVIN GAYE
☞ Marvin Gaye: What's Goin On and the
   Last Days of the Motown Town Sound,
   Ben Edmunds, Canangate Books; 2001.
Additional Information:
☞ Motown: Hot Wax, City Cool and Solid
   Gold, J. Randy Taraborelli, Doubleday;
   Garden City, New York, 1986.
☞ Ebony, Johnson Publishing; Chicago,
   June Edition 1994, p.92.
☞ Icons of Black Music: A History in
   Photographs 1900-2000, Charlotte
   Greig, Brown Partworks Ltd.; UK, 1999,
   pp.52-53.

98.
A) WESLEY SNIPES
☞ Ebony, Johnson Publishing; Chicago,
   May, 1994, pp.28-32.
Additional Information:
☞ The New York Times Guide to the Best
   1000 Movies Ever Made by Vincent
   Canby, Times Books; 1999
☞ The Essential Black Literature Guide,
   Published in association with the
   Schomburg Center for Research in
   Black Culture, Roger M. Valade II,
   Visible Ink Press; USA, 1996, p.223.
☞ Black Hollywood: From 1970 to Today,
   Gary Null, Citadel Press Books; 1993.

99.
C) MAD MAX 3
☞ The Tina Turner Experience: The
   Illustrated Biography, Chris Welch,
   Virgin Books; London, 1988.
Additional Information:
☞ Ebony, Johnson Publishing; Chicago,
   December, 2000, p.156.
☞ Icons of Black Music: A History in
   Photographs 1900-2000, Charlotte
   Greig, Brown Partworks Ltd.; UK, 1999,
   pp.160-61.
☞ Tina: The Tina Turner Story, Ron Wynn,
   Sidgwick & Jackson; London, 1985.

100.
B) STEVIE WONDER
☞ The Recording Academy, 5402 Pico
   Blvd, Santa Monica, California, USA,
   90405.
Additional Information:
☞ Stevie Wonder: Written Musiquarium;
   41 Hits Spanning His Career, Hal
   Leonard and Stevie Wonder, Hal
   Leonard Publishing Corporation; USA,
   1999.
☞ The Motown Album: An American
   Story, Elvis Mitchell, Virgin Books;
   London, 1990.
☞ 1997 Guinness Book of Records, Guinness
   Publishing Ltd.; UK, 1996, p.174.

101.
C) BABYFACE
☞ Time, Time Inc.; USA, April 28, 1997,
   pp.52-53.
Additional Information:
☞ Vibe, Quincy Jones and David Salzman
   Entertainment, Time Publishing Inc.;
   January, 1998, p.162.
☞ The New Nation, Western Hemisphere;
   London, February 3, 1997, pp.28-29.
☞ Ebony, Johnson Publishing; Chicago,
   USA, April 1996, pp.26-31.

102.
C) BIRD
☞ Today's Black Hollywood, James Robert
   Parish, Pinnacle Books, Windsor
   Publishing Corp.; USA, 1995, p.18.

Entertainment

Additional Information:
- ☞ The Voice, The Voice Group Ltd.; London, 14 April, 2003, p.23.
- ☞ Halliwell's Film Guide. Leslie Halliwell, 11th Edition, HarperCollins; 1995.
- ☞ Variety Movie Guide 96, Edited by Derek Ellery, Hamlyn Books; UK, 1995.

103.

A) SKA
- ☞ Roots Rock Reggae: An Oral History of Reggae Music from Ska to Dancehall, Chuck Foster, Billboard Books; 1999.

Additional Information:
- ☞ The Voice, The Voice Group Ltd.; London, 8 November 1994, p.3.
- ☞ Reggae Bloodlines: In Search of the Music and Culture of Jamaica, S. Davis and Peter Simon, HEB; 1984.
- ☞ Latin American Music Review, Volume 8, No. 1, "The Popular Music Culture of Kingston, Jamaica, Before Ska, Rocksteady and Reggae". Garth White, 1982, pp.1-25.

104.

A) LETHAL WEAPON
- ☞ Ebony, Johnson Publishing; Chicago, July, 1995, p.72.

Additional Information:
- ☞ Today's Black Hollywood, James Robert Parish, Pinnacle Books, Windsor Publishing Corp.; USA, 1995, p.15.
- ☞ The Weekly Journal, Voice Communications; London, 4 August 1994, p.9.
- ☞ Ebony, Johnson Publishing; Chicago, January, 1997, pp.32-34.

105.

C) THE ENTERTAINER
- ☞ King of Ragtime: Scott Joplin and His Era, Edward A. Berlin, Oxford University Press; New York, 1994.

Additional Information:
- ☞ Scott Joplin: The Man Who Made Ragtime, James Hawkins With Kathleen Benson, Robson Books; 1979.
- ☞ Ragtime: Its History, Composers and Music, John Edward Hasse, (ed.), Schirmer, New York, 1985.
- ☞ They Were Ragtime, Warren Forma, Grosset and Dunlap Books; New York, 1976.

106.

A) NIA LONG
- ☞ Ebony, Johnson Publishing; Chicago, July, 2000, p.140.

Additional Information:
- ☞ Ebony, Johnson Publishing; Chicago, December, 2000, p.146.
- ☞ Halliwell's Film Guide 2002. Leslie Halliwell, HarperCollins; UK, 2001.
- ☞ The New York Times Guide to the Best 1000 Movies Ever Made by Vincent Canby, Times Books; 1999

107.

B) CHUCK BERRY
- ☞ Chuck Berry: The Autobiography, Chuck Berry, Harmony Books; New York, 1987.

Additional Information:
- ☞ Chuck Berry: Mr. Rock N Roll, Krista Reese, Proteus Books; UK, 1982.
- ☞ Who's Who in Rock, Revised Edition Compiled and Edited by William York, Arthur Barker Ltd.; 1982, p.27.
- ☞ Ebony, Johnson Publishing; Chicago, January, 1997, pp.52-56.

108.

B) THE HARDER THEY COME
- ☞ The Harder They Come, Michael Thelwell, The X Press; 1996.

Additional Information:
- ☞ Icons of Black Music: A History in Photographs 1900-2000, Charlotte Greig, Brown Partworks Ltd.; UK, 1999, pp.24-25.
- ☞ Ex-iles. Essays on Caribbean Cinema, Edited by Mbye Cham, Africa World Press; NJ, 1992.
- ☞ Halliwell's Film Guide. Leslie Halliwell, 11th Edition, HarperCollins; 1995, p.502.

109.

A) BAD
- ☞ Michael Jackson: Body And Soul. An Illustrated Biography, by Geoff Brown, Virgin Books; London, 1988.

Additional Information:
- ☞ The Billboard Book of Number One Hits, Fred Bronson, Billboard Publications; New York, 1992.
- ☞ Upscale, Upscale Communications Inc.; August 1995.
- ☞ New Musical Express Who's Who in

Rock & Roll, Edited by John Tobler,
Hamlyn; 1991, pp.151-52.

110.
C) BARRY WHITE
☞ Stars of Soul and Rhythm & Blues: Top
Recording Artists and Showstopping
Performers, from Memphis and Motown
to Now. Lee Hildebrand, Billboard
Books; New York, 1994.
Additional Information:
☞ Ebony, Johnson Publishing; Chicago,
May, 1995, pp.52-58.
☞ The Enclopaedia of Pop, Rock and Soul,
Revised Edition, Irwin Stambler, St
Martin's Press; New York, 1989.
☞ Soul Music, A-Z. Hugh Gregory,
Blandford; London, 1991.

111.
C) THE DRIFTERS
☞ New Musical Express Who's Who in
Rock & Roll, Edited by John Tobler,
Hamlyn; 1991, p.199.
Additional Information:
☞ The Warner Guide to UK & US Hit
Singles, Compiled by Dave McAleer, A
Carlton/Little, Brown Book; UK, 1994.
☞ The Music of Black Americans. A
History, 2nd Edition, Eileen Southern,
W. W. Norton & Co.; 1983.
☞ Stars of Soul and Rhythm & Blues: Top
Recording Artists and Showstopping
Performers, from Memphis and Motown
to Now. Lee Hildebrand, Billboard
Books; New York, 1994.

112.
A) BEENIE MAN
☞ The Recording Academy, 5402 Pico Blvd,
Santa Monica, California, USA, 90405.
Additional Information:
☞ The Voice, The Voice Group Ltd.;
London, March 6, 2001, p.48.
☞ Hit Singles: Top 20 Charts from 1954 to
the Present Day, Dave McAleer,
Carlton; 2001.
☞ The Voice, The Voice Group Ltd.;
London, September 3, 2001, p.13.

113.
B) THE TEMPTATIONS
☞ The Temptations, (African American
Achievers), Ted Cox, Chelsea House
Publishing; 1997.

Additional Information:
☞ Ebony, Johnson Publishing; Chicago,
June, 2003, p.97.
☞ The Ultimate Soul Music Trivia Book:
501 Questions and Answers About
Motown, Rhythm & Blues, and More,
Bobby Bennett and Sarah A. Smith,
Citadel Press; 1997.
☞ Stars of Soul and Rhythm & Blues: Top
Recording Artists and Showstopping
Performers, from Memphis and Motown
to Now. Lee Hildebrand, Billboard
Books; New York, 1994.

114.
C) SECRETS AND LIES
☞ The Voice, The Voice Group Ltd.; May
5, 1997, pp.4-5.
Additional Information:
☞ The New Nation, Western Hemisphere;
London, May 12, 1997, p.3.
☞ The Hollywood Reporter, Weekly
International Edition, November 5,
1996, PS-1.
☞ Halliwell's Film Guide 2002. Leslie
Halliwell, HarperCollins; London, 2001.

115.
B) PARLIAMENT-FUNKADELIC
☞ Funk: The Music, The People and the
Rhythm of the One. Rickey Vincent, St.
Martin's Griffith, New York, 1996.
Additional Information:
☞ Icons of Black Music: A History in
Photographs 1900-2000, Charlotte
Greig, Brown Partworks Ltd.; UK, 1999,
pp.26-27, 151.
☞ Rap Attack 2: African Rap to New York
Hip Hop, David Toop, Serpents Tail;
1991, pp.42, 44, 137, 146, 191, 196.
☞ The Voice, The Voice Group Ltd.;
London, June 4, 1996, pp.17-18.

116.
A) GANGSTA'S PARADISE
☞ Fight the Power: Rap, Race and Reality.
Chuck D. with Yusuf Jah, Delacorte,
USA, 1997.
Additional Information:
☞ The Voice, The Voice Group Ltd.;
London, March 12, 1996, p.22.
☞ Between God and Gangsta Rap:
Bearing Witness to Black Culture,
Michael Eric Dyson, Oxford University
Press; New York and Oxford, 1996.

Entertainment

☞ Vibe History of Hip Hop, Alan Light, (ed.), Vibe Magazine, Three Rivers Press; USA, 1998.

117.
C) THE COSBY SHOW
☞ On the Real Side: A History of African American Comedy. Mel Watkins, Lawrence Hill; USA, 1999, pp.503, 508, 565.
Additional Information:
☞ Classic Sitcom: A Celebration of the Best in Primetime Comedy. Macmillan; New York, 1987.
☞ Ebony, Johnson Publishing; Chicago, May, 1992, pp.126-131.
☞ NBC Studios, Public Relations Department, 330 Bob Hope Drive, Burbank, CA

118.
C) HOLLYWOOD SHUFFLE
☞ Today's Black Hollywood, James Robert Parish, Pinnacle Books, Windsor Publishing Corp.; USA, 1995, p.15.
Additional Information:
☞ Ebony Man, Johnson Publishing; March, 1993, p.62.
☞ Halliwell's Film Guide. Leslie Halliwell, 11th Edition, HarperCollins; 1995, p.558.
☞ The New Nation, Western Hemisphere; London, April 28, 1997, p.51.

119.
A) KILLING ME SOFTLY
☞ Hit Singles: Top 20 Charts from 1954 to the Present Day, Dave McAleer, Carlton; 2001.
Additional Information:
☞ The Weekly Journal, Positive Time and Space Co.; London, 20th November 1996, p.19.
☞ Pride, London, September 1998, pp.18-22.
☞ New Musical Express Who's Who in Rock & Roll, Edited by John Tobler, Hamlyn; 1991, p.120.

120.
A) ICE CUBE
☞ Ebony, Johnson Publishing; Chicago, November, 2002, p.92.
Additional Information:
☞ Upscale, Upscale Communications Inc.; November 1995, p.30.

☞ Poetic Justice: Filmmaking South Central Style, John Singleton, Veronica Chambers, and Spike Lee, Dell Books; 1993.
☞ Time, Time Inc.; USA, March 23, 1992.

121.
A) GERMANY
☞ IFPI (Representing the Recording Industry Worldwide/World Music Awards), IFPI Secretariat, 54 Regents Street, London W1R, 5PJ.
Additional Information:
☞ Hit Singles: Top 20 Charts from 1954 to the Present Day, Dave McAleer, Carlton; 2001.
☞ National Academy of Recording Arts and Sciences, 6255 Sunset Blvd, Suite 1023, Hollywood, 90028.
☞ The Guardian, Guardian Newspapers; London, September 10, 2001.

122.
A) QUEEN LATIFAH
☞ Ebony, Johnson Publishing; Chicago, April, 2003, pp.152-156.
Additional Information:
☞ Ebony, Johnson Publishing; Chicago, June, 2003, p.134.
☞ The New York Times Guide to the Best 1000 Movies Ever Made by Vincent Canby, Times Books; 1999
☞ Halliwell's Film Guide 2002. Leslie Halliwell, HarperCollins; London, 2001.

123.
A) NAT KING COLE
☞ Icons of Black Music: A History in Photographs 1900-2000, Charlotte Greig, Brown Partworks Ltd.; UK, 1999, pp.28-29.
Additional Information:
☞ Ebony Pictorial History of Black America: Volume 3. Civil Rights Movement to Black Revolution, Johnson Publishing Company; 1974, pp.288, 291.
☞ On the Real Side: A History of African American Comedy. Mel Watkins, Lawrence Hill; USA, 1999, pp.301-2.
☞ The Black American Reference Book. Mabel M. Smyth, (ed.), Prentice-Hall Inc.; USA, 1976.

124.
B) BUMP AND GRIND
☞ Ebony, Johnson Publishing; Chicago, July, 1996, p.130.
Additional Information:
☞ The Voice, The Voice Group Ltd.; London, September 24, 2001, p.46.
☞ Ebony, Johnson Publishing; Chicago, July, 1996, pp.127-34.
☞ Hit Singles: Top 20 Charts from 1954 to the Present Day, Dave McAleer, Carlton; 2001.

125.
C) BLACKSTREET
☞ The Hollywood Reporter, Weekly International Edition, November 5, 1996, p.50.
Additional Information:
☞ The Voice, The Voice Group Ltd.; London, December 16, 1996, p.24.
☞ Ebony Man, Johnson Publishing; July, 1992, pp.34-37.
☞ Drummer's Guide to Hip Hop, House, New Jack Swing, Hip House and Soca House, Bill Elder, Warner Brothers Publications; USA, 1999.

126.
A) BUJU BANTON
☞ Words Like Fire: Dancehall Reggae and Ragga Muffin, Stascha Bader, Central Books; London, 1993.
Additional Information:
☞ Roots Rock Reggae: An Oral History of Reggae Music from Ska to Dancehall, Chuck Foster, Billboard Books; 1999.
☞ The Weekly Journal, Voice Communications; London, February 17, 1994, p.12.
☞ Caribbean Times, Hansib Publishing; London, May 9, 1996 p.11.

127.
B) B.E.T.
☞ Ebony, Johnson Publishing; Chicago, May, 2003, pp.36-37.
Additional Information:
☞ Today's Black Hollywood, James Robert Parish, Pinnacle Books, Windsor Publishing Corp.; USA, 1995, p.17.
☞ The Black Press in Britain, Ionie Benjamin, Trentham Books; London, 1995, 107.
☞ Jet, Johnson Publishing Co.; Chicago, October 16, 1989, p.40.

128.
B) LUCIANO
☞ The Voice, The Voice Group Ltd.; London, June 16, 1997, p.1.
Additional Information:
☞ The Rough Guide to Reggae, 2nd Edition, Peter Dalton and Orla Duane (eds.), Rough Guide Books; 2001.
☞ The Weekly Journal, Positive Time and Space Co.; London, November 20, 1996, p.13.
☞ The New Nation, Ethnic Media Group; London, 7 July, 2003, p.33.

129.
A) ELLA FITZGERALD
☞ Ella Fitzgerald. Stuart Nicholson, Victor Gollancz Publishing; London, 1993.
Additional Information:
☞ The Life and Times of Ella Fitzgerald, Sid Colin, Elm Tree Books; London, 1986.
☞ On the Real Side: A History of African American Comedy. Mel Watkins, Lawrence Hill; USA, 1999, pp.300, 386.
☞ Jazz Women: 1900 to the Present. Their Words, Lives and Music, Sally Placksin, Pluto Press; London and Sydney, 1982.

130.
C) DEEP SPACE NINE
☞ Deep Space Nine Companion (Star Trek), Terry J. Erdmann and Paula M. Block, Pocket Books; USA, 2001.
Additional Information:
☞ The New Nation, Western Hemisphere; London, February 17, 1997, p.23.
☞ Star Trek: Deep Space Nine, K. W. Jeter, Pocket Books; UK.
☞ Star Trek Deep Space Nine Technical Manual, Hermann Zimmerman, Rick Sternbach, Doug Drexler, and Ira Steven Behr, Pocket Books; USA, 1998.

131.
A) SLY AND ROBBIE
☞ The Guinness Who's Who of Reggae, Colin Larkin, Guinness Publishing; 1994.
Additional Information:
☞ This is Reggae Music, The Story of Jamaica's Music, Lloyd Bradley, Grove Press; 2001.

Entertainment

☞ The Voice, The Voice Group Limited; May 26, 1997, p.50.

☞ Roots Rock Reggae: An Oral History of Reggae Music from Ska to Dancehall, Chuck Foster, Billboard Books; 1999.

132.
A) DOROTHY DANDRIDGE
☞ Black Hollywood: The Negro in Motion Pictures, Gary Null, Lyle Stuart Press; USA, 1975.
Additional Information:
☞ The Voice, The Voice Group Ltd.; London, June 25, 1996, p.27.
☞ Ebony Pictorial History of Black America: Volume 3. Civil Rights Movement to Black Revolution, Johnson Publishing Company; 1974, pp.290-91.
☞ Ebony, Johnson Publishing; Chicago, August, 1995, p.115.

133.
A) JANET KAY
☞ The Warner Guide to UK & US Hit Singles, Compiled by Dave McAleer, A Carlton/Little, Brown Book; UK, 1994.
Additional Information:
☞ Pride, London, May 1997, pp.50-51.
☞ The Voice, The Voice Group Ltd.; London, September 10, 2001, p.3.
☞ There Ain't No Black in the Union Jack, Paul Gilroy, Hutchingson; UK, 1987.

134.
C) STARSKY AND HUTCH
☞ Black Hollywood: The Black Performer in Motion Pictures, Citadel Press Books, Carol Publishing; USA, 1990.
Additional Information:
☞ The Voice, The Voice Group Ltd.; London, July 2, 1996, p.29.
☞ Today's Black Hollywood, James Robert Parish, Pinnacle Books, Windsor Publishing Corp.; USA, 1995.
☞ The Voice, The Voice Group Ltd.; London, August 23, 1994, (Now Section p.2).

135.
A) OMAR EPPS
☞ Halliwell's Film Guide 2002. Leslie Halliwell, HarperCollins; London, 2001.
Additional Information:
☞ The Voice, The Voice Group Ltd.; London, December 4, 2000, p.40.

☞ The New York Times Guide to the Best 1000 Movies Ever Made by Vincent Canby, Times Books; 1999

☞ The Guardian, Guardian Newspapers; London, October 13, 2000.

136.
C) BEVERLEY HILLS COP III
☞ On the Real Side: A History of African American Comedy. Mel Watkins, Lawrence Hill; USA, 1999, pp.19-20, 563-65.
Additional Information:
☞ Halliwell's Film Guide. Leslie Halliwell, 11th Edition, HarperCollins; 1995.
☞ Today's Black Hollywood, James Robert Parish, Pinnacle Books, Windsor Publishing Corp.; USA, 1995, p.18.
☞ Roger Ebert's Movie Yearbook 2000 (Roger Eberts Movie Yearbook, 2000) by Roger Ebert, Andrews McMeel Publishing; 1999

137.
A) JOHN HOLT
☞ The Guinness Who's Who of Reggae, Colin Larkin, Guinness Publishing; 1994.
Additional Information:
☞ The Voice, The Voice Group Ltd.; London, July 25 1995, p.24.
☞ The Warner Guide to UK & US Hit Singles, Compiled by Dave McAleer, A Carlton/Little, Brown Book; UK, 1994.
☞ Reggae Bloodlines: In Search of the Music and Culture of Jamaica, S. Davis and Peter Simon, HEB; 1984.

138.
B) TAP
☞ Jazz Dance: The Story of American Venecular Dance, Marshall and Jean Stearns, Macmillan; New York, 1968.
Additional Information:
☞ Black Dance, Edward Thorpe, Chatto & Windus; London, 1989, p.99.
☞ A Pictorial History of Black America, Langston Hughes, Crown; NY, 1983.
☞ The Black American Reference Book. Mabel M. Smyth, (ed.), Prentice-Hall Inc.; USA, 1976.

139.
A) GHOSTS
☞ Today's Black Hollywood, James Robert Parish, Pinnacle Books, Windsor Publishing Corp.; USA, 1995, p.16.

Additional Information:
- Ebony, Johnson Publishing; Chicago, January Edition, 1997, pp.32-34.
- 1930-1990 Hollywood: Sixty Great Years. Prion, 1992, p.563.
- Woman in Comedy, Linda Martin and Kerry Segrave, Citadel Press; Secaucus, New Jersey, 1986.

140.
C) IN LIVING COLOR
- On the Real Side: A History of African American Comedy. Mel Watkins, Lawrence Hill; USA, 1999, p.566.

Additional Information:
- The Sunday ExPress; London, September 9, 2001, p.69.
- Today's Black Hollywood, James Robert Parish, Pinnacle Books, Windsor Publishing Corp.; USA, 1995, p.18.
- Savoy Magazine, Pro Circuit; USA, Aug 2001, (cover).

141.
C) COLORS
- Halliwell's Film Guide. Leslie Halliwell, 11th Edition, HarperCollins; 1995, p.237.

Additional Information:
- The New Nation, Western Hemisphere; London, July 7, 1997, p.46.
- The Guardian, Guardian Newspapers; London, November 24, 1999.
- East Side Stories: Gang Life in East L.A., Joseph Rodriguez, et al, Power House Cultural Entertainment; 1998.

142.
A) TONI BRAXTON
- Ebony, Johnson Publishing; Chicago, December, 2000, pp.164-70.

Additional Information:
- The Voice, The Voice Group Ltd.; London, July 9, 1996, p.23.
- Ebony, Johnson Publishing; Chicago, May, 1994, pp.134-138B.
- The Voice, The Voice Group Ltd.; December 4, 2000, p.3.

143.
C) INDEPENDENCE DAY
- Ebony, Johnson Publishing; Chicago, January, 1997, pp.32-34.

Additional Information:
- The Hollywood Reporter, Weekly International Edition, November 5. 1996, PI-7.
- Vibe, Quincy Jones and David Salzman Entertainment, Time Publishing Inc.; May, 1996, (cover).
- Today's Black Hollywood, James Robert Parish, Pinnacle Books, Windsor Publishing Corp.; USA, 1995.

144.
A) MOTOWN
- The Motown Story, Don Waller, Scribner; New York, 1985.

Additional Information:
- The Guardian, Guardian Newspapers; London, March 22, 1996, p.9.
- The Billboard Book of Number One Hits, Fred Bronson, Billboard Publications; New York, 1992.
- Motown: The History, Sharon Davis, Guinness Publications; Enfield, 1988.

145.
C) BOGLE
- Dancehall, Dancehall Newspapers Ltd.; London, November, 1996, p.7.

Additional Information:
- Reggae Island: Jamaican Music in the Digital Age, Tom Weber, Kingston Publications; Kingston, JA., 1992.
- Roots Rock Reggae: An Oral History of Reggae Music from Ska to Dancehall, Chuck Foster, Billboard Books; 1999.
- The Weekly Gleaner (U.K.), Library Archives Department, Elephant & Castle, London, SE1 6TE.

146.
A) WYNTON MARSALIS
- The Recording Academy, 5402 Pico Blvd, Santa Monica, California, USA, 90405.

Additional Information:
- Vibe, Quincy Jones and David Salzman Entertainment, Time Publishing Inc.; January, 1998, pp.54-57.
- Black Firsts: 2000 Years of Extraordinary Achievement. Jessie Carney Smith, Caspar L. Jordan and Robert L. Johns, Visible Ink Press; USA, 1994, p.28.
- The Essential Black Literature Guide, Published in association with the Schomburg Center for Research in

Entertainment

Black Culture, Roger M. Valade II,
Visible Ink Press; USA, 1996, p.192.

147.
A) STAND BY ME
☞ Too Close to Heaven, The Illustrated
History of Gospel Music, Viv
Broughton, British Broadcasting
Corporation; 1995.
Additional Information:
☞ In Search of Charles Tindley, Bernice
Johnson Reagon, National Museum of
American History, Program in Black
American Culture, Smithsonian
Institution Press; Washington, D.C.,
1981.
☞ Charles Albert Tindley: Prince of
Preachers. Ralph H. Jones, Abingdon
Press; Nashville, TN, 1982.
☞ We'll Understand it Better By and
By: Pioneering African American
Gospel Composers, Bernice Johnson
Reagon, Smithsonian Institution
Press; Washington and London,
1981.

148.
B) MAXWELL
☞ Ebony, Johnson Publishing; Chicago,
December, 2000, p.116.
Additional Information:
☞ Untold, Peter Akinti Publ.; London,
August/September, 1998, pp.76-81.
☞ The New Nation, Western Hemisphere;
London, February 17, 1997, p.27.
☞ The Voice, The Voice Group Ltd.;
London, September 3, 2001, pp.49-50.

149.
C) RUN DMC
☞ Black Noise: Rap Music and Black
Culture in Contemporary America,
Tricia Rose. Westeyan University Press;
1994, pp.3, 51-52.
Additional Information:
☞ Signifying Rappers: Rap and Race in
the Present, Mark Costello and David
Foster Wallace, Ecco Press; New York,
1990.
☞ The Billboard Book of Number One
Hits, Fred Bronson, Billboard
Publications; New York, 1992.
☞ Vibe History of Hip Hop, Alan Light,
(ed.), Vibe Magazine, Three Rivers
Press; USA, 1998.

150.
C) JOSEPH HAYDN
☞ Beethoven The Man, Haven Schauffler,
Volume 1, 1927, pp.27-8,
Additional Information:
☞ Sex and Race, Volume 3, J. A. Rogers,
5th Edition, H. M. Rogers Publishers;
USA, 1972, pp.306-7.
☞ The Boy Who Loved Music, David
Lasker, Viking Press; 1979.
☞ Haydn: His Life and Times, Neil
Butterworth, Paganiniana Books; 1980.

151.
B) THIN LIZZY
☞ The Best of Thin Lizzy, Warner Brothers
Publications; 1999.
Additional Information:
☞ New Musical Express Who's Who in
Rock & Roll, Edited by John Tobler,
Hamlyn; 1991.
☞ The Voice, The Voice Group Ltd.;
November 22, 1994, p.10.
☞ Who's Who in Rock, Revised Edition
Compiled and Edited by William York,
Arthur Barker Ltd.; 1982.

152.
C) JONES GIRLS
☞ Girl Groups: Fabulous Females That
Rocked the World, Krause Publications;
USA, 2000.
Additional Information:
☞ Hit Singles: Top 20 Charts from 1954 to
the Present Day, Dave McAleer,
Carlton; 2001.
☞ Facts on File Encyclopedia of Black
Women in America: Music (Volume 5),
Darlene Clark Hine and Kathleen
Thompson, (eds.), Facts of File, Inc.;
USA, 1997.
☞ Ladies of Soul, David Freeland, University
of Mississippi Press; USA, 2001.

153.
A) BRENDA FASSIE
☞ The Garland Handbook of African
Musicby Ruth M. Stone (Editor), et al,
Garland Publishing; 1999, p. 127.
Additional Information:
☞ The Voice, The Voice Group Ltd.;
London, 25 February, 2002, p.18.
☞ Christgau's Consumer Guide: Albums of
the 90s by Robert Christgau, Griffin,
2000, p.217.

- Africa (Garland Encyclopedia of World Music, Volume 1) by Ruth Stone, Editor), James Porter (Editor), Timothy Rice (Editor)Garland Publishing; 1997, p.431.

154.
B) THE BODYGUARD
- Upscale, Upscale Communications Inc.; November 1995, pp.22-27.
Additional Information:
- Diva: The Strictly Unauthorised Biography of Whitney Houston, Jeffrey Bowman, Headline; UK, 1994.
- Icons of Black Music: A History in Photographs 1900-2000, Charlotte Greig, Brown Partworks Ltd.; UK, 1999, pp.76-77.
- Pride, London, September 1998, pp.24-25.

155.
C) BESSIE SMITH
- Blues People: Negro Music in White America. Leroi Jones (Amiri Baraka), William Morrow; New York, 1963.
Additional Information:
- An Autobiography of Black Jazz, Dempsey J. Travis, Urban Research Institute Inc.; Chicago, 1983, pp.31-32, 70, 239, 324, 385.
- American Visions, Volume 11, No. 1, USA, February/March Edition, 1996, p.12.
- Jazz Women: 1900 to the Present. Their Words, Lives and Music, Sally Placksin, Pluto Press; London and Sydney, 1982.

156.
C) SO SOLID CREW
- The New Nation, Ethnic Media Group; London, 31 March, 2003, pp.28-29.
Additional Information:
- The Cultural Study of Music by Martin Clayton (Editor), et al Routledge, 1st edition, 2003. p.103.
- Fat Boy Slim, by Martin James, Sanctuary Publishing; 2002, p. 80, 90.
- The Big Issue, No. 532, U.K., 24-30 Mar, 2003, pp12-14.

157.
B) CONDUCTORS
- Blacks in Classical Music, Raoul Addul, Dodd, Mead & Co.; NY, 1977, pp.16, 191-93, 198-99.

Additional Information:
- The Times, London, February 26, 1996, p.19.
- Ebony Pictorial History of Black America: Volume 3. Civil Rights Movement to Black Revolution, Johnson Publishing Company; 1974, p.302.
- Class, June 21, 1993, USA, p.21.

158.
B) CHARLES MINGUS
- Jazz in its Time, Martin Williams, Oxford University Press; New York, Oxford, 1989, pp.54, 56, 75, 83, 152-53, 200, 239-40.
Additional Information:
- Vibe, Quincy Jones and David Salzman Entertainment, Time Publishing Inc.; January, 1998, p.172.
- The Picador Book of Blues and Jazz, Edited by James Campbell, Picador; London, 1995, pp.7, 266-79, 381, 384.
- Icons of Black Music: A History in Photographs 1900-2000, Charlotte Greig, Brown Partworks Ltd.; UK, 1999, pp.108-9.

159.
B) JADA PINKETT
- Ebony, Johnson Publishing; Chicago, August, 2003, p.41.
Additional Information:
- The Voice, The Voice Group Ltd.; London, July 23, 2001, pp.47-48.
- Ebony, Johnson Publishing; Chicago, February, 1997, p.57.
- Ebony, Johnson Publishing; Chicago, December, 2000, p.156.

160.
C) THE TIME MACHINE
- Hit Singles: Top 20 Charts from 1954 to the Present Day, Dave McAleer, Carlton; 2001.
Additional Information:
- The Voice, The Voice Group Ltd.; London, September 17, 2001, p.7.
- Cosmo, October, 2001, National Magazine Company; UK, p.10-14.
- The Voice, The Voice Group Ltd.; London, February 2, 2001, p.3.

161.
B) MORGAN FREEMAN
- Ebony, Johnson Publishing; Chicago, January, 1997, pp.32-34.

Additional Information:
☞ The Voice, The Voice Group Ltd.; London, June 28, 1994, pp.21-22.
☞ Today's Black Hollywood, James Robert Parish, Pinnacle Books, Windsor Publishing Corp.; USA, 1995.
☞ New African, September 2001, ICP Ltd.; London, p.38.

162.
A) A DRY WHITE SEASON
☞ Ex-iles, Essays on Caribbean Cinema, Edited by Mbye Cham, Africa World Press; NJ, 1992, p.155.
Additional Information:
☞ Jet, Johnson Publishing Co.; Chicago, November 18, 1991, p.162.
☞ Black Firsts: 2000 Years of Extraordinary Achievement. Jessie Carney Smith, Caspar L. Jordan and Robert L. Johns, Visible Ink Press; USA, 1994.
☞ Halliwell's Film Guide. Leslie Halliwell, 11th Edition, HarperCollins; 1995.

163.
A) THE HARLEM BROADCASTING CORPORATION
☞ This Was Harlem 1900-1950, Jervis Anderson, Farrah, Straus, Giroux; New York, 1982.
Additional Information:
☞ Voices of a Black Nation; Political Journalism in the Harlem Renaissance. Theodore G. Vincent, Africa World Press, Inc.; NJ, 1973.
☞ Black Firsts: 2000 Years of Extraordinary Achievement. Jessie Carney Smith, Caspar L. Jordan and Robert L. Johns, Visible Ink Press; USA, 1994.
☞ The Black American Reference Book. Mabel M. Smyth, (ed.), Prentice-Hall Inc.; USA, 1976.

164.
C) TRADING PLACES
☞ Richard Pryor: A Man and His Madness. A Biography, Beaufort Books; New York, 1984.
Additional Information:
☞ On the Real Side: A History of African American Comedy. Mel Watkins, Lawrence Hill; USA, 1999, pp.529-63.
☞ Today's Black Hollywood, James Robert Parish, Pinnacle Books, Windsor Publishing Corp.; USA, 1995, p.14.

☞ Blacks and White TV, Afro-Americans in Television Since 1948, J. Fred MacDonald, Nelson-Hall Publishing; Chicago, 1990, pp.189-91.

165.
B) MIAMI VICE
☞ Today's Black Hollywood, James Robert Parish, Pinnacle Books, Windsor Publishing Corp.; USA, 1995, p.15.
Additional Information:
☞ The Voice, The Voice Group Ltd.; London, June 18, 2001, p.5.
☞ Blacks and White TV, Afro-Americans in Television Since 1948, J. Fred MacDonald, Nelson-Hall Publishing; Chicago, 1990.
☞ Halliwell's Film Guide. Leslie Halliwell, 11th Edition, HarperCollins; 1995.

166.
C) SAMUEL L. JACKSON
☞ Ebony, Johnson Publishing; Chicago, January, 1997, pp.32-34.
Additional Information:
☞ Palais Des Festivals, Et Des Congress Es Plan Georges, Pompidou La Croisette.
☞ Today Newspaper, London, June 2, 1995, p.40.
☞ Halliwell's Film Guide 2002. Leslie Halliwell, HarperCollins; London, 2001.

167.
C) PULITZER
☞ Pulitzer Prizes, Columbia University, 709 Journalism Building, 2950 Broadway, New York, NY, 10027.
Additional Information:
☞ Wynton Marsalis: Skain's Domain: A Biography, Leslie, Schirmer Books; 2000.
☞ The Independent, Independent Newspapers; London, April 8, 1997, p.2.
☞ The Black Composer Speaks, Edited by David N. Baker, Et Al, The Scarecrow Press, Inc.; Metachen, New Jersey and London, 1978, pp.19, 192, 206, 373, 375-78, 357-77.

168.
A) WILLARD WHITE
☞ The Evening Standard, Associated Newspaper Group; London, April 28, 1997, p.15.

Additional Information:

☞ Black and British, David Bygott, Oxford University Press; 1992.

☞ Pride, London, May/June 1994, pp.73-74.

☞ The Voice, The Voice Group Ltd.; London, January 10, 1995, p.6.

169.

A) 239

☞ There Ain't No Black in the Union Jack, Paul Gilroy, Hutchingson; UK, 1987, p.209.

Additional Information:

☞ The Voice, The Voice Group Ltd.; London, June 4, 2001, p.53.

☞ Reggae Island: Jamaican Music in the Digital Age, Tom Weber, Kingston Publications; Kingston, JA., 1992.

☞ Words Like Fire: Dancehall Reggae and Ragga Muffin, Stascha Bader, Central Books; London, 1993.

170.

B) SMOKEY ROBINSON

☞ Smokey: Inside my Life, Smokey Robinson and David Ritz, Headline; London, 1989.

Additional Information:

☞ To Be loved, Berry Gordy, Headline Book Publishing; New York, London, 1994, pp.90-93, 101-3, 129-30, 268-69, 405-7.

☞ Ebony Pictorial History of Black America: Volume 3. Civil Rights Movement to Black Revolution, Johnson Publishing Company; 1974, pp.231, 300.

☞ Popular Music Magazine, Volume 14, No. 1, "Motown Crossover Hits, 1963-1966", Jon Fitzgerald, 1995, pp.1-11.

171.

C) LORRAINE HANSBERRY

☞ Lorraine Hansberry:Dramatist and Activist, Patricia McKissack, Delacorte Press; 1994.

Additional Information:

☞ Black Theatre: A Twentieth-Century Collection of the Work of Its Best Playwrights. Lindsay Patterson, New American Library; New York, 1971.

☞ Black Musical Theatre; From Coontown to Dream Girls. Allen Woll, Da =Capo Press; New York, 1989, pp.229, 251, 261-62.

☞ Hansberry's Drama: Commitment amid Complexity, Steven R. Carter, University of Illinois Press; 1991.

172.

B) SHAFT

☞ Gordon Parks: Black Photographer and Film Maker. Terry Harnan, Gerrard Publishing; 1971.

Additional Information:

☞ Reflections in Black: A history of Black Photographers, 1840 to the Present, Deborah Willis and Robin D. G. Kelley, W. W. Norton & Co.; New York, 2000.

☞ The Essential Black Literature Guide, Published in association with the Schomburg Center for Research in Black Culture, Roger M. Valade II, Visible Ink Press; USA, 1996, pp.222, 290.

☞ Gordon Parks, Midge Turk, Cromwell; 1971.

173.

A) DES'REE

☞ Upscale, Upscale Communications Inc.; November 1995, p.88.

Additional Information:

☞ The Weekly Journal, Voice Communications; London, August 4, 1994, p.3.

☞ Hit Singles: Top 20 Charts from 1954 to the Present Day, Dave McAleer, Carlton; 2001.

☞ Pride, London, May/June 1994.

174.

C) MAMA I WANNA SING

☞ The Voice, The Voice Group Ltd.; London, January 10, 1995, p.1.

Additional Information:

☞ Black Musical Theatre; From Coontown to Dream Girls. Allen Woll, Da Capo Press; New York, 1989, p.287.

☞ The Voice, The Voice Group Limited; June 27, 1995, pp.17-18.

☞ The Weekly Journal, Voice Communications; London, May 4, 1995, p.2.

175.

A) BEST SUPPORTING ACTOR

☞ Ebony Man, Johnson Publishing; July, 1992, pp.62-66.

Additional Information:
☞ Caribbean Times, Hansib Publishing; London, May 27, 1997, p.8.
☞ The Voice, The Voice Group Limited; May 26, 1997, p.22.
☞ Today's Black Hollywood, James Robert Parish, Pinnacle Books, Windsor Publishing Corp.; USA, 1995.

176.
B) NOTORIOUS B.I.G.
☞ Vibe, Quincy Jones and David Salzman Entertainment, Time Publishing Inc.; January, 1998, pp.106-8, 115.
Additional Information:
☞ Fight the Power: Rap, Race and Reality. Chuck D. with Yusuf Jah, Delacorte, USA, 1997.
☞ Ebony, Johnson Publishing; Chicago, August, 2003, pp.112-116.
☞ Icons of Black Music: A History in Photographs 1900-2000, Charlotte Greig, Brown Partworks Ltd.; UK, 1999, pp.118-19.

177.
A) FELA KUTI
☞ Fela Kuti: This Bitch of a Life. Carlos Moore, Allison & Busby; London, 1982.
Additional Information:
☞ Sterns Guide to Contemporary African Music, Ronnie Graham, Pluto Press; UK, 1989.
☞ African All Stars: The Pop Music of a continent, Chris Stapleton and Chris May, Paladin; London, Glasgow, Toronto, Sydney, Auckland, 1989.
☞ African Music: A People's Art, translated by Josephine Bennet, Lawrence Hill & Co.; Westport, UK, 1995.

178.
A) MUTABARUKA
☞ The Guinness Who's Who of Reggae, Colin Larkin, Guinness Publishing; 1994.
Additional Information:
☞ The Voice, The Voice Group Limited; March 10, 1997, p.29.
☞ The Voice, The Voice Group Limited; May 26, 1997, p.57.
☞ Roots Rock Reggae: An Oral History of Reggae Music from Ska to Dancehall, Chuck Foster, Billboard Books; 1999.

179.
A) CLEOPATRA JONES
☞ Today's Black Hollywood, James Robert Parish, Pinnacle Books, Windsor Publishing Corp.; USA, 1995, p.13.
Additional Information:
☞ To Find an Image: Black Films from Uncle Tom to Superfly. Bobbs-Merrill, New York, 1974.
☞ Blacks and White TV, Afro-Americans in Television Since 1948, J. Fred MacDonald, Nelson-Hall Publishing; Chicago, 1990, p.167.
☞ Black Hollywood: The Black Performer in Motion Pictures, Gary Null, Citadel Press Books, Carol Publishing; USA, 1990.

180.
B) COUNTRY AND WESTERN
☞ Country: The Biggest Music in America, Nick Tosches, Stein & Day; New York, 1977.
Additional Information:
☞ The Illustrated History of Country Music, Patrick Carr, Doubleday/Dolphin; Garden City, New York, 1980.
☞ The Voice, The Voice Group Ltd.; London, May 31, 1994, p.3.
☞ Country Music USA: A Fifty Year History, Revised Edition, Bill C. Malone, University of Texas Press; Austin and London, 1985.

181.
C) ACTING
☞ List: Showing the theaters and plays in various European cities where Ira Aldridge, the African Roscius, acted during the years 1824-1867, A. A. Schomburg, New York Public Libraries, New York, 1932.
Additional Information:
☞ On the Real Side: A History of African American Comedy. Mel Watkins, Lawrence Hill; USA, 1999, pp.105-6.
☞ Famous American Negroes, Langston Hughes, Popular Library Inc.; New York, 1962, pp.23-25.
☞ The Black American Reference Book. Mabel M. Smyth, (ed.), Prentice-Hall Inc.; USA, 1976, p.689.

182.
B) BILLY OCEAN
☞ Black and British, David Bygott, Oxford University Press; 1992, p.5.
Additional Information:
☞ The Warner Guide to UK & US Hit Singles, Compiled by Dave McAleer, A Carlton/Little, Brown Book; UK, 1994.
☞ The Voice, The Voice Group Ltd.; London, October 11, 1999, p.47.
☞ Soul Music, A-Z. Hugh Gregory, Blandford; London, 1991.

183.
C) MEMPHIS GROUP
☞ The Black American Reference Book. Mabel M. Smyth, (ed.), Prentice-Hall Inc.; USA, 1976.
Additional Information:
☞ The Warner Guide to UK & US Hit Singles, Compiled by Dave McAleer, A Carlton/Little, Brown Book; UK, 1994.
☞ Sweet Soul Music: Rhythm and Blues and the Southern Dream of Freedom, Paul Garolnick, Virgin Books; UK, 1986.
☞ The Soul Book, Tony Cummings, Ian Hoare and Simon Frith, (eds.), Methuen; London, 1975.

184.
A) N.W.A.
☞ Between God and Gangsta Rap: Bearing Witness to Black Culture, Michael Eric Dyson, Oxford University Press; New York and Oxford, 1996.
Additional Information:
☞ Newsweek, "The Rap Attitude", Jerry Adler, March 19, 1990, pp.56-59.
☞ Signifying Rappers: Rap and Race in the Present, Mark Costello and David Foster Wallace, Ecco Press; New York, 1990.
☞ The New Beats: Exploring the Music, Culture and Attitudes of Hip Hop. S. H. Fernando, Jr., Doubleday; New York, 1994.

185.
B) FRITZ THE CAT
☞ Today's Black Hollywood, James Robert Parish, Pinnacle Books, Windsor Publishing Corp.; USA, 1995, pp.13-14.
Additional Information:
☞ Complete Crumb: Life & Death of Fritz the Cat, Robert Crumb, Fantagraphic Books;

☞ Complete Crumb: Starring Fritz the Cat, Volume 3, Robert Crumb, Fantagraphic Books; 1988
☞ Encyclopedia of Animated Cartoons, Jeff Lenburg, Facts on File Ltd.; New York, and Oxford, 1991.

186.
B) BLUES BOY
☞ Icons of Black Music: A History in Photographs 1900-2000, Charlotte Greig, Brown Partworks Ltd.; UK, 1999, pp.92-93.
Additional Information:
☞ Nothing But the Blues: The Music and its Musicians, Lawrence Cohn (ed.), Abbeville Press; New York, 1993.
☞ Sweet Soul Music: Rhythm and Blues and the Southern Dream of Freedom, Paul Garolnick, Virgin Books; UK, 1986.
☞ The Black American Reference Book. Mabel M. Smyth, (ed.), Prentice-Hall Inc.; USA, 1976.

187.
B) MARLON
☞ A Pictorial History of Black America. Langston Hughes, Crown; NY, 1983.
Additional Information:
☞ New Musical Express Who's Who in Rock & Roll, Edited by John Tobler, Hamlyn; 1991.
☞ Ebony Pictorial History of Black America: Volume 3. Civil Rights Movement to Black Revolution, Johnson Publishing Company; 1974.
☞ The Billboard Book of Number One Hits, Fred Bronson, Billboard Publications; New York, 1992.

188.
C) BOOGIE WOOGIE
☞ Biographical Dictionary of American Music, Charles E. Claghorn, Parker Publishing Company; West Nayack, New York, 1973.
Additional Information:
☞ Riding on a Blue Note: Jazz and American Pop, Gary Giddins, Oxford University Press; New York and Oxford, 1981.
☞ The Illustrated Autobiography of Jazz, Brian Case, Stan Britt and Chrissie Murray, Revised Edition, Salamander Books; London, 1987.

Entertainment

☞ The Guinness Jazz Companion, Peter Clayton and Peter Gammand, Guinness Publishing; London, 1989.

189.
B) THREE
☞ The Cosby Wit: His Life and Humor. Bill Adler, Critic's Choice Paperbacks, New York, 1986.
Additional Information:
☞ Bill Cosby: In Words and Pictures, Robert E. Johnson, Johnson Publishing; 1987.
☞ Today's Black Hollywood, James Robert Parish, Pinnacle Books, Windsor Publishing Corp.; USA, 1995, p.12.
☞ Blacks and White TV, Afro-Americans in Television Since 1948, J. Fred MacDonald, Nelson-Hall Publishing; Chicago, 1990.

190.
C) LET'S DO IT AGAIN
☞ Today's Black Hollywood, James Robert Parish, Pinnacle Books, Windsor Publishing Corp.; USA, 1995, p.13.
Additional Information:
☞ Blacks and White TV, Afro-Americans in Television Since 1948, J. Fred MacDonald, Nelson-Hall Publishing; Chicago, 1990, p.167.
☞ To Find an Image: Black Films from Uncle Tom to Superfly. Bobbs-Merrill, New York, 1974.
☞ Ebony, Johnson Publishing; Chicago, December, 2000, p.120.

191.
A) HOUND DOG
☞ Icons of Black Music: A History in Photographs 1900-2000, Charlotte Greig, Brown Partworks Ltd.; UK, 1999, pp.158-59.
Additional Information:
☞ Ebony, Johnson Publishing; Chicago, June, 2003, p.191.
☞ The Weekly Journal, Voice Communications; London, July 28, 1994, p.5.
☞ Nile Valley Contributions to Civilization; Exploding the Myths, Volume 1, Anthony T. Browder, Institute of Khamic Guidance; Washington, D.C., 2000, p.160.

192.
B) MARCIA GRIFFITHS
☞ The Weekly Journal, Voice Communications; London, March 30, 1995, p.10.
Additional Information:
☞ Pride, London, September, 1997, pp.116-17.
☞ The Guinness Who's Who of Reggae, Colin Larkin, Guinness Publishing; 1994.
☞ This is Reggae Music, The Story of Jamaica's Music, Lloyd Bradley, Grove Press; 2001.

193.
B) VANESSA WILLIAMS
☞ Ebony, Johnson Publishing; Chicago, December, 2000, p.162.
Additional Information:
☞ The Weekly Journal, Voice Communications; London, April 27, 1995, p.11.
☞ Who's Who Among Black Americans, 1992-1993, USA, p.1537.
☞ Halliwell's Film Guide 2002. Leslie Halliwell, HarperCollins; London, 2001.

194.
B) EIGHT
☞ The 1997 Guinness Book of Records, Guinness Publishing Ltd.; UK, 1996, p.38.
Additional Information:
☞ The Recording Academy, 5402 Pico Blvd, Santa Monica, California, USA, 90405.
☞ Michael Jackson: Body and Soul. An Illustrated Biography, by Geoff Brown, Virgin Books; London, 1988.
☞ Motown: The History, Sharon Davis, Guinness Publications; Enfield, 1988.

195.
A) OMAR
☞ Hit Singles: Top 20 Charts from 1954 to the Present Day, Dave McAleer, Carlton; 2001.
Additional Information:
☞ The New Nation, Ethnic Media Group; London, May 5, 2003, p.30.
☞ The Weekly Journal, Positive Time and Space Co.; London, August 17, 1995, p.1.
☞ The Voice, The Voice Group Ltd.; London, 26 August, 2002, p.24.

196.
A) APOCALYPSE NOW
☞ Today's Black Hollywood, James Robert Parish, Pinnacle Books, Windsor Publishing Corp.; USA, 1995.
Additional Information:
☞ The Evening Standard, Associated Newspaper Group; London, 20 August 1997, p.26.
☞ Halliwell's Film Guide. Leslie Halliwell, 11th Edition, HarperCollins; 1995.
☞ Black Hollywood: From 1970 to Today, Gary Null, Citadel Press Books; 1993.

197.
B) FEELING HOT HOT HOT
☞ Latin American Music Review, Volume 15, No. 1, "Calypso as Rhetorical Performance: Trinidad Carnival 1993", John H. Patton, 1994, pp.55-74.
Additional Information:
☞ Drummer's Guide to Hip Hop, House, New Jack Swing, Hip House and Soca House, Bill Elder, Warner Brothers Publications; USA, 1999.
☞ The Steel Band Movement: The Forging of a National Art in Trinidad and Tobago. Stephen Stuempfle, Pennsylvania University Press; 1995.
☞ Hit Singles: Top 20 Charts from 1954 to the Present Day, Dave McAleer, Carlton; 2001.

198
C) BILL "BOJANGLES" ROBINSON
☞ On the Real Side: A History of African American Comedy. Mel Watkins, Lawrence Hill; USA, 1999, pp.230-34.
Additional Information:
☞ Black Hollywood: The Negro in Motion Pictures, Gary Null, Lyle Stuart Press; USA, 1975.
☞ Encyclopedia of Black America, W. A. Low and Virgil A. Clift, (eds.), Mcgraw-Hill; New York, 1981.
☞ Black Americana. Richard A. Long, Admiral; UK, 1985.

199.
C) SAMUEL COLERIDGE TAYLOR
☞ The Struggle for Black Arts in Britain, Kwesi Awusu, Comedia; 1986, p.110.

Additional Information:
☞ Distinguished Negroes Abroad, B. J. Flemming and M. J. Pryde, The Associated Publishers; Washington, D.C., 1946, pp.130-38.
☞ Black Londoners, 1890-1990, Susan Okokon, Sutton; UK, 1997, pp.9, 23, 65, 102, 109.
☞ Samuel Coleridge-Taylor, W. C. B. Sayers, Cassell; London, 1915.

200.
A) OTIS REDDING
☞ New Musical Express Who's Who in Rock & Roll, Edited by John Tobler, Hamlyn; 1991.
Additional Information:
☞ Icons of Black Music: A History in Photographs 1900-2000, Charlotte Greig, Brown Partworks Ltd.; UK, 1999, pp.132-33.
☞ Sweet Soul Music: Rhythm and Blues and the Southern Dream of Freedom, Paul Garolnick, Virgin Books; UK, 1986.
☞ The Soul Book, Tony Cummings, Ian Hoare and Simon Frith, (eds.), Methuen; London, 1975.

201.
A) THE MIGHTY SPARROW
☞ Sparrow: The Legend, Calypso King of the World, Inprint Publications;
Additional Information:
☞ The Trinidad Calypso, Keith Warner, Heinemann Educational Books; Kingston, Port of Spain, 1982.
☞ The New Nation, Western Hemisphere; London, March 17, 1997, p.17.
☞ Calypso Calaloo: Early Carnival Music in Trinidad and Tobago, Donald Hill, University Press of Florida; Gainsville, FL., 1993.

202.
B) LA BUTTERFLY
☞ Jazz Cleopatra: Josephine Baker in Her Time. Phyliss Rose, Doubleday; New York, 1989.
Additional Information:
☞ Naked at the Feast: A Biography of Josephine Baker, Lynn Haney, NY, 1981.
☞ Black Americana. Richard A. Long, Admiral; UK, 1985.
☞ A Pictorial History of Black America. Langston Hughes, Crown; NY, 1983.

Entertainment

203.

B) SWEDEN

☞ The Big Issue, No. 192, U.K., 29 July, 1996, p.8.

Additional Information:

☞ Black Noise: Rap Music and Black Culture in Contemporary America, Tricia Rose. Westeyan University Press; 1994.

☞ The Weekly Journal, Voice Communications; November 19, 1992, p.11.

☞ The Warner Guide to UK & US Hit Singles, Compiled by Dave McAleer, A Carlton/Little, Brown Book; UK, 1994.

204.

A) I'LL BE MISSING YOU-PUFF DADDY

☞ Bad Boy: The Influence of Sean "Puffy" Combs on the Music Industry, Ronin Ro, Pocket Books; USA, 2001.

Additional Information:

☞ Vibe History of Hip Hop, Alan Light, (ed.), Vibe Magazine, Three Rivers Press; USA, 1998.

☞ Vibe, Quincy Jones and David Salzman Entertainment, Time Publishing Inc.; January, 1998, (cover story).

☞ Hit Singles: Top 20 Charts from 1954 to the Present Day, Dave McAleer, Carlton; 2004.

205.

A) 1956

☞ Hit Singles: Top 20 Charts from 1954 to the Present Day, Dave McAleer, Carlton; 2001.

Additional Information:

☞ The Music of Black Americans. A History, 2nd Edition, Eileen Southern, W. W. Norton & Co.; 1983.

☞ The Soul Book, Tony Cummings, Ian Hoare and Simon Frith, (eds.), Methuen; London, 1975.

☞ Soul Music, A-Z. Hugh Gregory, Blandford; London, 1991.

206.

C) CHOICE FM

☞ The Black Press in Britain, Ionie Benjamin, Trentham Books; London, 1995, p.106.

Additional Information:

☞ Windrush: The Irresistible Rise of Multiracial Britain. Trevor Phillips, HarperCollins; 1998.

☞ Caribbean Times, Hansib Publishing; June 29, 1993, p.2.

☞ The Voice, The Voice Group Ltd.; London, January 3, 1995, pp.21-22.

207.

C) CLARINET

☞ World's Great Men of Color, Volume II, J. A. Rogers, Collier Macmillan Publishers; 1972, p.563.

Additional Information:

☞ The Black Press in Britain, Ionie Benjamin, Trentham Books; London, 1995, p.45.

☞ Festivals de Musique Américaine Dirigés Par Rudolph Dunbar, Marinette; Paris, 1945.

☞ Black Londoners, 1890-1990, Susan Okokon, Sutton; UK, 1997, pp.7, 24-25.

208.

B) COMMODORES

☞ Lionel Ritchie: An Illustrated Biography, David Nathan, Mcgraw-Hill; New York, 1985.

Additional Information:

☞ Hit Singles: Top 20 Charts from 1954 to the Present Day, Dave McAleer, Carlton; 2001.

☞ The Billboard Book of Number One Hits, Fred Bronson, Billboard Publications; New York, 1992.

☞ Soul Music, A-Z. Hugh Gregory, Blandford; London, 1991.

209.

C) LORENZO TUCKER

☞ On the Real Side: A History of African American Comedy. Mel Watkins, Lawrence Hill; USA, 1999, pp.342-343.

Additional Information:

☞ Slow to Fade: The Negro in American Film 1900-1942. Thomas Cripps, Oxford University Press; New York, 1977.

☞ 1999 Facts About Blacks: A Sourcebook of African American Accomplishment. Raymond M. Corbin, Beckham House Publishers; USA, 1st Edition, 1986, p.143.

☞ Black Hollywood: The Negro in Motion Pictures, Gary Null, Lyle Stuart Press; USA, 1975.

210.
B) FATS DOMINO
☞ Icons of Black Music: A History in Photographs 1900-2000, Charlotte Greig, Brown Partworks Ltd.; UK, 1999, pp.40-41.
Additional Information:
☞ The Billboard Book of Number One Hits, Fred Bronson, Billboard Publications; New York, 1992.
☞ Who's Who in Rock, Revised Edition Compiled and Edited by William York, Arthur Barker Ltd.; 1982.
☞ The Sound of the City: The Rise of Rock and Roll, Charlie Gillett, Pantheon; New York, 1983.

211.
B) JOHNNY NASH
☞ The Guinness Who's Who of Reggae, Colin Larkin, Guinness Publishing; 1994.
Additional Information:
☞ Reggae International, Steven Davis and Peter Simon, Thames & Hudson; London, 1982.
☞ The Warner Guide to UK & US Hit Singles, Compiled by Dave McAleer, A Carlton/Little, Brown Book; UK, 1994.
☞ Reggae Bloodlines: In Search of the Music and Culture of Jamaica, S. Davis and Peter Simon, HEB; 1984.

212.
B) AN OFFICER AND A GENTLEMAN
☞ 1999 Facts About Blacks: A Sourcebook of African American Accomplishment. Raymond M. Corbin, Beckham House Publishers; USA, 1st Edition, 1986, p.143.
Additional Information:
☞ The Academy Awards Handbook, Pinnacle Books, Windsor Publishing Corp.; USA, 1995.
☞ Black Hollywood: From 1970 to Today, Gary Null, Citadel Press Books; 1993.
☞ 1994 Radio Times, Film and Video Guide, Derek Winnert, Hodder & Stoughton; 1993.

213.
A) OH CAROLINA
☞ Ebony, Johnson Publishing; Chicago, May 2001, pp.116-20.

Additional Information:
☞ Hit Singles: Top 20 Charts from 1954 to the Present Day, Dave McAleer, Carlton; 2001.
☞ Ebony, Johnson Publishing; Chicago, February, 2001, p.75.
☞ The Voice, The Voice Group Ltd.; London, June 4, 2001, p.53.

214.
B) LAWS
☞ The Penguin Guide to Jazz on CD, LP and Cassette, Revised Edition, Richard Cook and Brian Morton, Penguin; London, 1994.
Additial Information:
☞ The Story of Jazz: From New Orleans to Rock Jazz, Joachim-Ernst Berendt, (ed.), Barrie & Jenkins; London, 1978.
☞ Riding on a Blue Note: Jazz and American Pop, Gary Giddins, Oxford University Press; New York and Oxford, 1981.
☞ The Illustrated Autobiography of Jazz, Brian Case, Stan Britt and Chrissie Murray, Revised Edition, Salamander Books; London, 1987.

215.
C) WEATHER REPORT
☞ 1999 Facts About Blacks: A Sourcebook of African American Accomplishment. Raymond M. Corbin, Beckham House Publishers; USA, 1st Edition, 1986.
Additional Information:
☞ The Guinness Jazz Companion, Peter Clayton and Peter Gammand, Guinness Publishing; London, 1989.
☞ The Story of Jazz: From New Orleans to Rock Jazz, Joachim-Ernst Berendt, (ed.), Barrie & Jenkins; London, 1978.
☞ Dancing in Your Head: Jazz, Blues, Rock and Beyond, Gene Santoro, Oxford University Press; New York and Oxford, 1994.

216.
A) DRUMS
☞ Ebony Pictorial History of Black America: Volume 3. Civil Rights Movement or Black Revolution, Johnson Publishing Company; 1974.

Entertainment

Additional Information:

☞ An Autobiography of Black Jazz, Dempsey J. Travis, Urban Research Institute, Inc.; Chicago, 1983.

☞ Jazz in its Time, Martin Williams, Oxford University Press; New York, Oxford, 1989.

☞ The Picador Book of Blues and Jazz, Edited by James Campbell, Picador; London, 1995.

217.
A) KENNY GAMBLE AND LEON HUFF

☞ The Sound of Philadelphia, Tony Cummings, Methuen; London, 1975.

Additional Information:

☞ Encyclopedia of Black America, W. A. Low and Virgil A. Clift, (eds.), Mcgraw-Hill; New York, 1981.

☞ Sweet Soul Music: Rhythm and Blues and the Southern Dream of Freedom, Paul Garolnick, Virgin Books; UK, 1986.

☞ Black Noise: Rap Music and Black Culture in Contemporary America, Tricia Rose. Westeyan University Press; 1994.

218.
B) ROGERS AND EDWARDS

☞ New Musical Express Who's Who in Rock & Roll, Edited by John Tobler, Hamlyn; 1991.

Additional Information:

☞ Black Noise: Rap Music and Black Culture in Contemporary America, Tricia Rose. Westeyan University Press; 1994.

☞ The Billboard Book of Number One Hits, Fred Bronson, Billboard Publications; New York, 1992.

☞ Hit Singles: Top 20 Charts from 1954 to the Present Day, Dave McAleer, Carlton; 2001.

219.
A) PHYLICIA RASHAD

☞ The Los Angeles Times, Monday 7th June, 2004

Additional Information:

☞ The Voice, The Voice Group Ltd.; London, June 12, 2004.

☞ Tony, Grammy, Emmy, Country: A Broadway, Television and Records Award, Reference. Compiled by Don Franks, USA.

☞ Today's Black Hollywood, James Robert Parish, Pinnacle Books, Windsor Publishing Corp.; USA, 1995

220.
B) ISLEY BROTHERS

☞ New Musical Express Who's Who in Rock & Roll, Edited by John Tobler, Hamlyn; 1991.

Additional Information:

☞ Ebony Man, Johnson Publishing; July, 1992, p.8.

☞ The Billboard Book of Number One Hits, Fred Bronson, Billboard Publications; New York, 1992.

☞ Sweet Soul Music: Rhythm and Blues and the Southern Dream of Freedom, Paul Garolnick, Virgin Books; UK, 1986.

221.
B) MOVIE STAR

☞ "Well, I Heard It on the Radio and I Saw It on the Television:" An Essay for the Australian Film Commission on the Politics and of Filmmaking by and About Aboriginal People, Marcia Langton, Australia.

Additional Information:

☞ The Encyclopedia of Aboriginal Australia, Australian Institute of Aboriginal and Torrest Straight Islander State, Edited by David Horton, Australia, 1994.

☞ "Tudawali", March 1997, British Broadcasting Corporation, Library Archives, White City, London, W12

☞ Aboriginal Cultural Heritage, 18 Kilda Street, Baxter, Victoria, Melbourne, Au.

222.
C) ERYKAH BADU

☞ Hip-Hop Divas, Vibe Magazine, (ed.), Three Rivers Press; USA, 2001.

Additional Information:

☞ Vibe, Quincy Jones and David Salzman Entertainment, Time Publishing Inc.; August, 1997, (cover story).

☞ Ebony, Johnson Publishing; Chicago, December, 2000, p.124.

☞ Pride, London, May 1997, p.43.

223.
C) CHAKA KHAN

☞ The Warner Guide to UK & US Hit Singles, Compiled by Dave McAleer, A Carlton/Little, Brown Book; UK, 1994.

Additional Information:

☞ Ebony Man, Johnson Publishing; July, 1992, p.6.

☞ Icons of Black Music: A History in Photographs 1900-2000, Charlotte Greig, Brown Partworks Ltd.; UK, 1999, pp.90-91.

☞ Enclopaedia of Pop, Rock and Soul, Revised Edition, Irwin Stambler, St Martin's Press; New York, 1989.

224.
B) MY BOY LOLLIPOP

☞ Roots Rock Reggae: An Oral History of Reggae Music from Ska to Dancehall, Chuck Foster, Billboard Books; 1999.

Additional Information:

☞ The Warner Guide to UK & US Hit Singles, Compiled by Dave McAleer, A Carlton/Little, Brown Book; UK, 1994.

☞ The Voice, The Voice Group Ltd.; July 14, 1997, pp.20-21.

☞ Reggae International, Steven Davis and Peter Simon, Thames & Hudson; London, 1982.

Entertainment

A

Science & Engineering

Answers and Sources

225.

C) BACK OF THE HEAD

☞ Ben Carson, Gregg Lewis and Deborah Shaw Lewis Zondervan Books; US, 2002.

Additional Information:

☞ Ebony, Johnson Publishing; Chicago, January, 2003, pp.38-41.

☞ Gifted Hands, Ben Carson with Cecil Murphey, Zondervan Books; US, 1996.

☞ Think Big, Ben Carson with Cecil B. Murphey, Zondervan Books; US, 1996.

226.

A) 3.1 BILLION CALCULATIONS PER SECOND

☞ New African, July/August 1996, ICP Ltd.; London, pp.8-11 (cover story).

Additional Information:

☞ "Pioneer of the Year", March 1996, National Society of Black Engineers, 1454 Duke Street, Alexandria, Virginia, 22314.

☞ New African, April 2000, ICP Ltd.; London, p.25.

☞ "Computer Scientist of the year Award 1993", National Technical Association, Brooklyn, NY, USA.

227.

A) 3

☞ IBM Research Division, Thomas J. Watson Research Center, PO Box 218, Yorktown Heights, New York 10598

Additional Information:

☞ Black Scientists and Inventors, Volume 1, Ava Henry and Michael Williams, (eds.), BIS Publications; London, 1999.

☞ The Customer-Centered Enterprise: How IBM and Other World-Class Companies Achieve Extraordinary Results by Putting Customers First, Harvey Thompson McGraw-Hill Trade; 1st edition, 1999

☞ Black Inventors Museum, Jeffers Associates, 50 Markham Rd, Unit 3, Toronto, Ontario, M1M 2Z4

228.

C) APOLLO 16

☞ NASA H.Q., Administrators Office, Code-A, Washington, D.C., 20546, USA.

Additional Information:

☞ Space Astronomy in the Shuttle Era. George R. Carruthers, National Technical Association, Journal 2, January 1978.

☞ 1999 Facts About Blacks: A Sourcebook of African American Accomplishment. Raymond M. Corbin, Beckham House Publishers; USA, 1st Edition, 1986, pp.47-48.

☞ Black Makers of History. The Real McCoy, Frank Forde, Lesnah Hall and Virginia McLean, The Book Place; 1988, p.99.

229.

A) KENYA

☞ Science Awakening, B. L. Van Der Waerden, Vol. II, Oxford University Press;

Additional Information:

☞ Crash Course in Black History: 150 Important Facts About African Peoples, Zak A. Kondo, Nubia Press; USA, 1988, p.4.

☞ The Voice, The Voice Group Ltd.; London, October 18, 1999, p.18.

☞ The Ruins of Empire, Count Constantine de Volney, Black Classic Press; Baltimore, MD, 1990.

230.

B) CATERACTS

☞ Ebony, Johnson Publishing; Chicago, February, 2000.

Additional Information:

☞ DuPont Building, 1007 Market Street, Wilmington, DE, USA, 19898

☞ New African, April 2000, ICP Ltd.; London, p.23.

☞ National Library of Medicine, 8600 Rockville Pike, Rockville, Maryland, 20894, USA.

231.

B) GLIDER

☞ Journal of African Civilization, Transactions Periodicals Consortium; Rutgers University, New Brunswick, New Jersey, "African Observers of the Universe. The Sirius Question", Hunter Adams III, Vol. 1., No. 2., November 1979, p.x.

Additional Information:

☞ Blacks in Science: Ancient and Modern, Ivan Van Sertima, (ed.), Transaction; USA, 1985, pp.92-99.

☞ What They Never Told You in History Class, Indus Khamit-Kush, Luxorr Publications; USA, 1983, p.114.

☞ Egyptian Museum, Cairo, Room No. 22, Model 6347.

232.
A) FOUNTAIN PEN
☞ Assistant Commissioner for Patents; United States Patent Office, Archive Records, Washington, D.C., 20231, January 7, 1890, Patent No. 419,065.
Additional Information:
☞ Ebony, Johnson Publishing; Chicago, February, 1997, p.40.
☞ Black Inventors of America, McKinley Burt, National Book Co; Oregon, 1969.
☞ Blacks in Science: Astrophysicist to Zoologist. Hattie Carwell, USA, 1977, p.87.

233.
C) HIV/AIDS
☞ The British Patent Office, Archive Records, Southampton Buildings, Chancery Lane, London, WC2, August 20, 1992, Mariandina A, B & J, Patent No. 2224649.
Additional Information:
☞ The Medical Review, Vol 2., No. 1, Jan/Feb 1996, Uganda, East Africa.
☞ The Journal of Transfigural Mathematics, Vol. 2, Berlin, 1996
☞ Black Scientists and Inventors Millennium Calendar 1999, BIS Publications; P.O. Box 14918, London, N17 8WJ.

234.
A) ELEVATOR
☞ Assistant Commissioner for Patents; United States Patent Office, Archive Records, Washington, D.C., 20231, October 11, 1887 Patent No. 371, 278.
Additional Information:
☞ Blacks in Science: Astrophysicist to Zoologist. Hattie Carwell, USA, 1977, p.83.
☞ Black Inventors of America, McKinley Burt, National Book Co; Oregon, 1969.
☞ Pride, London, May 1997, pp.118-19.

235.
C) ENDEAVOR
☞ Find Where the Wind Goes: Moments from My Life, Dr. Mae Jemison, Scholastic Trade Publications; 2001.

Additional Information:
☞ Jet, Johnson Publishing; Chicago, September 14, 1992, pp.34-38.
☞ African-American Astronauts, Stanley P. Jones, Octavia L. Trip, Fred Amram, and Susan K. Henderson, Capstone Press; 1998.
☞ Ebony, Johnson Publishing; Chicago, December, 1992, pp.118-24.

236.
B) GARDENER
☞ Groote Schuur Hospital, Main Road, Observatory, 7925, Cape Town, South Africa.
Additional Information:
☞ The Guardian, Guardian Newspapers; London, April 25, 2003.
☞ Linda Goodman's Sun Signs, Linda Goodman, Bantam Books; Reissue edition, 1985, p.414.
☞ Building Moral Intelligence: The Seven Essential Virtues that Teach Kids to Do the Right Thing, Michele Borba, Jossey-Bass Publications; 2002.

237.
C) BURGLER ALARM
☞ Blacks in Science: Astrophysicist to Zoologist. Hattie Carwell, USA, 1977, p.90.
Additional Information:
☞ Black Inventors of America, McKinley Burt, National Book Co; Oregon, 1969.
☞ Assistant Commissioner for Patents; United States Patent Office, Archive Records, Washington, D.C.
☞ Black Scientists and Inventors Millennium Calendar 1999, BIS Publications; P.O. Box 14918, London, N17 8WJ.

238.
C) EYE GLASSES
☞ African Presence in Early Europe, Edited by Ivan Van Sertima, Transaction; 1986, pp.157-59.
Additional Information:
☞ History of Science: Ancient and Medieval, Rene Taton, (ed.), Basic Books; 1957, USA.
☞ The Golden Age of the Moor. Light of Europe's Dark Age, Ivan Van Sertima, Transaction; New Jersey, 1991.
☞ A History of the Interlectual Development of Europe, J.W. Draper, London, 1864.

239.
A) MATHEMATICS
☞ Blacks in Science: Ancient and Modern, Ivan Van Sertima, (ed.), Transaction; USA, 1985, pp.111-13.
Additional Information:
☞ Musee de' Histoire Naturelle, Brussels.
☞ Africa Counts: Number and Patern in African Culture. Prindlee, Weber & Scmidt; USA.
☞ What They Never Told You in History Class, Indus Khamit-Kush, Luxorr Publications; USA, 1983.

240.
A) THE FIRST U.S. SPACE SHUTTLE
☞ NASA H.Q., Administrators Office, Code-A, Washington, D.C., 20546, USA.
Additional Information:
☞ Blacks in Science: Ancient and Modern, Ivan Van Sertima, (ed.), Transaction; USA, 1985, pp.246-248.
☞ What They Never Told You in History Class, Indus Khamit-Kush, Luxorr Publications; USA, 1983, p.304.
☞ Black Makers of History. The Real McCoy, Frank Forde, Lesnah Hall and Virginia McLean, The Book Place; 1988, p.39.

241.
B) BULL RING
☞ African Presence in Early Europe, Edited by Ivan Van Sertima, Transaction; 1986, p.195.
Additional Information:
☞ Africa in Portugal, Flamingo; London, February 1962.
☞ The Golden Age of the Moor. Light of Europe's Dark Age, Ivan Van Sertima, Transaction; New Jersey, 1991.
☞ Nature Knows No Color Line. J. A. Rogers, 3rd Edition, H. M. Rogers Publishers; 1952.

242.
A) SWAZILAND
☞ The New York Times, February 8, 1970, p.6.
Additional Information:
☞ Great African Thinkers Volume 1, Cheikh Anta Diop, Edited by Ivan Van Sertima, Transaction; USA, 1987, p.83.
☞ What They Never Told You in History Class, Indus Khamit-Kush, Luxorr Publications; USA, 1983, p.118.

☞ Blacks in Science: Ancient and Modern, Ivan Van Sertima, (ed.), Transaction; USA, 1985, p.110.

243.
B) X RAYS
☞ Crisis, Vol. 46, No. 6, pp.167-69.
Additional Information:
☞ Blacks in Science: Astrophysicist to Zoologist. Hattie Carwell, USA, 1977, pp.68-69.
☞ The Voice, The Voice Group Ltd.; London, November 8, 1999.
☞ Black Pioneers of Science and Invention, Louis Haber, Harcourt, Brace & World, Inc.; 1970.

244.
B) MARINE BIOLOGY
☞ Black Apollo of Science: The Life of Ernest Just. Kenneth R. Manning, Oxford University Press; 1983, pp.67-114.
Additional Information:
☞ Encyclopedia of Black America, W. A. Low and Virgil A. Clift, (eds.), Mcgraw-Hill; New York, 1981, pp.481, 807.
☞ Great Negroes: Past and Present. Russell L. Adams, Afro-Am Publishing Company; Chicago, Illinois, 3rd Edition (1981).
☞ Portraits in color, Mary White Ovington, The Viking Press; 1927.

245.
C) CAESAREAN SECTION
☞ Great African Thinkers. Volume 1, Cheikh Anta Diop, Edited by Ivan Van Sertima, Transaction; USA, 1987, p.86.
Additional Information:
☞ Blacks in Science: Ancient and Modern, Ivan Van Sertima, (ed.), Transaction; USA, 1985, pp.23-24, 151-52.
☞ Black Makers of History. The Real McCoy, Frank Forde, Lesnah Hall and Virginia McLean, The Book Place; 1988, p.15.
☞ Edinburgh Medical Journal, 1884

246.
B) NASA'S MOON BUGGY
☞ Blacks in Science: Ancient and Modern, Ivan Van Sertima, (ed.), Transaction; USA, 1985, pp.249-51.

Additional Information:
- ☞ Ideology of Racism. Samuel Kennedy Yeboah, Hansib Publishing; 1988, UK, p.222.
- ☞ New African, April 2000, ICP Ltd.; London, p.24.
- ☞ What They Never Told You in History Class, Indus Khamit-Kush, Luxorr Publications; USA, 1983, p.307.

247.
C) DOUBLE REMEN
- ☞ Great African Thinkers. Volume 1, Cheikh Anta Diop, Edited by Ivan Van Sertima, Transaction; USA, 1987, p.77.

Additional Information:
- ☞ Blacks in Science: Ancient and Modern, Ivan Van Sertima, (ed.), Transaction; USA, 1985, p.184.
- ☞ Nile Valley Contributions to Civilization; Exploding the Myths, Volume 1, Anthony T. Browder, Institute of Khamic Guidance; Washington, D.C., 2000, p.128.
- ☞ Stolen Legacy. George G. M. James, Philosophical Libraries; NY, 1988.

248.
A) ROLLER COASTER
- ☞ Assistant Commissioner for Patents; United States Patent Office, Archive Records, Washington, D.C., 20231,December 19, 1899, Patent No. 639, 692.

Additional Information:
- ☞ Black Inventors of America, McKinley Burt, National Book Co; Oregon, 1969.
- ☞ Blacks in Science: Ancient and Modern, Ivan Van Sertima, (ed.), Transaction; USA, 1985, p.215, 220.
- ☞ Ebony, Johnson Publishing; Chicago, February, 1997, p.40.

249.
A) 1893
- ☞ Black Makers of History. The Real McCoy, Frank Forde, Lesnah Hall and Virginia McLean, The Book Place; 1988, p.77.

Additional Information:
- ☞ Great Negroes: Past and Present. Russell L. Adams, Afro-Am Publishing Company; Chicago, Illinois, 3rd Edition (1981).
- ☞ Black Firsts: 2000 Years of Extraordinary Achievement. Jessie Carney Smith, Caspar L. Jordan and Robert L. Johns, Visible Ink Press; USA, 1994.

- ☞ Black Scientists of America, R. X. Donovan, National Book Company; USA, 1990.

250.
B) LUBRICATION FLUID
- ☞ Black Firsts: 2000 Years of Extraordinary Achievement. Jessie Carney Smith, Caspar L. Jordan and Robert L. Johns, Visible Ink Press; USA, 1994.

Additional Information:
- ☞ Black Inventors from Africa to America, C. R. Gibbs, Three Dimentional Publishing; USA, 1995.
- ☞ Black Scientists of America, R. X. Donovan, National Book Company; USA, 1990.
- ☞ Black Makers of History. The Real McCoy, Frank Forde, Lesnah Hall and Virginia McLean, The Book Place; 1988.

251.
C) TRAFFIC LIGHTS
- ☞ Assistant Commissioner for Patents; United States Patent Office, Archive Records, Washington, D.C., 20231, November 20, 1923, Patent No. 1, 475,024.

Additional Information:
- ☞ Black Inventors from Africa to America, C. R. Gibbs, Three Dimentional Publishing; USA, 1995.
- ☞ Black Scientists of America, R. X. Donovan, National Book Company; USA, 1990.
- ☞ Black Scientists and Inventors, Ava Henry and Michael Williams, (eds.), BIS Publications; London, 1999.

252.
A) SIRIUS B
- ☞ Journal of African Civilization, Transactions Periodicals Consortium; Rutgers University, New Brunswick, New Jersey, "African Observers of the Universe. The Sirius Question", Hunter Adams III, Vol. 1., No. 2., November 1979, pp.1-20.

Additional Information:
- ☞ The African Origin of Civilization: Myth or Reality, Cheikh Anta Diop (translated by Mercer Cook), Lawrence Hill & Company; 1974, pp.136-37, 141-42, 179, 234, 301.

☞ Black Makers of History. The Real McCoy, Frank Forde, Lesnah Hall and Virginia McLean, The Book Place; 1988, p.25.

☞ Star Maps, William R. Fix, Octopus Books Ltd.; London, 1979.

253.
A) SHOES
☞ Black Pioneers of Science and Invention, Louis Haber, Harcourt, Brace & World, Inc.; New York, 1970, pp.225-33.
Additional Information:
☞ Amsterdam News, NY, April 20, 1932.
☞ Black Inventors from Africa to America, C. R. Gibbs, Three Dimentional Publishing; USA, 1995.
☞ Assistant Commissioner for Patents; United States Patent Office, Archive Records, Washington, D.C., 20231, February 25, 1896, Patent No. 421, 954.

254.
B) SUGAR FROM SUGAR CANE
☞ Black Inventors from Africa to America, C. R. Gibbs, Three Dimentional Publishing; USA, 1995.
Additional Information:
☞ Black Scientists of America, R. X. Donovan, National Book Company; USA, 1990.
☞ Ideology of Racism. Samuel Kennedy Yeboah, Hansib Publishing; UK, 1988, pp.194-95.
☞ Assistant Commissioner for Patents; United States Patent Office, Archive Records, Washington, D.C., 20231, December 10, 1846, Patent No. 4, 879.

255.
C) CAMBRIDGE
☞ Biochemical Journal, "The Biological Activity of Pure Peptides Obtained by Enzymic Hydrolysis of Insulin", D. S. H. W. Nicol, Volume 75, 1960, pp.395-401.
Additional Information:
☞ Nature: "Amino-acid sequence of human insulin". D. S. H. W. Nicol and L. F. Smith, Volume 187, 1960, pp.483-485.
☞ Cambridge University, Medical Archive Records, Department of Medicine, Level 5, Addensbrooke's Hospital, Box 157, Hills Road, Cambridge, CB2 2QQ.

☞ The Voice, The Voice Group Ltd.; London, August 2, 1999, p.42.

256.
C) UNDER WATER CLOCK
☞ Black Scientists of America, R. X. Donovan, National Book Company; USA, 1990.
Additional Information:
☞ Ideology of Racism. Samuel Kennedy Yeboah, Hansib Publishing; UK, 1988, pp.199-200.
☞ Black Inventors of America, McKinley Burt, National Book Co; Oregon, 1969.
☞ Blacks in Science: Astrophysicist to Zoologist. Hattie Carwell, USA, 1977, pp.80-81.

257.
A) BERNARD HARRIS
☞ African-American Astronauts, Stanley P. Jones, Octavia L. Trip, Fred Amram, and Susan K. Henderson, Capstone Press; 1998.
Additional Information:
☞ NASA H.Q., Administrators Office, Code-A, Washington, D.C., 20546, USA.
☞ The Voice, The Voice Group Ltd.; London, February 28, 1995, p.17.
☞ What They Never Told You in History Class, Indus Khamit-Kush, Luxorr Publications; USA, 1983, p.310.

258.
A) HEAR
☞ Blacks in Science: Astrophysicist to Zoologist. Hattie Carwell, USA, 1977 pp.24-25.
Additional Information:
☞ Great Negroes: Past and Present. Russell L. Adams, Afro-Am Publishing Company; Chicago, Illinois, 3rd Edition (1981).
☞ National Library of Medicine, 8600 Rockville Pike, Rockville, Maryland,0894, USA.
☞ Ideology of Racism. Samuel Kennedy Yeboah, Hansib Publishing; 1988, UK, p.220.

259.
A) CLOTHES DRYER
☞ Blacks in Science: Ancient and Modern, Ivan Van Sertima, (ed.), Transaction; USA, 1985.

Additional Information:
- ☞ Assistant Commissioner for Patents; United States Patent Office, Archive Records, Washington, D.C., 20231, January 7, 1890, Patent No. 476, 416.
- ☞ Black Inventors of America, McKinley Burt, National Book Co; Oregon, 1969.
- ☞ Blacks in Science: Astrophysicist to Zoologist. Hattie Carwell, USA, 1977, p.86.

260.
C) THE HAIR WEAVE
- ☞ Pride, London, May 1997, p.119.

Additional Information:
- ☞ Black Stars: African American Women Scientists and Inventors, Otha Richard Sullivan, Jim Haskins Wiley; US, 2001
- ☞ Good Hair (For Colored Girls Who've Considered Weaves When the Chemicals Became to Ruff), Lonnice B. Bonner, Crown Publishing; New York, 1994.
- ☞ Hair Story: Untangling the Roots of Black Hair in America, Lori L. Tharps and Ayana D. Byrd, St Martin's Press; 2001.

261.
A) DRY CLEANING SOLVENT
- ☞ Outward Dreams: Black Inventors and Their Inventions, J. Haskins, USA, 1991, pp.4-5.

Additional Information:
- ☞ Pride, London, May 1997, p.118.
- ☞ Black Firsts: 2000 Years of Extraordinary Achievement. Jessie Carney Smith, Caspar L. Jordan and Robert L. Johns, Visible Ink Press; USA, 1994, p.343.
- ☞ Eyewitness: The Negro in America, William L. Katz, Pittman Publishing; New York, 1968, pp.98-99, 139.

262.
C) SOY BEAN
- ☞ Black Scientists of America, R. X. Donovan, National Book Company; USA, 1990.

Additional Information:
- ☞ Ideology of Racism. Samuel Kennedy Yeboah, Hansib Publishing; UK, 1988, p.198.
- ☞ Blacks in Science: Astrophysicist to Zoologist. Hattie Carwell, USA, 1977, p.48.

- ☞ National Library of Medicine, 8600 Rockville Pike, Rockville, Maryland, 20894, USA.

263.
B) FIBRE OPTIC ENDOSCOPE
- ☞ Blacks in Science: Astrophysicist to Zoologist. Hattie Carwell, USA, 1977, p.30.

Additional Information:
- ☞ Who's Who Among Black Americans, 1992-1993, USA, p.64.
- ☞ National Library of Medicine, 8600 Rockville Pike, Rockville, Maryland, 20894, USA.
- ☞ Black Firsts: 2000 Years of Extraordinary Achievement. Jessie Carney Smith, Caspar L. Jordan and Robert L. Johns, Visible Ink Press; USA, 1994, p.355.

264.
B) ROCKET
- ☞ NASA H.Q., Administrators Office, Code-A, Washington, D.C., 20546, USA.

Additional Information:
- ☞ Blacks in Science: Astrophysicist to Zoologist. Hattie Carwell, USA, 1977, p.91.
- ☞ 1999 Facts About Blacks: A Sourcebook of African American Accomplishment. Raymond M. Corbin, Beckham House Publishers; USA, 1st Edition, 1986, p.38.
- ☞ The Voice, The Voice Group Ltd.; London, October 18, 1999, p.18.

265.
A) LEWIS LATIMER
- ☞ Assistant Commissioner for Patents; United States Patent Office, Archive Records, Washington, D.C., 20231, September 13, 1881, Patent No. 247,097.

Additional Information:
- ☞ Black Scientists of America, R. X. Donovan, National Book Company; USA, 1990.
- ☞ The New York Times, December 12, 1928 (Obituary Notice).
- ☞ Black Makers of History. The Real McCoy, Frank Forde, Lesnah Hall and Virginia McLean, The Book Place; 1988, p.61.

Science & Engineering

266.
B) HE WAS A MATHEMATICS GENIUS
☞ The Great White Lie-Slavery, Emancipation, Changing Racial Attitudes, Jack Gratus, Monthly Review Press; 1973, p.254.

Additional Information:
☞ Gentleman's Magazine, LVIII (1788), England, p.112.
☞ Ideology of Racism. Samuel Kennedy Yeboah, Hansib Publishing; 1988, UK, p.185.
☞ Black Scientists and Inventors, Ava Henry and Michael Williams, (eds.), BIS Publications; London, 1999.

267.
B) STONEHENGE
☞ The Story of England: Makers of the Realm, Arthur byant, Collins; London, 1953.

Additional Information:
☞ Ancient and Modern Britons. David MacRitchie, Volume 1, Keegan Paul, Trench & Co.; 1985.
☞ Anacalypsis, Godfrey Higgins, Volume 1, Book 1, New Hyde Park; New York, 1965, Chapter 4.
☞ The hidden truth "Free your mind", Andrew Muhammad Hakiki publishing; London, 2004, pp.42.

268.
B) THEONINE
☞ The Journal of Biological chemistry, Issue 119, 1937, US, pp.109-119, 121-131.

Additional Information:
☞ American Health Dilemma: Race, Medicine, Health Care in the United States, W. Michael Byrd, Brunner-Routledge; 1st edition, 2001, p.258
☞ Educator's Sourcebook of African American Heritage (J-B Ed: Book of Lists), Johnnie H. Miles, Juanita J. Davis, Sharon E. Ferguson-Roberts and Rita G. Giles, Jossey-Bass Publishers; 2002, p.156
☞ Under the Knife: How a Wealthy Negro Surgeon Wielded Power in the Jim Crow South, Hugh Pearson, Free Press; 2002, p.106

269.
C) SMALLPOX
☞ Ideology of Racism. Samuel Kennedy Yeboah, Hansib Publishing; 1988, UK, p.220.

Additional Information:
☞ Black Firsts: 2000 Years of Extraordinary Achievement. Jessie Carney Smith, Caspar L. Jordan and Robert L. Johns, Visible Ink Press; USA, 1994, p.350.
☞ Great Negroes: Past and Present. Russell L. Adams, Afro-Am Publishing Company; Chicago, Illinois, 3rd Edition (1981) p.59.
☞ Black Inventors from Africa to America, C. R. Gibbs, Three Dimentional Publishing; USA, 1995.

270.
C) IMHOTEP
☞ Blacks in Science: Ancient and Modern, Ivan Van Sertima, (ed.), Transaction; USA, 1985, p.129.

Additional Information:
☞ The Daily Telegraph, London, March 28, 1989, p.19.
☞ Africa: Mother of Western Civilisation, Dr. Yosef A. A. Ben Jochannon, Black Classic Press; Baltimore, MD, 1988, p.271.
☞ Herodotus: The Histories. Great Books of the Western World, Encyclopaedia Brittanica; Chicago, 1952, pp.49-50, 60-65, 69-70.

271.
B) MARY SEACOLE
☞ The Wonderful Adventures of Mary Seacole in Many Lands, Mary Seacole, J. Blackwood; London, 1857.

Additional Information:
☞ Makers of History, The Real McCoy, Frank Forde, Lesnah Hall and Virginia McLean, The Book Place; 1988, p.91.
☞ Roots of the Future: The Ethnic Diversity in the Making of Britain. CRE; UK, 1996.
☞ The New Nation, Western Hemisphere; London, January 6, 1997, p.6.

272.
A) BICYCLE
☞ Assistant Commissioner for Patents; United States Patent Office, Archive Records, Washington, D.C., 20231, Patent No. 634, 823; and No. 639, 708.

Additional Information:
☞ Blacks in Science: Astrophysicist to Zoologist. Hattie Carwell, USA, 1977, p.90.

☞ Black Inventors of America, McKinley Burt, National Book Co; Oregon, 1969.
☞ Black Scientists and Inventors Millennium Calendar 1999, BIS Publications; P.O. Box 14918, London, N17 8WJ

273.
C) SICKLE CELL
☞ New African, September 2001, ICP Ltd.; London, pp.40-43.
Additional Information:
☞ The Woman A-Z of family Health, Anne-Marie Sapsted, Grafton Books, Collins; London, Toronto, Auckland, 1987, p.282-83.
☞ Cambridge Encyclopedia, David Crystal, Cambridge University Press; 1990, p.1105.
☞ Third World Impact. 8th Edition, Edited by Arif Ali, Hansib Publishing; 1988, p.11.

274.
A) CHARLES DREW
☞ Black Firsts: 2000 Years of Extraordinary Achievement. Jessie Carney Smith, Caspar L. Jordan and Robert L. Johns, Visible Ink Press; USA, 1994.
Additional Information:
☞ National Library of Medicine, 8600 Rockville Pike, Rockville, Maryland, 20894, USA.
☞ The Black American Reference Book. Mabel M. Smyth, (ed.), Prentice-Hall Inc.; USA, 1976, p.895.
☞ Blacks in Science: Ancient and Modern, Ivan Van Sertima, (ed.), Transaction; USA, 1985, pp.228, 258.

275.
C) 325
☞ George Washington Carver: God's Ebony Scientist, B. G. Miller, Zon Deruam Publishing House; Grand Rapids, Michigan, 1943.
Additional Information:
☞ Modern Americans in science and Invention, Enda Yost, Frederick A. Stokes Company; New York, 1941, pp.147-62.
☞ Wizard of Tuskegee, David Manber, Crowell-Collier Press; New York, 1967.
☞ Ideology of Racism. Samuel Kennedy Yeboah, Hansib Publishing; 1988, UK, pp.204-220.

276.
B) 1980
☞ Jet, Johnson Publishing Co.; Chicago, October 9, 1980, p.8.
Additional Information:
☞ Class, USA, December, 1983.
☞ The Voice, The Voice Group Ltd.; London, October 18, 1999, p.18.
☞ Black Firsts: 2000 Years of Extraordinary Achievement. Jessie Carney Smith, Caspar L. Jordan and Robert L. Johns, Visible Ink Press; USA, 1994, p.360.

277.
C) ALGEBRA
☞ Women Scientists from Antiquity to the Present, Carol Herzburg, Locust Hill Press; West Cornwall Ct., 1986, p.xviii
Additional Information:
☞ Black Women in Antiquity, Edited by Ivan Van Sertima, Transaction; 7th Edition, 1992, p.155.
☞ Herodotus: The Histories. Great Books of the Western World, Encyclopaedia Brittanica; Chicago, 1952, pp.49-50, 60-65, 69-70.
☞ Blacks in Science: Ancient and Modern, Ivan Van Sertima, (ed.), Transaction; USA, 1985, p.105.

278.
A) ISLE OF LEWIS
☞ Ancient and Modern Britons. David MacRitchie, Volume 1, Keegan Paul, Trench & Co.; 1985.
Additional Information:
☞ The Black Celts, A. Ali & I. Ali, Punite Publications; Cardiff, 1993.
☞ Your History: From the Beginning of Time to the Present, J. A. Rogers, Black Classic Press; Baltimore, MD, 1983, p.91.
☞ Archaeology of Scotland, D. Wilson, Edinburgh, 1851.

279.
B) FARMING
☞ A Short History of Western Civilization, by Professors Harrison, Sullivan and Sherman, Alfred A. Knoff Publishers; New York.
Additional Information:
☞ Blacks in Science: Ancient and Modern, Ivan Van Sertima, (ed.), Transaction; USA, 1985, pp.58-64.

☞ Black Makers of History. The Real McCoy, Frank Forde, Lesnah Hall and Virginia McLean, The Book Place; 1988, p.35.

☞ Und Afrika Sprach, Leo Frobenius, Germany, 1910.

280.
B) CHEMOTHERAPY
☞ Black Makers of History. The Real McCoy, Frank Forde, Lesnah Hall and Virginia McLean, The Book Place; 1988, p.109.
Additional Information:
☞ Against the Odds: Blacks in the Profession of Medicine in the United States. Wilbur H. Watson, Transaction; 1999.
☞ Blacks in Science: Astrophysicist to Zoologist. Hattie Carwell, USA, 1977, p.58.
☞ Facts on File Encyclopedia of Black Women in America: Science Health, and Medicine (Volume 11), Darlene Clark Hine and Kathleen Thompson, (eds.), Facts on File, Inc.; USA, 1997.

281.
A) IRONING BOARD
☞ Assistant Commissioner for Patents; United States Patent Office, Archive Records, Washington, D.C., 20231, April 26, 1892 Patent No. 473, 653.
Additional Information:
☞ Blacks in Science: Astrophysicist to Zoologist. Hattie Carwell, USA, 1977, p.76.
☞ Black Stars: African American Women Scientists and Inventors, Otha Richard Sullivan, Jim Haskins Wiley; US, 2001
☞ Salute to Black Women Inventors, Black Science Activity Books; Chandler/White Publishers; Chicago, 1990.

282.
C) GAS INTO ELECTRICITY
☞ Black Inventors from Africa to America, C. R. Gibbs, Three Dimentional Publishing; USA, 1995.
Additional Information:
☞ Blacks in Science: Astrophysicist to Zoologist. Hattie Carwell, USA, 1977, pp.50-51.
☞ Black Inventors of America, McKinley Burt, National Book Co; Oregon, 1969.

☞ Blacks in Science: Ancient and Modern, Ivan Van Sertima, (ed.), Transaction; USA, 1985, pp.192, 215, 224, 226-27.

283.
A) HOLOGRAMS
☞ Encyclopaedia Britannica, 1976 Edition, "Holography", p.605.
Additional Information:
☞ Journal of the Optical Society of America, "Interferometric Vibration Analysis by Wavefront Reconstruction", Robert L. Powell and Karl A. Stetson, 1965.
☞ Blacks in Science: Astrophysicist to Zoologist. Hattie Carwell, USA, 1977, p.33.
☞ Holograms and Holography, John R. Vacca, Charles River Media; 2001.

284.
C) 93 MILLION MILES
☞ Hutchingson Encyclopedia, 8th Edition, Hutchingson; UK, 1988.
Additional Information:
☞ The 1997 Guinness Book of Records, Guinness Publishing Ltd.; UK, 1996, p.14.
☞ Seeing the Stars: The BBC Television Series, Patrick Moor, British Broadcasting Company; pp.4, 8-9.
☞ Cambridge Encyclopedia, David Crystal, Cambridge University Press; 4th Edition, 2000.

285.
A) ELBERT ROBERTSON
☞ Blacks in Science: Astrophysicist to Zoologist. Hattie Carwell, USA, 1977, p.36.
Additional Information:
☞ Great Negroes: Past and Present. Russell L. Adams, Afro-Am Publishing Company; Chicago, Illinois, 3rd Edition (1981), p.59.
☞ Black Inventors of America, McKinley Burt, National Book Co; Oregon, 1969.
☞ Black Scientists and Inventors Millennium Calendar 1999, BIS Publications; P.O. Box 14918, London, N17 8WJ

286.
A) 1885
☞ Pride, London, May 1997, p.119.

Additional Information:
- ☞ Blacks in Science: Astrophysicist to Zoologist. Hattie Carwell, USA, 1977, p.79.
- ☞ Black Firsts: 2000 Years of Extraordinary Achievement. Jessie Carney Smith, Caspar L. Jordan and Robert L. Johns, Visible Ink Press; USA, 1994, p.346.
- ☞ Salute to Black Women Inventors, Black Science Activity Books; Chandler/White Publishers; Chicago, 1990.

287.
A) ASPIRIN
- ☞ Blacks in Science: Ancient and Modern, Ivan Van Sertima, (ed.), Transaction; USA, 1985, p.22.

Additional Information:
- ☞ Journal of African Civilisations, Volume 1, No. 2, USA, 1979.
- ☞ They Came Before Columbus: African Presence in Ancient America, Ivan Van Sertima, Random House; USA, 1976.
- ☞ New! Encyclopaedia Britannica Print Set, 2002 Edition (Aspirin).

288.
B) SUBMARINE TORPEDO DISCHARGER
- ☞ Ebony, Johnson Publishing; Chicago, February, 1997, p.40.

Additional Information:
- ☞ Salute to Black Women Inventors, Black Science Activity Books; Chandler/White Publishers; Chicago, 1990.
- ☞ The Voice, The Voice Group Ltd.; London, November 15, 1999, p.42.
- ☞ Black Stars: African American Women Scientists and Inventors, Otha Richard Sullivan, Jim Haskins Wiley; US, 2001

289.
C) DIESEL
- ☞ Black Scientists and Inventors, Volume 1, Ava Henry and Michael Williams, (eds.), BIS Publications; London, 1999.

Additional Information:
- ☞ New African, April 2000, ICP Ltd.; London, p.25.
- ☞ The Voice, The Voice Group Ltd.; London, August 2, 1999, p.42.
- ☞ The Complete Who's Who of Test Cricketers, C. Martin-Jenkins, Orbus Publishing; London, 1983.

290.
A) FIRST GLOBAL SATELLITE
- ☞ NASA H.Q., Administrators Office, Code-A, Washington, D.C., 20546, USA.

Additional Information:
- ☞ Blacks in Science: Astrophysicist to Zoologist. Hattie Carwell, USA, 1977.
- ☞ Assistant Commissioner for Patents; United States Patent Office, Archive Records, Washington, D.C., 20231.
- ☞ Commercial Observation Satellites: At the Leading Edge of Global Transparency, Kevin M O'Connel, Ray A. Williamson, John C. Baker, (eds.), Rand Corporation; 2001.

291.
B) R
- ☞ Native Tongues, Charles Berlitz, Panther Books; U.K., 1984, p.128.

Additional Information:
- ☞ The Daily Telegraph, London, Tuesday March 28, 1989, p.19.
- ☞ Nile Valley Contributions to Civilization; Exploding the Myths, Volume 1, Anthony T. Browder, Institute of Khamic Guidance; Washington, D.C., 2000, p.127.
- ☞ Black Man of the Nile and His Family. Dr. Yosef A. A. Ben Jochannon, Black Classic Press; Baltimore, MD, 1988.

292.
C) VANILLA
- ☞ Giant Steps Discoveries Series, Brian Thompson (ed.), Longman Books; UK, 1976, pp.24-25.

Additional Information:
- ☞ Vanilla, Chocolate, & Strawberry: The Story of Your Favorite Flavors, Bonnie Busenberg, Lerner Publications Company; 1994.
- ☞ Heaven's Delight-Vanilla, Luis M. Mendoza de Carvalho, Ethnobotanical Leaflets, (Journal on-line) "http://www.siu.edu/"
- ☞ American Home Garden Book and Plant Encyclopedia, American Home Editors, M. Evans & Company, Incorporated; USA, 1972

293.
B) LAWN MOWER
- ☞ Assistant Commissioner for Patents; United States Patent Office, Archive Records, Washington, D.C., 20231, May 1899 Patent No. 624, 749.

Additional Information:
☞ Black Inventors of America, McKinley Burt, National Book Co; Oregon, 1969.
☞ Blacks in Science: Ancient and Modern, Ivan Van Sertima, (ed.), Transaction; USA, 1985, p.218.
☞ Blacks in Science: Astrophysicist to Zoologist. Hattie Carwell, USA, 1977, p.76.

294.
B) KIDNEY
☞ Blacks in Science: Astrophysicist to Zoologist. Hattie Carwell, USA, 1977, pp.40-41.
Additional Information:
☞ Great Negroes: Past and Present. Russell L. Adams, Afro-Am Publishing Company; Chicago, Illinois, 3rd Edition (1981).
☞ National Library of Medicine, 8600 Rockville Pike, Rockville, Maryland, 20894, USA.
☞ 1999 Facts About Blacks: A Sourcebook of African American Accomplishment. Raymond M. Corbin, Beckham House Publishers; USA, 1st Edition, 1986, p.50

295.
B) THE STARS
☞ Science, Volume 200, May 16, 1978, USA.
Additional Information:
☞ Black Makers of History. The Real McCoy, Frank Forde, Lesnah Hall and Virginia McLean, The Book Place; 1988, p.17.
☞ Nile Valley Contributions to Civilization; Exploding the Myths, Volume 1, Anthony T. Browder, Institute of Khamic Guidance; Washington, D.C., 2000, pp.75
☞ Crash Course in Black History: 150 Important Facts About African Peoples, Zak A. Kondo, Nubia Press; USA, 1988.

296.
A) QUANTUM PHYSICS
☞ Science Magazine, "Elmer Samuel Imes", W. F. G. Swann, December 26, 1941, USA, pp.600-1.
Additional Information:
☞ (HF Zietschrift Fur Natur Forschug Teil A Physik, Physikair Sche, Chemmie, Kosmophy,) "Vibrational Analysis of Polymeric Hydrogen Fluoride Cylclic", S. J. Cyvin, et al, Norway, 1973, p.1781.

☞ Ideology of Racism. Samuel Kennedy Yeboah, Hansib Publishing; 1988, UK, p.221.
☞ Journal of African Civilizations, Transactions Periodicals Consortium; Rutgers University, New Brunswick, New Jersey, "Black Space", James G. Spady, September 1980, p.263.

297.
C) PRINTING PRESS
☞ Assistant Commissioner for Patents; United States Patent Office, Archive Records, Washington, D.C., 20231. September 17, 1878 Patent No. 208, 208.
Additional Information:
☞ Blacks in Science: Astrophysicist to Zoologist. Hattie Carwell, USA, 1977, p.81.
☞ Black Scientists and Inventors Millennium Calendar 1999, BIS Publications; P.O. Box 14918, London, N17 8WJ.
☞ Great Negroes: Past and Present. Russell L. Adams, Afro-Am Publishing Company; Chicago, Illinois, 3rd Edition (1981) p.59.

298.
C) RICHARD HILL
☞ A Bibliography of Richard Hill: Negro Scholar, Scientist, Native of Spanish Town, Jamaica. William Almon Griffey, Matuchen Books; New Jersey, 1932.
Additional Information:
☞ Staying Power, Peter Fryer, Pluto Press; 2nd Edition, UK, 1985, p.437.
☞ World's Great Men of Color, Volume II, J. A. Rogers, Collier Macmillan Publishers; 1972, pp.258- 61.
☞ A Naturalist's Sojourn in Jamaica, Philip Henry and Richard Hill, Longman, Brown Green and Longmans; London, 1851.

299.
C) GUINEA-WORM DISEASE
☞ New African, April 2000, ICP Ltd.; London, p.24.
Additional Information:
☞ Norwegian Nobel Committee, Drammensveien 19, N/0255, Oslow, Norway.
☞ Our Story: A Hand Book of African History and Contemporary Issues, Edited by Akyaaba Addai-Sebo and Ansel Wong, London Strategic Policy; 1988, pp.62-93.

☞ The Swiss Contribution to Western Civilization, Raphael E. G. Armattoe, W. Tempest; Dundalk, 1944.

300.
B) SPARK PLUG
☞ Blacks in Science: Astrophysicist to Zoologist. Hattie Carwell, USA, 1977, p.90.
Additional Information:
☞ Black Inventors of America, McKinley Burt, National Book Co; Oregon, 1969.
☞ Assistant Commissioner for Patents; United States Patent Office, Archive Records, Washington, D.C.
☞ Black Scientists and Inventors Millennium Calendar 1999, BIS Publications; P.O. Box 14918, London, N17 8WJ.

301.
B) CONTROL UNIT FOR PACEMAKERS
☞ Blacks in Science: Astrophysicist to Zoologist. Hattie Carwell, USA, 1977.
Additional Information:
☞ Blacks in Science: Ancient and Modern, Ivan Van Sertima, (ed.), Transaction; USA, 1985, pp.215, 226.
☞ 1999 Facts About Blacks: A Sourcebook of African American Accomplishment. Raymond M. Corbin, Beckham House Publishers; USA, 1st Edition, 1986, p.38.
☞ Ideology of Racism. Samuel Kennedy Yeboah, Hansib Publishing; 1988, UK, p.202.

302.
A) GENES
☞ Blacks in Science: Astrophysicist to Zoologist. Hattie Carwell, USA, 1977, p.25.
Additional Information:
☞ National Library of Medicine, 8600 Rockville Pike, Rockville, Maryland, 20894, USA.
☞ Peninsula Bulletine, February 7, 1976.
☞ Negroes in Science: National Science Doctorates 1876-1969. James M. Jay, Balamp Publishing; Detroit, 1971.

303.
C) REFRIGERATOR
☞ Assistant Commissioner for Patents; United States Patent Office, Archive Records, Washington, D.C., 14th July 1891, Patent No. 455, 891.

Additional Information:
☞ Ebony, Johnson Publishing; Chicago, February, 1997, pp.42-46.
☞ Blacks in Science: Astrophysicist to Zoologist. Hattie Carwell, USA, 1977.
☞ Great Negroes: Past and Present. Russell L. Adams, Afro-Am Publishing Company; Chicago, Illinois, 3rd Edition (1981) p.59.

304.
C) THE EDWIN SMITH PAPYRUS
☞ Nile Valley Contributions to Civilization; Exploding the Myths, Volume 1, Anthony T. Browder, Institute of Khamic Guidance; Washington, D.C., 2000, p.125.
Additional Information:
☞ Ancient Times, James H. Breasted, Ginn & Company; Boston, Mass., 1935.
☞ Journal of African Civilizations. Vol. 1., Transactions Periodicals Consortium; Rutgers University, New Brunswick, New Jersey, November 1979.
☞ The African Background to Medical Science Essays in African History, Science & Civilisation, Charles S. Finch, Karnak House; London, 1990.

305.
B) PROXIMA CENTAURI
☞ Hutchingson Encyclopedia, 8th Edition, Hutchingson; UK, 1988.
Additional Information:
☞ The 1997 Guinness Book of Records, Guinness Publishing Ltd.; UK, 1996, p.11.
☞ Seeing the Stars: The BBC Television Series, Patrick Moor, British Broadcasting Company.
☞ New! Encyclopaedia Britannica Print Set, 2002 Edition.

306.
A) AIRSHIP
☞ Assistant Commissioner for Patents; United States Patent Office, Archive Records, Washington, D.C., 20231, February 20, 1900, Patent No. 643, 975.
Additional Information:
☞ Black Scientists and Inventors, Ava Henry and Michael Williams, (eds.), BIS Publications; London, 1999.
☞ Blacks in Science: Astrophysicist to Zoologist. Hattie Carwell, USA, 1977, p.84.

☞ Black Inventors of America, McKinley Burt, National Book Co; Oregon, 1969.

307.
B) KERATIN

☞ The African Origin of Civilization: Myth or Reality, Cheikh Anta Diop, translated by Mercer Cook, Lawrence Hill & Company; 1974, p.281.

Additional Information:

☞ Vitamins and Minerals, From A-Z, Dr. Jewel Pookram, A & B Publishers; Brooklyn, NY, 1993.

☞ Melanin, A key to Freedom, UB & US Communications Systems, Inc.; Second Printing, Virginia, 1995.

☞ Melanin, The Chemical Key to Black Greatness, The Harmful Effects of Toxic Drugs on Melanin Centers Within the Black Human, Melanin Technologies; Texas, 1988.

308.
A) HENRIETTA LACKS

☞ A Conspiracy of Cells: One Woman's Immortal Legacy and the Medical Scandal it Caused, Michael Gold, State University of New York Press; 1986.

Additional Information:

☞ The Sunday Times Magazine, London, March 16, 1997, pp.47-51.

☞ National Library of Medicine, 8600 Rockville Pike, Rockville, Maryland, 20894, USA.

☞ The Voice, The Voice Group Ltd.; London, January 24, 1995, p.21.

309.
C) SHIPS FOR THE U.S. NAVY

☞ Assistant Commissioner for Patents; United States Patent Office, Archive Records, Washington, D.C., 20231, No. 451,086.

Additional Information:

☞ Black Inventors of America, McKinley Burt, National Book Co; Oregon, 1969.

☞ Blacks in Science: Astrophysicist to Zoologist. Hattie Carwell, USA, 1977, p.88.

☞ Black Pioneers of Science and Invention, Louis Haber, Harcourt, Brace & World, Inc.; New York, 1970.

310.
A) SEED PLANTER

☞ Blacks in Science: Ancient and Modern, Ivan Van Sertima, (ed.), Transaction; USA, 1985, p.217.

Additional Information:

☞ Assistant Commissioner for Patents; United States Patent Office, Archive Records, Washington, D.C., 20231.

☞ The Colored Inventor, Henry Baker, Arno Press; New York, 1969.

☞ Negro Almanac 1989, USA, pp.1079-1424.

311.
A) TRAIN ALARM

☞ Assistant Commissioner for Patents; United States Patent Office, Archive Records, Washington, D.C., 20231, No. 584, 540.

Additional Information:

☞ Blacks in Science: Ancient and Modern, Ivan Van Sertima, (ed.), Transaction; USA, 1985, p.218.

☞ Black Inventors of America, McKinley Burt, National Book Co; Oregon, 1969.

☞ Black Scientists and Inventors, Ava Henry and Michael Williams, (eds.), BIS Publications; London, 1999.

312.
B) STEAM ENGINE

☞ History of Science: Ancient and Medieval, Rene Taton, (ed.), Basic Books; 1957, USA.

Additional Information:

☞ Blacks in Science: Ancient and Modern, Ivan Van Sertima, (ed.), Transaction; USA, 1985, pp.190-91.

☞ A Short History of Greek Mathematics, James Gow, G. E. Stechert & Co.; New York, 1923, p.285.

☞ Nile Valley Contributions to Civilization; Exploding the Myths, Volume 1, Anthony T. Browder, Institute of Khamic Guidance; Washington, D.C., 2000, p.163.

313.
C) PAPYRUS OF MOSCOW

☞ Great African Thinkers. Volume 1, Cheikh Anta Diop, Edited by Ivan Van Sertima, Transaction; USA, 1987, p.74.

Additional Information:
- ☞ Blacks in Science: Ancient and Modern, Ivan Van Sertima, (ed.), Transaction; USA, 1985.
- ☞ Journal of African Civilizations. Vol. 1., Transactions Periodicals Consortium; Rutgers University, New Brunswick, New Jersey, November 1979.
- ☞ Africa Counts: Number and Patern in African Culture. Prindlee, Weber & Scmidt; USA.

314.
B) QUARANTINE AND SANITATION
- ☞ African Presence in Early Europe, Edited by Ivan Van Sertima, Transaction; 1986, p.194.

Additional Information:
- ☞ Centenary Edition on the Birth of Sousa Martins (Imprensa Medica Centenario Do Nascimento Do José Tomaz De Sousa Martins) Ano, No. 5, March 10, 1943.
- ☞ World's Great Men of Color, Volume II, J. A. Rogers, Collier Macmillan Publishers; 1972, pp.138- 41.
- ☞ Medicos Portuguese Revista Bio-Bibliographica, Volume 1, No. 3, May 1926.

315.
C) MEHARRY MEDICAL COLLEGE
- ☞ Meharry Medical College, 1005 D. B. Todd Blvd., Nashville, TN., 37208-3599.

Additional Information:
- ☞ Against the Odds: Blacks in the Profession of Medicine in the United States. Wilbur H. Watson, Transaction; 1999.
- ☞ Ebony Pictorial History of Black America: Volume 3. Civil Rights Movement to Black Revolution, Johnson Publishing Company; 1974.
- ☞ 1999 Facts About Blacks: A Sourcebook of African American Accomplishment. Raymond M. Corbin, Beckham House Publishers; USA, 1st Edition, 1986, p.33.

316.
A) THE ROUND TOWER OF ABERNATHY
- ☞ Ancient and Modern Britons. David MacRitchie, Volume 1, Keegan Paul, Trench & Co.; 1985, p.110.

Additional Information:
- ☞ The Black Celts, A. Ali & I. Ali, Punite Publications; Cardiff, 1993.
- ☞ Archaeology of Scotland, D. Wilson, Edinburgh, 1851.
- ☞ Celtic Scotland, William F. Skene, Vols. 1-3, Freeport, New York, 1876.

317.
A) INTERNATIONAL RED CROSS
- ☞ Third World Impact. 8th Edition, Edited by Arif Ali, Hansib Publishing; 1988, p.236.

Additional Information:
- ☞ The Black Press in Britain, Ionie Benjamin, Trentham Books; London, 1995, p.16.
- ☞ Black Settlers in Britain, 1555-1958, Nigel File and Chris, Power, Heinemann Educational Books; UK, 1981.
- ☞ Staying Power, Peter Fryer, Pluto Press; UK, 2nd Edition, 1985.

318.
B) $50,000
- ☞ 1999 Facts About Blacks: A Sourcebook of African American Accomplishment. Raymond M. Corbin, Beckham House Publishers; USA, 1st Edition, 1986, p.5.

Additional Information:
- ☞ The Colored Inventor, Henry Baker, Arno Press; New York, 1969.
- ☞ Blacks in Science: Astrophysicist to Zoologist. Hattie Carwell, USA, 1977, p.75.
- ☞ Black Inventors of America, McKinley Burt, National Book Co; Oregon, 1969.

319.
A) NATIONAL MEDICAL ASSOCIATION
- ☞ Against the Odds: Blacks in the Profession of Medicine in the United States. Wilbur H. Watson, Transaction; 1999.

Additional Information:
- ☞ Ebony, Johnson Publishing; Chicago, July, 1995, p.122.
- ☞ 1999 Facts About Blacks: A Sourcebook of African American Accomplishment. Raymond M. Corbin, Beckham House Publishers; USA, 1st Edition, 1986.
- ☞ Ebony Pictorial History of Black America: Volume 3. Civil Rights Movement to Black Revolution, Johnson Publishing Company; 1974.

Science & Engineering

320.
C) SYPHILIS
☞ 1999 Facts About Blacks: A Sourcebook of African American Accomplishment. Raymond M. Corbin, Beckham House Publishers; USA, 1st Edition, 1986, p.11.
Additional Information:
☞ World's Great Men of Color, J. A. Rogers, Volume II, Collier Macmillan Publishers; 1972, p.561.
☞ Blacks in Science: Astrophysicist to Zoologist. Hattie Carwell, USA, 1977, p.58.
☞ Against the Odds: Blacks in the Profession of Medicine in the United States Wilbur H. Watson, Transaction; 1999.

321.
B) TELEPHONE
☞ 1999 Facts About Blacks: A Sourcebook of African American Accomplishment. Raymond M. Corbin, Beckham House Publishers; USA, 1st Edition, 1986, p.11.
Additional Information:
☞ Black Inventors of America, McKinley Burt, National Book Co; Oregon, 1969.
☞ Blacks in Science: Astrophysicist to Zoologist. Hattie Carwell, USA, 1977, p.85.
☞ Black Scientists and Inventors, Ava Henry and Michael Williams, (eds.), BIS Publications; London, 1999.

322.
C) 105
☞ 1999 Facts About Blacks: A Sourcebook of African American Accomplishment. Raymond M. Corbin, Beckham House Publishers; USA, 1st Edition, 1986, p.14.
Additional Information:
☞ Blacks in Science: Astrophysicist to Zoologist. Hattie Carwell, USA, 1977, pp.27-28.
☞ National Library of Medicine, 8600 Rockville Pike, Rockville, Maryland, 20894, USA.
☞ Eyewitness: The Negro in America, William L. Katz, Pittman Publishing; New York, 1968.

323.
A) LETTER BOX
☞ Assistant Commissioner for Patents; United States Patent Office, Archive Records, Washington, D.C., 20231, October 27, 1891, Patent No. 462,093 and October 4, 1892, Patent No. 483, 525.
Additional Information:
☞ Blacks in Science: Astrophysicist to Zoologist. Hattie Carwell, USA, 1977, pp.27-28.
☞ Black Inventors of America, McKinley Burt, National Book Co; Oregon, 1969.
☞ Black Scientists and Inventors, Ava Henry and Michael Williams, (eds.), BIS Publications; London, 1999.

324.
B) BISON
☞ The Black Cowboy: The Life and Legend of George McJunkin, By Franklin Folson, US (www.amazon.com)
Additional Information:
☞ The Voice, The Voice Group Ltd.; London, 10 February, 2003, p.23.
☞ The Black Cowboys (African-American Achievers), Gina De Angelis, Chelsea House Publishers; 1997.
☞ The Negro Cowboys, Philip Durham and Everett L. Jones (Photographer), University of Nebraska Press; 1983.

325.
B) AUTOMATIC GEAR SHIFT
☞ Assistant Commissioner for Patents; United States Patent Office, Archive Records, Washington, D.C., 20231, December 6, 1932 Patent No. 1, 889, 814.
Additional Information:
☞ New African, April 2000, ICP Ltd.; London, p.24.
☞ Blacks in Science: Astrophysicist to Zoologist. Hattie Carwell, USA, 1977, p.87.
☞ Black Inventors of America, McKinley Burt, National Book Co; Oregon, 1969.

326.
C) INDUCTION RAILWAY TELEGRAPH
☞ 1999 Facts About Blacks: A Sourcebook of African American Accomplishment. Raymond M. Corbin, Beckham House Publishers; USA, 1st Edition, 1986, p.81.

Additional Information:

☞ Black Inventors of America, McKinley Burt, National Book Co; Oregon, 1969.

☞ Blacks in Science: Ancient and Modern, Ivan Van Sertima, (ed.), Transaction; USA, 1985, pp.215, 220.

☞ Ideology of Racism. Samuel Kennedy Yeboah, Hansib Publishing; UK, 1988, p.192.

327.
B) NIGERIA

☞ Financial Times, London, July 6, 2001.

Additional Information:

☞ The Voice, The Voice Group Ltd.; September 10, 2001, pp.1, 4.

☞ Reuters News Agency, August 1, 2001.

☞ African Business, December 1998, No.238, ICP Ltd.; London.

328.
C) ALZHEIMER'S

☞ Ebony, Johnson Publishing; Chicago, February, 2000.

Additional Information:

☞ New African, April 2000, ICP Ltd.; London, p.25.

☞ 1999 Facts About Blacks: A Sourcebook of African American Accomplishment. Raymond M. Corbin, Beckham House Publishers; USA, 1st Edition, 1986, p.41.

☞ Blacks in Science: Astrophysicist to Zoologist. Hattie Carwell, USA, 1977, p.48.

329.
B) PENCIL SHARPENER

☞ Assistant Commissioner for Patents; United States Patent Office, Archive Records, Washington, D.C., 20231, October 11, 1897 Patent No. 594, 114.

Additional Information:

☞ Blacks in Science: Astrophysicist to Zoologist. Hattie Carwell, USA, 1977, p.82.

☞ Black Inventors of America, McKinley Burt, National Book Co; Oregon, 1969.

☞ Pride, London, May 1997, 118-19.

330.
A) SATELLITE TRACKER

☞ NASA H.Q., Administrators Office, Code-A, Washington, D.C., 20546, USA.

Additional Information:

☞ Black Contributions to the Engineering and Science Fields at NASA Lewis Research Center, Cleveland, NASA Lewis Research Center, 1975.

☞ The Voice, The Voice Group Ltd.; London, October 18, 1999, p.18.

☞ Blacks in Science: Astrophysicist to Zoologist. Hattie Carwell, USA, 1977, p.90.

331.
B) STREET SWEEPER

☞ Assistant Commissioner for Patents; United States Patent Office, Archive Records, Washington, D.C., 20231, Patent No. 556, 711; and No. 560, 154; and No. 558, 719.

Additional Information:

☞ Black Inventors of America, McKinley Burt, National Book Co; Oregon, 1969.

☞ Blacks in Science: Astrophysicist to Zoologist. Hattie Carwell, USA, 1977, p.76.

☞ Black Scientists and Inventors, Ava Henry and Michael Williams, (eds.), Publications; London, 1999.

332.
B) CLOCK

☞ The Black American Reference Book. Mabel M. Smyth, (ed.), Prentice-Hall Inc.; USA, 1976, pp.20, 411, 453.

Additional Information:

☞ The Life of Benjamin Banneker, Silvio A. Bendini, USA, 1972.

☞ Black Makers of History. The Real McCoy, Frank Forde, Lesnah Hall and Virginia McLean, The Book Place; 1988, p.71.

☞ Black Scientists and Inventors, Ava Henry and Michael Williams, (eds.), BIS Publications; London, 1999.

General Knowledge

Answers and Sources

333.
B) FOR US BY US
☞ FUBU, The Collection, 350 Fifth Avenue, Suite 6617, New York, NY, 10118
Additional Information:
☞ Crain's Book of Lists 2001, New York, NY, USA, 2000.
☞ Smart Money Magazine (SmartMoney.com) December 27, 2000.
☞ Vibe, Quincy Jones and David Salzman Entertainment, Time Publishing Inc.; February, 1996, p.14.

334.
B) IMAN
☞ Who's Who of Black Achievers, John Hughes, (ed.), Ethnic Media Group; UK, 1999, p.67.
Additional Information:
☞ The Mirror, Mirror Newspaper Group; August 3, 1999, p.25.
☞ Ebony, Johnson Publishing; Chicago, August, 1995, pp.116-22.
☞ Vogue Magazine, Library Archives, 350 Maddison Avenue, New York, NY, 10017, USA.

335.
A) THIRD MONDAY IN JANUARY
☞ African American Holidays, James C. Anyike, Volume 1, Popular Truth, Inc.; Chicago, IL, 1991.
Additional Information:
☞ Ebony, Johnson Publishing; Chicago, January, 1997, p.31.
☞ Chronicle of the Twentieth Century, Jacques Legrand, Longman Books; 1988, p.1262.
☞ Ebony, Johnson Publishing; Chicago, February, 2001, p.126.

336.
B) ILLUSIONIST
☞ Mysterious Stranger: A Book of Magic, David Blaine, Villard Pulishing, 1st edition, 2002.
Additional Information:
☞ The Evening Standard, Associated Newspaper Group; London, 30 September, 2003, p.23.
☞ David Blaine – Fearless: DVD, Buena Vista Home Video, USA (Canada), 2002.

☞ The Evening Standard, Associated Newspaper Group; London, 20 October, 2003.

337.
C) ICE CREAM
☞ 999 Facts About Blacks: A Sourcebook of African American Accomplishment. Raymond M. Corbin, Beckham House Publishers; USA, 1st Edition, 1986, p.46.
Additional Information:
☞ The Voice, The Voice Group Ltd.; London, December 6, 1999, p.57.
☞ Ice Cream, W. S. Arbuckle, Chapman & Hall; USA, 1986, p.3.
☞ Assistant Commissioner for Patents; United States Patent Office, Archive Records, Washington, D.C., 20231, February 2, 1897, Patent No. 576, 395. "Ice Cream Mold/Scooper",

338.
A) MISS AMERICA
☞ The Miss America Organization, 2 Miss America Way, Suite 1000, Atlantic City, NJ, 08401, USA.
Additional Information:
☞ Black Firsts: 2000 Years of Extraordinary Achievement. Jessie Carney Smith, Caspar L. Jordan and Robert L. Johns, Visible Ink Press; USA, 1994, p.259.
☞ Ebony, Johnson Publishing; Chicago, August, 1995, pp.120-22.
☞ Black Women in America, USA, pp.409, 1266-1268.

339.
C) BLACK STAR SHIPPING LINE
☞ Marcus Garvey, 1887-1940, Adolph Edwards, New Beacon Publishers; London, 1967.
Additional Information:
☞ Marcus Garvey: Message to the People. Edited by Tony Martin, Foreword by The Honorary Charles L. James, New Marcus Garvey Library; Book No. 7, 1986.
☞ The Black Press in Britain, Ionie Benjamin, Trentham Books; London, 1995, p.18.
☞ Garvey and Garveyism, Amy Jacques Garvey, Kingston, Jamaica, 1963, Collier Books; New York, 1970.

340.
B) BAGGY CLOTHES
☞ The Voice, The Voice Group Ltd.;
London, November 15, 1994, p.14.
Additional Information:
☞ Vibe, Quincy Jones and David Salzman
Entertainment, Time Publishing Inc.;
February, 1996, p.83.
☞ The Weekly Journal, Voice
Communications; London, June 23,
1994, p.9.
☞ Karl Kani, Sales Dept., 1385 Broadway,
New York, New York, 10018.

341.
A) HIBISCUS
☞ The Well Planned Garden, Sue Phillips,
Weidenfield & Nicolson; London, 1988,
pp.113-14.
Additional Information:
☞ The Voice, The Voice Group Limited;
May 19, 1997, p.5.
☞ Jamaica: The Fairest Isle, Phillip
Sherlock and Berber Preston, UK.
☞ Cambridge Encyclopedia, David Crystal,
Cambridge University Press; 4th Edition,
2000.

342.
B) WASHINGTON, D.C.
☞ The Black American Reference Book.
Mabel M. Smyth, (ed.), Prentice-Hall
Inc.; USA, 1976, pp.20, 411, 453.
Additional Information:
☞ Black Makers of History. The Real
McCoy, Frank Forde, Lesnah Hall and
Virginia McLean, The Book Place;
1988, p.71.
☞ Eyewitness: The Negro in America,
William L. Katz, Pittman Publishing;
New York, 1968.
☞ Seven Black American Scientists, Robert
C. Hayden, Addisonian Press;
Massachusettes, 1970.

343.
B) RESURRECTION AND IMMORTALITY
☞ The Gods of the Egyptians, E. A. Wallis
Budge, Dover Publications Inc.; NY,
1969.
Additional Information:
☞ Nile Valley Contributions to Civilization;
Exploding the Myths, Volume 1, Anthony
T. Browder, Institute of Khamic Guidance;
Washington, D.C., 2000, p.83.

☞ Black Athena: The Afroasiatic Roots of
Classical Civilsation, Vols. 1 & 2, Martin
Bernal, FAB; London, 1991.
☞ Black Man of the Nile and His Family.
Dr. Yosef A. A. Ben Jochannon, Black
Classic Press; Baltimore, MD, 1988.

344.
C) THE OLYMPIC RINGS
☞ International Olympic Committee, Public
Relations department, Avenue de la
Gare, No. 10, 1003 Lausanne,
Switzerland.
Additional Information:
☞ Olympics: Facts and Feats, Stan
Greenberry, Guinness Publishing; 1996,
p.94.
☞ Chronicle of the Twentieth Century,
Jacques Legrand, Longman Books; 1988,
pp.1110-1111.
☞ Chronicle of the Olympics, 1896-1996,
Dorling Kindersley Publishing; UK, 1996.

345.
A) PLANT
☞ Nomads Who Cultivate Beauty, Mette
Bovin, Transaction; New Jersey, 2001.
Additional Information:
☞ The Encyclopedia of Africa, Franklin
Watts, Inc.; New York and London,
1976.
☞ Cambridge Encyclopedia, David Crystal,
Cambridge University Press; 1990,
p.200.
☞ African Kingdoms, Basil Davidson, Time-
Life Books; (Nederland), 1980.

346.
B) JOHANNESBURG
☞ Macdonalds Encyclopedia of Africa,
Macdonald Educational Ltd.; UK, 1986.
Additional Information:
☞ Tutu: Voice of the Voiceless, Shirley Du
Boulay, Hodder & Stoughton; 1988.
☞ African Political Facts Since 1945, Cook
& Killingray, Macmillan Press Ltd.; 1983.
☞ Steve Biko: Black Consciousness in South
Africa, Millard Arnold, Vintage Books;
New York, 1979.

347.
A) THUMB PIANO
☞ The Music of Africa, J. H. Kwabena
Nketia, Victor Gollancz Ltd.; London,
1979, pp.77- 84.

Additional Information:
- African History for Beginners, Herb Boyd, Writers & Readers Publishing, Inc.; London, New York, 1994, p.21.
- African Music: A People's Art, translated by Josephine Bennet, Lawrence Hill & Co.; Westport, UK, 1995.
- African All Stars: The Pop Music of a continent, Chris Stapleton and Chris May, Paladin; London, Glasgow, Toronto, Sydney, Auckland, 1989.

348.
A) FOXWOODS RESORT
- Foxwoods Resort, P.O. Box 3777, Mashantuzket, CN., 06332, USA.
Additional Information:
- Ebony, Johnson Publishing; Chicago, June, 1995, pp.46-50.
- The New Nation, Western Hemisphere; London, March 17, 1997, p.17.
- Without Reservation: The Making of America's Most Powerful Indian Tribe and Foxwoods, the World's Largest Casino, Jeff Benedict, HarperCollins; USA, 2001.

349.
C) ISLAM
- Islam: A Short History, Karen Armstrong, Random House; New York, 2000.
Additional Information:
- The Guardian, Guardian Newspapers; London, December 7, 1996.
- A Book of Beliefs, John Allen, John Butterworth, Myrtle Langley, Lion Publishing; UK, 1981.
- Islam Today: A Short Introduction to the Muslim World, Akbar S. Ahmed, I. B. Tauris & Co Ltd.; UK, 1999.

350.
C) CHESS
- Lasker Chess Manual, Emmanuel Lasker, Fitzhouse Books; 1991, p.1.
Additional Information:
- Sports and Games of Ancient Egypt, Wolfgang Deike (translated by Allen Guttmann), Yale University Press; New Haven and London, 1992.
- Women in Chess: Players of the Modern Age, John Graham, MacFarland & Company, Inc.; USA, 1987.
- Chess History, Harry Golombek, G. P. Putnam's Sons; New York, 1976.

351.
B) APOLLO THEATRE
- Amateur Night at the Apollo: Ralph Cooper Presents Five decades of Great Entertainment. Ralph Cooper with Steve Dougherty, HarperCollins; New York, 1990.

Additional Information:
- This Was Harlem 1900-1950, Jervis Anderson, Farrah, Straus, Giroux; New York, 1982.
- On the Real Side: A History of African American Comedy. Mel Watkins, Lawrence Hill; USA, 1999, pp.503-4, 518-19.
- Showtime at the Apollo, Ted Fox, Holt, Rhinehart and Winston; USA, 1983.

352.
A) BOOKER T. WASHINGTON
- Booker T. Washington and the Negro's Place in American Life, Samuel R. Spencer, Little, Brown; Boston, USA, 1955.
Additional Information:
- Jet, Johnson Publishing Co.; Chicago, June 28, 1993, pp.48-51.
- Booker T. Washington. Shirley Graham, Messner; New York, 1955.
- They Showed the Way Up, Charlemae Hill Rollins, Thomas Y. Crowell Company; New York, 1964, pp.141-42.

353.
A) TALLEST PEOPLE
- The Guinness Book of Records 2003, Guinness Publishing Ltd.; UK, 2002.
Additional Information:
- The Voice, The Voice Group Ltd.; London, 18 February 2002, p.7.
- Tall Clubs International, 741 Winterside Circle, San Ramon, CA 94583, USA.
- Irish Examiner, February 19, 2002.

354.
A) MEXICO
- Mysteries of the Mexican Pyramids, Harper & Row; London, 1976.
Additional Information:
- Mexico, Robert Marett, Thames & Hudson; London, 1971, pp.16, 44, 48.
- The 1997 Guinness Book of Records, Guinness Publishing Ltd.; UK, 1996, p.229.

They Came Before Columbus: African Presence in Ancient America, Ivan Van Sertima, Random House; USA, 1976, pp.155-56, 227.

355.
B) THE PJS
☞ Growing Up Laughing With Eddie Murphy, Harris Haith, Authorhouse Publishers; US, 2003
Additional Information:
☞ www.pazsaz.com/pjs.html
☞ www.nyls.edu/docs/collier.text
☞ Eddie Murphy: The Life and Times of a Comic on the Edge, Frank Sanello, Birch Lane Press; US, 1997

356.
B) MORRIS DANCING
☞ Ancient and Modern Britons. David MacRitchie, Volume 1, Keegan Paul, Trench & Co.; 1985, pp.53-54, 351, 390, 397.
Additional Information:
☞ Black Britannia: A History of Black People in Britain, Edward Scobie, Johnson Publishing Co.; 1972.
☞ Nature Knows No Color Line. J. A. Rogers, 3rd Edition, H. M. Rogers Publishers; 1952, p.87.
☞ History of Scotland, Buchanan, Book 1, Chapter 1, Pxxxiii.

357.
A) GORILLA
☞ My Apingi Kingdom, Paul Du Chaillu and Paul Belloni, Harper; New York, 1928.
Additional Information:
☞ Memories, Edward Clodd, Chapham and Hall; London, 1916.
☞ 100 Amazing Facts About the Negro: With Complete Proof, J. A. Rogers, H. M. Rogers Publishers; USA, 1995, p.66.
☞ The Black American Reference Book. Mabel M. Smyth, (ed.), Prentice-Hall Inc.; USA, 1976.

358.
B) ATLANTIC OCEAN
☞ Professor Arno Peters's Atlas of the World, Longman; London, 1989.
Additional Information:
☞ The Times of London Concise Atlas of the World, Times of London, (ed.), Crown Publishing; 2001.

New! Encyclopaedia Britannica Print Set, 2002 Edition.
☞ The Encyclopedia of Africa, Franklin Watts, Inc.; New York and London, 1976.

359.
B) REGINALD LEWIS
☞ Why Should White Guys Have All the Fun, Reginald Lewis and Blair S. Walker, John Wiley & Sons, Inc.; 1995.
Additional Information:
☞ Black Entrepreneurship in America, Shelly Green and Paul Pryde, Transaction; New Jersey, 1996.
☞ Ebony, Johnson Publishing; Chicago, USA, February 1994, p.90.
☞ TLC Beatrice, 9 West 57th Street, New York, NY, 10019, USA.

360.
C) SWASTIKA
☞ African Kingdoms, Basil Davidson, Time-Life Books; (Nederland), 1980, pp.134-35.
Additional Information:
☞ The Isis Papers, Dr. Frances Cress Welsing, Third World Press; Chicago, 1991, p.67.
☞ Africa: Mother of Western Civilisation, Dr. Yosef A. A Ben Jochannon, Black Classic Press; Baltimore, MD, 1988, p.438.
☞ Your History: From the Beginning of Time to the Present, J. A. Rogers, Black Classic Press; Baltimore, MD, 1983, p.33.

361.
A) COSMETICS
☞ Black Firsts: 2000 Years of Extraordinary Achievement. Jessie Carney Smith, Caspar L. Jordan and Robert L. Johns, Visible Ink Press; USA, 1994, pp.56-57, 58.
Additional Information:
☞ New African, April 2000, ICP Ltd.; London, p.25.
☞ Black Makers of History. The Real McCoy, Frank Forde, Lesnah Hall and Virginia McLean, The Book Place; 1988, p.10.
☞ Black Women for Beginners, Sandra Sharp, Writers and Readers Publishing, Inc.; New York, 1993, p.199.

General Knowledge

362.
B) BRUCE OLDFIELD
☞ The Mirror, Mirror Newspaper Group; April 24, 1997, p.24.

Additional Information:

☞ The Weekly Journal, Voice Communications; London, November 5, 1992, p.10.

☞ The Evening Standard, Associated Newspaper Group; London, January 20, 1997, p.58.

☞ The Voice, The Voice Group Ltd.; November 22, 1994, p.21.

363.
A) HIPPOPOTAMUS
☞ The Cambridge Encyclopedia of Africa, Cambridge University Press; 1981.

Additional Information:

☞ Macdonalds Encyclopedia of Africa, Macdonald Educational Ltd.; UK, 1986.

☞ Cambridge Encyclopedia, David Crystal, Cambridge University Press; 1990, p.569.

☞ Children's Encyclopedia, Harold Boswell Taylor, (ed.), Treasure Press; 1985, p.168.

364.
B) MOREHOUSE COLLEGE
☞ Ebony, Johnson Publishing; Chicago, May, 2003, pp.60-73.

Additional Information:

☞ Ebony, Johnson Publishing; Chicago, February, 1994, pp.50-56.

☞ Ebony Pictorial History of Black America: Volume 3. Civil Rights Movement to Black Revolution, Johnson Publishing Company; 1974, pp.137, 145.

☞ Encyclopedia of Black America, W. A. Low and Virgil A. Clift, (eds.), Mcgraw-Hill; New York, 1981.

365.
B) ST. LUCIA
☞ Caribbean Times, Hansib Publishing; London, December 17, 1994, p.8.

Additional Information:

☞ Jet, Johnson Publishing Co.; Chicago, November 1, 1979.

☞ The Black Press in Britain, Ionie Benjamin, Trentham Books; London, 1995, p.97.

☞ Time, Time Inc.; USA, October 19, 1992, pp.24, 65.

366.
C) ARABIC
☞ Cambridge Encyclopedia, David Crystal, Cambridge University Press; 4th Edition, 2000.

Additional Information:

☞ Caribbean and African Languages, Morgan Dalphinus, Karia Press; 1985.

☞ Africa A-Z, Robert S. Kane, Doubleday and Company Inc.; New York, 1972.

☞ The Africans, David Lamb, New York, Vintage Books; New York, 1983.

367.
C) FANNIE MAE
☞ Ebony, Johnson Publishing; Chicago, April, 2001, pp.106-112.

Additional Information:

☞ Fortune 500, Norman Pearlstine, (ed.), Michael Freberley Publ.; USA, 2000.

☞ Time, Time Inc.; February 10, 1997.

☞ FannieMae, 3900 Wisconsin Avenue, N.W., Washington, D.C., 20016, USA.

368.
C) FUNKI DREADS
☞ Who's Who of Black Achievers, John Hughes, (ed.), Ethnic Media Group; UK, 1999, p.32.

Additional Information:

☞ The Weekly Journal, Voice Communications; November 5, 1993, p.10.

☞ The New Nation, Western Hemisphere; London, September 8, 1997, pp.16, 45.

☞ NAACP, Educational Department, 260 Fifth Avenue, NY, NY 10001-6408.

369.
B) BILL PICKETT
☞ Guts: Legendary Black Rodeo Cowboy Bill Pickett, Cecil Johnson, Bill Pickett, June Ford, (ed.), Summit Publications; 1994.

Additional Information:

☞ The Guardian, Guardian Newspapers; London, September 8, 1983.

☞ Upscale, Upscale Communications Inc.; November 1995, p.105.

☞ Rodeo Cowboys in the North American Imagination, (Wilbur S. Shepperson Series in History and Humanities), Michael Allen, University of Nevada Press; 1998.

370.

A) BARBIE

☞ Mattel Inc.; 333 Continental Blvd., El Segundo, California, USA, 90245-5012

Additional Information:

☞ The Black Heritage Book of Trivia, Morgan White Jr., Quinlan Press; Boston, 1985, pp.91, 173.

☞ Ebony, Johnson Publishing; Chicago, September, 2001, p.83.

☞ Barbie, Reader's Digest Children's Books; Reader's Digest Publishing; UK, 2000.

371.

A) POTATO CHIP CRISPS

☞ Before the Mayflower: A History of Black America. Lerone Bennett Jr., 5th Edition, Penguin Books; 1984, p.650.

Additional Information:

☞ 1999 Facts About Blacks: A Sourcebook of African American Accomplishment. Raymond M. Corbin, Beckham House Publishers; USA, 1st Edition, 1986, pp.45, 46.

☞ Famous First Facts About Negroes, Romeo B. Garrett, Arno Press; USA, 1972.

☞ The Voice, The Voice Group Ltd.; London, December 6, 1999, p.57.

372.

C) MARIJUANA

☞ Rasta and Resistance, H. Campbell, Hansib Publishing Limited; UK, 1986.

Additional Information:

☞ The Voice, The Voice Group Limited; April 14, 1997, p.32.

☞ A Book of Beliefs, John Allen, John Butterworth, Myrtle Langley, Lion Publishing; UK, 1981, p.118.

☞ The Voice, The Voice Group Limited; June 6, 1995, pp.25-26.

373.

A) MOROCCO

☞ Macdonalds Encyclopedia of Africa, Macdonald Educational Ltd.; UK, 1986.

Additional Information:

☞ African Civilizations, Grakam Connah, Cambridge University Press; 1989.

☞ African Kingdoms, Basil Davidson, Time-Life Books; (Nederland), 1980.

☞ Cambridge Encyclopedia, David Crystal, Cambridge University Press; 1990, p.223.

374.

B) SCOTTISH

☞ Nature Knows No Color Line. J. A. Rogers, 3rd Edition, H. M. Rogers Publishers; 1952, p.32.

Additional Information:

☞ Your History: From the Beginning of Time to the Present, J. A. Rogers, Black Classic Press; Baltimore, MD, 1983, p.37.

☞ A Dictionary of World Mythology, Arthur Cotterell, Winward; UK, 1979.

☞ The Enclopaedia of Myths and Legends of all Nations, H. S. Robinson, Kaye & Ward, Ltd.; London, 1950.

375.

B) BRAZIL

☞ Professr Arno Peters's Atlas of the World, Longman; London, 1989. UK.

Additional Information:

☞ The Negro in Brazil, Arthur Romas, translated by Richard Datee, The Associated Publishers; Washington, D.C., 1951.

☞ Historia Do Brazil, Rocha Pombo, Volume 4, San Paulo, 1918.

☞ The Penguin Atlas of World History; From the Beginning to the Eve of the French Revolution. Vol. 1., Herman Kinder and Werner Hilgemann.

376.

C) JOHNSON PRODUCTS

☞ Jet, Johnson Publishing Co.; Chicago, November 18, 1995, p.16.

Additional Information:

☞ Encyclopedia of Black America, W. A. Low and Virgil A. Clift, (eds.), Mcgraw-Hill; New York, 1981, p.473.

☞ Ebony Success Library, Vol 2, Johnson Publishing; USA, pp.126-29.

☞ Famous First Blacks, Sterlin G. Alford, USA, p.76.

377.

B) BLACK HOLOCAUST MUSEUM

☞ A Time of Terror. A Survivors Story. James Cameron, Writers & Readers; London, 1995.

Additional Information:

☞ The Weekly Journal, Voice Communications; London, 22nd June 1995, p.12.

☞ "Everyman:" 'Unforgiven. The Legacy of a Lynching', June 18, 1995, British-Broadcasting Corporation, Library Archives, W12.

☞ America's Black Holocaust Museum, 2233 North Fourth Street, Milwaukee, 53212, USA.

378.
C) KALAHARI
☞ Cambridge Encyclopedia, David Crystal, Cambridge University Press; 1990, p.650.
Additional Information:
☞ Professor Arno Peters's Atlas of the World, Longman; London, 1989. UK.
☞ The Encyclopedia of Africa, Franklin Watts, Inc.; New York and London, 1976.
☞ Africa A-Z, Robert S. Kane, Doubleday and Company Inc.; New York, 1972.

379.
A) CHICAGO
☞ What They Never Told You in History Class, Indus Khamit-Kush, Luxorr Publications; USA, 1983, p.278.
Additional Information:
☞ Your History: From the Beginning of Time to the Present, J. A. Rogers, Black Classic Press; Baltimore, MD, 1983, p.87.
☞ The Black American Reference Book. Mabel M. Smyth, (ed.), Prentice-Hall Inc.; USA, 1976.
☞ The Black Heritage Book of Trivia, Morgan White Jr., Quinlan Press; Boston, 1985, pp.4, 119.

380.
B) GODDESS OF CHASTITY
☞ Black Women in Antiquity, Edited by Ivan Van Sertima, Transaction; 7th. Edition, 1992, pp.127, 164
Additional Information:
☞ Book of the Beginnings, Gerald Massey, Volume 1, New York, 1930, p.18.
☞ Sex and Race, Volume 1., J. A. Rogers, 9th Edition, H. M. Rogers Publishers; USA, 1968, p.279.
☞ Scientific Monthly, Volume 73, "The Black Madonna: An Example of Culture Borrrowing", Leonard W. Moss and Stephen C. Cappannari, 1953.

381.
B) TUSKEGEE INSTITUTE
☞ Up From Slavery; An Autobiography, Booker T. Washington, Transaction; New Jersey, 1991.
Additional Information:
☞ The Man Farthest Down, Booker T. Washington and Robert E. Park, Transaction; New Jersey, 1983.
☞ Booker T. Washington and the Negro's Place in American Life, Samuel R. Spencer, Little, Brown; Boston, USA, 1955.
☞ They Showed the Way Up, Charlemae Hill Rollins, Thomas Y. Crowell Company; New York, 1964, pp.141-42.

382.
A) DIAMOND
☞ The 1997 Guinness Book of Records, Guinness Publishing Ltd.; UK, 1996, p.104.
Additional Information:
☞ The Voice, The Voice Group Ltd.; March 29, 1994, p.5.
☞ Cambridge Encyclopedia, David Crystal, Cambridge University Press; 1990, p.324.
☞ Tower of London, General Enquiries, Tower Hill, London, EC1.

383.
C) LUCY
☞ Lucy: The Beginning of Human Kind. D. C. Johnson and M. A. Eden, Granada; 1981.
Additional Information:
☞ Life Magazine, November 1981, USA.
☞ The New York Times, June 11, 1982.
☞ The Daily ExPress; London, November 5, 1992.

384.
A) FALCON
☞ The Gods of the Egyptians, E. A. Wallis Budge, Dover Publications Inc.; NY, 1969.
Additional Information:
☞ A Dictionary of World Mythology, Arthur Cotterell, Winward; UK, 1979.
☞ Nile Valley Contributions to Civilization; Exploding the Myths, Volume 1, Anthony T. Browder, Institute of Khamic Guidance; Washington, D.C., 2000, p.55.

The Power of Myth, Joseph Campbell with Bill Moyers, Doubleday; New York, NY, 1988.

385.
B) ACKEE
☞ The Weekly Journal, Voice Communications; London, June 22, 1995, p.3.
Additional Information:
☞ Vegetarian Cooking Caribbean Style, Annette Norma, Angela Royal Publishing; Kent, UK, 1996.
☞ The Complete Caribbean Cookbook: Totally Tropical Recipes From the Paradise Islands, Beverley Le Blanc, (ed.), The Apple Press; UK, 1996.
☞ Jamaica: The Fairest Isle, Phillip Sherlock and Barbara Preston, UK.

386.
A) LIMBO
☞ Callaloo, Calypso & Carnival: The Cuisine of Trinidad and Tobago,Dave Dewitt, Mary Jane Wilan, Ten Speed Press; 1993
Additional Information:
☞ Carnival Undercover, Bret Witter and Lorelei Sharkey, Plume Books; 2003.
☞ After the Dance: A Walk Through Carnival in Jacmel, Haiti. Edwidge Danticat, Crown Publishers; 1st edition, 2002.
☞ Carnival in Rio, Helmut Teissl, Abbeville Press; Book & CD edition 2000

387.
C) BORN ON A SUNDAY
☞ The Book of African Names, Molefi Kete Asante, Africa World Press Inc.; NJ, 1991.
Additional Information:
☞ African Names, Julia Stewart, Carol Publishing; Citadel Book Press; USA, 1996.
☞ Names from Africa, Ogonna Chuks-Orji, Johnson Publishing; Chicago, 1972.
☞ The Voice, The Voice Group Ltd.; London, June 21, 1994, p.14.

388.
C) SOFT SHEEN
☞ Soft Sheen/Carson Products, 1000 E. 87th Street, Chicago, IL, 60619

Additional Information:
☞ Hype Hair, "Word Up!", Video Productions, Inc.; USA.
☞ The Black Press in Britain, Ionie Benjamin, Trentham Books; London, 1995, p.80.
☞ Black Beauty and Hair Magazine, Hawker Consumer Publications; 13 Park House, 140 Battersea Park Road, London, SW11 4NB.

389.
A) SEAN JEAN COMBS
☞ Vogue Magazine, Library Archives, 350 Maddison Avenue, New York, NY, 10017, USA.
Additional Information:
☞ Sean "Puffy" Combs (Black Americans of Achievement), Elizabeth Atkins Bowman, Chelsea House Publishers; 2001.
☞ The Voice, The Voice Group Ltd.; London, September 24, 2001, p.6.
☞ Now Magazine, June 6, 2001, IPC Media Ltd.; London, p.74.

390.
B) NILE
☞ Professor Arno Peters's Atlas of the World, Longman; London, 1989.
Additional Information:
☞ Nile Valley Contributions to Civilization; Exploding the Myths, Volume 1, Anthony T. Browder, Institute of Khamic Guidance; Washington, D.C., 2000, pp.45-46.
☞ National Geographic Magazine, Volume 165, No. 5, May 1985.
☞ The Encyclopedia of Africa, Franklin Watts, Inc.; New York and London, 1976.

391.
A) ADMIRAL
☞ 100 Amazing Facts About the Negro: With Complete Proof, J. A. Rogers, H. M. Rogers Publishers; USA, 1995, p.49.
Additional Information:
☞ Staying Power, Peter Fryer, Pluto Press; UK, 2nd Edition, 1985.
☞ Your History: From the Beginning of Time to the Present, J. A. Rogers, Black Classic Press; Baltimore, MD, 1983, p.10.
☞ Pirates: Old and New, J. Gollomb, London, 1931, p.11.

392.
C) NOTTING HILL CARNIVAL
☞ The Struggle for Black Arts in Britain, Kwesi Awusu, Comedia; 1986, p.7.
Additional Information:
☞ Black Londoners, 1890-1990, Susan Okokon, Sutton; UK, 1997, pp.110, 124-26.
☞ Black and British, David Bygott, Oxford University Press; 1992.
☞ New African, October 2001, ICP Ltd.; London, p.11.

393.
C) ENGLAND
☞ BBC History Magazine, BBC Worldwide, April 2001, Vol. 2, No. 4, pp.50-51.
Additional Information:
☞ A Biographical Dictionary of the Saints, by the Rt. Rev. F. G. Holweck, Herder Book Company; 1969 (Originally Published 1924).
☞ Nile Valley Contributions to Civilization; Exploding the Myths, Volume 1, Anthony T. Browder, Institute of Khamic Guidance; Washington, D.C., 2000, p.97.
☞ George of Lydda, Written by Isabel Hill Elder, London, 1949.

394.
A) CO-CHIEF OPERATIONS DIRECTOR
☞ Time Warner, Inc.; Public Relations Department, 75 Rockerfeller Plaza, New York, USA.
Additional Information:
☞ Ebony, Johnson Publishing; Chicago, October, 2002, p.94.
☞ USA Today, European Edition, June 4, 1997, Sports Section, p.10B.
☞ Planet AOL: From 'Anywhere' to 'Everywhere' With Time Warner & Beyond, Terry Wooten, USA, 2001.

395.
A) MONTSERRAT
☞ Montserrat: Emerald Isle of the Caribbean, Howard A. Fergus, Macmillan; 1986.
Additional Information:
☞ The Complete Caribbean Cookbook: Totally Tropical Recipes From the Paradise Islands, Beverley Le Blanc, (ed.), The Apple Press; UK, 1996.

☞ New! Encyclopaedia Britannica Print Set, 2002 Edition.
☞ Anguilla to Dominica: Including Anguilla, St. Martin, St. Barts, Saba, Statia, St. Kitts, Nevis, Antigua, Montserrat, Redonda, Guadeloupe, and Dominica, Donald M. Street, USA, 2001.

396.
B) EGYPT
☞ Freemasonry and Judaism, Vicomte Leon De Poncins, A & B Book Publishers; Brooklyn, NY, 1994.
Additional Information:
☞ Freemasonry-The Brotherhood, Stephen Knight, Granada Publishing; UK, 1984, pp.15-16.
☞ Ancient Egypt and the Islamic Destiny, by Mustapher El-Amin, First Edition, New Mind Productions; New Jersey, 1988.
☞ The Origin of Freemasonary Connected With the Origin and Evolution of the Human Race, Albert Churchward, G. Allen and Goodwin, Ltd.; London, 1920.

397.
C) EUROPA
☞ Herodotus: The Histories, Great Books of the Western World, Encyclopaedia Brittanica, Chicago, 1952.
Additional Information:
☞ The Enclopaedia of Myths and Legends of all Nations, H. S. Robinson, Kaye & Ward, Ltd.; London, 1950.
☞ Who's Who in the Ancient World, Betty Radice, Penguin; 1982, pp.80, 114.
☞ Dictionary of World Mythology, Arthur A. Cotterell, G. P. Putman and Sons; New York, 1980.

398.
C) GYPSIES
☞ Gypsies: An Illustrated History, Jean-Pierre Liégeois, Al Saqi Books; 1986.
Additional Information:
☞ Ancient and Modern Britons. David MacRitchie, Volume 1, Keegan Paul, Trench & Co.; 1985, pp.139-43.
☞ The Enclopaedia of Myths and Legends of all Nations, H. S. Robinson, Kaye & Ward, Ltd.; London, 1950.
☞ African Presence in Early Europe, Edited by Ivan Van Sertima, Transaction; 1986, p.260.

399.

B) LOWER EGYPT

☞ Nile Valley Contributions to Civilization; Exploding the Myths, Volume 1, Anthony T. Browder, Institute of Khamic Guidance; Washington, D.C., 2000, p.85.

Additional Information:

☞ African Origin of the Major Western Religions, Dr. Yosef A. A. Ben Jochannon, Black Classic Press; Baltimore, MD, 1988.

☞ Wonderful Ethiopians of the Ancient Cushite Empire, Drusilla Dunjee Houston, Black Classic Press; Baltimore, Maryland, 1989.

☞ Kemet and Other Ancient African Civilisation, Vivian Verdell Gordon, Third World Press; Chicago. IL., 1991.

400.

B) YAM

☞ The African Cookbook, by Bea Sandler, Diane and Lee Dillon (Illustrators), Citadel Press; 1993.

Additional Information:

☞ The Complete Caribbean Cookbook: Totally Tropical Recipes From the Paradise Islands, Beverley Le Blanc, (ed.), The Apple Press; UK, 1996.

☞ The Voice, The Voice Group Ltd.; London, August 16, 1994, p.5.

☞ Cambridge Encyclopedia, David Crystal, Cambridge University Press; 1990, p.1319.

401.

B) BRAZIL

☞ Encyclopedia of Latin America, Edited by Helen Delpar, Macgraw-Hill Book Company; 1974.

Additional Information:

☞ The Negro in American Civilisation, Nathaniel Weyl, Public Affairs Press; Washington, D.C., 1960.

☞ Negroes in Brazil, Donald Pierson, Southern Illinois University Press; Feffer & Simons, Inc.; London and Amsterdam, 1942.

☞ Sex and Race, Vols. 1-3, J. A. Rogers, H. M. Rogers Publishers; USA, 1967.

402.

A) ABUJA

☞ Identity Transformation and Identity Politics Under Structural Adjustment in Nigeria, Attahiru Jega, Transaction; New Jersey, 2000.

Additional Information:

☞ Macdonalds Encyclopedia of Africa, Macdonald Educational Ltd.; UK, 1986.

☞ Cambridge Encyclopedia, David Crystal, Cambridge University Press; 4th Edition, 2000.

☞ African Political Facts Since 1945, Cook & Killingray, Macmillan Press Ltd.; 1983.

403.

B) GHANA

☞ New! Encyclopaedia Britannica Print Set, 2002 Edition.

Additional Information:

☞ Africa Must Unite, Kwame Nkruma, New York, International Publishers; 1972.

☞ Macdonalds Encyclopedia of Africa, Macdonald Educational Ltd.; UK, 1986.

☞ African Encyclopedia, The Oxford University Press; 1974.

404.

C) AFRICAN FEMINIST

☞ An African Victorian Feminist, Adelaide Cromwell, Frank Cass & Co. Ltd.; 1981.

Additional Information:

☞ Daughters of Africa: An International Anthology of Words and Writings by Women of African Descent from the Ancient Egyptian to the Present. Edited by Margaret Busby, Vintage Books; 1993, pp.153-54.

☞ Black Women for Beginners, Sandra Sharp, Writers and Readers Publishing, Inc.; New York, 1993.

☞ Staying Power, Peter Fryer, Pluto Press; UK, 2nd Edition, 1985.

405.

B) ISIS

☞ Black Women in Antiquity, Edited by Ivan Van Sertima, Transaction; 7th Edition, 1992, p.9.

Additional Information:

☞ Museums of Egypt, Robert S. Branchi, Newsweek, Inc.; 1980, p.162.

☞ Black Athena: The Afroasiatic Roots of Classical Civilsation, Vols. 1 & 2, Martin Bernal, FAB; London, 1991.

☞ Return to the African Mother Principle of Male and Female Equality, Vol. 1., Oba T. Shaka, Pan African Publishers and Distributors; 1995.

General Knowledge

406.
A) GALASIUS
☞ Liber Pontificalis (Book of Popes) translated by L. R. Loomis, New York, 1916, pp.17, 110.
Additional Information:
☞ African Presence in Early Europe, Edited by Ivan Van Sertima, Transaction; 1986, pp.104-7.
☞ Journal of African Civilization, Transactions Periodicals Consortium; Rutgers University, New Brunswick, New Jersey, "African Popes", Edward Scobie, Volume 4, No. 1., April, 1982.
☞ Blacks Who Died for Jesus, A History Book, Mark Hyman, Winston-Derek Publishers, Inc.; USA, 1983, pp.21-25.

407.
C) AFRICAN BOARD GAME
☞ African History for Beginners, Herb Boyd, Writers & Readers Publishing, Inc.; New York, 1994, p.46.
Additional Information:
☞ The New Nation, Western Hemisphere; London, April 7, 1997, p.3
☞ Sports and Games of Ancient Egypt, Wolfgang Deike (translated by Allen Guttmann), Yale University Press; New Haven and London, 1992.
☞ Black Business and Culture, Issue 3, London, August-November 1997, p.3.

408.
A) SENEGAL
☞ The African Origin of Civilization: Myth or Reality, Cheikh Anta Diop, translated by Mercer Cook, Lawrence Hill & Company; 1974.
Additional Information:
☞ The Africans, David Lamb, New York, Vintage Books; New York, 1983.
☞ Macdonalds Encyclopedia of Africa, Macdonald Educational Ltd.; UK, 1986.
☞ The Music of Africa, J. H. Kwabena Nketia, Victor Gollancz Ltd.; London, 1979.

409.
B) ASSEGAI
☞ World's Great Men of Color, J. A. Rogers, Volume I, Collier Macmillan Publishers; 1972, pp.265-274.

Additional Information:
☞ Caribbean Times, Hansib Publishing; London, 8th October 1994, p.19.
☞ The Washing of the Spears, Donald R. Morris, Simon and Schuster; New York, 1965, pp.40-67.
☞ Makers of South Africa. B. L. W. Brett, T. Nelson; London, 1944, pp.19-27.

410.
B) JAMAICA
☞ The Jamaica Daily Gleaner, July 2, 2000.
Additional Information:
☞ Reggae Bloodlines: In Search of the Music and Culture of Jamaica, S. Davis and Peter Simon, HEB; 1984.
☞ Jamaica: The Fairest Isle, Philip Sherlock and Barbara Preston, UK.
☞ The Book of Jamaica, Russell Banks, HarperCollins; 1996.

411.
A) ROME
☞ Nile Valley Contributions to Civilization; Exploding the Myths, Volume 1, Anthony T. Browder, Institute of Khamic Guidance; Washington, D.C., 2000, pp.121, 191.
Additional Information:
☞ Cleopatra's Needle; With a Preliminary Sketch of the History, Erection Uses and Signification, Charles E. Moldenke, The Lancaster Press, Inc.; 1935.
☞ The Magic of the Obelisks, Peter Tompkins, Harper & Row; 1981.
☞ The Obelisks of Egypt: Skyscrapers of the Past, Labib Habachi, The American University of Cairo Press; Cairo, Egypt, 1984.

412.
C) DALLAS
☞ American Visions, Volume 11, No. 1, USA, February/March Edition, 1996, p.32.
Additional Information:
☞ Ebony, Johnson Publishing; Chicago, February, 2003, pp.52-59.
☞ African American Museum, P.O. Box 150153, Dallas, Texas, 75315.
☞ History Outreach: Programs for Museums, Historical Organizations, and Academic History Departments. J. D. Britton and Diane F. Britton, Krieger Publishers; Malabar, Fla., 1994.

413.

B) LIBYA

☞ Flags of the World, Edited by E. M. C. Barraclough and W. G. Grampton, Frederick Warne Ltd.; London, 1981, p.85.

Additional Information:

☞ Flags, Eric Inglefield, Kingfisher Books; London, 1981.

☞ Africa A-Z, Robert S. Kane, Doubleday and Company Inc.; New York, 1972.

☞ Cambridge Encyclopedia, David Crystal, Cambridge University Press; 4th Edition, 2000.

414.

C) THE WINDWARD ISLANDS

☞ Cambridge Encyclopedia, David Crystal, Cambridge University Press; 1990, pp.529, 763, 1306.

Additional Information:

☞ Professor Arno Peters's Atlas of the World, Longman; London, 1989.

☞ The Times of London Concise Atlas of the World, Times of London, (ed.), Crown Publishing; 2001.

☞ Black Skin White Masks, Frantz Fanon (translated by Charles Lam Markmann), Paladin; London, 1970.

415.

A) MALI

☞ Timbuctoo: The Mysterious, F. Dobois, London, 1896.

Additional Information:

☞ African Encyclopedia, The Oxford University Press; 1974.

☞ The Africans: A Triple Heritage, Ali A. Mazrui, BBC Publications; 1986.

☞ Africa A-Z, Robert S. Kane, Doubleday and Company Inc.; New York, 1972.

416.

C) BAGPIPES

☞ Ancient and Modern Britons. David MacRitchie, Volume 1, Keegan Paul, Trench & Co.; 1985, pp.302-7.

Additional Information:

☞ African Peoples Contribution to World History: Shattering the Myth, Vol. 1, Paul L. Hamilton, R. A. Renaissance Publications; USA, 1993.

☞ History of Scotland, Buchanan, Book 1, Chapter 1, Pxxxiii.

☞ What They Never Told You in History Class, Indus Khamit-Kush, Luxorr Publications; USA, 1983.

417.

B) LAKE VICTORIA

☞ Africa: Mother of Western Civilisation, Dr. Yosef A. A Ben Jochannon, Black Classic Press; Baltimore, MD, 1988, p.44.

Additional Information:

☞ The Encyclopedia of Africa, Franklin Watts, Inc.; New York and London, 1976. Macdonald Educational Ltd.; 1986.

☞ Nile Valley Contributions to Civilization; Exploding the Myths, Volume 1, Anthony T. Browder, Institute of Khamic Guidance; Washington, D.C., 2000, p.45.

☞ The Times of London Concise Atlas of the World, Times of London, (ed.), Crown Publishing; 2001.

418.

C) VERONICA WEBB

☞ The Weekly Journal, Voice Communications; London, April 27, 1995, p.13.

Additional Information:

☞ Pride, Voice Communications; September/October Edition 1994.

☞ The Voice, The Voice Group Limited; March 28, 1995, pp.4-5.

☞ The Weekly Journal, Voice Communications; London, October 20, 1994, p.10.

419.

B) MANASSEH AND EPHRAIM

☞ King James Bible, Genesis, Chapter 41, Verse 45.

Additional Information:

☞ Black Characters and References of the Holy Bible, F. S. Rhoades, First Edition, Vantage Press; New York, 1980.

☞ The Black Biblical Heritage, John L. Johnson, Winston-Derek Publishers, Inc.; 1974.

☞ The Original African Heritage Study Bible, Dr. Cain Hope Felder, (ed.), World Bible Punlishing Co.; USA, 1993.

420.

C) OPRAH WINFREY

☞ Oprah Winfrey-The Real Story, George Mair, Birch Lane Press; UK, 1995.

Additional Information:
- ☞ The Essential Black Literature Guide, Published in association with the Schomburg Center for Research in Black Culture, Roger M. Valade II, Visible Ink Press; USA, 1996, p.386.
- ☞ Ebony, Johnson Publishing; Chicago, July, 1995, pp.22-28.
- ☞ Who's Who Among Black Americans, 1992-1993, USA, p.1556.

421.
A) ZAMBEZI RIVER
- ☞ Cambridge Encyclopedia, David Crystal, Cambridge University Press; 1990, p.1267.

Additional Information:
- ☞ National Geographic, Volume 165, No. 5, May 1985.
- ☞ Professor Arno Peters's Atlas of the World, Longman; London, 1989.
- ☞ An Atlas of African History, J. D. Fage, Edward Arnold; UK, 1958-61.

422.
B) OKRA
- ☞ Entertaining With Style, Prue Leith and Pooly Tyrer, Macdonald Books; London and Sydney, 1986, p.188.

Additional Information:
- ☞ The African Cookbook, by Bea Sandler, Diane and Lee Dillon (Illustrators), Citadel Press; 1993.
- ☞ Mango Spice; 44 Caribbean Songs, A & C Black Ltd.; London, 1981, (Introduction).
- ☞ The Complete Caribbean Cookbook: Totally Tropical Recipes From the Paradise Islands, Beverley Le Blanc, (ed.), The Apple Press; UK, 1996.

423.
A) AUSTRAL ASIA
- ☞ Professor Arno Peters's Atlas of the World, Longman; London, 1989, UK.

Additional Information:
- ☞ World Travel Guide, 1997-1998, Worldwide Edition, Columbus Press Ltd.; 1997.
- ☞ Cambridge Encyclopedia, David Crystal, Cambridge University Press; 4th Edition, 2000.
- ☞ The Times of London Concise Atlas of the World, Times of London, (ed.), Crown Publishing; 2001.

424.
A) SCOTLAND
- ☞ Early Christian Art, Andre Grabar, Odyssey Press; New York, 1968.

Additional Information:
- ☞ Sex and Race, Volume 1, J. A. Rogers, H. M. Rogers Publishers; USA, 1966, p.197.
- ☞ Celtic Scotland, William F. Skene, Vols. 1-3, Freeport, New York, 1876.
- ☞ African Presence in Early Europe, Edited by Ivan Van Sertima, Transaction; 1986, p.128.

425.
C) JAMAICA
- ☞ Jamaica: The Fairest Isle, Phillip Sherlock and Barbara Preston, UK.

Additional Information:
- ☞ The Book of Jamaica, Russell Banks, HarperCollins; 1996.
- ☞ Reggae Bloodlines: In Search of the Music and Culture of Jamaica, S. Davis and Peter Simon, HEB; 1984.
- ☞ Caribbean Companion: The A-Z Reference, Brian Dyde, The MacMillan Press, Ltd.; London, 1992.

426.
B) SUDAN
- ☞ Professor Arno Peters's Atlas of the World, Longman; London, 1989.

Additional Information:
- ☞ Africa A-Z, Robert S. Kane, Doubleday and Company Inc.; New York, 1972.
- ☞ The Africans: A Triple Heritage, Ali A. Mazrui, BBC Publications; 1986.
- ☞ Africa, Phyllis Martin and Patrick O'Meara, Indiana University Press; Bloomington, 1986.

427.
B) TAKE MY HAND PRECIOUS LORD
- ☞ Ebony, Johnson Publishing; Chicago, February, 1997, p.90.

Additional Information:
- ☞ Too Close to Heaven, The Illustrated History of Gospel Music, Viv Broughton, British Broadcasting Corporation; 1995.
- ☞ We'll Understand it Better By and By: Pioneering African American Gospel Composers, Bernice Johnson Reagon, Smithsonian Institution Press; Washington and London, 1981.

☞ Serials Review, Volume 20, No. 4. "From Spirituals to Gospel Rap", Timothy Dodge, Gospel Music Periodicals; 1994, pp.67-78.

428.
A) INDONESIA
☞ The Pesantren Tradition: The Role of the Kyai in the Maintenance of Traditional Islam in Java, Zamakhsyari Dhofier, Arizona State University Program Forum; 1999.
Additional Information:
☞ Indonesia in Transition: Muslim Intellectuals and National Development, Howard M. Federspiel, Nova Science Publishers. Inc.; 1998.
☞ Japan's Colonialism and Indonesia, Aziz Muhammed Abdul, M. Nijhoff (publ.), The Hague, 1955.
☞ Muslim's through Discourse, John R. Bowen, Princeton University Press; 1993.

429.
B) LION MOUNTAIN
☞ Rough Guide to West Africa, Jim Hudgens and Richard Trillo, Rough Guides Limited; 4th edition, 2003
Additional Information:
☞ West Africa before the Colonial Era: A History to 1850, Basil Davidson, Pearson Education; 1998
☞ Sojourns in West Africa, Steven E Keenan, Universe; 2004
☞ Macdonalds Encyclopedia of Africa, Macdonald Educational Ltd.; UK, 1986.

430.
A) XYLOPHONE
☞ The Music of Africa, J. H. Kwabena Nketia, Victor Gollancz Ltd.; London, 1979, pp.81, 84.
Additional Information:
☞ African Music: A People's Art, translated by Josephine Bennet, Lawrence Hill & Co.; Westport, UK, 1995.
☞ African All Stars: The Pop Music of a continent, Chris Stapleton and Chris May, Paladin; London, Glasgow, Toronto, Sydney, Auckland, 1989.
☞ African Kingdoms, Basil Davidson, Time-Life Books; (Nederland), 1980.

431.
A) ETHIOPIA
☞ The Holy Bible, King James Version.
Additional Information:
☞ Black Characters and References of the Holy Bible, F. S. Rhoades, First Edition, Vantage Press; New York, 1980.
☞ The Black Biblical Heritage, John L. Johnson, Winston-Derek Publishers, Inc.; 1974.
☞ The Original African Heritage Study Bible, Dr. Cain Hope Felder, (ed.), World Bible Punlishing Co.; USA, 1993.

432.
A) MISS ITALY
☞ Corriera Della Sera, September 10, 1996.
Additional Information:
☞ The Voice, The Voice Group Ltd.; London, September 24, 1996, p.11.
☞ La Repubblica, September 10, 1996.
☞ Pride, London, September 1997, p.15.

433.
C) 60 MINUTES
☞ Who's Who Among Black Americans, 1992-1993, USA, p.143.
Additional Information:
☞ CBS, Public Relations Department, 7800 Beverley Blvd., Los Angeles, CA.
☞ Ebony Man, Johnson Publishing; March, 1993, p.43.
☞ The Essential Black Literature Guide, Published in association with the Schomburg Center for Research in Black Culture, Roger M. Valade II, Visible Ink Press; USA, 1996, pp.205, 328.

434.
C) APOLLO
☞ Herodotus: The Histories. Great Books of the Western World, Encyclopaedia Brittanica, Chicago, 1952, pp.49-50, 60-65, 69-70.
Additional Information:
☞ Who's Who in the Ancient World, Betty Radice, Penguin; 1982, pp.80, 114.
☞ Anacalypsis, Godfrey Higgins, Volume 1, New Hyde Park; New York, 1965.
☞ Greek Myths, Robert Graves, Volume 1, Penguin Books;

General Knowledge

435.

A) AFRICAN METHODIST EPISCOPAL CHURCH

☞ Ebony, Johnson Publishing; Chicago, February, 2001, p.119.

Additional Information:

☞ Too Close to Heaven, The Illustrated History of Gospel Music, Viv Broughton, British Broadcasting Corporation; 1995.

☞ Ebony, Johnson Publishing; Chicago, February, 1995, p.80.

☞ Ebony Pictorial History of Black America: Volume 3. Civil Rights Movement to Black Revolution, Johnson Publishing Company; 1974, p.243.

436

B) FORTY-TWO

☞ Nile Valley Contributions to Civilization; Exploding the Myths, Volume 1, Anthony T. Browder, Institute of Khamic Guidance; Washington, D.C., 2000, pp.90-92.

Additional Information:

☞ The Book of the Dead, Edited and translated by Ernest A. Wallis Budge, Dover Publications; New York, NY, 1967.

☞ The Negative Confessions, Bell Publishing Co.; New York, 1960.

☞ What They Never Told You in History Class, Indus Khamit-Kush, Luxorr Publications; USA, 1983, p.213.

437.

A) THE CHARLESTON

☞ Black Dance, Edward Thorpe, Chatto & Windus; London, 1989.

Additional Information:

☞ Cambridge Encyclopedia, David Crystal, Cambridge University Press; 1990, p.243.

☞ The Black Heritage Book of Trivia, Morgan White Jr., Quinlan Press; Boston, 1985.

☞ Black Manhattan, James Weldon Johnson, Atheneum; New York, 1968, pp.189-90.

438.

B) SUDAN

☞ The Music of Africa, J. H. Kwabena Nketia, Victor Gollancz Ltd.; London, 1979, pp.251- 53.

Additional Information:

☞ The Dinka of Sudan, Francis Mading Deng, Waveland Press Inc.; Illionois, 1972.

☞ African Kingdoms, Basil Davidson, Time-Life Books; (Nederland), 1980.

☞ Macdonalds Encyclopedia of Africa, Macdonald Educational Ltd.; 1986.

439.

A) TWENTY

☞ Vernon Can Read! A Memoir, Vernon E. Jordan and Annette Gordon-Reed, Jr., Public Affairs Publ.; USA, 2001.

Additional Information:

☞ Ebony, Johnson Publishing; Chicago, November, 2000, p.73.

☞ Ebony, Johnson Publishing; Chicago, October, 1994, pp.36-42.

☞ The Voice, The Voice Group Ltd.; July 23, 1996, p.11.

440.

A) ELAMITES

☞ History of Egypt, (Gaston Maspero) translated by M. L. London, Volume 4, The Grollier Society; 1903.

Additional Information:

☞ The Struggle of the Nations: Egypt, Syria and Assyria, Gaston Maspero, D. Appleton & Co.; 1987.

☞ The Black Biblical Heritage, John L. Johnson, Winston-Derek Publishers, Inc.; 1974.

☞ Black Characters and References of the Holy Bible, F. S. Rhoades, First Edition, Vantage Press; New York, 1980.

441.

C) MISS GREAT BRITAIN

☞ The Voice, The Voice Group Ltd.; London, October 9, 2000, p.59.

Additional Information:

☞ The Voice, The Voice Group Ltd.; July 23, 1996, p.11.

☞ The Weekly Journal, Voice Communications; London, December 22, 1994, p.22.

☞ The Voice, The Voice Group Ltd.; October 18, 1994, p.3.

442.

B) REPUBLIC OF CYPRUS

☞ The New York Voice, July 2, 1980.

Additional Information:
- ☞ Blacks Who Died for Jesus, A History Book, Mark Hyman, Winston-Derek Publishers, Inc.; USA, 1983, p.25-28.
- ☞ Sex and Race, Volume 1, J. A. Rogers, H. M. Rogers Publishers; USA, 1968, p.95.
- ☞ No Green Pasters, Roi Ottley, John Murray Books; London, 1952.

443.
A) 7
- ☞ Professor Arno Peters's Atlas of the World, Longman; London, 1989.

Additional Information:
- ☞ Upscale, Upscale Communications, Inc.; November 1995, pp.62-64.
- ☞ The Times of London Concise Atlas of the World, Times of London, (ed.), Crown Publishing; 2001.
- ☞ Cambridge Encyclopedia, David Crystal, Cambridge University Press; 1990, pp.208-9.

444.
A) 1958
- ☞ The Struggle for Black Arts in Britain, Kwesi Awusu, Comedia; 1986, p.7.

Additional Information:
- ☞ The Voice, The Voice Group Limited; 26th May 1997, p.5.
- ☞ The Weekly Journal, Voice Communications; London, 27th May 1993, p.6.
- ☞ Africa Must Unite, Kwame Nkruma, New York, International Publishers; 1972.

445.
C) TALKING DRUM
- ☞ African Music, Volume 5, No. 1, "Standard Drum Patterns in Nigeria" Samuel Akpabot, 1971, pp.37-39.

Additional Information:
- ☞ African History for Beginners, Herb Boyd, Writers & Readers Publishing, Inc.; London, New York, 1994, p.82.
- ☞ The Music of Africa, J. H. Kwabena Nketia, Victor Gollancz Ltd.; London, 1979.
- ☞ African Music: A People's Art, translated by Josephine Bennet, Lawrence Hill & Co.; Westport, UK, 1995.

446.
B) GLADIATORS
- ☞ The Voice, The Voice Group Ltd.; February 10, 1997, p.35.

Additional Information:
- ☞ American Gladiators (Who's Hot), G. Dinero, A Bantam Classic and Loveswept Publication; USA, 1993.
- ☞ The Voice, The Voice Group Ltd.; London, July 7, 1997, p.5.
- ☞ The American Gladiators and The Gladiators, London Weekend Television, Library Archives, Kent House, Upper Ground, Southbank, London SE1.

447.
C) WORLD ATLAS
- ☞ Professor Arno Peters's Atlas of the World, Longman; London, 1989.

Additional Information:
- ☞ The Daily Telegraph, March 20, 1989, p.18.
- ☞ Nile Valley Contributions to Civilization; Exploding the Myths, Volume 1, Anthony T. Browder, Institute of Khamic Guidance; Washington, D.C., 2000, pp.38-39.
- ☞ The New Atlas of African History, G. S. P. Freeman-Grenville, Simon & Schuster; New York, 1991.

448.
A) LIFT EVERY VOICE AND SING
- ☞ Lift Every Voice and Sing: A Celebration of the Negro National Anthem, 100 Years, 100 Voices, Julian Bond and Sondra K. Wilson, (eds.), Random House; New York, 2000.

Additional Information:
- ☞ Lift Every Voice and Sing: A Pictorial Tribute to the Negro National Anthem, James Weldon Johnson, Jump at the Sun Publications; USA, 2001.
- ☞ Lift Every Voice and Sing, James Weldon Johnson, Walker & Co.; USA, 1993.
- ☞ Lift Every Voice and Sing: Selected Poems, James Weldon Johnson, Sondra Kathryn Wilson, (preface), Penguin; USA, 2000.

449
B) PORT OF SPAIN
- ☞ Adventure Guide: Trinidad & Tobago, Kathleen O'Donnell and Stassi Pefkaros, Hunter Publishing, Inc.; 2000.

Additional Information:
- A Brief History of the Caribbean, Jan Rogozinskii, Facts on File; 1992.
- Caribbean Companion: The A-Z Reference, Brian Dyde, The MacMillan Press, Ltd.; London, 1992.
- The Cambridge Encyclopedia of Latin America and the Caribbean, Cambridge University Press; 1989.

450.
C) NIGERIA
- Sunday Times, South Africa, Johnic Publishing; November 18, 2001.

Additional Information:
- The Voice, The Voice Group Ltd.; November 18, 2001, p.3.
- The Sunday Observer, London, November 18, 2001.
- The Miss America Organization, 2 Miss America Way, Suite 1000, Atlantic City, NJ, 08401, USA.

451.
B) THE GUINEA
- Black and British, David Bygott, Oxford University Press; 1992.

Additional Information:
- Your History: From the Beginning of Time to the Present, J. A. Rogers, Black Classic Press; Baltimore, MD, 1983, p.2.
- History of the Black Presence in London, GLC; London, 1986, p.9.
- Black and White-The Negro and English Society 1555-1945, James Walvin, Allen Lane, The Penguin Press; 1973.

452.
B) TANZANIA
- The Music of Africa, J. H. Kwabena Nketia, Victor Gollancz Ltd.; London, 1979, pp.251- 53.

Additional Information:
- African Kingdoms, Basil Davidson, Time-Life Books; (Nederland), 1980.
- Africa, Phyllis Martin and Patrick O'Meara, Indiana University Press; Bloomington, 1986.
- Macdonalds Encyclopedia of Africa, Macdonald Educational Ltd.; 1986.

453.
B) LOUIS ARMSTRONG
- Louis Armstrong: An American Genius.

James L. Collier, Oxford University Press; New York, 1983.

Additional Information:
- Black Americana. Richard A. Long, Admiral; UK, 1985, pp.48, 51-52, 135, 137-39, 146.
- The Music of Black Americans. A History, 2nd Edition, Eileen Southern, W. W. Norton & Co.; 1983, pp.373-77.
- Jazz in the Movies: A Guide to Jazz Musicians 1917-1977, David Meeker, (ed.), Talisman; London, 1977.

454.
A) TWA
- Black Man of the Nile and His Family. Dr. Yosef A. A. Ben Jochannon, Black Classic Press; Baltimore, MD, 1988.

Additional Information:
- African Kingdoms, Basil Davidson, Time-Life Books; (Nederland), 1980, pp.20-21, 62-63.
- The Africans, David Lamb, New York, Vintage Books; New York, 1983.
- The Weekly Journal, Voice Communications; London, May 5, 1994, p.3.

455.
B) BENIN
- African Kingdoms, Basil Davidson, Time-Life Books; (Nederland), 1980, pp.100-1, 109-11.

Additional Information:
- African Encyclopedia, The Oxford University Press; 1974.
- Black Kingdoms Black People, Fambamigbe Publishers; Nigeria, 1979.
- Africa A-Z, Robert S. Kane, Doubleday and Company Inc.; New York, 1972.

456.
C) NEGEV
- Cambridge Encyclopedia, David Crystal, Cambridge University Press; 1990, p.838.

Additional Information:
- Professor Arno Peters's Atlas of the World, Longman; London, 1989. UK.
- Macdonalds Encyclopedia of Africa, Macdonald Educational Ltd.; 1986.
- The New Atlas of African History, G. S. P. Freeman-Grenville, Simon & Schuster; New York, 1991.

457.
C) AFRICAN WOMEN SOLDIERS
☞ Palace of Minos, Sir A. Evans, Volume 2, Part 2, London, 1928, pp.348, 755-57.
Additional Information:
☞ Nature Knows No Color Line. J. A. Rogers, 3rd Edition, H. M. Rogers Publishers; 1952, p.34.
☞ The Amazons, G. C. Rotherery, London, 1910, pp.8, 10.
☞ A Dictionary of World Mythology, Arthur Cotterell, Winward; UK, 1979.

458.
A) MOROCCO
☞ Cambridge Encyclopedia, David Crystal, Cambridge University Press; 1990, pp.813-14.
Additional Information:
☞ Professor Arno Peters's Atlas of the World, Longman; London, 1989.
☞ Macdonalds Encyclopedia of Africa, Macdonald Educational Ltd.; 1986.
☞ Africa, Phyllis Martin and Patrick O'Meara, Indiana University Press; Bloomington, 1986.

459.
B) MOUNT KILIMANJARO
☞ Kilimanjaro and Mount Kenya: A Climbing and Trekking Guide, Cameron M. Burns, Mountaineers Books; 1998.
Additional Information:
☞ Cambridge Encyclopedia, David Crystal, Cambridge University Press; 1990, p.661.
☞ Macdonalds Encyclopedia of Africa, Macdonald Educational Ltd.; 1986.
☞ Nile Valley Contributions to Civilization; Exploding the Myths, Volume 1, Anthony T. Browder, Institute of Khamic Guidance; Washington, D.C., 2000, p.45.

460.
C) BERBER
☞ Macdonalds Encyclopedia of Africa, Macdonald Educational Ltd.; UK, 1986.
Additional Information:
☞ The Africans, Ali A. Muzuri, A Triple Heritage, BBC Publications; London, 1986.
☞ Cambridge Encyclopedia, David Crystal, Cambridge University Press; 1990, p.1234.

☞ The Origin of the Tuaregs, F. Rodd, Geographical Journal; Volume 67.

461.
C) IRON SMITHS
☞ The Ancient Black Christians, Martin de Porres Walsh, Julian Richardson Associates, Publishers; San Francisco, 1969.
Additional Information:
☞ St Mauritius, W. S. Seiferth, Phylon; 1941, pp.370-76.
☞ World's Great Men of Color, Volume II, J. A. Rogers, Collier Macmillan Publishers; 1972, pp.10-15.
☞ Blacks Who Died for Jesus, A History Book, Mark Hyman, Winston-Derek Publishers, Inc.; USA, 1983, p.11.

462.
A) WEST AFRICA
☞ The Music of Africa, J. H. Kwabena Nketia, Victor Gollancz Ltd.; London, 1979, p.256.
Additional Information:
☞ African History for Beginners, Herb Boyd, Writers & Readers Publishing, Inc.; London, New York, 1994, p.7.
☞ African Music: A People's Art, translated by Josephine Bennet, Lawrence Hill & Co.; Westport, UK, 1995.
☞ African All Stars: The Pop Music of a continent, Chris Stapleton and Chris May, Paladin; London, Glasgow, Toronto, Sydney, Auckland, 1989.

463.
B) DEADWOOD DICK
☞ Africa's Gift to America, The Afro-American in the Making and Saving of the United States, Joel A. Rogers, H. M. Rogers Publishers; NY, 1959.
Additional Information:
☞ The American Cowboy, Lonn Taylor and Ingrid Maar, Harper & Row; USA, 1983.
☞ The Voice, The Voice Group Ltd.; London, February 8, 1994, p.19.
☞ The Guardian, Guardian Newspapers; London, September 8, 1983.

464.
A) FASHION DESIGNERS MOVEMENT
☞ CNN News (cnn.com) October 9, 2000.

Additional Information:
- ☞ The Weekly Journal, Voice Communications; London, November 19, 1992, p.11.
- ☞ New African, October 2001, ICP Ltd.; London, p.11.
- ☞ The African Music Encyclopedia: Music from Africa and the Africa Diaspora, "Papa Wemba", Janet Planet, africanmusic.org., 1995.

465.
A) ERITREA
- ☞ African Political Facts Since 1945, Cook & Killingray, Macmillan Press Ltd.; 1983, pp.242-43.

Additional Information:
- ☞ Macdonalds Encyclopedia of Africa, Macdonald Educational Ltd.; UK, 1986.
- ☞ African Encyclopedia, The Oxford University Press; 1974.
- ☞ The Africans, David Lamb, New York, Vintage Books; New York, 1983.

466.
B) FASHION CAFE
- ☞ The Evening Standard, Associated Newspaper Group; London, April 27, 1997, pp.12-13.

Additional Information:
- ☞ Pearson Communications Ltd.; Southbank House, Black Prince Road, London, SE1 7SJ.
- ☞ Model, Michael Gross, Bantum Books; UK, 1995.
- ☞ Ebony, Johnson Publishing; Chicago, December, 2000, p.144.

467.
A) SICILY
- ☞ Blacks Who Died for Jesus, A History Book, Mark Hyman, Winston-Derek Publishers, Inc.; USA, 1983, p.98.

Additional Information:
- ☞ No Green Pasters, Roi Ottley, John Murray Books; London, 1952.
- ☞ The Black Saint, Brother Ernest, Dujarie Press; Notre Dame, 1949.
- ☞ World's Great Men of Color, J. A. Rogers, Collier Macmillan Publishers; 1972, pp.17-22.

468.
C) COMMANDER IN CHIEF OF THE RUSSIAN ARMY
- ☞ The Sunday Times, London, June 6, 1999, p.11.

Additional Information:
- ☞ Great Negroes: Past and Present. Russell L. Adams, Afro-Am Publishing Company; Chicago, Illinois, 3rd Edition (1981), p.5.
- ☞ Negro History Bulletin, "Alexander Pushkin", Ruth Kemp, Association for the Study of Negro Life, Washington, D.C., December, 1940, pp.57-79, 61-62.
- ☞ An Introduction to the Economic History of Ethiopia from Early Times to 1800, Richard Keir, Patrick Pankhurst; London, 1961, pp.423-426.

469.
A) KENYA
- ☞ African Political Facts Since 1945, Cook & Killingray, Macmillan Press Ltd.; 1983.

Additional Information:
- ☞ Macdonalds Encyclopedia of Africa, Macdonald Educational Ltd.; UK, 1986.
- ☞ New! Encyclopaedia Britannica Print Set, 2002 Edition.
- ☞ Africa A-Z, Robert S. Kane, Doubleday and Company Inc.; New York, 1972.

470.
C) LA LEGION NOIRE
- ☞ African Presence in Early Europe, Edited by Ivan Van Sertima, Transaction; 1986, pp.317-28.

Additional Information:
- ☞ Biographies from Tuesday Magazine, "Le Chevalier de St. Georges", Bantum Pathfinder, New York, Toronto, London, 1968, pp.60-67.
- ☞ Negro History Bulletin, "Chevalier de St. Georges", Washington, D.C., December 1937, p.7.
- ☞ Nature Knows No Color Line. J. A. Rogers, 3rd Edition, H. M. Rogers Publishers; 1952, p.92.

471.
B) ANUBIS
- ☞ The Gods of the Egyptians, E. A. Wallis Budge, Dover Publications Inc.; NY, 1969.

Additional Information:
☞ A Dictionary of World Mythology, Arthur Cotterell, Winward; UK, 1979.
☞ Black Athena: The Afroasiatic Roots of Classical Civilsation, Vols. 1 & 2, Martin Bernal, FAB; London, 1991.
☞ The Book of the Dead, Edited and translated by Ernest A. Wallis Budge, Dover Publications; New York, NY, 1967.

472.
B) MARY PRINCE
☞ The History of Mary Prince: A West Indian Slave Related by Herself, Edited by Moira Ferguson, Pandora, London, 1987.
Additional Information:
☞ The Voice, The Voice Group Ltd.; March 30, 1993, p.16.
☞ Black British Literature. An Annoted Bibliography, Prahbu Guptara, Dangaroo Press; London, 1986, p.139.
☞ We Are Your Sisters: Black Women in the Nineteenth Century, Dorothy Sterlin, W.W. Norton; New York, 1984.

473.
A) TRINIDAD AND TOBAGO
☞ Black Firsts: 2000 Years of Extraordinary Achievement. Jessie Carney Smith, Caspar L. Jordan and Robert L. Johns, Visible Ink Press; USA, 1994, p.259.
Additional Information:
☞ Essence, April 1978, p.32.
☞ Jet, Johnson Publishing Co.; Chicago, November 10, 1977.
☞ Trinidad ExPress; Library Archives, 35 Independence Square, Box 1252, Port of Spain, Trinidad.

474.
A) KAMPALA
☞ African Political Facts Since 1945, Cook & Killingray, Macmillan Press Ltd.; 1983.
Additional Information:
☞ Cambridge Encyclopedia, David Crystal, Cambridge University Press; 4th Edition, 2000.
☞ Macdonalds Encyclopedia of Africa, Macdonald Educational Ltd.; UK, 1986.
☞ Africa A-Z, Robert S. Kane, Doubleday and Company Inc.; New York, 1972.

475.
C) SAUCES
☞ Black Women for Beginners, Sandra Sharp, Writers and Readers Publishing, Inc.; New York, 1993, p.159.
Additional Information:
☞ Who's Who of Black Achievers, John Hughes, (ed.), Ethnic Media Group; UK, 1999, p.105.
☞ The Weekly Journal, Voice Communications; London, September 9, 1993, p.14.
☞ Black Londoners, 1890-1990, Susan Okokon, Sutton; UK, 1997, p.56.

476.
A) LIFE
☞ The Ankh: African Origin of Electromagnetism. Nur Ankh Amen, Nur Ankh Amen Co.; New York, 1993.
Additional Information:
☞ Nile Valley Contributions to Civilization; Exploding the Myths, Volume 1, Anthony T. Browder, Institute of Khamic Guidance; Washington, D.C., 2000, p.67.
☞ The Signs and Symbols of Primordial Man, Albert Churchward, E. P. Dutton and Co.; New York, 1910.
☞ Meter Neter, Volume 1, Ra Un Nefer Amen, Khamit Group; Bronx, NY, 1990.

477.
C) GHANA
☞ African History: An Illustrated Handbook, Earl Sweeting and Lez Edmond, London Strategic Policy Unit; 1988, p.21.
Additional Information:
☞ The Africans, David Lamb, New York, Vintage Books; New York, 1983.
☞ Africa: Its Empires, Nations and People, Mary Penick Motley, Wayne State University Press; Detroit, 1969.
☞ West Africa, London, 28th September-4th October 1993, p.1646.

478.
B) 1970
☞ The Grenadian Voice, December 4, 1970, St George's, Grenada.
Additional Information:
☞ Famous First Facts About Negroes, Romeo B. Garrett, Arno Press; USA, 1972, p.23.

☞ Black Firsts: 2000 Years of Extraordinary Achievement. Jessie Carney Smith, Caspar L. Jordan and Robert L. Johns, Visible Ink Press; USA, 1994, p.257.

☞ The Daily Mirror, London, December 4, 1970.

479.

C) OSTRICH

☞ The 1997 Guinness Book of Records, Guinness Publishing Ltd.; UK, 1996, p.38.

Additional Information:

☞ The Discovery of Animal Behaviour, John Sparks, Collins; London, Glasgow, Sydney, Auckland, Toronto, Johannesburg, 1982, pp.22, 76, 214-16.

☞ Children's Encyclopedia, Harold Boswell Taylor, (ed.), Treasure Press; 1985, p.257.

☞ Ostriches, Anthony Wooton, Wayland Publishers Ltd.; London, 1981.

480.

C) 1962

☞ History of Black Saints in the United States, Cyprian Davis, Crossroad/Herder & Herder; 1995, pp.25-27.

Additional Information:

☞ Black Firsts: 2000 Years of Extraordinary Achievement. Jessie Carney Smith, Caspar L. Jordan and Robert L. Johns, Visible Ink Press; USA, 1994, pp.315-16.

☞ The Voice, The Voice Group Ltd.; London, April 26, 1999, p.38.

☞ Dictionary of Saints, John J. Delaney, Doubleday; New York, 1980, p.477.

481.

A) ENGLISH

☞ Cambridge Encyclopedia, David Crystal, Cambridge University Press; 4th Edition, 2000.

Additional Information:

☞ Macdonalds Encyclopedia of Africa, Macdonald Educational Ltd.; UK, 1986.

☞ The Africans, David Lamb, New York, Vintage Books; New York, 1983.

☞ African Political Facts Since 1945, Cook & Killingray, Macmillan Press Ltd.; 1983.

482.

B) MALARIA

☞ The 1997 Guinness Book of Records, Guinness Publishing Ltd.; UK, 1996, p.47.

Additional Information:

☞ Manson's Tropical Diseases, 18th Edition, Manson-Bahr and Apted, Baillére Tindall; London, 1982.

☞ West Africa, London, London, November 25 – December 1, 1991, pp.1918-19.

☞ General Pathology, J. B. Walter and M. S. Israel, Churchill Livingstone Books, Longman; Edinburgh and London, 1974.

483.

C) NAIRA

☞ Credit, Currencies and Culture: African Financial Institutions in Historical Perspective, Endre Stiansen and Jane I. Guyer, (eds.), Transaction; New Jersey, 2000.

Additional Information:

☞ Naira Power, Buchi Emecheta, Macmillan; UK, 1982.

☞ African Encyclopedia, The Oxford University Press; 1974.

☞ World Travel Guide, 1997-1998, Worldwide Edition, Columbus Press Ltd.; 1997.

484.

A) AN ORAL HISTORIAN

☞ The Griot's Craft. An Essay on Oral Tradition and Diplomacy, Jan Jansen, Transaction; New Jersey, 2001.

Additional Information:

☞ African history for Beginners, Herb Boyd, Writers & Readers Publishing, Inc.; London, New York, 1994.

☞ Macdonalds Encyclopedia of Africa, Macdonald Educational Ltd.; UK, 1986.

☞ The Africans, David Lamb, New York, Vintage Books; New York, 1983.

485.

B) AMHARIC

☞ The Languages of the World, Kenneth Katzner, Funk & Wagnalls; New York, 1975.

Additional Information:

☞ Africa A-Z, Robert S. Kane, Doubleday and Company Inc.; New York, 1972.

- Caribbean and African Languages, Morgan Dalphinus, Karia Press; 1985.
- Africa: Its Empires, Nations and People, Mary Penick Motley, Wayne State University Press; Detroit, 1969.

486.
B) HARARE
- African Political Facts Since 1945, Cook & Killingray, Macmillan Press Ltd.; 1983.

Additional Information:
- Macdonalds Encyclopedia of Africa, Macdonald Educational Ltd.; UK, 1986.
- New! Encyclopaedia Britannica Print Set, 2002 Edition.
- Africa, Phyllis Martin and Patrick O'Meara, Indiana University Press; Bloomington, 1986.

487.
A) REGGAE SUNSPLASH
- The New Nation, Western Hemisphere; London, May 26, 1997, p.15.

Additional Information:
- The Weekly Journal, Voice Communications; London, January 12, 1995, p.6.
- Reggae Bloodlines: In Search of the Music and Culture of Jamaica, S. Davis and Peter Simon, HEB; 1984.
- Reggae Island: Jamaican Music in the Digital Age, Tom Weber, Kingston Publications; Kingston, JA., 1992.

488.
A) GRENADA
- Grenada: Spice Paradise, Roger Brathwaite, Caribbean Publications; 2002

Additional Information:
- The Cambridge Encyclopedia of Latin America and the Caribbean, Cambridge University Press; 1989, p.524.
- Caribbean Companion: The A-Z Reference, Brian Dyde, The MacMillan Press, Ltd.; London, 1992.
- A Brief History of the Caribbean, Jan Rogozinskii, Facts on File; 1992.

489.
A) THE VICTORIA CROSS
- Your History: From the Beginning of Time to the Present, J. A. Rogers, Black Classic Press; Baltimore, MD, 1983, p.17.

Additional Information:
- They Came to Britain, The History of a Multi-Cultural Nation, Philip Page and Heather Newman, Edward Arnold; UK, 1985, p.26.
- Staying Power, Peter Fryer, Pluto Press; 2nd Edition, UK, 1985.
- Black Britannia: A History of Black People in Britain, Edward Scobie, Johnson Publishing Co.; 1972.

490.
B) NIGERIA
- Identity Transformation and Identity Politics Under Structural Adjustment in Nigeria, Attahiru Jega, Transaction; New Jersey, 2000.

Additional Information:
- Cambridge Encyclopedia, David Crystal, Cambridge University Press; 4th Edition, 2000.
- Macdonalds Encyclopedia of Africa, Macdonald Educational Ltd.; UK, 1986.
- African Political Facts Since 1945, Cook & Killingray, Macmillan Press Ltd.; 1983.

491.
B) BEER
- A History of Egypt, James Henry Breasted, Bantam Matrix Books; New York, NY, 1967, p.88.

Additional Information:
- National Geographic Magazine, October 1941, p.454.
- African History: An Illustrated Handbook, Earl Sweeting and Lez Edmond, London Strategic Policy Unit; 1988, p.15.
- Popular Account of the Ancient Egyptians, Volume 1, Sir J. G. Wilkingson, 1854, p.53.

492.
C) DESIGNING THE HARPSICHORD
- African Presence in Early Europe, Edited by Ivan Van Sertima, Transaction; 1986, p.159.

Additional Information:
- The Moors in Spain, Stanley Lane-Pool, T. Fisher Unwin; London, 1887.
- A Tropical Dependency, Lora L. Shaw (Lady Lugard), p.45.
- Golden Trade of the Moors, E. W. Bovill, Oxford University Press; London, 1968.

General Knowledge

493.
A) MOUNTAINS
☞ The Book of Goddesses and Heroines,
Patricia Monaghan, Dutton; New York,
1981, pp.7-8, 76-77.
Additional Information:
☞ Black Women in Antiquity, Edited by
Ivan Van Sertima, Transaction; 7th
Edition, 1992, p.75.
☞ Mountain Names, Robert Hixson
Julyan, The Mountaineers; Seattle,
1984.
☞ Man, "A Few Notes on the Neolithic
Egyptians and Ethiopians", V. Guiffrida-
Ruggeri, Volume 16, No. 55, pp.87-90.

494.
C) TREVOR McDONALD
☞ International Television News, 200
Grays Inn Road, London WC1X 8XZ.
Additional Information:
☞ Who's Who of Black Achievers, John
Hughes, (ed.), Ethnic Media Group; UK,
1999, p.118.
☞ Black and British, David Bygott, Oxford
University Press; 1992, p.3.
☞ The Mirror, Mirror Newspaper Group;
Mar 5, 1999, p.15

495.
B) FRANCE
☞ African-American Aviators: Bessie
Coleman, William J. Powell, James
Herman Banning, Benjamin O. Davis,
Jr., General Daniel James, Jr., Stanley P.
Jones, Octavia L. Trip, Fred Amram, and
Susan K. Henderson, Capstone Press;
1998.
Additional Information:
☞ Black Women for Beginners, Sandra
Sharp, Writers and Readers Publishing,
Inc.; New York, 1993.
☞ Black Firsts: 2000 Years of Extraordinary
Achievement. Jessie Carney Smith,
Caspar L. Jordan and Robert L. Johns,
Visible Ink Press; USA, 1994, p.255.
☞ Notable Black American Women, Jessie
Carney Smith, (ed.), USA, 1991,
pp.202-203.

Literature & Art

Answers and Sources

496.

B) EMPEROR OF OCEAN PARK

☞ The Emperor of Ocean Park, Stephen L. Carter, Alfred A. Knopf; New York, 2002.

Additional Information:

☞ Ebony, Johnson Publishing; Chicago, December, 2002, p.102.

☞ Integrity, Stephen L. Carter, HarperPerennial; NY, 1997

☞ God's Name in Vain: The Wrongs and Rights of Religion in Politics, Stephen L. Carter, Basic Books; US, 2000.

497.

C) TERRY McMILLAN

☞ Waiting to Exhale, Terry McMillan, Black Swan Publishing; USA, 1992.

Additional Information:

☞ Daughters of Africa: An International Anthology of Words and Writings by Women of African Descent from the Ancient Egyptian to the Present. Edited by Margaret Busby, Vintage Books; New York, 1993, p.828.

☞ The Essential Black Literature Guide, Published in association with the Schomburg Center for Research in Black Culture, Roger M. Valade II, Visible Ink Press; USA, 1996, pp.111, 366.

☞ Ebony, Johnson Publishing; Chicago, April, 2001, pp.154-58.

498.

B) WHITE TEETH

☞ Pride, Voice Communications; September Edition, 2002, p.146.

Additional Information:

☞ The Evening Standard, Associated Newspaper Group; London, 27 January, 2003, p.9.

☞ White Teeth: A Novel, Zadie Smith, Penguin; UK, 2001.

☞ Zadie Smith's White Teeth: A Reader's Guide (Continuum Contemporaries), Claire Squires, Continuum Pub Group; 2002.

499.

B) HIEROGLYPHS

☞ Palaeography, by Bernard Quaritch, London 1894, p.5.

Additional Information:

☞ The Penguin Atlas of World History; From the Beginning to the Eve of the French Revolution. Vol. 1., Herman Kinder and Werner Hilgemann, p.23.

☞ Egypt During the Golden Age, Legrand H. Clegg and Karima Ahmed, The Clegg Series; Compton, CA., 1991.

☞ Nile Valley Contributions to Civilization; Exploding the Myths, Volume 1, Anthony T. Browder, Institute of Khamic Guidance; Washington, D.C., 2000, pp.54, 67, 88.

500.

C) STATUE OF LIBERTY

☞ The Journey of the Songhai People, Calvin Robinson, Brittle, and Robinson, Farmer Press; Washington D.C., 1987. p.193.

Additional Information:

☞ Black Women for Beginners, Sandra Sharp, Writers and Readers Publishing, Inc.; New York, 1993, p.60.

☞ The New York Times, May 8, 1986, Part 2.

☞ The New York Post, June 17, 1986.

501.

A) ICEBERG SLIM

☞ Pimp: The Story of My Life, Iceberg Slim, Pay Back Press; Edinburgh, 1996.

Additional Information:

☞ The Ice Opinion, Ice T., Pan Books; London, 1994.

☞ The Naked Soul of Iceberg Slim, Iceberg Slim, Pay Back Press; Edinburgh, 1996.

☞ Pride, London, Jan/Feb 1997, p.39.

502.

C) RUSSIAN

☞ Pushkin: A Biography, David Magarshak, Grove Press; New York, 1969.

Additional Information:

☞ Great Negroes: Past and Present. Russell L. Adams, Afro-Am Publishing Company; Chicago, Illinois, 3rd Edition (1981) p.119.

☞ Negro History Bulletin, "The Negro's Literary influence on Masterpieces of Music", John Duncun, Washington, D.C., March 1948, pp.134-37.

☞ The Essential Black Literature Guide, Published in association with the Schomburg Center for Research in Black Culture, Roger M. Valade II, Visible Ink Press; USA, 1996, p.212.

503.

C) NELSON MANDELA

☞ The Long Walk to Freedom: The Autobiography of Nelson Mandela, Back Bay Books, Little, Brown; 1995.

Additional Information:

☞ Mandela, Charlene Smith with Desmond Tutu, New Holland/Struik; 2000.

☞ Higher than Hope: Nelson Mandela, Fatimox Meer, Hamish Hamilton Limited; 1989.

☞ Nelson Mandela. The Man and the Movement, Mary Benson, W. W. Norton & Co.; New York and London, 1986.

504.

B) THE NEW NATION

☞ The New Nation, Western Hemisphere; London, November 25, 1996.

Additional Information:

☞ The Evening Standard, Associated Newspaper Group; London, August 22, 1997, pp.25-26.

☞ Who's Who of Black Achievers, John Hughes, (ed.), Ethnic Media Group; UK, 1999, pp.124-152.

☞ Ethnic Media Group; 148 Cambridge Heath Road, London E1, 5QJ.

505.

C) DEVIL IN A BLUE DRESS

☞ Devil in a Blue Dress, Walter Mosley, Pan Books; 1990.

Additional Information:

☞ Ebony, Johnson, Publishing; Chicago, December, 1995, pp.106-12.

☞ A Little Yellow Dog: An Easy Rawlins Mystery, Walter Mosley, Pocket Books; 1997.

☞ The Essential Black Literature Guide, Published in association with the Schomburg Center for Research in Black Culture, Roger M. Valade II, Visible Ink Press; USA, 1996, p.260.

506.

B) DIME

☞ Black Women for Beginners, Sandra Sharp, Writers and Readers Publishing, Inc.; New York, 1993, p.158.

Additional Information:

☞ National Association of State Treasurers, Library Archives, North Cap Street, 444 Washington, D.C., 20090.

☞ Notable Black American Women, Jessie Carney Smith, (ed.), USA, 1991, pp.128-30.

☞ Facts on File Encyclopedia of Black Women in America: Business and Professions (Volume 4), Darlene Clark Hine and Kathleen Thompson, (eds.), Facts of File, Inc.; USA, 1997.

507.

B) THE AUTOBIOGRAPHY OF MISS JANE PITTMAN

☞ The Essential Black Literature Guide, Published in association with the Schomburg Center for Research in Black Culture, Roger M. Valade II, Visible Ink Press; USA, 1996, p.146.

Additional Information:

☞ 1999 Facts About Blacks: A Sourcebook of African American Accomplishment. Raymond M. Corbin, Beckham House Publishers; USA, 1st Edition, 1986.

☞ Black Hollywood: From 1970 to Today, Gary Null, Citadel Press Books; 1993.

☞ The Black Heritage Book of Trivia, Morgan White Jr., Quinlan Press; Boston, 1985.

508.

A) GRAFFITI

☞ Basquiat: A Quick Killing in Art. Phoebe Hobay, Quartet Books; 1998.

Additional Information:

☞ Warhol, Victor Bokis, Frederick Miller Publishing; London, Sydney, Auckland, Johannesburg, 1989.

☞ Evening Standard, Associated Newspaper Group; London, March 27, 1997, p.22.

☞ American Visions, 1156 15th Street, NW, Suite 615, Washington, D.C., 20005.

509.

C) VIBE

☞ Who's Who of Black Achievers, John Hughes, (ed.), Ethnic Media Group; UK, 1999, p.60.

Additional Information:

☞ Vibe Magazine, Quincy Jones and David Salzman Entertainment, Time Publishing, Inc.; Public Relations Department, 75 Rockerfeller Plaza, New York, NY. USA.

☞ Tupac Amaru Shakur 1971-1996, Quincy Jones, Editors of Vibe Magazine (ed.), Three Rivers Press; USA, 1998.

☞ Q: The Autobiography of Quincy Jones, Quincy Jones, Doubleday; New York, 2001.

510.
B) IF WE MUST DIE
☞ Claude McKay: The Black Poet at War, Gayle Addison Jr., Broadside; 1972.
Additional Information:
☞ A Long Way From Home, Claude McKay, An Autobiography, Harcourt, Brace & World, Inc.; 1970.

☞ The Essential Black Literature Guide, Published in association with the Schomburg Center for Research in Black Culture, Roger M. Valade II, Visible Ink Press; USA, 1996, pp.167, 252.

☞ The Black Press in Britain, Ionie Benjamin, Trentham Books; London, 1995, p.18.

511.
A) DENNIS RODMAN
☞ Bad As I Wanna Be, Dennis Rodman with Tim Keown, Delacorte Press; US, 1996.
Additional Information:
☞ The Evening Standard, Associated Newspaper Group; London, May 12, 1997, p.70.

☞ Words from the Worm: An Unauthorized Trip Through the Mind of Dennis Rodman, Dennis Rodman and Dave Whitaker, Bonus Books; 1997.

☞ The New Nation, Western Hemisphere; London, December 23, 1996, p.61.

512.
B) MAAT
☞ Garvey's Last Soldier, David Simon, Ebony Books; UK, 1999, p.4.
Additional Information:
☞ Meter Neter, Volume 1, Ra Un Nefer Amen, Khamit Group; Bronx, NY, 1990.

☞ Nile Valley Contributions to Civilization; Exploding the Myths, Volume 1, Anthony T. Browder, Institute of Khamic Guidance; Washington, D.C., 2000, p.267.

☞ The Gods of the Egyptians, E. A. Wallis Budge, Dover Publications Inc.; NY, 1969.

513.
C) NAOMI CAMPBELL
☞ Swan, Naomi Campbell and Carol Mcintyre, London, 1994.
Additional Information:
☞ Pearson Communications Ltd.; Southbank House, Black Prince Road, London, SE1 7SJ.

☞ The Voice, The Voice Group Ltd.; London, September 13, 1994, p.1.

☞ The Evening Standard, Associated Newspaper Group; London, April 10, 1997, p.13.

514.
B) POETRY
☞ Sappho's Lyre: Archaic Lyric and Woman Poets of Ancient Greece, Diane J. Rayor, University of California Press; Berkley and Los Angeles California, 1991.
Additional Information:
☞ Black Women in Antiquity, Edited by Ivan Van Sertima, Transaction; 7th Edition, 1992, p.145.

☞ Cambridge Encyclopedia, David Crystal, Cambridge University Press; 1990, p.1066.

☞ African Presence in Early Europe, Edited by Ivan Van Sertima, Transaction; 1986, p.213.

515.
A) YOUR BLUES AIN'T LIKE MINE
☞ Your Blues Ain't Like Mine, Bebe Moore Campbell, Ballantine Books; 1993.
Additional Information:
☞ Brothers and Sisters, Bebe Campbell Moore, Heinemann; UK, 1994.

☞ The Essential Black Literature Guide, Published in association with the Schomburg Center for Research in Black Culture, Roger M. Valade II, Visible Ink Press; USA, 1996, p.68.

☞ The Weekly Journal, Voice Communications; London, February 9, 1995, p.15.

516.
A) ACTS OF FAITH
☞ Acts of Faith, Iyanla Vanzant, Simon and Schuster; Fireside, USA, 1993.
Additional Information:
☞ Value in the Valley, Iyanla Vanzant, Simon and Schuster; Fireside, USA, 1995.

☞ Inspired, Inspired Publishing; Issue No. 2, London, May 1995.

☞ Ebony, Johnson Publishing; Chicago, November, 2000, p.96.

517.
C) THE FINAL CALL
☞ The Final Call, 734 West 79th Street, Chicago, Illinois, 60620.
Additional Information:
☞ The Voice, The Voice Group Ltd.; London, April 4, 1995, pp.21-22.
☞ Inside the Nation of Islam: A Historical and Personal Testimony by a Black Muslim, Vibert L. White, University of Florida Press; 2001.
☞ The Nation of Islam: An American Millenarian Movement, Martha F. Lee, Syracuse University Press; 1996.

518.
B) BELOVED
☞ Beloved, Toni Morrison, Picador, Pan Books; 1988.
Additional Information:
☞ Ebony, Johnson Publishing; Chicago, March, 1994, pp.48-50.
☞ Black Womens Writer at Work, Edited by Claudia Tate, Oldcastle Books; England, 1985.
☞ Ebony, Johnson Publishing; Chicago, November, 2000, p.82.

519.
B) BUCHI EMECHETA
☞ In the Ditch, Buchi Emecheta, Allison & Busby; London, 1979.
Additional Information:
☞ Second Class Citizen, Buchi Emecheta, G. Braziller; New York, 1982.
☞ The Essential Black Literature Guide, Published in association with the Schomburg Center for Research in Black Culture, Roger M. Valade II, Visible Ink Press; USA, 1996, p.131.
☞ Daughters of Africa: An International Anthology of Words and Writings by Women of African Descent from the Ancient Egyptian to the Present. Edited by Margaret Busby, Vintage Books; New York, 1993, p.656.

520.
A) ZORA NEALE HURSTON
☞ Dust Tracks on a Road, Zora Neale Hurston, HarperCollins; New York, 1996.

Additional Information:
☞ Their Eyes Were Watching God: A Novel (Perennial Classic), Zora Neale Hurston, Perennial Classics; 1999.
☞ The Complete Stories, Zora Neale Hurston, HarperPerennial Library; USA, 1996.
☞ New Essays on Their Eyes Were Watching God (The American Novel), Michael Awkward, (ed.), Cambridge University Press; 1991.

521.
A) BRITAIN
☞ The Oxford Illustrated Encyclopedia of the Arts, Edited by John Julius Norwich, Oxford University Press; 1990, p.9.
Additional Information:
☞ The Arts of Black Africa, by Jean Laude (translated by Jean Devock), University of California Press; Berkeley, LA, London, 1971.
☞ Cambridge Encyclopedia, David Crystal, Cambridge University Press; 1990, p.129.
☞ Nigerian Imagies: The Splendour of African Sculpture. William B. Fagg, Praeger; New York, 1963.

522.
B) DOVES
☞ The African Origin of Civilization: Myth or Reality, Cheikh Anta Diop, translated by Mercer Cook, Lawrence Hill & Company; 1974, pp.1, 110, 242.
Additional Information:
☞ Black Women in Antiquity, Edited by Ivan Van Sertima, Transaction; 7th Edition, 1992, p.138.
☞ The Life of Greece, Durant Will, Simon & Schuster; New York, 1966.
☞ Nile Valley Contributions to Civilization; Exploding the Myths, Volume 1, Anthony T. Browder, Institute of Khamic Guidance; Washington, D.C., 2000, pp.138.

523.
C) NOTRE DAME OF KAZAN
☞ Black Women in Antiquity, Edited by Ivan Van Sertima, Transaction; New Jersey, 7th Edition, 1992, pp.182-83.
Additional Information:
☞ The New York Sunday News, 'Spain's Black Madonna Venerated for Years', Ben Carruthers, October 7, 1973.

☞ Arts of Russia, Abraam L. Kaganovich, World Publishing Company; Cleveland, 1969.

☞ Christian Art, C. R. Morey, Norton; New York, 1958.

524.
C) INVISIBLE MAN

☞ Invisible Man, Ralph Ellison, Random House; Thirtieth aniversary edition, 1982.

Additional Information:

☞ New Essay's on "Invisible Man". Robert O'Meally, (ed.), Cambridge University Press; New York, 1988.

☞ Afro-American Literature in the Twentieth Century, Michael J. Cook, Yale University Press; New Haven 1984.

☞ Ralph Ellison: A Collection of Critical Essays. John Hersey, (ed.), Prentice-Hall; New Jersey, 1974.

525.
A) THOTH

☞ The Gods of the Egyptians, E. A. Wallis Budge, Dover Publications Inc.; NY, 1969.

Additional Information:

☞ Egypt, Gift of the Nile, Walter A. Fairservis, The Macmillan Co.; New York, 1963, pp.74-75.

☞ Stolen Legacy. George G. M. James, Philosophical Libraries; NY, 1988, p.108.

☞ Black Man of the Nile and His Family. Dr. Yosef A. A. Ben Jochannon, Black Classic Press; Baltimore, MD, 1988.

526.
B) JUAN DE PAREJA

☞ The Guinness Book of Records, Guinness Publishing Ltd.; UK, 1976, pp.85-86.

Additional Information:

☞ History of Black Americans; From Africa to the Emergence of the Cotton Kingdoms. Philip S. Foner, Greenwood Press; 1975, p.98.

☞ Your History: From the Beginning of Time to the Present, J. A. Rogers, Black Classic Press; Baltimore, MD, 1983.

☞ "Portrait of Juan de Parega, the Assistant to Valézquez", The Minneapolis Institute of Arts, 2400 Third Avenue South, Minneapolis, Minnesota, 55404, USA.

527.
A) JAMES BALDWIN

☞ James Baldwin: A Biography. David Leeming, Knopf; USA, 1994.

Additional Information:

☞ The Price of the Ticket: Collected Nonfiction 1948-1985, James Baldwin, St. Martins Press; Marek, New York, 1985.

☞ The Essential Black Literature Guide, Published in association with the Schomburg Center for Research in Black Culture, Roger M. Valade II, Visible Ink Press; USA, 1996, p.29.

☞ Afro-American Literature in the Twentieth Century, Michael J. Cook, Yale University Press; New Haven 1984.

528.
B) THE 4 MUSKETEERS

☞ Photographic Records Department, Sotheby Park Bernet, New York, USA (Photograph by Gaspard Felix Tournachon).

Additional Information:

☞ Five French Negro Authors, Mercer Cook, The Associated Publishers; Washington, D.C., 1943.

☞ My Memoirs, Alexandre Dumas, 6 Vols., New York, 1907-1908.

☞ The Incredible Marquis, Herbert Sherman Gorman, Farrar and Rinehart, Inc.; New York, 1929.

529.
B) THE COLOR PURPLE

☞ Afro-American Literature in the Twentieth Century, Michael J. Cook, Yale University Press; New Haven 1984.

Additional Information:

☞ Black Womens Writer at Work, Edited by Claudia Tate, Oldcastle Books; England, 1985.

☞ Black Americana. Richard A. Long, Admiral; UK, 1985, p.116.

☞ Revolutionary Petunias and other Poems, Alice Walker, The Woman's Press; London, 1988.

530.
A) SPIDER

☞ Mango Spice; 44 Caribbean Songs, A & C Black Ltd.; London, 1981, pp.40-44.

Additional Information:

☞ Jamaican Song and Story, Collected and Edited by Walter Jekyll, Dover Publications, Inc.; New York, 1966.

☞ African Kingdoms, Basil Davidson, Time-Life Books; (Nederland), 1980, p.150.

☞ The Essential Black Literature Guide, Published in association with the Schomburg Center for Research in Black Culture, Roger M. Valade II, Visible Ink Press; USA, 1996, p.361.

531.
C) ASHANTI

☞ The Africans, David Lamb, New York, Vintage Books; New York, 1983.

Additional Information:

☞ African Kingdoms, Basil Davidson, Time-Life Books; (Nederland), 1980, pp.107, 126.

☞ Our Story: A Hand Book of African History and Contemporary Issues, Edited by Akyaaba Addai-Sebo and Ansel Wong, London Strategic Policy; 1988.

☞ The Encyclopedia of Africa, Franklin Watts, Inc.; New York and London, 1976.

532.
B) BILAL

☞ Dictionary of Islam, D. P. Hughes, PBH Publishers; 1885.

Additional Information:

☞ An Introduction to African Civilizations, Willis N. Huggins, Avon House; New York, 1937, p.71, 97.

☞ World's Great Men of Color, J. A. Rogers, Volume 1, Collier Macmillan Publishers; 1972, pp.143-147.

☞ African Origin of the Major Western Religions, Dr. Yosef A. A. Ben Jochannon, Black Classic Press; Baltimore, MD, 1988.

533.
A) FREEDOM'S JOURNAL

☞ Your History: From the Beginning of Time to the Present, J. A. Rogers, Black Classic Press; Baltimore, MD, 1983, p.58.

Additional Information:

☞ 1999 Facts About Blacks: A Sourcebook of African American Accomplishment. Raymond M. Corbin, Beckham House Publishers; USA, 1st Edition, 1986.

☞ The Essential Black Literature Guide, Published in association with the Schomburg Center for Research in Black Culture, Roger M. Valade II, Visible Ink Press; USA, 1996, p.205.

☞ Black Firsts: 2000 Years of Extraordinary Achievement. Jessie Carney Smith, Caspar L. Jordan and Robert L. Johns, Visible Ink Press; USA, 1994, p.219.

534.
A) PHILADELPHIA TRIBUNE

☞ Encyclopedia of Black America, W. A. Low and Virgil A. Clift, (eds.), Mcgraw-Hill; New York, 1981, p.642.

Additional Information:

☞ The Black Press: 1827-1890. Martin E. Dann, (ed.), G. P. Putnam's Sons; New York, 1971.

☞ 1999 Facts About Blacks: A Sourcebook of African American Accomplishment. Raymond M. Corbin, Beckham House Publishers; USA, 1st Edition, 1986.

☞ Alexander's Magazine, Number 6, (editorial), August 15, 1908, USA.

535.
B) YARDIE

☞ Yardie, Victor Headley, The X Press; UK, 1991.

Additional Information:

☞ Who's Who of Black Achievers, John Hughes, (ed.), Ethnic Media Group; UK, 1999, pp.18, 80.

☞ The New Nation, Western Hemisphere; London, January 6, 1997, p.34.

☞ The Black Press in Britain, Ionie Benjamin, Trentham Books; London, 1995, p.78.

536.
A) LUCY MORGAN

☞ The Complete Works of William Shakespeare, George Lyman Kittredge, (ed.), Grolier; New York, 1958 (Sonnets 127, 131 & 132).

Additional Information:

☞ The Illustrated Stratford Shakespeare; All 37 Plays, All 160 Sonnets and Poems, Chancellor Press; UK, 1982, pp.1020-21.

☞ Black Britannia: A History of Black People in Britain, Edward Scobie, Johnson Publishing Co.; 1972, p.6.

Literature & Art

☞ Roots in Britain, Ziggi Alexander and Audrey Dewjee, Brent Library Service; 2nd Edition, 1981.

537.
C) ROOTS
☞ Roots, Alex Haley, Vintage Press; UK, 1991.

Additional Information:
☞ Ebony Pictorial History of Black America: Volume 3. Civil Rights Movement to Black Revolution, Johnson Publishing Company; 1974, p.271.
☞ The New Nation, Western Hemisphere; London, March 17, 1997, p.2.
☞ The Essential Black Literature Guide, Published in association with the Schomburg Center for Research in Black Culture, Roger M. Valade II, Visible Ink Press; USA, 1996, pp.160, 317.

538.
B) 16
☞ Dopefiend, Holloway, Donald Goines, Holloway House Publishers; US, Reissued, 2000.

Additional Information:
☞ The New Nation, Ethnic Media Group; London, 7 June, 2004, p.27.
☞ Never Die Alone, Donald Goines, Holloway House Publishers; US, 2000.
☞ Daddy Cool, Donald Goines, Holloway House Publishers; US, 2003

539.
A) C. L. R. JAMES
☞ Minty Alley, C. L. R. James, New Beacon Books Ltd.; London, and Port of Spain, 1971.

Additional Information:
☞ The Essential Black Literature Guide, Published in association with the Schomburg Center for Research in Black Culture, Roger M. Valade II, Visible Ink Press; USA, 1996, p.191.
☞ The Black Jacobins, C. L. R. James, Allison & Busby; 1984.
☞ Black British Literature, An Annotated Bibliography, Prahbu Guptara, Dangaroo Press; London, 1986, pp.100-2.

540.
A) ROCK THIS
☞ Rock This, Chris Rock, Littlem, Brown & Company; 1998.

Additional Information:
☞ African American Humor: The Best Black Comedy from Slavery to Today, (Library of Black America, Mel Watkins, Lawrence Hill & Co.; 2002.
☞ African American Viewers and the Black Situation Comedy: Situation Racial Humor (Studies in African American History and Culture), Robin R. Means Coleman, Garland Publishing; USA, 2000.
☞ On the Real Side: A History of African American Comedy. Mel Watkins, Lawrence Hill; USA, 1999.

541.
C) LOUISE BENNETT
☞ Black Women for Beginners, Sandra Sharp, Writers and Readers Publishing, Inc.; New York, 1993, p.174.

Additional Information:
☞ Jamaica Labish, Louise Bennet, Sangster's Book Stores; Jamaica, 1966.
☞ Daughters of Africa: An International Anthology of Words and Writings by Women of African Descent from the Ancient Egyptian to the Present. Edited by Margaret Busby, Vintage Books; New York, 1993, p.278.
☞ Blaze a Fire: Significant Contributions of Caribbean Woman, Nesha Z. Haniff, Sister Vision; Toronto, 1988.

542.
C) ANDROMEDA
☞ Greek Myths, Robert Graves, Volume 1, Penguin Books;

Additional Information:
☞ Black Women in Antiquity, Edited by Ivan Van Sertima, Transaction; 7th Edition, 1992, pp.5, 13-14.
☞ Herodotus: The Histories. Great Books of the Western World, Encyclopaedia Brittanica; Chicago, 1952.
☞ Blacks in Antiquity: Ethiopians in the Greco-Roman Experience, Frank M. Snowden Jr., The Belcap Press of Harvard University Press; Cambridge, Mass., 1970.

543.
B) GWENDOLYNE BROOKS
☞ Pulitzer Prizes, Columbia University, 709 Journalism Building, 2950 Broadway, New York, NY, 10027.

Additional Information:
☞ The Essential Black Literature Guide, Published in association with the Schomburg Center for Research in Black Culture, Roger M. Valade II, Visible Ink Press; USA, 1996, p.11.
☞ Daughters of Africa: An International Anthology of Words and Writings by Women of African Descent from the Ancient Egyptian to the Present. Edited by Margaret Busby, Vintage Books; New York, 1993, p.268.
☞ Afro-American Literature in the Twentieth Century, Michael J. Cook, Yale University Press; New Haven 1984.

544.
C) THE KEBRA NEGAST
☞ Kebra Nagast (tanslated by Sir Wallis Budge), Oxford University Press; London, 1932.

Additional Information:
☞ Black Characters and References of the Holy Bible, F. S. Rhoades, First Edition, Vantage Press; New York, 1980.
☞ Wonderful Ethiopians of the Ancient Cushite Empire, Drusilla Dunjee Houston, Black Classic Press; Baltimore, Maryland, 1989.
☞ The Black Biblical Heritage, John L. Johnson, Winston-Derek Publishers, Inc.; 1974.

545.
A) 1920s
☞ This Was Harlem 1900-1950, Jervis Anderson, Farrah, Straus, Giroux; New York, 1982.

Additional Information:
☞ Ebony Pictorial History of Black America: Volume 3. Civil Rights Movement to Black Revolution, Johnson Publishing Company; 1974, pp.263-65, 268.
☞ A Pictorial History of Black America. Langston Hughes, Crown; NY, 1983.
☞ Black Artists of the New Generation, Elton C. Fax, Dodd, Mead; & Co.; New York, 1977.

546.
C) THE SAGA PRIZE
☞ The Weekly Journal, Voice Communications; London, August 17, 1995, p.2.

Additional Information:
☞ Real Life, Marsha Hunt, Chatto & Windus; 1986.
☞ Joy, Marsha Hunt, Plume; 1992.
☞ Some Kind of Black, Diran Adebayo, London, 1994, (First winner of SAGA prize).

547.
A) CHICAGO
☞ 1999 Facts About Blacks: A Sourcebook of African American Accomplishment. Raymond M. Corbin, Beckham House Publishers; USA, 1st Edition, 1986, pp.83, 86.

Additional Information:
☞ Wall of Respect, Mary & Leigh Block Museum of Art, 1967 Sheridan Road, Evanstan, IL, 60208.
☞ The Explosion of Chicago Black Street Gangs, Useni Eugene Perkins, Third World Press; USA.
☞ Black Artists of the New Generation, Elton C. Fax, Dodd, Mead; & Co.; New York, 1977.

548.
B) LATIN
☞ The Comedies (Penguin Classics), Terence Afer Publius Terentius, Betty Radice (trans.), Viking Press; 1976.

Additional Information:
☞ The Forgotten Great Africans 3000 B.C.-1959 A.D., G. K. Osei, London, 1965, p.8.
☞ What They Never Told You in History Class, Indus Khamit-Kush, Luxorr Publications; USA, 1983, p.278.
☞ Sex and Race, Volume 1, J. A. Rogers, 9th Edition, H. M. Rogers Publishers; USA, 1968, p.88.

549.
B) EDWARD WILMOT BLYDEN
☞ Black Spokesman. Edward Wilmot Blyden, Edited by Hollis R. Lynch, Frank Cass & Co. Ltd.; 1971.

Additional Information:
☞ Staying Power, Peter Fryer, Pluto Press; 2nd Edition, UK, 1985, pp.275-77.

Literature & Art

- Edward Wilmot Blyden, Hollis R. Lynch, Oxford University Press; London and New York, 1967.
- Blyden of Liberia, Edith Holden, Vantage Press; New York, 1966.

550.
A) BLACK
- Christ and Krishna, John M. Robertson, London, 1889, p.16.

Additional Information:
- Book of the Beginnings, Gerald Massey, Volume 1, New York, 1930.
- What They Never Told You in History Class, Indus Khamit-Kush, Luxorr Publications; USA, 1983.
- Elevation to Krishna Consciousness, A. C. Bhaktivedanta Swami Prabhupada, Bhaktivedanta Book Trust; Los Angeles, 1973.

551.
C) ROBERT BROWNING
- World's Great Men of Color, Volume II, J. A. Rogers, Collier Macmillan Publishers; 1972, pp.550-51

Additional Information:
- Ebony, Johnson Publishing; Chicago, May, 1995, pp.96-100.
- Browning Society Papers, February 28, 1890, pp.31-36.
- Sex and Race, Volume 2, J. A. Rogers, 7th Edition, H. M. Rogers Publishers; USA, 1980, pp.122-33.

552.
C) LINTON KWESI JOHNSON
- Black and British, David Bygott, Oxford University Press; 1992.

Additional Information:
- Black British Literature, An Annotated Bibliography, Prahbu Guptara, Dangaroo Press; London, 1986, p.104.
- The Weekly Journal, Voice Communications; London, March 23, 1995, p.15.
- Voices of the Living and the Dead, L. K. Johnson, Race Today Publications; Revised Edition, 1983.

553.
B) BILLIE HOLIDAY
- Billie's Blues, John Chilton, Quartet Books; London 1975.

Additional Information:
- Wishing on the Moon: The Life and Times of Billie Holiday, Donald Clarke, Viking, 1994.
- Daughters of Africa: An International Anthology of Words and Writings by Women of African Descent from the Ancient Egyptian to the Present. Edited by Margaret Busby, Vintage Books; New York, 1993, p.259.
- Jazz Women: 1900 to the Present. Their Words, Lives and Music, Sally Placksin, Pluto Press; London and Sydney, 1982.

554.
B) AESOP
- Blacks in Antiquity, Frank M. Snowden Jr., Harvard University Press; Cambridge, Mass., 1970, pp.5-7, 188, 197.

Additional Information:
- African History, Earl Sweeting and Lez Edmond, London Strategic Policy Unit; 1988, p.27.
- World's Great Men of Color, Volume 1, J. A. Rogers, Collier Macmillan Publishers; 1972, pp.73-80.
- Lives of Eminent Philosophers, Laertius Diogenes, Vols.1-2, G. P. Putnam's Sons; New York, 1925.

555.
C) MAYA ANGELOU
- I Know Why the Cage Bird Sings, Maya Angelou, Random House; New York, 1970.

Additional Information:
- The Heart of a Woman, Maya Angelou, Bantam Books; New York-Toronto-London-Sydney-Auckland, 1994.
- Jet, Johnson Publishing Co.; Chicago, February 8, 1993, pp.4-10.
- Womens Writer at Work, Edited by Claudia Tate, Oldcastle Books; England, 1985.

556.
A) 20,000
- Black Britannia: A History of Black People in Britain, Edward Scobie, Johnson Publishing Co.; 1972, p.13.

Additional Information:
- Staying Power, Peter Fryer, Pluto Press; 2nd Edition, UK, 1985.

- ☞ The New Nation, Western Hemisphere; London, January 20, 1997, p.36.
- ☞ Black Settlers in Britain, 1555-1958, Nigel File and Chris, Power, Heinemann Educational Books; UK, 1981.

557.
A) LAND OF THE LOTUS EATER
- ☞ Negroes: Past and Present. Russell L. Adams, Afro-Am Publishing Company; Chicago, Illinois, 3rd Edition (1981).

Additional Information:
- ☞ They Showed the Way Up, Charlemae Hill Rollins, Thomas Y. Crowell Company; New York, 1964, pp.121-125.
- ☞ World's Great Men of Color, Volume II, J. A. Rogers, Collier Macmillan Publishers; 1972.
- ☞ Henry Ossawa Tanner: Illustrated Catalogue of Religious Paintings by The Great Distinguished American Artist, Mr. Henry O. Tanner, American Art Association, New York, 1908.

558.
B) THINGS FALL APART
- ☞ Things Fall Apart, Chinua Achebe, Heinemann; UK, 1989.

Additional Information:
- ☞ Talking With African Writers, Jane Wilkingson, Heinemann Educational Books, Inc.; 1992, p.91.
- ☞ Chinua Achebe, David Carroll, Macmillan; 1990.
- ☞ American, African and Caribbean Authors, A Bio Bibliography, Libraries UnLimited; 1985.

559.
A) THREE
- ☞ Cambridge Encyclopedia, David Crystal, Cambridge University Press; 4th Edition, 2000.

Additional Information:
- ☞ The African Origin of Civilization: Myth or Reality, Cheikh Anta Diop, translated by Mercer Cook, Lawrence Hill & Company; 1974, p.45.
- ☞ Hutchingson Encyclopedia, 8th Edition, Hutchingson; UK, 1988.
- ☞ Nile Valley Contributions to Civilization; Exploding the Myths, Volume 1, Anthony T. Browder, Institute of Khamic Guidance; Washington, D.C., 2000, p.182.

560.
C) ETHIOPIANS
- ☞ What They Never Told You in History Class, Indus Khamit-Kush, Luxorr Publications; USA, 1983.

Additional Information:
- ☞ The Iliad. Chapter I, "The Quarrel", translated by E. V. Rieu, Penguin Classics; 1988.
- ☞ Herodotus: The Histories. Great Books of the Western World, Encyclopaedia Brittanica; Chicago, 1952.
- ☞ Wonderful Ethiopians of the Ancient Cushite Empire, Drusilla Dunjee Houston, Black Classic Press; Baltimore, Maryland, 1989.

561.
B) KINGS
- ☞ King James Bible, II Kings, Chapter 19, Verse 9.

Additional Information:
- ☞ African Kingdoms, Basil Davidson, Time-Life Books; (Nederland), 1980, p.36.
- ☞ The Black Biblical Heritage, John L. Johnson, Winston-Derek Publishers, Inc.; 1974.
- ☞ Black Characters and References of the Holy Bible, F. S. Rhoades, First Edition, Vantage Press; New York, 1980.

562.
B) FOURTEEN
- ☞ Cleopatra's Needle; With a Preliminary Sketch of the History, Erection Uses and Signification, Charles E. Moldenke, The Lancaster Press, Inc.; 1935.

Additional Information:
- ☞ The Book of the Dead, Edited and translated by Ernest A. Wallis Budge, Dover Publications; New York, NY, 1967.
- ☞ Nile Valley Contributions to Civilization; Exploding the Myths, Volume 1, Anthony T. Browder, Institute of Khamic Guidance; Washington, D.C., 2000, p.89.
- ☞ Stories From Ancient Egypt, Marguerite Divin, Burke Books; London, 1965, pp.41-42.

563.
C) GERALD BOYD
- ☞ St. Petersburg Times, June 6, 2003

- Burning Down My Masters' House: My Life at the New York Times by Jayson Blair, New Millennium; 2004, NY, 2004.

Additional Information:

- The Sunday Times, London, March 24, Section 5, P.4., 2004
- Gray Lady Down: Jayson Blair and How the New York Times Lost Touch With America, William McGowan, Encounter Books; 2004

564.
C) ETHIOPS

- Herodotus: The Histories. Great Books of the Western World, Encyclopaedia Brittanica; Chicago, 1952, pp.49-50, 60-65, 69-70.

Additional Information:

- African Presence in Early Europe, Edited by Ivan Van Sertima, Transaction; 1986, p.213.
- Celtic Druids, Godfrey Higgins, London, 1829, p.162.
- Nile Valley Contributions to Civilization; Exploding the Myths, Volume 1, Anthony T. Browder, Institute of Khamic Guidance; Washington, D.C., 2000, p.139.

565.
A) 1992

- Omeros, Derek Walcott, Faber; UK, 1990.

Additional Information:

- Critical Perspectives on Derek Walcott, Robert D. Hamner, Three Continents; 1993.
- Jet, Johnson Publishing Co.; Chicago, October 26, 1992, p.14.
- Time, Time Inc.; USA, October 19, 1992, p.24, 65.

566.
B) $10,000

- Walker's Appeal, David Walker, Arno Press and The New York Times, 1969.

Additional Information:

- 1999 Facts About Blacks: A Sourcebook of African American Accomplishment. Raymond M. Corbin, Beckham House Publishers; USA, 1st Edition, 1986.
- On the Real Side: A History of African American Comedy. Mel Watkins, Lawrence Hill; USA, 1999, pp.404, 413.

- Chronology of African American History, Hornsby, USA, p.16.

567.
C) IT CONTAINED NO PUNCTUATION

- Sassafrass, Cypress and Indigo, Ntozake Shange, Mathuen; London, 1983.

Additional Information:

- Black Women for Beginners, Sandra Sharp, Writers and Readers Publishing, Inc.; New York, 1993.
- The Essential Black Literature Guide, Published in association with the Schomburg Center for Research in Black Culture, Roger M. Valade II, Visible Ink Press; USA, 1996, p.332.
- 1999 Facts About Blacks: A Sourcebook of African American Accomplishment. Raymond M. Corbin, Beckham House Publishers; USA, 1st Edition, 1986.

568.
A) CONFESSIONS

- Augustine. His Life and Thoughts, Warren Thomas Smith, John Knox Press; Atlanta, 1980.

Additional Information:

- The Confessions of St. Augustine, Aurelius Augustine, Chatto and Windus, London, 1909.
- Saints Who Made History, Maisie Ward, Sheed and Ward, London, 1960.
- A Biographical Dictionary of the Saints, by the Rt. Rev. F. G. Holweck, Herder Book Company; 1969 (Originally Published 1924).

569.
A) CARTER G. WOODSON

- Carter Goodwin Woodson:The Father of Black HIstory, Patricia McKissack and Frederick McKissack, Enslow, 1991.

Additional Information:

- The Essential Black Literature Guide, Published in association with the Schomburg Center for Research in Black Culture, Roger M. Valade II, Visible Ink Press; USA, 1996, p.385.
- Great Negroes: Past and Present. Russell L. Adams, Afro-Am Publishing Company; Chicago, Illinois, 3rd Edition (1981) p.114.
- Negro History, "Place of Carter G. Woodson in American Historiography", John Hope Franklin, Bulletin, Washington, D.C., May 1950, pp.174-76.

570.
A) SAMURAI WARRIOR
☞ The African Origin of Civilization: Myth or Reality, Cheikh Anta Diop, translated by Mercer Cook, Lawrence Hill & Company; 1974, p.281.
Additional Information:
☞ African Presence in Asian Antiquity, Runoko Rashadi, Nile Valley Civilizations, Edited by Ivan Van Sertima, Journal of African Civilization Ltd.; Inc.; NJ, 1985.
☞ Prehistoric Japan, Professor Munro, Yokohama, 1911.
☞ African Presence in Early Asia, Edited by Ivan Van Sertima, Transaction; New Brunswick (USA), Oxford (UK), 1985.

571.
B) THIRTY-FIRST
☞ The Quran, (Chatper 31) Dar Al-Choura, Clemeenceau St. Tajer Bldg., Beirut, 1980.
Additional Information:
☞ World's Great Men of Color, Volume 1, J. A. Rogers, Collier Macmillan Publishers; 1972, pp.67-72.
☞ Folk-Lore of the Holy Land, J. E. Hanauer, London, 1907, pp.19-22.
☞ Islam: A Short History, Karen Armstrong, Random House; New York, 2000.

572.
C) PUBLISH A BOOK
☞ Phillis Wheatley, America's First Black Poetess, M. M. Fuller, Gerrad Publishing Co.; USA, 1971.
Additional Information:
☞ Black Women for Beginners, Sandra Sharp, Writers and Readers Publishing, Inc.; New York, 1993.
☞ Black Firsts: 2000 Years of Extraordinary Achievement. Jessie Carney Smith, Caspar L. Jordan and Robert L. Johns, Visible Ink Press; USA, 1994, p.418.
☞ Daughters of Africa: An International Anthology of Words and Writings by Women of African Descent from the Ancient Egyptian to the Present. Edited by Margaret Busby, Vintage Books; New York, 1993.

573.
B) PROVERBS
☞ World Civilizations: Their History and Their Culture, Philip Lee Ralph, (ed. et al), 9th edition, Volume 1, W. W. Norton & Co.; New York, 1997.
Additional Information:
☞ African Origin of the Major Western Religions, Dr. Yosef A. A. Ben Jochannon, Black Classic Press; Baltimore, MD, 1988.
☞ New African, April 2001, ICP Ltd.; London, p.20.
☞ The Dawn of Consciousness, James H. Breasted, C. Scribner & Sons; New York, 1933.

574.
B) 15,000 YEARS
☞ A History of Art, E. Faure, Volume 1, New York, 1931, p.13.
Additional Information:
☞ Sex and Race, Volume 1, J. A. Rogers, 9th Edition, H. M. Rogers Publishers; USA, 1968, p.170.
☞ Cambridge Encyclopedia, David Crystal, Cambridge University Press; 1990, p.1302.
☞ Black Women in Antiquity, Edited by Ivan Van Sertima, Transaction; 7th Edition, 1992, pp.99.

575.
C) POLAND
☞ Washington Post, May 4, 1979, USA.
Additional Information:
☞ Jet, Johnson Publishing Co.; Chicago, February 15, 1982.
☞ Black Women in Antiquity, Edited by Ivan Van Sertima, Transaction; 7th Edition, 1992, p.180, 181.
☞ Time, Time Inc.; USA, June 11, 1979.

576.
C) RA
☞ The Gods of the Egyptians, E. A. Wallis Budge, Dover Publications Inc.; NY, 1969.
Additional Information:
☞ Black Athena: The Afroasiatic Roots of Classical Civilsation, Vols. 1 & 2, Martin Bernal, FAB; London, 1991.
☞ African Origin of the Major Western Religions, Dr. Yosef A. A. Ben Jochannon, Black Classic Press; Baltimore, MD, 1988.
☞ Man and His Gods, Homer W. Smith, Little, Brown; Boston, 1952.

577.

A) EBONY

☞ Black Entrepreneurship in America, Shelly Green and Paul Pryde, Transaction; New Jersey, 1996.

Additional Information:

☞ The Black Press in Britain, Ionie Benjamin, Trentham Books; London, 1995, pp.101-3.

☞ Ebony Pictorial History of Black America: Volume 3. Civil Rights Movement to Black Revolution, Johnson Publishing Company; 1974, pp.37, 223-24, 229, 278, 287.

☞ The Black American Reference Book. Mabel M. Smyth, (ed.), Prentice-Hall Inc.; USA, 1976.

578.

C) THE WIND DONE GONE

☞ United States Court of Appeals, 11th Circuit, 56 Forsyth Street N.W., Atlanta, 30303.

Additional Information:

☞ The Voice, The Voice Group Ltd.; London, October 22, 2001, p.11.

☞ The Wind Done Gone, Alice Randall, Houghton and Mufflin; USA, 2001.

☞ The Voice, The Voice Group Ltd.; London, June 11, 2001, p.10.

579.

B) THE KA'ABA

☞ Dictionary of Islam, T. P. Hughes, PBH Publishers; 1885.

Additional Information:

☞ Ancient Egypt and the Islamic Destiny, by Mustapher El-Amin, First Edition, New Mind Productions; New Jersey, 1988.

☞ Folk-Lore of the Holy Land, J. E. Hanauer, London, 1907.

☞ Islam: A Short History, Karen Armstrong, Random House; New York, 2000.

580.

B) THE JAMAICA GLEANER

☞ The Black Press in Britain, Ionie Benjamin, Trentham Books; London, 1995, pp.65-66.

Additional Information:

☞ The Story of the Gleaner, Linda D. Cameron, Kingston, Jamaica, 2001.

☞ The Book of Jamaica, Russell Banks, HarperCollins; 1996.

☞ The Daily Gleaner, 7 North Street, P.O. Box 40, Kingston, Jamaica.

581.

A) RITA DOVE

☞ Ebony, Johnson Publishing; Chicago, May, 1995, p.20.

Additional Information:

☞ Pulitzer Prizes, Columbia University, 709 Journalism Building, 2950 Broadway, New York, NY, 10027.

☞ Daughters of Africa: An International Anthology of Words and Writings by Women of African Descent from the Ancient Egyptian to the Present. Edited by Margaret Busby, Vintage Books; New York, 1993, p.825.

☞ Ebony, Johnson Publishing; Chicago, March, 1994, p.48.

582.

B) HE USED ELEPHANT DUNG

☞ Brooklyn Museum of Art, 200 Eastern Parkway, Brooklyn, NY, 11238.

Additional Information:

☞ The Turner Prize, Virginia Button, Tate Publishing; London, 2001.

☞ Tate Britain, Millbank, London, SW1P 4RG.

☞ The Times, London, December 2, 1998.

583.

A) ESSENCE

☞ The Black Press in Britain, Ionie Benjamin, Trentham Books; London, 1995, p.103

Additional Information:

☞ Lessons in Living, Susan L. Taylor, USA, 1996.

☞ The Voice, The Voice Group Ltd.; London, July 9, 1996, p.18.

☞ The New Nation, Western Hemisphere; London, May 26, 1997, p.7.

584.

B) SHORTHAND WRITING

☞ Shorthand, Heffey Collection, New York Public Library; I.D. 5 D.V. 261, pp.8-10.

Additional Information:

☞ The Conquest of Civilization, James H. Breasted, Harper & Brothers; New York, 1926, p.53.

☞ New African, April 2000, ICP Ltd.; London, p.23.

☞ African History, Earl Sweeting and Lez Edmond, London Strategic Policy Unit; 1988, p.22.

585.
B) EBONICS
☞ The Real Ebonics Debate: Power, Language, and the Education of African-American Children, Theresa Perry and Lisa Delpit, (ed.), Beacon Press; USA, 1998.
Additional Information:
☞ The Old Fat White Guy's Guide to Ebonics, I. B. White, Cliff Carle (ed.), CCC Publications; USA, 1987.
☞ Black Communications: Breaking Down the Barriers, Evelyn B. Dandy, African American Images; Chicago, 1991.
☞ Ebony, Johnson Publishing; Chicago, August, 2000, p.156-58.

586.
C) TO KILL A MOCKINGBIRD
☞ Harper Lee's To Kill A Mocking Bird (Barron's Book Notes), Joyce Milton, Barron's Educational Series, 1984.
Additional Information:
☞ To Kill A Mocking Bird, Reissued Edition, Harper Lee, Prentice Hall; 1988.
☞ The Black Heritage Book of Trivia, Morgan White Jr., Quinlan Press; 1985.
☞ Iron Cages: Race and Culture in Nineteenth-Century America, Ronal T. Takaki, Alfred A. Knopf; New York, 1979.

587.
C) MALORIE BLACKMAN (BAFTA-British Art/ Films and TV Awards)
☞ Hacker, Malarie Blackman, Corgi; 1994.
Additional Information:
☞ The Weekly Journal, Voice Communications; London, April 21, 1994, p.12.
☞ Thief, Malarie Blackman, Corgi; 1995.
☞ Pig Heart Boy, Malarie Blackman, Doubleday; 1996.

588.
A) ST. MATTHEW
☞ King James Bible, St. Matthew, Chapter 1.
Additional Information:
☞ The Black Biblical Heritage, John L. Johnson, Winston-Derek Publishers, Inc.; 1974.

☞ The Original African Heritage Study Bible, Dr. Cain Hope Felder, (ed.), World Bible Punlishing Co.; USA, 1993.
☞ Black Characters and References of the Holy Bible, F. S. Rhoades, First Edition, Vantage Press; New York, 1980.

589.
B) LES HONNEURS PERDUS
☞ Les Honneurs Perdus, Calixthe Beyala, Roman Books; 1995.
Additional Information:
☞ The Weekly Journal, Positive Time and Space Co.; London, December 4, 1996, p.18.
☞ The Sun Hath Looked Upon Me, (African Writers Series), Calixthe Beyala, Marjolijn De Jaeger, (trans.), Heinemann; 1996.
☞ Mon Afrique: Photographs of Sub-Saharan Africa, Pascal Maitre, Calix Beyala (Preface), Aperture, 2000.

590.
A) HARVARD
☞ Ebony, Johnson Publishing; Chicago, November, 2000, p.62.
Additional Information:
☞ The Essential Black Literature Guide, Published in association with the Schomburg Center for Research in Black Culture, Roger M. Valade II, Visible Ink Press; USA, 1996, pp.149-50.
☞ Colored People, Louis Gates, USA, 1994.
☞ The Slave's Narrative: Texts and Contexts. Henry Louis Gates and Charles T. Davis, (eds.), Oxford University Press; New York, 1972.

591.
C) SIR GALAHAD
☞ Nature Knows No Color Line. J. A. Rogers, 3rd Edition, H. M. Rogers Publishers; 1952, p.75.
Additional Information:
☞ Story of King Arthur and His Knights, Howard Pyle, Dover Publications; 1982.
☞ The World of King Arthur and His Court: People, Places, Legend, and Law, Kevin Crossley-Holland, Dutton Books; 1999.
☞ King Arthur and His Knights: Selected Tales by Sir Thomas Malory, (A Galaxy Book; 434), Eugene Vinaver, (ed.), Oxford University, 1983

Literature & Art

592.
B) WOLE SOYINKA
☞ Wole Soyinka Revisited, Derek Wright, Twayne; 1993.
Additional Information:
☞ Talking With African Writers, Jane Wilkingson, Heinemann Educational Books, Inc.; 1992, p.91.
☞ Aké: The Years of Childhood, Wole Soyinka, Random House; New York, 1981.
☞ Myth, Literature, and the African Myth, Wole Soyinka, Cambridge University Press; New York, 1976.

593.
A) LOIS MAILOU JONES
☞ The Life and Art of Lois Mailou Jones, Tritobia Hayes Benjamin and Lois Mailou Jones, Pomengranate; 1997.
Additional Information:
☞ Ebony, Johnson Publishing; Chicago, January, 1997, pp.100-5.
☞ Persistent Women Artists, Pablita Velarde, Mine Okubo, Lois Mailou Jones, Presented by Batty LaDuke, USA, NTSC Formats (video) Only, 1996.
☞ Wonders: The Best Children's Poems of Effie Lee Newsome, By Effie Lee Newsome, Lois Mailou Jones, (illustrator), Rudine Sims Bishop, (ed.), Boyds Mills Press; 1999.

594.
C) MINE BOY
☞ Mine Boy, Peter Abrahams, Heinemann; 1963.
Additional Information:
☞ The Black Experience in the 20th Century: An Autobiography, Peter Abrahams, Indiana University Press; 2001.
☞ A Wreath For Udomo, Peter Abrahams, Knopf; New York.
☞ African Literature in the 20th Century, O. R. Dawthorne, Heinemann; 1974.

595.
C) CAPITALISM AND SLAVERY
☞ Capitalism and Slavery, Erik Williams, Andre Deutsch Ltd.; London, 1964.
Additional Information:
☞ Black Londoners, 1890-1990, Susan Okokon, Sutton; UK, 1997, p.28.
☞ The Cambridge Encyclopedia of Latin America and the Caribbean, Cambridge University Press; 1989.

☞ African and Caribbean Politics: From Kwame Nkruma to the Grenada Revolution, Manning Marable, Verso; London, 1987.

596.
B) PAUL LAURENCE DUNBAR
☞ Paul Laurence Dunbar. Black Americans of Achievement, Tony Gentry, Chelsea House Publishers; New York, Philadelphia, 1989, p.105.
Additional Information:
☞ Paul Laurence Dunbar, Peter Revell, Twayne;, 1979.
☞ A Pictorial History of Black America. Langston Hughes, Crown; NY, 1983.
☞ The Essential Black Literature Guide, Published in association with the Schomburg Center for Research in Black Culture, Roger M. Valade II, Visible Ink Press; USA, 1996, p.122.

597.
A) ARTHUR ASHE
☞ Days of Grace: A Memoir, Arthur Ashe and Arnold Rampersad, Heinemann; London, 1993.
Additional Information:
☞ Jet, Johnson Publishing Co.; Chicago, June 12, 1993, pp.51, 58.
☞ The Observer, London, April 20, 1997, (Sport) p.12.
☞ Off the Court, Arthur Ashe with Neil Amdur, New American Library; New York, 1981.

598.
A) GUYANA
☞ Black British Literature, An Annotated Bibliography, Prahbu Guptara, Dangaroo Press; London, 1986, pp.89-94.
Additional Information:
☞ Palace of the Peacock, Wilson Harris, Faber; London, 1960.
☞ Selected Black American, African and Caribbean Authors, A Bio Bibliography, Libraries UnLimited; 1985.
☞ The Waiting Room, Wilson Harris, Faber; London, 1967.

599.
B) POETRY
☞ The Selected Poems of Nikki Giovanni, Nikki Giovanni, William Morrow & Co.; 1996.

Additional Information:
- ☞ Ebony Pictorial History of Black America: Volume 3. Civil Rights Movement to Black Revolution, Johnson Publishing Company; 1974, p.278.
- ☞ Black Womens Writer at Work, Edited by Claudia Tate, Oldcastle Books; England, 1985.
- ☞ Love, Nikki Giovanni, William Morrow & Co.; 1997.

600.
A) FREDERICK DOUGLASS
- ☞ The Life and Times of Frederick Douglass: Written by Himself. Federick Douglass, Citidal Press; New Jersey, 1983.

Additional Information:
- ☞ They Showed the Way Up, Charlemae Hill Rollins, Thomas Y. Crowell Company; New York, 1964, pp.46-52.
- ☞ Frederick Douglass: Slave-Fighter-Freeman, Arna Bontemps, Knopf; New York, 1959.
- ☞ Twelve Americans: Their Lives and Times, Howard Carroll, Harper; New ork, 1883, pp.263-99.

601.
B) A LIBRARY
- ☞ African History, Earl Sweeting and Lez Edmond, London Strategic Policy Unit; 1988, p.17.

Additional Information:
- ☞ Rosicrution Digest, June 1964, USA, p.208.
- ☞ A History of Libraries, Alfred Hessel, Reuben Pliss (trans.), The Scarecrow Press; New Brunswick, N.J., 1955.
- ☞ Nile Valley Contributions to Civilization; Exploding the Myths, Volume 1, Anthony T. Browder, Institute of Khamic Guidance; Washington, D.C., 2000.

602.
A) LANGSTON HUGHES
- ☞ The Big Sea: An Autobiography. Langston Hughes, Alfred A. Knopf; New York, 1940.

Additional Information:
- ☞ Langston Hughes: Before and Beyond Harlem, Faith Berry, Lawrence Hill & Company; Connecticut, 1983.

- ☞ The Black Literature Guide, Published in association with the Schomburg Center for Research in Black Culture, Roger M. Valade II, Visible Ink Press; USA, 1996, p.3178.
- ☞ American, African and Caribbean Authors, A Bio Bibliography, Libraries UnLimited; 1985.

603.
C) SATIRE
- ☞ The Golden Asse, Lucius Apulius, (R. Graves, trans.) Farrar, Straus & Giroux; New York, 1951.

Additional Information:
- ☞ The Cambridge Encyclopedia, Cambridge University Press; Edited by David Crystal, 1990, p.61.
- ☞ Black Women in Antiquity, Edited by Ivan Van Sertima, Transaction; 7th Edition, 1992, pp.65, 68.
- ☞ Satire and Society in Ancient Rome: Exeter Studies in History, Susan H. Braund, University of Exeter Press; 1989.

604.
A) THE BAPTISM OF THE EUNUCH
- ☞ The Hidden Rembrant, J. Bolton and H. Bolten-Rampt, Phaidon Press; Oxford, 1978, p.11.

Additional Information:
- ☞ Romanticism and Art, William Vaughn, Thames & Hobson; UK, 1994.
- ☞ Cambridge Encyclopedia, David Crystal, Cambridge University Press; 1990, p.1016.
- ☞ The Holy Bible, Acts 8: 27-39.

605.
C) TITUS ANDRONICUS
- ☞ The Complete Works of William Shakespeare, George Lyman Kittredge, (ed.), Grolier; New York, 1958.

Additional Information:
- ☞ The Illustrated Stratford Shakespeare; All 37 Plays, All 160 Sonnets and Poems, Chancellor Press; UK, 1982, pp.678-700.
- ☞ Titus Andronicus, H. Fuller, Modern Language Association, Volume 16, No. 1, UK.
- ☞ Nature Knows No Color Line. J. A. Rogers, 3rd Edition, H. M. Rogers Publishers; 1952, p.75.

606.
B) ARENA
☞ Arena Magazine, 3rd Floor, Block A, Exmouth House, Pine Street, London, EC1R 0JL.
Additional Information:
☞ Who's Who of Black Achievers, John Hughes, (ed.), Ethnic Media Group; UK, 1999, p.111.
☞ The Voice, The Voice Group Ltd.; London, October 8, 2001, p.19.
☞ Untold, Peter Akinti Publ.; London, July/August, 2000, p.42.

607.
C) THE BLUEST EYE
☞ The Unfinished Quest of Richard Wright, by Michael Fabre, William Morrow & Co. Inc.; NY, 1973
Additional Information:
☞ On the Real Side: A History of African American Comedy. Mel Watkins, Lawrence Hill; USA, 1999, pp.424-25.
☞ Afro-American Literature in the Twentieth Century, Michael J. Cook, Yale University Press; New Haven 1984.
☞ Black Boy, Richard Wright, Perennial Classics; New York, 1966.

608.
A) AFRICAN GEOGRAPHY
☞ The History and Description of Africa, Joannes Leo Africanus, Vols. 1-3, Hakluyt Society; London, 1896.
Additional Information:
☞ African Kingdoms, Basil Davidson, Time-Life Books; (Nederland), 1980, p.85.
☞ World's Great Men of Color, Volume II, J. A. Rogers, Collier Macmillan Publishers; 1972, pp.547-48.
☞ The Map of Africa by Treaty, Vols. 1-3, Edward Hertslet, Harrison and Sons; London, 1909.

609.
A) JOAN RILEY
☞ A Kindness to the Children, Joan Riley, The Women's Press; UK, 1993.
Additional Information:
☞ Daughters of Africa: An International Anthology of Words and Writings by Women of African Descent from the Ancient Egyptian to the Present. Edited by Margaret Busby, Vintage Books; New York, 1993, p.909.

☞ Black British Literature, An Annoted Bibliography, Prahbu Guptara, Dangaroo Press; London, 1986, p.141.
☞ Waiting in the Twilight, Joan Riley, The Women's Press; UK, 1988.

610.
B) THE QURAN
☞ Staying Power, Peter Fryer, Pluto Press; 2nd Edition, UK, 1985.
Additional Information:
☞ Your History: From the Beginning of Time to the Present, J. A. Rogers, Black Classic Press; Baltimore, MD, 1983, p.4.
☞ Black Settlers in Britain, 1555-1958, Nigel File and Chris, Power, Heinemann Educational Books; UK, 1981.
☞ Black and White-The Negro and English Society 1555-1945, James Walvin, Allen Lane, The Penguin Press; 1973.

611.
B) 1991
☞ The Essential Black Literature Guide, Published in association with the Schomburg Center for Research in Black Culture, Roger M. Valade II, Visible Ink Press; USA, 1996, pp.137, 283.
Additional Information:
☞ West Africa, London, December 9-15, 1991, p.2053.
☞ Black Londoners, 1890-1990, Susan Okokon, Sutton; UK, 1997, p.108.
☞ West Africa, London, November 4-10, 1991, p.1842.

612.
A) SIMON OF CYRENE
☞ King James Bible, St. Luke, Chapter 23, Verse 26.
Additional Information:
☞ King James Bible, St. Mark, Chapter 15, Verse 21.
☞ World's Great Men of Color, J. A. Rogers, Volume II, Collier Macmillan Publishers; 1972, p.13.
☞ Black Characters and References of the Holy Bible, F. S. Rhoades, First Edition, Vantage Press; New York, 1980.

613.
B) SCHOMBURG CENTER FOR RESEARCH IN BLACK CULTURE
☞ Ebony, Johnson Publishing; Chicago, November, 2000, pp.144-50.

Additional Information:
☞ New National Black Monitor, USA, July 8, 1982.
☞ Arthur A. Schomburg, The Freemason, Harry Albro Williamson, Williamson Masonic Collection; New York, 1941.
☞ Ebony, Johnson Publishing; Chicago, February, 1995, p.88.

Sport

Answers and Sources

614.
A) EVANDER HOLYFIELD
☞ Evander Holyfield: Heavyweight Champion, Rob Kirkpatrick, Powerkids Press; 2001.
Additional Information:
☞ Boxing's Most Wanted: The Top 10 Book of Champs, Chumps, and Punch-Drunk Palookas (Brassey's Most Wanted). Mike Fitzgerald Jr., and Davil L. Hudson, Jr, Brasseys, Inc.; 2003
☞ An Illustrated History of Boxing, Nat Fleischer and Sam Andre, Updated by Nigel Collins, Citadel Press; 2002.
☞ The Gloves: A Boxing Chronicle, Robert Anasi, North Point Press; 2002.

615.
C) SERENA WILLIAMS
☞ Time, Time Inc.; USA, September 3, 2001, (cover).
Additional Information:
☞ The New York Times, September 8, 2001.
☞ The Sunday Times, London, September 9, 2001.
☞ Ebony, Johnson Publishing; Chicago, May, 2003, pp.156-160.

616.
C) WALTER PAYTON
☞ The 1997 Guinness Book of Records, Guinness Publishing Ltd.; UK, 1996, p.251.
Additional Information:
☞ Walter Payton, Philip Kaslow, Chelsea House; USA, 1994.
☞ Ebony, Johnson Publishing; Chicago, August, 1992, p.96.
☞ NFL's Greatest: Pro Football's Best Players, Teams, and Games. National Football League, (ed.), Phil Barber and John Fawaz, DK Publishing; 2000.

617.
A) PELE
☞ Pele: My Life and the Beautiful Game, Pele with Robert L. Fish, New English Library; 1977.
Additional Information:
☞ I Was There: 20 Great Sporting Memories from the Writers of the Daily Telegraph and Sunday Telegraph, Edited by Norman Barrett, London, 1985, pp.9-15.

☞ The Hamlyn Encyclopedia of Soccer, Ian Morrison, Hamlyn; London, 1989, pp.116-19.
☞ The Observer, London, April 20, 1997, (Sport) p.12.

618.
C) SAN FRANCISCO GIANTS
☞ San Francisco Giants, 24 Willie Mays Plaza, San Francisco, California, 94107
Additional Information:
☞ The San Francisco Chronicle, October 8, 2001.
☞ Ebony, Johnson Publishing; Chicago, November, 2002, p.66.
☞ Barry Bonds: Baseball's Complete Player, Miles Harvey, Children's Press; USA, 1994.

619.
B) BOBSLEIGH
☞ The New Nation, Western Hemisphere; London, March 17, 1997, p.57.
Additional Information:
☞ The Collins Quiz Book, Carol P. Shaw, HarperCollins Publishers; Glasgow, 1996, pp.33, 143.
☞ International Olympic Committee, Archive Records Department, Avenue de la Gare, No. 10, 1003 Lausanne, Switzerland.
☞ The Weekly Journal, Voice Communications; London, December 9, 1993, p.1.

620.
C) SLAM DUNK
☞ A Hard Road to Glory: A History of the African American Athlete. Volume 2, Arthur Ashe, USA, 1988. pp.55-56.
Additional Information:
☞ Ebony, Johnson Publishing; Chicago, August, 1992, p.66.
☞ Black Americana. Richard A. Long, Admiral; UK, 1985.
☞ The 1997 Guinness Book of Records, Guinness Publishing Ltd.; UK, 1996, p.255.

621.
C) ENGLISH CHANNEL
☞ Ebony, Johnson Publishing; Chicago, August, 1992, p.80.

Additional Information:

☞ Channel Swimmers Association, The Hermitage, 12 Vale Square, Ramsgate, Kent, CT11 9BX.

☞ Captain Webb and 100 Years of Channel Swimming, Margaret A. Jarvis, USA.

☞ Swimming the Channel, Jill Neville, St.Martin's Press; New York, 1994.

622.
B) MOUNT EVEREST

☞ The Sunday Times, South Africa, 1 June, 2003.

Additional Information:

☞ The Sunday Times, South Africa, 8 June, 2003.

☞ BBC News, London, Monday, 26 May, 2003.

☞ The Sunday Times, South Africa, 23 March, 2003.

623.
C) 100 METER BUTTERFLY

☞ Olympics: Facts and Feats, Stan Greenberry, Guinness Publishing; 1996, p.181.

Additional Information:

☞ Chronicle of the Olympics, 1896-1996, Dorling Kindersley Publishing; UK, 1996.

☞ The Observer, London, April 20, 1997, (Sport) p.12.

☞ USA Today, October 3, 1988.

624.
B) POLO

☞ The Voice, The Voice Group Ltd.; London, 21 February, 2002, p.44.

Additional Information:

☞ Royal County of Berkshire Polo Club, Windsor, United Kingdom.

☞ Scottish Daily Record, September 5, 2002

☞ The Post.IE, the Sunday Business Post (online), 19 August, 2001.

625.
B) QUARTERBACK

☞ Ebony, Johnson Publishing; Chicago, August, 1992, pp.74, 96.

Additional Information:

☞ Jet, Johnson Publishing Co.; Chicago, April 16, 1990, p.51.

☞ NFL 2001 Record and Fact Book, National Football League, Workman Publishing Company; 2001.

☞ NFL's Official Encyclopedia History of Professional Football, National Football League; USA.

626.
A) AC MILAN

☞ Ruud Gullit, Portrait of a Genius, Harry Harris, Collins Willow; UK, 1996.

Additional Information:

☞ The Guinness Record of World Soccer. Guy Oliver, Guinness Publishing; UK, 1992.

☞ European Football Yearbook, 95/96, Sports Project Ltd.; UK, 1995, p.610.

☞ The Evening Standard, Associated Newspaper Group; London, May 12, 1997, pp.68-69.

627.
B) 12 STROKES

☞ The Times, London, April 17, 1997, p.24.

Additional Information:

☞ The Observer, London, April 20, 1997, (Sport) p.12.

☞ The New Nation, Western Hemisphere; London, 10th February 1997, p.12.

☞ Time, Time Inc.; USA, April 28, 1997, pp.38-39.

628.
C) FRANK WORRELL

☞ The Complete Who's Who of Test Cricketers, C. Martin-Jenkins, Orbus Publishing; London, 1983.

Additional Information:

☞ Cricket Facts and Feats, Bill Frindall, 4th Edition, Guinness Publishing; UK, 1996.

☞ The Weekly Journal, Voice Communications; London, March 23, 1995, p.24.

☞ 100 Great Westindian Test Cricketers, by Bridgette Lawrence With Reg Scarlett, Hansib Publishing Ltd.; UK.

629.
A) WRESTLING

☞ Black Stars of Professional Wrestling, Julian L. D. Shabazz, Awesome Records, 1999.

Additional Information:

☞ Jet, Johnson Publishing Co.; Chicago, September 21, 1992, p.50.

☞ The Encyclopedia of Professional Wrestling: 100 Years of the Good, the Bad and the Unforgettable, Kristian Pope and Ray Whebbe Jr., Krause Publications; 2001.

☞ Black Firsts: 2000 Years of Extraordinary Achievement. Jessie Carney Smith, Caspar L. Jordan and Robert L. Johns, Visible Ink Press; USA, 1994.

630.
A) SOCCER PREMIER LEAGUE
☞ The F.A. Premier League, 11 Connought Place, London W2 2ET
Additional Information:
☞ The New Nation, Western Hemisphere; London, July 14, 1997, p.6.
☞ The Weekly Journal, Voice Communications; London, February 9, 1995, p.24.
☞ The Voice, The Voice Group Ltd.; February 12, 2001, p.60.

631.
A) THE KENTUCKY DERBY
☞ The Black American Reference Book. Mabel M. Smyth, (ed.), Prentice-Hall Inc.; USA, 1976, p.957.
Additional Information:
☞ Ebony Pictorial History of Black America: Volume 3. Civil Rights Movement to Black Revolution, Johnson Publishing Company; 1974, p.251.
☞ A Hard Road to Glory: A History of the African American Athlete. Volume 1, Arthur Ashe, USA, 1988. pp.47-49.
☞ Dictionary of American Negro Biography, Rayford W. Logan and Michael R. Winston, W. W. Norton & Co.; New York, 1993, pp.462-63.

632.
B) FLORENCE GRIFFITH-JOYNER
☞ Florence Griffith-Joyner: Olympic Runner, Rob Kirkpatrick, Powerskids Press; USA, 2001.
Additional Information:
☞ African Americans in Sport, Gary A. Sailes, (ed.), Transaction; New Jersey, 1998.
☞ Facts on File Encyclopedia of Black Women in America: Dance, Sports, and Visual Arts (Volume 3), Darlene Clark Hine and Kathleen Thompson, (eds.), Facts of File, Inc.; USA, 1997.

☞ Olympics: Facts and Feats, Stan Greenberry, Guinness Publishing; 1996.

633.
B) TWENTY-THREE
☞ The Ultimate Encyclopedia of Tennis: The Definitive Illustrated Guide to World Tennis, John Parsons, Carlton Books; 1999.
Additional Information:
☞ The Weekly Journal, Voice Communications; London, November 19, 1992.
☞ Ebony, Johnson Publishing; Chicago, October, 1995, p.139.
☞ The Black Heritage Book of Trivia, Morgan White Jr., Quinlan Press; Boston, 1985, pp.89, 172.

634.
C) 400 METER HURDLES
☞ Chronicle of the Olympics, 1896-1996, Dorling Kindersley Publishing; UK, 1996.
Additional Information:
☞ The Guinness Encyclopedia of International Sports, Records and Results. Peter Matthews, 3rd Edition, Guinness Publishing; 1993.
☞ African Americans in Sport, Gary A. Sailes, (ed.), Transaction; New Jersey, 1998.
☞ A Hard Road to Glory: A History of the African American Athlete. Volume 2, Arthur Ashe, USA, 1988.

635.
B) RICKY HENDERSON
☞ The 1997 Guinness Book of Records, Guinness Publishing Ltd.; UK, 1996, p.253.
Additional Information:
☞ Ebony, Johnson Publishing; Chicago, August, 2001, pp.62-65.
☞ A Hard Road to Glory: A History of the African American Athlete. Volume 2, Arthur Ashe, USA, 1988. pp.26-27.
☞ 1999 Facts About Blacks: A Sourcebook of African American Accomplishment. Raymond M. Corbin, Beckham House Publishers; USA, 1st Edition, 1986, p.125.

636.
A) WINGER
☞ Blood and Thunder: The Unofficial Biography of Jonah Lomu, Phil Shirley, Trafalgar Square; UK, 1999.

Additional Information:
- Daily Mail, London, November 28, 1996, p.75.
- Inside the All Blacks, Robin McConnell, HarperCollins; New Zealand, 1999.
- The Weekly Journal, Voice Communications; London, June 22, 1995, p.20.

637.
C) CHICAGO WHITESOX
- Chicago Whitesox, 333 West 35th Street, Chicago Illinois, 60616.

Additional Information:
- African Americans in Sport, Gary A. Sailes, (ed.), Transaction; New Jersey, 1998.
- USA Today, European Edition, June 7, 1997, Sports Section.
- 2001 ESPN Information Please Sports Almanac, ESPN; espn.com

638.
B) EUSEBIO
- The Hamlyn Encyclopedia of Soccer, Ian Morrison, Hamlyn; London, 1989, pp.43-44.

Additional Information:
- The Guinness Record of World Soccer. Guy Oliver, Guinness Publishing; UK, 1992.
- The Guinness Encyclopedia of International Sports, Records and Results. Peter Matthews, 3rd Edition, Guinness Publishing; 1993.
- Fédération Internationale De Football Association, Library Records Dept., Higzigueg 11, P.O. Box 85, 8030, Zurich.

639.
A) THE ROCK
- The Rock Says, The Rock and WWF, Regan Books; US, 2000.

Additional Information:
- Ebony, Johnson Publishing; Chicago, June, 2003, p.136.
- WWF SmackDown! "Just Bring It": Prima's Official Strategy Guide, Prima (Ed.), et al, Prima Lifestyles, US, 2001.
- The World Wrestling Entertainment Yearbook 2003, Michael McAvennie, WWE Books; 2003.

640.
B) MOST HOME RUNS
- The 1997 Guinness Book of Records, Guinness Publishing Ltd.; UK, 1996, p.252.

Additional Information:
- Ebony, Johnson Publishing; Chicago, August, 1992, p.58.
- A Hard Road to Glory: A History of the African American Athlete. Volume 2, Arthur Ashe, USA, 1988. pp.18-19.
- Hank Aaron, James Tackach, Chelsea House; USA, 1992.

641.
C) 501
- Beating the Field, Brian Lara with Brian Scovell, Corgi Books; UK, 1996.

Additional Information:
- The 1997 Guinness Book of Records, Guinness Publishing Ltd.; UK, 1996, p.256.
- Cricket Facts and Feats, Bill Frindall, 4th Edition, Guinness Publishing; UK, 1996, pp.33-35, 128, 161-62, 166.
- The Weekly Journal, Voice Communications; London, April 21, 1994 p.1.

642.
C) WIMBLEDON
- The Ultimate Encyclopedia of Tennis: The Definitive Illustrated Guide to World Tennis, John Parsons, Carlton Books; 1999.

Additional Information:
- Wimbledon: The Official History, John Barrett, Trafalgar Square; 2001.
- The Wimbledon Compendium 1995, Alan Little, Honorary librarian, Wimbledon Lawn Tennis Museum, The All England Tennis and Croquet Club; 1995.
- The Encyclopedia of Aboriginal Australia, Australian Institute of Aboriginal and Torrest Straight Islander State, Edited by David Horton, Australia, 1994.

643.
B) LIBERIA
- Prosports African Football Yearbook, Filippo Maria Ricci, (ed.), Third Edition, 2001.

Additional Information:
- The New Nation, Western Hemisphere; January 20, 1997, p.56.
- The Voice, The Voice Group Ltd.; London, July 2, 1996, pp.62-63.
- Prosports of the African Cup of Nations 1957-2000, Filippo Maria Ricci, (ed.), 2000.

644.
A) THE SPRINGBOKS
- Rugby and the South African Nation: Sport, Cultures, Politics and Power in the Old and New South Africas, John Nauright and David R. Black, Manchester University Press; 1998.

Additional Information:
- The Guinness Encyclopedia of International Sports, Records and Results. Peter Matthews, 3rd Edition, Guinness Publishing; 1993.
- Rugby League: An Illustrated History, Robert Gate, Arthur Baker Publishing; London, 1989.
- The Sunday Times Illustrated History of Twentieth Century Sport, Chris Nawrat, Steve Hutchings and Greg Struthers, Hamlyn; 1992, p.405.

645.
B) 19.32 SECONDS
- Michael Johnson: Sprinter Deluxe, Bert Rosenthal, GHB Publisher's LLC; 2000.

Additional Information:
- Slaying the Dragon, Michael Johnson, Piatikus; USA, 1996.
- African Americans in Sport, Gary A. Sailes, (ed.), Transaction; New Jersey, 1998.
- The 1997 Guinness Book of Records, Guinness Publishing Ltd.; UK, 1996, p.330.

646.
B) 107 YARDS
- M&T Bank Stadium, Baltimore Ravens, 1101 Russell Street Baltimore, MD 21230.

Additional Information:
- USA Today, 1 October, 2002.
- Cicinnati Post, "Back up do in Bengals", 11 November, 2002.
- The Guinness Book of Records 2004, Guinness Publishing Ltd.; UK, 2003.

647.
C) MIKE POWELL
- IAAF, 17 Rue Princesse, Florestine, B.P. 359, 98007, Monaco.

Additional Information:
- African Americans in Sport, Gary A. Sailes, (ed.), Transaction; New Jersey, 1998.
- The Guinness Encyclopedia of International Sports, Records and Results. Peter Matthews, 3rd Edition, Guinness Publishing; 1993.
- The 1997 Guinness Book of Records, Guinness Publishing Ltd.; UK, 1996, p.234.

648.
B) HAILE GEBRSELASSIE
- World Record Breakers in Track & Field Athletics, Gerald Lawson, Human Kinetics Publishing; 1997.

Additional Information:
- The 1997 Guinness Book of Records, Guinness Publishing Ltd.; UK, 1996, p.330.
- 2001 ESPN Information Please Sports Almanac, ESPN; espn.com.
- (Zeke's Olympic Pocket Guide) Athletics, Track: 100 Meters, 200 Meters, Relays, Hurdle, & Lots, Lots More, Jason Page, Lerner Publishing Group; USA, 2000.

649.
C) WEST AFRICA
- Prosports African Football Yearbook, Filippo Maria Ricci, (ed.), Third Edition, 2001.

Additional Information:
- The 1997 Guinness Book of Records, Guinness Publishing Ltd.; UK, 1996, p.338.
- New African, September 2001, ICP Ltd.; London, p.49.
- Africa Today, May/June Edition 1997, Volume 3, No. 3, p.24.

650.
C) BASKETBALL
- The Biographical History of Basketball: Over 500 Portraits of the most significant on and off Court Personalities of the Games Past and Present, Peter C. Bjarkman, Mcgraw-Hill; 1999.

Additional Information:
- Sepia, December, 1974, p.62.
- Ebony, Johnson Publishing; Chicago, January, 1975, p.97.
- 1999 Facts About Blacks: A Sourcebook of African American Accomplishment. Raymond M. Corbin, Beckham House Publishers; USA, 1st Edition, 1986, p.106.

651.
A) CLARENCE SEEDORF
- Encyclopedia of Sports Culture, Ellis Cashmore, Routledge Books; 2002.

Additional Information:
- The New Nation, Ethnic Media Group; London, May 26, 2003, p.54.
- Fédération Internationale De Football Association, Library Records Dept., Higzigueg 11, P.O. Box 85, 8030, Zurich.
- Ultimate Encyclopedia Of Soccer, Keir Radnedge, Carlton; 8th edition, 2002.

652.
B) IAN WRIGHT
- Arsenal Football Club, Avenell Road, Highbury, London N5 1BU.

Additional Information:
- Mr. Wright: The Explosive Autobiography of Ian Wright, Collins Willow; UK, 1996.
- The Sunday Times, London, September 14, 1997, Section 2.
- European Football Yearbook, 95/96, Sports Project Ltd.; UK, 1995, p.308.

653.
B) NEW YORK RENAISSANCE FIVE
- Ebony Pictorial History of Black America: Volume 3. Civil Rights Movement to Black Revolution, Johnson Publishing Company; 1974.

Additional Information:
- Black Americana. Richard A. Long, Admiral; UK, 1985.
- The Biographical History of Basketball: Over 500 Portraits of the most significant on and off Court Personalities of the Games Past and Present, Peter C. Bjarkman, Mcgraw-Hill; 1999.
- A Pictorial History of Black America. Langston Hughes, Crown; NY, 1983.

654.
B) TAMPA BAY ROWDIES
- Tampa Bay Rowdies Soccer Club, Personal Records Office, Tampa Bay, Florida, USA.

Additional Information:
- The Hamlyn Encyclopedia of Soccer, Ian Morrison, Hamlyn; London, 1989.
- Black Pearls of Soccer, Al Hamilton, Harrap; London, 1982.
- The Voice, The Voice Group Ltd.; November 20, 2000, p.60.

655.
B) TWENTY
- The 1997 Guinness Book of Records, Guinness Publishing Ltd.; UK, 1996, p.303.

Additional Information:
- The Sunday Times Illustrated History of Twentieth Century Sport, Chris Nawrat, Steve Hutchings and Greg Struthers, Hamlyn; 1992, p.351.
- Vibe, Quincy Jones and David Salzman Entertainment, Time Publishing Inc.; September, 1995.
- African Americans in Sport, Gary A. Sailes, (ed.), Transaction; New Jersey, 1998.

656.
B) ALTHEA GIBSON
- I Always Wanted to be Somebody, Althea Gibson, Harper Row; USA, 1958.

Additional Information:
- World of Tennis, John Barret, Colins Willow; UK, 1993, p.373.
- The Wimbledon Compendium 1995, Alan Little, Honorary librarian, Wimbledon Lawn Tennis Museum, The All England Tennis and Croquet Club; 1995.
- The Observer, London, April 20, 1997, (Sport) p.12.

657.
C) BASKETBALL
- See How She Runs: Marian Jones & the Making of a Champion, Ron Rapoport, Algonquin Books; USA, 2000.

Additional Information:
- Ebony, Johnson Publishing; Chicago, October, 2000, pp.122-23, 128.
- Marian Jones: The Fastest Woman in the World, Bill Gutman, Pocket Books; USA, 2000.
- The Voice, The Voice Group Ltd.; July 14, 1997, p.51.

Sport

658.
B) MARIA CARIDAD COLON
☞ Chronicle of the Olympics, 1896-1996, Dorling Kindersley Publishing; UK, 1996.
Additional Information:
☞ International Olympic Committee, Archive Records Department, Avenue de la Gare, No. 10, 1003 Lausanne, Switzerland.
☞ (Zeke's Olympic Pocket Guide) Athletics, Field: Pole Vault, Long Jump, Hammer, Javelin, & Lots, Lots More, Jason Page, Lerner Publishing Group; USA, 2000.
☞ Olympics: Facts and Feats, Stan Greenberry, Guinness Publishing; 1996.

659.
A) DUKE McKENZIE
☞ The Voice, The Voice Group Limited; London, June 8, 1993, p.56.
Additional Information:
☞ The Total Sports Illustrated Book of Boxing, Nathan Ward, (ed.), Total Sports; 1999.
☞ The Voice, The Voice Group Ltd.; London, (24 Hours Section), January 24, 1995, p.11.
☞ An Illustrated History of Boxing, Nat Fleischer and Sam Andre, Updated by Nigel Collins, Citadel Press; 2002.

660.
B) JOE FRAZIER
☞ Ghosts of Manila: The Fateful Blood Feud Between Muhammad Ali and Joe Frazier, Mark Kram, HarperCollins; 2001.
Additional Information:
☞ I Was There: 20 Great Sporting Memories from the Writers of the Daily Telegraph and Sunday Telegraph, Edited by Norman Barrett, London, 1985.
☞ The Total Sports Illustrated Book of Boxing, Nathan Ward, (ed.), Total Sports; 1999.
☞ A Century of Boxing Greats: Inside the Ring With the 100 Best Boxers, Patrick Myler, Robson Books Ltd.; 1998.

661.
A) HIT THIRTY-SIX RUNS OFF A SIX BALL OVER
☞ Cricket Facts and Feats, Bill Frindall, 4th Edition, Guinness Publishing; UK, 1996, pp.29-30, 32-36, 56-58, 161-62.

Additional Information:
☞ The 1997 Guinness Book of Records, Guinness Publishing Ltd.; UK, 1996, p.256.
☞ 100 Great Westindian Test Cricketers, by Bridgette Lawrence With Reg Scarlett, Hansib Publishing Ltd.; UK.
☞ The Daily Telegraph Chronicle of Cricket, Edited by Norman Barrett, Guinness Publishing; 1994.

662.
C) TEN
☞ Wilma Unlimited: How Wilma Rudolph Became the World's Fastest Woman. Kathleen Krull, Scott Foresman Publishers; 1996.
Additional Information:
☞ A Hard Road to Glory: A History of the African American Athlete. Volume 2, Arthur Ashe, USA, 1988, pp.182, 185, 187, 201.
☞ Ebony, Johnson Publishing; Chicago, July, 1996, p.62.
☞ Jet, Johnson Publishing Co.; Chicago, July 12, 1993, pp.56-58.

663.
C) COLIN McMILLAN
☞ Fight the Power, An Autobiography, Colin McMillan, UK, 2000.
Additional Information:
☞ Audley Harrison: Realising the Dream, Granada Media; 2001.
☞ The Professional Boxing Authority, 88 Lee High Road, London SE28.
☞ An Illustrated History of Boxing, Nat Fleischer and Sam Andre, Updated by Nigel Collins, Citadel Press; 2002.

664.
B) HIGH JUMP
☞ The 1997 Guinness Book of Records, Guinness Publishing Ltd.; UK, 1996, p.234, 238.
Additional Information:
☞ The Weekly Journal, Voice Communications; London, September 9,1993, p.16.
☞ The Weekly Journal, Voice Communications; London, March 30, 1995, p.22.
☞ Chronicle of the Olympics, 1896-1996, Dorling Kindersley Publishing; UK, 1996.

665.

A) TWENTY-FIVE

☞ The 1997 Guinness Book of Records, Guinness Publishing Ltd.; UK, 1996, p.251.

Additional Information:

☞ Ebony, Johnson Publishing; Chicago, November, 2002, pp.106.

☞ NFL 2001 Record and Fact Book, National Football League, Workman Publishing Company; 2001.

☞ NFL's Greatest: Pro Football's Best Players, Teams, and Games. National Football League, (ed.), Phil Barber and John Fawaz, DK Publishing; 2000.

666.

A) BO JACKSON

☞ Bo Jackson, Bill Gutman, Lisa Clancy, (ed.), Archway Books; 1991.

Additional Information:

☞ The Weekly Journal, Voice Communications; London, September 30, 1993, p.16.

☞ Bo Jackson: Overcoming the Odds, Jon Kramer, Raintree/Steck Vaughn; 1996.

☞ 2001 ESPN Information Please Sports Almanac, ESPN; espn.com.

667.

B) SAN FRANSICO 49ERS

☞ African Americans in Sport, Gary A. Sailes, (ed.), Transaction; New Jersey, 1998.

Additional Information:

☞ NFL's Greatest: Pro Football's Best Players, Teams, and Games. National Football League, (ed.), Phil Barber and John Fawaz, DK Publishing; 2000, p.31.

☞ The Voice, The Voice Group Ltd.; London, September 10, 1996, p.59.

☞ The 1997 Guinness Book of Records, Guinness Publishing Ltd.; UK, 1996, p.251.

668.

C) VIV RICHARDS

☞ The Complete Who's Who of Test Cricketers, C. Martin-Jenkins, Orbus Publishing; London, 1983.

Additional Information:

☞ The 1997 Guinness Book of Records, Guinness Publishing Ltd.; UK, 1996, p.258.

☞ Cricket Facts and Feats, Bill Frindall, 4th Edition, Guinness Publishing; UK, 1996.

☞ The Daily Telegraph Chronicle of Cricket, Edited by Norman Barrett, Guinness Publishing; 1994.

669.

B) DENISE LEWIS

☞ Personal Best: The Autobiography of and Amazing Woman, Denise Lewis, Century Books; UK, 2001.

Additional Information:

☞ The Evening Standard, Associated Newspaper Group; London, August 2, 2001, p.71.

☞ International Olympic Committee, Public Relations department, Avenue de la Gare, No. 10, 1003 Lausanne, Switzerland.

☞ The Voice, The Voice Group Ltd.; London, April 9, 2001, pp.58-59.

670.

B) EDMONTON OILERS

☞ A Hard Road to Glory: A History of the African American Athlete. Volume 3, Arthur Ashe, USA, 1988, p.222.

Additional Information:

☞ Champions: The Making of the Edmonton Oilers, Kevin Lowe, 1982.

☞ Ebony, Johnson Publishing; Chicago, August, 1992, p.80.

☞ Edmonton Oilers, 11230 110 Street, Edmonton, Alberta, T5G 3G8.

671.

B) KELLY HOLMES

☞ The Sunday Times, London, August 29, 2004.

Additional Information:

☞ The British Olympic Association, Educational Dept., Committee, 1 Wandsworth Plain, London, SW18 1EH

☞ Daily Mail, London, August 30, 2004.

☞ The Evening Standard, Associated Newspaper Group; London, August 30, 2004.

672.

B) QUADRUPLE

☞ The 1997 Guinness Book of Records, Guinness Publishing Ltd.; UK, 1996, p.300

Additional Information:

☞ The Weekly Journal, Voice Communications; London, February 9, 1995, pp.1, 24.

☞ IAAF, 17 Rue Princesse, Florestine, B.P.

359., 98007, Monaco.
☞ The Voice, The Voice Group Ltd.;
London, May 25, 1993, p.21.

673.
A) L. A. RAIDERS
☞ Jet, Johnson Publishing Co.; Chicago,
October 23, 1989, p.48.
Additional Information:
☞ Sport Illustrated, USA, October 23, 1989.
☞ The Voice, The Voice Group Ltd.;
London, February 14, 1995.
☞ Jet, Johnson Publishing Co.; Chicago,
February 26, 1990, p.48.

674.
A) 2 MILES
☞ The Times, London, Monday July 21,
1997, p.28.
Additional Information:
☞ USA Today, July 20, 1997 (Sports
Section).
☞ The Voice, The Voice Group Ltd.; July 7,
1997, p.63.
☞ 2001 ESPN Information Please Sports
Almanac, ESPN; espn.com.

675.
C) WBU (WORLD BOXING UNION)
☞ An Illustrated History of Boxing, Nat
Fleischer and Sam Andre, Updated by
Nigel Collins, Citadel Press; 2002.
Additional Information:
☞ A Hard Road to Glory: A History of the
African American Athlete. Volume 3,
Arthur Ashe, USA, 1988, pp.215-16.
☞ Who's Who Among Black Americans,
1992-1993, USA, p.633.
☞ A Century of Boxing Greats: Inside the
Ring With the 100 Best Boxers, Patrick
Myler, Robson Books Ltd.; 1998

676.
C) BLACK DRAGON
☞ Senpaku Shinko Building, No.2, 1-11-2
Poranomon, Minato-Ku, Tokyo 105,
Japan.
Additional Information:
☞ Manual of the Martial Arts, Ron Van Clief,
Wade Books; USA, 1981.
☞ The Black Heroes, A & B Publishers;
Brooklyn, NY, 1996.
☞ Black Belt, "Chinese Goju"-Vols. 1-2, Ron
Van Clief, ancientwarriorvideos.com.

677.
A) OPEN
☞ Nippon, (Sumo Governing Body) Sumo
Kyokai, Kokugikan Ryogoku, Sumida-
Ku, Tokyo, Japan.
Additional Information:
☞ The Weekly Journal, Voice
Communications; London, December
17, 1992, p.5.
☞ Sumo Showdown: The Hawaiian
Challenge, Philip Sandoz, USA.
☞ Dynamic Sumo, Clyde Newton,
Kodansha International; 2000.

678.
C) GYMNASTICS
☞ Magnificent Seven: The Authorized
Story of American Gold, Nancy
Kleinbaum, Et Al, A Bantam Doubleday
Dell Publication; 1996.
Additional Information:
☞ 2001 ESPN Information Please Sports
Almanac, ESPN; espn.com.
☞ Jet, Johnson Publishing Co.; Chicago,
August 17, 1992, p.48.
☞ American Gymnasts: Gold Medal
Dreams, Chip Lovitt, Archway Books;
2000.

679.
B) SEATTLE MARINERS
☞ Ebony, Johnson Publishing; Chicago,
July, 2000, pp.46-51.
Additional Information:
☞ Cincinnati Reds, 100 Cinergy Fields,
Cincinnati, Ohio, 45202.
☞ Ken Griffey Jr., Lois Nicholson, Chelsea
House; USA, 1997.
☞ Seattle Mariners, P.O. Box 4100,
Seattle, Washington, 98104

680.
B) NEW YORK NICKS
☞ The Voice, The Voice Group Ltd.;
London, July 2, 1996, p.60.
Additional Information:
☞ Ebony, Johnson Publishing; Chicago,
August, 1992, p.64.
☞ African Americans in Sport, Gary A.
Sailes, (ed.), Transaction; New Jersey,
1998.
☞ New Bill James Historical Baseball
Abstract, Bill James, Simon & Schuster;
2001.

681.
B) WORLD CHAMPIONSHIP ATHLETICS
☞ International Amateur Athletics Federation, 17 Rue Princesse, Florestine, B.P. 359, 98007, Monaco.
Additional Information:
☞ 2001 ESPN Information Please Sports Almanac, ESPN; espn.com.
☞ La Tercera, October 15, 2000, Terra Networks, Chile, South America.
☞ Athletics in Action: The Official International Amateur Athletics Federation Book on Track and Field Techniques, Howard Payne, (ed.), USA.

682.
A) CAMEROON
☞ Prosports African Football Yearbook, Filippo Maria Ricci, (ed.), Third Edition, 2001.
Additional Information:
☞ The Weekly Journal, Voice Communications; London, June 16, 1994, p.8.
☞ West Africa, London, May 31, - June 6, 1993, p.929.
☞ Fédération Internationale De Football Association, Library Records Dept., Higzigueg 11, P.O. Box 85, 8030, Zurich.

683.
C) JACK JOHNSON
☞ Black Champion: The Life and Times of Jack Johnson, Fanis Farr, Scribner; New York, 1964.
Additional Information:
☞ Jack Johnson and His Times, Fenzil Bachelor, Phoenix Sports Books; London, 1956.
☞ The Observer, London, April 20, 1997, (Sport) p.12.
☞ Before the Mayflower: A History of Black America. Lerone Bennett Jr., 5th Edition, Penguin Books; 1984, p.634.

684.
A) HOUSTON ROCKETS
☞ USA Today, European Edition, December 3, 1996, Sports Section, p.1.
Additional Information:
☞ Ebony, Johnson Publishing; Chicago, February, 1994, p.142.
☞ The Weekly Journal, Voice Communications; London, June 23, 1994, p.18.

☞ The Voice, The Voice Group Limited; London, September 8, 1997, p.63.

685.
B) NINE
☞ A Hard Road to Glory: A History of the African American Athlete. Volume 3, Arthur Ashe, USA, 1988, pp.201-2.
Additional Information:
☞ Facts and Feats, Stan Greenberry, Guinness Publishing; 1996.
☞ International Olympic Committee, Archive Records Department, Avenue de la Gare, No. 10, 1003 Lausanne, Switzerland.
☞ The Observer, London, April 20, 1997, (Sport) p.12.

686.
B) HASIM RAHMAN
☞ The Times, London, November 17, 2001.
Additional Information:
☞ An Illustrated History of Boxing, Nat Fleischer and Sam Andre, Updated by Nigel Collins, Citadel Press; 2002.
☞ A Century of Boxing Greats: Inside the Ring With the 100 Best Boxers, Patrick Myler, Robson Books Ltd.; 1998.
☞ The Greatest: Who is Britain's Top Sport Star, Daley Thompson, Stewart Binns and Tom Lewis, Bextree; Channel 4 Television Corporation, London, 1996, pp.150-52.

687.
A) ROLAND BUTCHER
☞ The Sunday Times Illustrated History of Twentieth Century Sport, Chris Nawrat, Steve Hutchings and Greg Struthers, Hamlyn; 1992, p.312.
Additional Information:
☞ The Complete Who's Who of Test Cricketers, C. Martin-Jenkins, Orbus Publishing; London, 1983, p.31.
☞ The Daily Telegraph Chronicle of Cricket, Edited by Norman Barrett, Guinness Publishing; 1994.
☞ Third World Impact. 8th Edition, Edited by Arif Ali, Hansib Publishing; 1988.

688.
A) JOE LOUIS
☞ African Americans in Sport, Gary A. Sailes, (ed.), Transaction; New Jersey, 1998.

Sport

Additional Information:

☞ Great American Sports Stories, Edited by Carswell Adams, Stamford House; New York, 1947.

☞ The Sunday Times Illustrated History of Twentieth Century Sport, Chris Nawrat, Steve Hutchings and Greg Struthers, Hamlyn; 1992.

☞ The Observer, London, April 20, 1997, (Sport) p.12.

689.
C) GAIL DEVERS

☞ Chronicle of the Olympics, 1896-1996, Dorling Kindersley Publishing; UK, 1996.

Additional Information:

☞ Ebony, Johnson Publishing; Chicago, October, 2000, p.124.

☞ Olympics: Facts and Feats, Stan Greenberry, Guinness Publishing; 1996, p.94.

☞ Gail Devers: Over Coming the Odds, Bill Gutman, Raintree/Steck Vaughn; 1996.

690.
B) TABLE TENNIS

☞ Third World Impact. 8th Edition, Edited by Arif Ali, Hansib Publishing; 1988.

Additional Information:

☞ The Voice, The Voice Group Ltd.; London, April 5, 1994, p.51.

☞ The Weekly Journal, Voice Communications; London, March 23, 1995, p.24.

☞ The Voice, The Voice Group Ltd.; August 20, 2001, p.55.

691.
A) THREE

☞ The Times, London, April 17, 1997, p.24.

Additional Information:

☞ The New Nation, Western Hemisphere; London, February 10, 1997, p.12.

☞ Time, Time Inc.; USA, April 28, 1997, pp.38-39.

☞ The Evening Standard, Associated Newspaper Group; London, November 21, 1996, p.71.

692.
B) 400 METERS

☞ Chronicle of the Olympics, 1896-1996, Dorling Kindersley Publishing; UK, 1996.

Additional Information:

☞ The Voice, The Voice Group Ltd.; London, December 23, 1996, p.51.

☞ International Olympic Committee, Archive Records Department, Avenue de la Gare, No. 10, 1003 Lausanne, Switzerland.

☞ The Voice, The Voice Group Ltd.; London, July 2, 2001, p.64.

693.
A) LA LAKERS

☞ Magic Johnson, Sean Dolan, Chelsea House Publishers; NY, 1993.

Additional Information:

☞ Ebony, Johnson Publishing; Chicago, August, 1992, p.64.

☞ The Guinness Encyclopedia of International Sports, Records and Results. Peter Matthews, 3rd Edition, Guinness Publishing; 1993, p.94.

☞ Ebony, Johnson Publishing; Chicago, November, 2000, p.72.

694.
B) PAUL INCE

☞ Who's Who of Black Achievers, John Hughes, (ed.), Ethnic Media Group; UK, 1999, p.55.

Additional Information:

☞ Black Pearls of Soccer, Al Hamiilton, Harrap; London, 1982.

☞ European Football Yearbook, 95/96, Sports Project Ltd.; UK, 1995, p.319.

☞ Third World Impact. 8th Edition, Edited by Arif Ali, Hansib Publishing; 1988.

695.
B) DEFENDER

☞ Ooh Aah Paul Mcgrath: The Black Pearl of Inchicore, Paul McGrath and Cathal Dervan, UK.

Additional Information:

☞ The New Nation, Western Hemisphere; London, February 3, 1997, p.54.

☞ European Football Yearbook, 95/96, Sports Project Ltd.; UK, 1995, p.308.

☞ The F.A. Premier League, 11 Connought Place, London W2 2ET.

696.
C) FULHAM

☞ Fulham Football Club, Craven Cottage, Stevenage Road, London, SW6

Additional Information:
- ☞ The Sunday Times, London, November 4, 2001 (Sports Section).
- ☞ The Voice, The Voice Group Ltd.; London, March 24, 1997.
- ☞ The Guinness Record of World Soccer. Guy Oliver, Guinness Publishing; UK, 1992.

697.
A) REAL MADRID
- ☞ The Sunday Times, (Orient Express Section) London, October 7, 2001, p.13.

Additional Information:
- ☞ Black Pearls of Soccer, Al Hamilton, Harrap; London, 1982.
- ☞ Fédération Internationale De Football Association, Library Records Dept., Higzigueg 11, P.O. Box 85, 8030, Zurich.
- ☞ Black Sportsmen, Ernest Cashmore, Routlege & Keegan Paul; UK, 1982, p.30.

698.
C) KOBE BRYANT
- ☞ LA Lakers, 555 North Nash Street, El Segundo, California, 90245

Additional Information:
- ☞ The Biographical History of Basketball: Over 500 Portraits of the most significant on and off Court Personalities of the Games Past and Present, Peter C. Bjarkman, Mcgraw-Hill; 1999.
- ☞ The Voice, The Voice Group Ltd.; London, September 3, 2001, pp.62-63.
- ☞ 2001 ESPN Information Please Sports Almanac, ESPN; espn.com.

699.
B) THE AMERICAS CUP
- ☞ Americas Cup Museum, 5 Siska Court, Halls Head, Western Australia, 6210.

Additional Information:
- ☞ Black Firsts: 2000 Years of Extraordinary Achievement. Jessie Carney Smith, Caspar L. Jordan and Robert L. Johns, Visible Ink Press; USA, 1994, p.403.
- ☞ A Century Under Sail: Selected Photographs by Morris Rosenfeld and Stanley Rosenfeld Legendary Photographers of the Americas Cup Races, Stanley Rosenfeld, Mystic Seaport Museum Publications; 2001.
- ☞ Emerge, October, USA, 1992, p.38.

700.
C) MR. OCTOBER
- ☞ Reggie Jackson, by Eddie Stone, Holloway House Publishing Co.; LA, 1980.

Additional Information:
- ☞ The 1997 Guinness Book of Records, Guinness Publishing Ltd.; UK, 1996, p.253.
- ☞ Ebony, Johnson Publishing; Chicago, August, 1992, p.96.
- ☞ The Guinness Encyclopedia of International Sports, Records and Results. Peter Matthews, 3rd Edition, Guinness Publishing; 1993.

701.
B) BASEBALL'S NATIONAL LEAGUE
- ☞ Ebony, Johnson Publishing; Chicago, August, 1992, pp.52-54.

Additional Information:
- ☞ In the Ballpark: The Working Lives of Baseball People, George Gmelch and J. J. Weiner, Smithsonian Institute Press; 1999.
- ☞ Ebony, Johnson Publishing; Chicago, June, 1994, pp.116-18.
- ☞ Total Baseball, The Official Encyclopedia of Major League Baseball, John Thorn, Pete Palmer, Michael Gersham, 7th Edition, Total Sports; 2001.

702.
A) MICHAEL MOORER
- ☞ Ebony, Johnson Publishing; Chicago, July, 1995, pp.86-92.

Additional Information:
- ☞ The Evening Standard, Associated Newspaper Group; London, May 8, 1997, p.68.
- ☞ An Illustrated History of Boxing, Nat Fleischer and Sam Andre, Updated by Nigel Collins, Citadel Press; 2002.
- ☞ A Century of Boxing Greats: Inside the Ring With the 100 Best Boxers, Patrick Myler, Robson Books Ltd.; 1998.

703.
A) FIVE
- ☞ Suger Ray. The Sugar Ray Robinson Story, Sugar Ray Robinson and Dave Anderson, Revised Edition, Robsons, 1996.

Additional Information:

☞ A Century of Boxing Greats: Inside the Ring With the 100 Best Boxers, Patrick Myler, Robson Books Ltd.; 1998.

☞ Encyclopedia of Boxing, Maurice Golesworthy, 7th Edition, Robert Hale; London, 1983.

☞ The Sunday Times Illustrated History of Twentieth Century Sport, Chris Nawrat, Steve Hutchings and Greg Struthers, Hamlyn; 1992.

704.
B) DECATHLON

☞ The Greatest: Who is Britain's Top Sport Star, Daley Thompson, Stewart Binns and Tom Lewis, Bextree; Channel 4 Television Corporation, London, 1996, pp.226-29.

Additional Information:

☞ The Guinness Encyclopedia of International Sports, Records and Results. Peter Matthews, 3rd Edition, Guinness Publishing; 1993.

☞ The Sunday Times Illustrated History of Twentieth Century Sport, Chris Nawrat, Steve Hutchings and Greg Struthers, Hamlyn; 1992.

☞ Chronicle of the Olympics, 1896-1996, Dorling Kindersley Publishing; UK, 1996.

705.
C) HEPTATHLON

☞ Jackie Joyner-Kersee: Record-Breaking Runner, Liza N. Burby, Powerkids Press; 1998.

Additional Information:

☞ Ebony, Johnson Publishing; Chicago, July, 2001, p.80.

☞ Ebony, Johnson Publishing; Chicago, March, 1994, pp.48-50.

☞ Jackie Joyner-Kersee: Sports Superstars Series, Richard Rambeck, Child's World Books; 1997.

706.
A) DETROIT PISTONS

☞ Bad As I Wanna Be, Dennis Rodman with Tim Keown, Delacorte Press; USA, 1996.

Additional Information:

☞ The Voice, The Voice Group Ltd.; London, October 22, 1996, p.16.

☞ African Americans in Sport, Gary A. Sailes, (ed.), Transaction; New Jersey, 1998.

☞ Words from the Worm: An Unauthorized Trip Through the Mind of Dennis Rodman, Dennis Rodman and Dave Whitaker, Bonus Books; 1997.

707.
C) NEW YORK YANKEES

☞ USA Today-Sports Section, August 2, 1996, p.1B.

Additional Information:

☞ Ebony, Johnson Publishing; Chicago, August, 1992, p.60.

☞ New Bill James Historical Baseball Abstract, Bill James, Simon & Schuster; 2001.

☞ Total Baseball, The Official Encyclopedia of Major League Baseball, John Thorn, Pete Palmer, Michael Gersham, 7th Edition, Total Sports; 2001.

708.
A) INTERNATIONAL CRICKET COUNCIL

☞ The Weekly Journal, Voice Communications; London, July 15, 1993, p.8.

Additional Information:

☞ Cricket Facts and Feats, Bill Frindall, 4th Edition, Guinness Publishing; UK, 1996, pp.35, 41, 43, 162.

☞ The Complete Who's Who of Test Cricketers, C. Martin-Jenkins, Orbus Publishing; London, 1983.

☞ 100 Great Westindian Test Cricketers, by Bridgette Lawrence With Reg Scarlett, Hansib Publishing Ltd.; UK.

709.
A) SAMOA

☞ Rugby and the South African Nation: Sport, Cultures, Politics and Power in the Old and New South Africas (International Studies in the History of Sport), by John Nauright, Manchester University Press; UK, 1998.

Additional Information:

☞ Encyclopedia of Sports Culture, Ellis Cashmore, Routledge Books; 2002.

☞ Country of My Skull: Guilt, Sorrow, and the Limits of Forgiveness in the New South Africa, Antjie Krog, Luke Mitchell (Ed.) Times Books; 2000, p.349.

☞ Negotiating the Past: The Making of Memory in South Africa, Sarah Nuttall (Ed.), et al, Oxford University Press; 1998.

710.
C) WEIGHT LIFTING
☞ The 1997 Guinness Book of Records, Guinness Publishing Ltd.; UK, 1996, p.245.
Additional Information:
☞ International Olympic Committee, Archive Records Department, Avenue de la Gare, No. 10, 1003 Lausanne, Switzerland.
☞ The Guinness Encyclopedia of International Sports, Records and Results, Peter Matthews, 3rd Edition, Guinness Publishing; 1993.
☞ Chronicle of the Olympics, 1896-1996, Dorling Kindersley Publishing; UK, 1996.

711.
C) HIGH JUMP
☞ Encyclopedia of Black America, W. A. Low and Virgil A. Clift, (eds.), Mcgraw-Hill; New York, 1981, p.143.
Additional Information:
☞ Ebony, Johnson Publishing; Chicago, July, 1996 p.62.
☞ Chronicle of the Olympics, 1896-1996, Dorling Kindersley Publishing; UK, 1996.
☞ The Sunday Times Illustrated History of Twentieth Century Sport, Chris Nawrat, Steve Hutchings and Greg Struthers, Hamlyn; 1992.

712.
B) DEION SANDERS
☞ Deion Sanders, B. Chadwick, Chelsea House; USA, 1996.
Additional Information:
☞ Upscale, Upscale Communications, Inc.; November 1995, p.14.
☞ African Americans in Sport, Gary A. Sailes, (ed.), Transaction; New Jersey, 1998.
☞ The Voice, The Voice Group Ltd.; London, February 27, 1996, p.59.

713.
B) ARROWS
☞ Arrows Formula One Team, Leafield Cricket Centre, Leafield, Witney, Oxon, OX29, 9PF.
Additional Information:
☞ The New Nation, Ethnic Media Group; London, March 8, 1999, p.1.

☞ British Racing Drivers Club, Silverstone Circuit, Towcaster, Northampton, NN12 8TN.
☞ Untold, Peter Akinti Publ.; London, August/September, 1998, pp.110-11.

714.
B) JUSTIN GATLIN
☞ The Evening Standard, Associated Newspaper Group; London, August 23, 2004.
Additional Information:
☞ Daily Mail, London, August 23, 2004.
☞ The New Nation, Ethnic Media Group; London, August 30, 2004.
☞ The New York Times, August 23, 2004.

715.
C) HEAVYWEIGHT BOXING
☞ International Olympic Committee, Archive Records Department, Avenue de la Gare, No. 10, 1003 Lausanne, Switzerland.
Additional Information:
☞ Chronicle of the Olympics, 1896-1996, Dorling Kindersley Publishing; UK, 1996.
☞ Olympics: Facts and Feats, Stan Greenberry, Guinness Publishing; 1996, p.113.
☞ An Illustrated History of Boxing, Nat Fleischer and Sam Andre, Updated by Nigel Collins, Citadel Press; 2002.

716.
A) 400 METER HURDLES
☞ USA Today, August 2, 1996, p.9B.
Additional Information:
☞ Chronicle of the Olympics, 1896-1996, Dorling Kindersley Publishing; UK, 1996.
☞ International Olympic Committee, Archive Records Department, Avenue de la Gare, No. 10, 1003 Lausanne, Switzerland.
☞ The Voice, The Voice Group Ltd.; London, April 9, 2001, p.58.

717.
B) FENCING
☞ Roots in Britain, Ziggi Alexander and Audrey Dewjee, Brent Library Service; 2nd Edition, 1981, p.10.
Additional Information:
☞ Staying Power, Peter Fryer, Pluto Press; UK, 2nd Edition, UK, 1985.

- Sex and Race, Volume 1, J. A. Rogers, 9th Edition, H. M. Rogers Publishers; USA, 1968, p.202.
- Black Britannia: A History of Black People in Britain, Edward Scobie, Johnson Publishing Co.; 1972.

718.
B) PRESTON NORTH END
- The First Black Footballer: Arthur Wharton 1865-1930: An Absence of Memory, (Cass Series-Sports in the Global Society, 11.) Phil Vasili, Frank Cass & Co.; 1998.

Additional Information:
- The New Nation, Western Hemisphere; London, March 17, 1997, p.59.
- The Voice, The Voice Group Ltd.; London, April 28, 1997, p.71.
- Preston North End Football Club, Lowthorpe Road, Deepdale, PR1 6RU, UK.

719.
B) WORLD CHAMPIONSHIPS
- The Voice, The Voice Group Limited; February 15, 1994, p.59.

Additional Information:
- IAAF, 17 Rue Princesse, Florestine, B.P. 359, 98007, Monaco.
- The Weekly Journal, Voice Communications; London, January 19, 1995, p.18.
- The National Association of Ice Skating UK Ltd.; 15-27 Gee Street, London, EC1V 3RE.

720.
B) KAREEM ABDUL-JUBBAR
- The 1997 Guinness Book of Records, Guinness Publishing Ltd.; UK, 1996, p.255.

Additional Information:
- The Biographical History of Basketball: Over 500 Portraits of the most significant on and off Court Personalities of the Games Past and Present, Peter C. Bjarkman, Mcgraw-Hill; 1999.
- Ebony, Johnson Publishing; Chicago, August, 1992, p.64.
- The Guinness Encyclopedia of International Sports, Records and Results. Peter Matthews, 3rd Edition, Guinness Publishing; 1993, p.94.

721.
A) CYCLING
- Major Taylor: Andrew Ritchie, Bicycle Books, Mill Valley Books; California.

Additional Information:
- The Penguin Book of the Bicycle, Roderick Watson and Martin Gray, Penguin Books Ltd.; UK, 1978.
- A Hard Road to Glory: A history of the African American Athlete. Volume 1, Arthur Ashe, USA, 1988, pp.54-57.
- Your History: From the Beginning of Time to the Present, J. A. Rogers, Black Classic Press; Baltimore, MD, 1983, p.18.

722.
C) MARATHON
- Ebony, Johnson Publishing; Chicago, October, 2000, p.134.

Additional Information:
- The 1997 Guinness Book of Records, Guinness Publishing Ltd.; UK, 1996, p.330.
- Ebony, Johnson Publishing; Chicago, January, 1997, p.92.
- International Olympic Committee, Archive Records Department, Avenue de la Gare, No. 10, 1003 Lausanne, Switzerland.

723.
C) MICHAEL JOHNSON
- Slaying The Dragon, Michael Johnson, Piatikus; USA, 1996.

Additional Information:
- Ebony, Johnson Publishing; Chicago, July, 1996, p.88.
- African Americans in Sport, Gary A. Sailes, (ed.), Transaction; New Jersey, 1998.
- The Evening Standard, Associated Newspaper Group; London, April 16, 1997, p.73.

724.
B) COURTNEY WALSH
- International Cricket Council, Clock Tower, Lords Cricket Ground, London, NW8 8QN.

Additional Information:
- Cricket Facts and Feats, Bill Frindall, 4th Edition, Guinness Publishing; UK, 1996.

- The Voice, The Voice Group Ltd.; London, 26 August, 2002, p.32.
- The Daily Telegraph Chronicle of Cricket, Edited by Norman Barrett, Guinness Publishing; 1994.

725.
B) FLOYD PATTERSON
- A Hard Road to Glory: A History of the African American Athlete. Volume 3, Arthur Ashe, USA, 1988, pp.347-50
Additional Information:
- The Sunday Times Illustrated History of Twentieth Century Sport, Chris Nawrat, Steve Hutchings and Greg Struthers, Hamlyn; 1992.
- Ebony Pictorial History of Black America: Volume 3. Civil Rights Movement to Black Revolution, Johnson Publishing Company; 1974, pp.251, 259.
- The Guinness Encyclopedia of International Sports, Records and Results. Peter Matthews, 3rd Edition, Guinness Publishing; 1993.

726.
C) ELERY HANLEY
- Who's Who of Black Achievers, John Hughes, (ed.), Ethnic Media Group; UK, 1999, p.114.
Additional Information:
- The Greatest: Who is Britain's Top Sport Star, Daley Thompson, Stewart Binns and Tom Lewis, Bextree; Channel 4 Television Corporation, London, 1996, pp.116-18.
- The Sunday Times Illustrated History of Twentieth Century Sport, Chris Nawrat, Steve Hutchings and Greg Struthers, Hamlyn; 1992, p.380.
- Rugby League: An Illustrated History, Robert Gate, Arthur Baker Publishing; London, 1989, p.140.

727.
A) COLIN JACKSON
- The Voice, The Voice Group Ltd.; London, 14 April, 2003, p.31.
Additional Information:
- The Greatest: Who is Britain's Top Sport Star, Daley Thompson, Stewart Binns and Tom Lewis, Bextree; Channel 4 Television Corporation, London, 1996, pp.132-34.
- The 1997 Guinness Book of Records, Guinness Publishing Ltd.; UK, 1996, p.238.

- The Evening Standard, Associated Newspaper Group; London, May 12, 1997, p.67.

728.
A) TEN
- Linford Christie: An Autobiography, Linford Christie and Tony Ward, UK.
Additional Information:
- The Greatest: Who is Britain's Top Sport Star, Daley Thompson, Stewart Binns and Tom Lewis, Bextree; Channel 4 Television Corporation, London, 1996, pp.51-54.
- The Sunday Times Illustrated History of Twentieth Century Sport, Chris Nawrat, Steve Hutchings and Greg Struthers, Hamlyn; 1992.
- Olympics: Facts and Feats, Stan Greenberry, Guinness Publishing; 1996.

729.
C) COMMONWEALTH GAMES 1994
- The Voice, The Voice Group Ltd.; London, October 4, 1994, p.19.
Additional Information:
- The Weekly Journal, Voice Communications; London, May 25, 1995, p.20.
- Cathy Freeman, By Beth Dolan. Australia.
- (Zeke's Olympic Pocket Guide) Athletics, Field: Pole Vault, Long Jump, Hammer, Javelin, & Lots, Lots More, Jason Page, Lerner Publishing Group; USA, 2000.

730.
C) NINE
- Martin Offiah: A Blaze of Glory, David Lawrence, UK.
Additional Information:
- The Greatest: Who is Britain's Top Sport Star, Daley Thompson, Stewart Binns and Tom Lewis, Bextree; Channel 4 Television Corporation, London, 1996, pp.189-90.
- The Voice, The Voice Group Ltd.; London, December 23, 1996, p.51.
- Rugby League: An Illustrated History, Robert Gate, Arthur Baker Publishing; London, 1989, p.140.

Sport

731.
C) RANDOLPH TURPIN
☞ The Greatest: Who is Britain's Top Sport Star, Daley Thompson, Stewart Binns and Tom Lewis, Bextree; Channel 4 Television Corporation, London, 1996, pp.236-237.
Additional Information:
☞ The Total Sports Illustrated Book of Boxing, Nathan Ward, (ed.), Total Sports; 1999.
☞ Encyclopedia of Boxing, Maurice Golesworthy, 7th Edition, Robert Hale; London, 1983.
☞ McIvanney on Boxing, Hugh McIvanney, Mainstream Publishing; Edinburgh and London, 1996.

732.
A) 1947
☞ Crossing the Line: Black Major Leaguers, 1947-1959, Larry Moffi and Jonathon Kronstadt, University of Iowa Press; 1996.
Additional Information:
☞ Illustrated History of Baseball, Alex Chadwick, Brompton; 1988.
☞ Baseball and Softball, Ian Smyth, The Crowood Press; England, 1995, p.9.
☞ Black Americana. Richard A. Long, Admiral; UK, 1985, p.179.

733.
B) TORONTO BLUE JAYS
☞ Ebony, Johnson Publishing; Chicago, USA, February 1994, p.90.
Additional Information:
☞ Baseball and Softball, Ian Smyth, The Crowood Press; England, 1995, p.10.
☞ Ebony, Johnson Publishing; Chicago, USA, August 1992, p.54.
☞ Ebony, Johnson Publishing; Chicago, USA, May 1994, p.146.

734.
C) DENMARK
☞ World Record Breakers in Track & Field Athletics, Gerald Lawson, Human Kinetics Publishing; 1997.
Additional Information:
☞ The Voice, The Voice Group Ltd.; July 14, 1997, p.51.
☞ (Zeke's Olympic Pocket Guide) Athletics, Track: 100 Meters, 200 Meters, Relays, Hurdle, & Lots, Lots More, Jason Page, Lerner Publishing Group; USA, 2000.
☞ The Voice, The Voice Group Ltd.; July 7, 1997, p.63.

735.
B) OLIVER McCALL
☞ Frank Bruno: From Zero To Hero, Frank Bruno With Norman Giller, Andre Deutsch; UK, 1996.
Additional Information:
☞ An Illustrated History of Boxing, Nat Fleischer and Sam Andre, Updated by Nigel Collins, Citadel Press; 2002.
☞ The Greatest: Who is Britain's Top Sport Star, Daley Thompson, Stewart Binns and Tom Lewis, Bextree; Channel 4 Television Corporation, London, 1996, pp.41-42.
☞ McIvanney on Boxing, Hugh McIvanney, Mainstream Publishing; Edinburgh and London, 1996.

736.
B) SOCCER
☞ Prosports of the African Cup of Nations 1957-2000, Filippo Maria Ricci, (ed.), 2000.
Additional Information:
☞ West Africa, London, January 6-12, 1992, pp.19-34.
☞ New African, September 2001, ICP Ltd.; London, p.49.
☞ Prosports African Football Yearbook, Filippo Maria Ricci, (ed.), Third Edition, 2001.

737.
C) MAURICE GREEN
☞ The Guinness Book of Records 2001, Guinness Publishing Ltd.; UK, 2000.
Additional Information:
☞ (Zeke's Olympic Pocket Guide) Athletics, Track: 100 Meters, 200 Meters, Relays, Hurdle, & Lots, Lots More, Jason Page, Lerner Publishing Group; USA, 2000.
☞ Ebony, Johnson Publishing; Chicago, December, 2000, p.136.
☞ The New Nation, Ethnic Media Group; London, May 5, 2003, p.52.

738.
A) O. J. SIMPSON
☞ NFL's Greatest: Pro Football's Best Players, Teams, and Games. National Football League, (ed.), Phil Barber and John Fawaz, DK Publishing; 2000.
Additional Information:
☞ NFL's Official Encyclopedia History of Professional Football, National Football League. USA.

☞ The Gridiron UK Guide to American Football: All the Greats. Ross Biddiscombe, Patrick Stevens, UK, 1986.

☞ The NFL Official History of Pro Football, Beau Riffenburgh and Jack Clary, Hamlyn; 1996.

739.
B) SIX

☞ The Greatest: Who is Britain's Top Sport Star, Daley Thompson, Stewart Binns and Tom Lewis, Bextree; Channel 4 Television Corporation, London, 1996, pp.217-18.

Additional Information:

☞ Chronicle of the Olympics, 1896-1996, Dorling Kindersley Publishing; UK, 1996.

☞ Olympics: Facts and Feats, Stan Greenberry, Guinness Publishing; 1996.

☞ The Voice, The Voice Group Ltd.; London, September 24, 2001, p.6.

740.
A) ORLANDO MAGIC

☞ Ebony, Johnson Publishing; Chicago, USA, May 1996, pp.26-32.

Additional Information:

☞ Ebony, Johnson Publishing; Chicago, November, 2000, p.88.

☞ Orlando Magic, 8701 Maitland Summit Blvd., Orlando, Florida, USA, 32810.

☞ L. A. Lakers, 555 North Nash Street, Elsegundo, California, 90245

741.
B) HENRY ARMSTRONG

☞ 1999 Facts About Blacks: A Sourcebook of African American Accomplishment. Raymond M. Corbin, Beckham House Publishers; USA, 1st Edition, 1986, p.128.

Additional Information:

☞ Black Firsts: 2000 Years of Extraordinary Achievement. Jessie Carney Smith, Caspar L. Jordan and Robert L. Johns, Visible Ink Press; USA, 1994, p.381.

☞ The Black American Reference Book. Mabel M. Smyth, (ed.), Prentice-Hall Inc.; USA, 1976.

☞ Encyclopedia of Boxing, Maurice Golesworthy, 7th Edition, Robert Hale; London, 1983.

742.
C) 400 METERS

☞ Daily Mail, London, August 25, 2004.

Additional Information:

☞ The New Nation, Ethnic Media Group; London, August 30, 2004.

☞ The Mail on Sunday; London, August 26, 2004.

☞ "The 2004 Olympics", August 24, 2004, British Broadcasting Corporation, Library Archives, White City, London, W12.

743.
A) FRANK ROBINSON

☞ Frank Robinson, Norman Macht, Chelsea House; USA, 1991.

Additional Information:

☞ Ebony, Johnson Publishing; Chicago, June, 1995, p.40.

☞ Before the Mayflower: A History of Black America. Lerone Bennett Jr., 5th Edition, Penguin Books; 1984, p.636.

☞ Ebony, Johnson Publishing; Chicago, August, 2000, pp.48-50.

744.
A) PROFESSIONAL FOOTBALL ASSOCIATION

☞ Black and British, David Bygott, Oxford University Press; 1992, p.74.

Additional Information:

☞ The Weekly Journal, Voice Communications; London, September 29, 1994, p.8.

☞ English Football Association, Library Records Dept., Lancaster House, Lancaster Gate, Paddington W2, London.

☞ The New Nation, Western Hemisphere; London, April 28, 1997, p.57.

745.
C) LONG JUMP

☞ Ebony, Johnson Publishing; Chicago, April, 1996, pp.68-72.

Additional Information:

☞ The Sunday Times Illustrated History of Twentieth Century Sport, Chris Nawrat, Steve Hutchings and Greg Struthers, Hamlyn; 1992.

☞ Chronicle of the Twentieth Century, Jacques Legrand, Longman Books; 1988.

☞ Ebony, Johnson Publishing; Chicago, October, 2000, pp.131, 183.

746.

A) LYNETTE WOODWARD

☞ Ebony, Johnson Publishing; Chicago, August, 1992, p.64.

Additional Information:

☞ A Hard Road to Glory: A History of the African American Athlete. Volume 3, Arthur Ashe, USA, 1988, pp.64, 253.

☞ Ebony, Johnson Publishing; Chicago, February Edition 1997, pp.156-60.

☞ Black Firsts: 2000 Years of Extraordinary Achievement. Jessie Carney Smith, Caspar L. Jordan and Robert L. Johns, Visible Ink Press; USA, 1994, p.401.

747.

A) BASEBALL

☞ Ebony, Johnson Publishing; Chicago, August, 1992.

Additional Information:

☞ New Bill James Historical Baseball Abstract, Bill James, Simon & Schuster; 2001.

☞ Crossing the Line: Black Major Leaguers, 1947-1959, Larry Moffi and Jonathon Kronstadt, University of Iowa Press; 1996.

☞ Encyclopedia of Black America, W. A. Low and Virgil A. Clift, (eds.), Mcgraw-Hill; New York, 1981.

748.

C) EMPIRE

☞ A Hard Road to Glory: A History of the African American Athlete. Volume 2, Arthur Ashe, USA, 1988, p.32.

Additional Information:

☞ Ebony Pictorial History of Black America: Volume 3. Civil Rights Movement to Black Revolution, Johnson Publishing Company; 1974.

☞ Encyclopedia of Black America, W. A. Low and Virgil A. Clift, (eds.), Mcgraw-Hill; New York, 1981, p.635.

☞ Ebony, Johnson Publishing; Chicago, August, 1992, p.58.

749.

A) CHARLIE SIFFORD

☞ Encyclopedia of Black America, W. A. Low and Virgil A. Clift, (eds.), Mcgraw-Hill; New York, 1981, p.635.

Additional Information:

☞ Ebony, Johnson Publishing; Chicago, August, 1992, p.78.

☞ The Black Heritage Book of Trivia, Morgan White Jr., Quinlan Press; Boston, 1985.

☞ 1999 Facts About Blacks: A Sourcebook of African American Accomplishment. Raymond M. Corbin, Beckham House Publishers; USA, 1st Edition, 1986.

750.

B) CHELSEA

☞ Chelsea Football Club, Stanford Bridge, Fulham Road, London, SW6 1HS.

Additional Information:

☞ The Independent on Sunday, Independent Newspapers; London, May 18, 1997.

☞ The Times, London, Monday May 19, 1997 (Sports Section).

☞ Ruud Gullit, Portrait of a Genius, Harry Harris, Collins Willow; UK, 1996.

751.

A) NATIONAL BASKETBALL ASSOCIATION

☞ And the Walls Came Tumbling Down: The Basketball Game That Changed American Sports, Frank Fitzpatrick, Bison Books Corporation, USA, 2000.

Additional Information:

☞ Ebony, Johnson Publishing; Chicago, August, 1992, p.62.

☞ Before the Mayflower: A History of Black America. Lerone Bennett Jr., 5th Edition, Penguin Books; 1984, p.634.

☞ 1999 Facts About Blacks: A Sourcebook of African American Accomplishment. Raymond M. Corbin, Beckham House Publishers; USA, 1st Edition, 1986, p.99.

752.

A) ARISTIDES

☞ A Hard Road to Glory: A History of the African American Athlete. Volume 1, Arthur Ashe, USA, 1988.

Additional Information:

☞ The Black Heritage Book of Trivia, Morgan White Jr., Quinlan Press; Boston, 1985.

☞ 1999 Facts About Blacks: A Sourcebook of African American Accomplishment. Raymond M. Corbin, Beckham House Publishers; USA, 1st Edition, 1986.

☞ Black Firsts: 2000 Years of Extraordinary Achievement. Jessie Carney Smith, Caspar L. Jordan and Robert L. Johns, Visible Ink Press; USA, 1994.

753.
B) LIGHT HEAVYWEIGHT
☞ Sugar Ray Leonard & Other Noble Warriors, Sam Toperoff, McGraw Hill Book Co.; New York, 1987.
Additional Information:
☞ Sugar Ray Leonard, James Haskins, Lothrop Lee & Shepard; USA, 1982.
☞ A Century of Boxing Greats: Inside the Ring With the 100 Best Boxers, Patrick Myler, Robson Books Ltd.; 1998.
☞ An Illustrated History of Boxing, Nat Fleischer and Sam Andre, Updated by Nigel Collins, Citadel Press; 2002.

754.
B) SHOW JUMPING
☞ Jumping the Odds, Memoirs of a Rastafarian Show Jumper, Oliver Skeete with the assistance of Peter Holt, Headline Books; UK, 1995.
Additional Information:
☞ Jet, Johnson Publishing Co.; Chicago, January 21, 1991, p.48.
☞ Black Firsts: 2000 Years of Extraordinary Achievement. Jessie Carney Smith, Caspar L. Jordan and Robert L. Johns, Visible Ink Press; USA, 1994.
☞ The Observer, London, April 20, 1997, (Sport) p.12.

755.
C) ZINA GARRISON
☞ Zina: My Life in Women's Tennis, Zina Garrison and Doug Smith, Frog Ltd.; 2000.
Additional Information:
☞ Jet, Johnson Publishing Co.; Chicago, July 23, 1990, p.51
☞ Zina Garrison: Ace, A. P. Porter, USA, 1991.
☞ Chronicle of the Olympics, 1896-1996, Dorling Kindersley Publishing; UK, 1996.

756.
C) PATRICK KLUIVERT
☞ Brilliant Orange: The Neurotic Genius of Dutch Football, David Winner, Bloomsbury Publications Ltd.; UK, 2000.
Additional Information:
☞ The Rough Guide European Football 2000-2001: A Fan's Handbook (Rough Guide), Peterjon Cresserll, Simon Evans, Dan Goldstein, (eds.), Rough Guides; 2000.

☞ De top 100: De Beste Nederlandse Voetballers Van Deze Eeuw, Henk Spaan. Netherlands.
☞ European Football Yearbook, 95/96, Sports Project Ltd.; UK, 1995.

757.
B) WARREN MOON
☞ Ebony, Johnson Publishing; Chicago, August, 1992, p.68.
Additional Information:
☞ 1999 Facts About Blacks: A Sourcebook of African American Accomplishment. Raymond M. Corbin, Beckham House Publishers; USA, 1st Edition, 1986, p.101.
☞ The Guinness Encyclopedia of International Sports, Records and Results. Peter Matthews, 3rd Edition, Guinness Publishing; 1993.
☞ The 1997 Guinness Book of Records, Guinness Publishing Ltd.; UK, 1996, p.251.

758.
B) JERSEY JOE WALCOTT
☞ Encyclopedia of Boxing, Maurice Golesworthy, 7th Edition, Robert Hale; London, 1983.
Additional Information:
☞ 1999 Facts About Blacks: A Sourcebook of African American Accomplishment. Raymond M. Corbin, Beckham House Publishers; USA, 1st Edition, 1986, p.101.
☞ McIvanney on Boxing, Hugh McIvanney, Mainstream Publishing; Edinburgh and London, 1996.
☞ The Total Sports Illustrated Book of Boxing, Nathan Ward, (ed.), Total Sports; 1999.

759.
A) SIX
☞ 1999 Facts About Blacks: A Sourcebook of African American Accomplishment. Raymond M. Corbin, Beckham House Publishers; USA, 1st Edition, 1986.
Additional Information:
☞ The Black American Reference Book. Mabel M. Smyth, (ed.), Prentice-Hall Inc.; USA, 1976.
☞ American Negro Reference Book, John P. Davis, Prentice Hall; New Jersey, 1966.

Sport

A Hard Road to Glory: A History of the African American Athlete. Volume 1, Arthur Ashe, USA, 1988.

760.
B) EMLEN TUNNEL
Ebony, Johnson Publishing; Chicago, August, 1992, pp.68, 72.
Additional Information:
Before the Mayflower: A History of Black America. Lerone Bennett Jr., 5th Edition, Penguin Books; 1984.
1999 Facts About Blacks: A Sourcebook of African American Accomplishment. Raymond M. Corbin, Beckham House Publishers; USA, 1st Edition, 1986.
A Hard Road to Glory: A History of the African American Athlete. Volume 3, Arthur Ashe, USA, 1988, pp.130-31, 355-56.

761.
B) FIGURE SKATING
Ebony, Johnson Publishing; Chicago, February, 1995, p.134.
Additional Information:
The Weekly Journal, Voice Communications; London, February 9, 1995, pp.1, 24.
Ebony, Johnson Publishing; Chicago, August, 1992, p.80.
A Hard Road to Glory: A History of the African American Athlete. Volume 3, Arthur Ashe, USA, 1988. pp.224, 257.

762.
A) JOHN RUIZ
The New Nation, Ethnic Media Group; London, May 5, 2003, p.54.
Additional Information:
Boxing's Most Wanted: The Top 10 Book of Champs, Chumps, and Punch-Drunk Palookas (Brassey's Most Wanted). Mike Fitzgerald Jr., and Davil L. Hudson, Jr, Brasseys, Inc.; 2003
Let's Go to the Videotape: All The Plays and Replays From My Life in Sports, Larry Warner and Weisman Wolf, Warner Books; 2000, p.163, 171.
The Hardest Game: McIlvanney on Boxing, by Hugh McIlvanney McGraw-Hill/Contemporary Books; 2001, p.270.

763.
B) SIX
Ebony, Johnson Publishing; Chicago, August, 1992, p.72.
Additional Information:
NFL's Official Encyclopedia History of Professional Football, National Football League. USA.
NFL 2001 Record and Fact Book, National Football League, Workman Publishing Company; 2001.
NFL's Greatest: Pro Football's Best Players, Teams, and Games. National Football League, (ed.), Phil Barber and John Fawaz, DK Publishing; 2000.

764.
A) THE ENGLISH SWEEPSTAKES
A Hard Road to Glory: A History of the African American Athlete. Volume 1, Arthur Ashe, USA, 1988, p.49.
Additional Information:
Encyclopedia of Black America, W. A. Low and Virgil A. Clift, (eds.), Mcgraw-Hill; New York, 1981.
1999 Facts About Blacks: A Sourcebook of African American Accomplishment. Raymond M. Corbin, Beckham House Publishers; USA, 1st Edition, 1986, p.114.
The Black American Reference Book. Mabel M. Smyth, (ed.), Prentice-Hall Inc.; USA, 1976.

765.
B) LEON SPINKS
King of the World: Muhammad Ali and the Rise of An American Hero, David Remnick, Vintage Books; New York, 1999.
Additional Information:
Muhammad Ali: His Life and Times, Thomas Hauser, Touchstone Books; 1992.
More Than a Hero: Muhammad Ali's Life Lessons Presented Through His Daughter's Eyes, Muhammad Ali and Hana Ali, Pocket Books; 2000.
Ghosts of Manila: The Fateful Blood Feud Between Muhammad Ali and Joe Frazier, Mark Kram, HarperCollins; 2001.

766.
A) AUSTRALIA
Sweet Chariot: The complete book of the rugby world cup, Ian Robertson,, Mainstream Publishing Company Ltd.; UK, 2004

Additional Information:
☞ Independent Sports Travel Guides: Rugby World Cup 2003, Jo Metcalfe and Matthew McGrory, Johanna Publishing Limited; 2003
☞ The History of the Rugby World Cup, Gerald Davies, John Eales Sanctuary Publishing Ltd.; 2004
☞ The Australian Rugby Companion: The Game They Play in Heaven, Gordon Bray, Penguin Books Australia Ltd;

767.
A) BOXING
☞ Roots of the Future: The Ethnic Diversity in the Making of Britain. CRE; UK, 1996.
Additional Information:
☞ Ebony Pictorial History of Black America: Volume 3. Civil Rights Movement to Black Revolution, Johnson Publishing Company; 1974, p.251.
☞ Staying Power, Peter Fryer, Pluto Press; UK, 2nd Edition, 1985.
☞ Nature Knows No Color Line. J. A. Rogers, 3rd Edition, H. M. Rogers Publishers; 1952, p.171.

768.
B) DALLAS MAVERICKS
☞ Independent on Sunday, London, 8 February 2004, (Sports Week) p.10.
Additional Information:
☞ Orlando Magic, 8701 Maitland Summit Blvd., Orlando, Florida, USA, 32810.
☞ The Voice, The Voice Group Ltd.; London, May 21, 2001, p.63.
☞ Utah Jazz, 301 West South Temple, Salt Lake City, Utah, 84101.

769.
B) KIP KEINO
☞ Chronicle of the Olympics, 1896-1996, Dorling Kindersley Publishing; UK, 1996.
Additional Information:
☞ The Voice, The Voice Group Ltd.; London, April 30, 2001, p.10.
☞ Olympics: Facts and Feats, Stan Greenberry, Guinness Publishing; 1996.
☞ World Record Breakers in Track & Field Athletics, Gerald Lawson, Human Kinetics Publishing; 1997.

770.
C) MARVIN HAGLER
☞ Marvelous Marvin Hagler, (Scu-2/ Sports Clubs-Ups), Carolyn Gloeckner, Howard Schroeder; USA.
Additional Information:
☞ A Century of Boxing Greats: Inside the Ring With the 100 Best Boxers, Patrick Myler, Robson Books Ltd.; 1998.
☞ The Total Sports Illustrated Book of Boxing, Nathan Ward, (ed.), Total Sports; 1999.
☞ An Illustrated History of Boxing, Nat Fleischer and Sam Andre, Updated by Nigel Collins, Citadel Press; 2002.

771.
A) 1000 METERS
☞ The 1997 Guinness Book of Records, Guinness Publishing Ltd.; UK, 1996, p.239.
Additional Information:
☞ The Weekly Journal, Voice Communications; London, May 20, 1995, p.20.
☞ New African, September 2001, ICP Ltd.; London, p.48.
☞ The Voice, The Voice Group Ltd.; London, November 6, 2000, p.62.

772.
C) 1982
☞ Jet, Johnson Publishing Co.; Chicago, February 20, 1984, p.40.
Additional Information:
☞ A Hard Road to Glory: A history of the African American Athlete. Volume 3, Arthur Ashe, USA, 1988, p.234.
☞ Rodeo Cowboys in the North American Imagination, (Wilbur S. Shepperson Series in History and Humanities), Michael Allen, University of Nevada Press; 1998.
☞ American Rodeo: From Buffalo Bill to Big Business, Kristine Fredriksson Texas A & M University Press; 1993.

773.
A) GOLF TEE
☞ Assistant Commissioner for Patents; United States Patent Office, Archive Records, Washington, D.C., 20231, 12th December 1899, Patent No. 638, 920.

Additional Information:

- Vibe, Quincy Jones and David Salzman
  Entertainment, Time Publishing Inc.;
  February, 1996, p.59.
- Blacks in Science: Astrophysicist to
  Zoologist. Hattie Carwell, USA, 1977,
  p.79.
- 1999 Facts About Blacks: A Sourcebook
  of African American Accomplishment.
  Raymond M. Corbin, Beckham House
  Publishers; USA, 1st Edition, 1986,
  p.38.

History

Answers and Sources

774.

B) HE WAS THE FIRST AFRICAN POPE

☞ Liber Pontificalis (Book of Popes) translated by L. R. Loomis, New York, 1916, pp.17, 40.

Additional Information:

☞ The New York Voice, July 2, 1980.

☞ African Presence in Early Europe, Edited by Ivan Van Sertima, Transaction; 1986, pp.97-100.

☞ Journal of African Civilization, Transactions Periodicals Consortium; Rutgers University, New Brunswick, New Jersey, "African Popes", Edward Scobie, Volume 4, No. 1., April, 1982.

775.

B) GRANDMOTHER

☞ The Sunday Times, London, June 6, 1999, p.11.

Additional Information:

☞ Debretts "Kings and Queens of Britain", by David Williamson, Webb Bower; 1986, p.165.

☞ Black Women in Antiquity, Edited by Ivan Van Sertima, Transaction; 7th Edition, 1992, pp.136-37.

☞ Nature Knows No Color Line. J. A. Rogers, 3rd Edition, H. M. Rogers Publishers; 1952 (Cover), p.93.

776.

A) THE ALPS

☞ Hannibal: A History of the Art of War Among the Carthagonians and Romans Down to the Battle of Pydna, 168b.c., Theodore Ayrault Dodge, Da Capo Press; New York, 1995.

Additional Information:

☞ African Glory: The Story of Vanished Negro Civilisation, J. C. De Graft-Johnson, Walker and Company; New York, 1954, pp.20-21, 130-31, 184-85.

☞ The Penguin Atlas of World History; From the Beginning to the Eve of the French Revolution. Vol. 1., Herman Kinder and Werner Hilgemann, pp.81-85.

☞ Scipio Africanus: The Conqueror of Hannibal (Selections from Livy: Books 26-30), Livy, T. A. Buckney (ed.), Bolchazy Carducci; 1987.

777.

B) NUBIA

☞ Nubian Twighlight, Rex Keating, R. Hart-Davis; London, 1962.

Additional Information:

☞ Cambridge Encyclopedia, David Crystal, Cambridge University Press; 1990, p.673.

☞ Nile Valley Contributions to Civilization; Exploding the Myths, Volume 1, Anthony T. Browder, Institute of Khamic Guidance; Washington, D.C., 2000, p.54.

☞ African Kingdoms, Basil Davidson, Time-Life Books; (Nederland), 1980, p.34.

778.

A) JAMESTOWN, VIRGINIA

☞ Before the Mayflower: A History of Black America. Lerone Bennett Jr., 5th Edition, Penguin Books; 1984, pp.194, 441.

Additional Information:

☞ Your History: From the Beginning of Time to the Present, J. A. Rogers, Black Classic Press; Baltimore, MD, 1983, p.73.

☞ Ebony, Johnson Publishing; Chicago, February, 2001, p.116.

☞ 1999 Facts About Blacks: A Sourcebook of African American Accomplishment. Raymond M. Corbin, Beckham House Publishers; USA, 1st Edition, 1986, p.3.

779.

B) ETHIOPIA

☞ The Encyclopedia of Africa, Franklin Watts, Inc.; New York and London, 1976.

Additional Information:

☞ The Africans, Ali A. Muzuri, A Triple Heritage, BBC Publications; London, 1986.

☞ The Destruction of Black Civilization: Great Issues of a Race from 4500 B.C. to 2000 A.D., Chancellor Williams, Third World Press; Chicago, 1976, p.267.

☞ Cambridge Encyclopedia, David Crystal, Cambridge University Press; 1990, p.974.

780.

A) MEMPHIS

☞ Ancient Egypt: The Light of the World, Volume 1, Gerald Massey, Black Classic Press; Baltimore, MD, 1992.

Additional Information:
- ☞ A History of Egypt, James Henry Breasted, Bantam Matrix Books; New York, NY, 1967.
- ☞ The African Origin of Civilization: Myth or Reality, Cheikh Anta Diop, translated by Mercer Cook, Lawrence Hill & Company; 1974, pp.93-95, 207-8, 219-21.
- ☞ Ancient Records of Egypt: Historical Documents From the Earliest Times to the Persian Conquest, Vols. 1-5, James H. Breasted, The University of Chicago Press; Chicago, 1906-1907.

781.
C) GORMUND
- ☞ African Presence in Early Europe, Edited by Ivan Van Sertima, Transaction; 1986, p.227.

Additional Information:
- ☞ Ancient and Modern Britons. David MacRitchie, Volume 1, Keegan Paul, Trench & Co.; 1985.
- ☞ History of the Kings of Britain, Geoffrey of Monmouth, Translated by Sebastian Evans, E.P. Dutton; New York, 1958, pp.239-41.
- ☞ Folklore As an Historical Science, George Laurence Gomme, Gordon Press Publications; 1990, p.119.

782.
A) CRISPUS ATTUCKS
- ☞ Crispus Attucks: Black Leader of Colonial Patriots, Dharathula Millender, Econo-Clad Books; USA, 1999.

Additional Information:
- ☞ Chronicle of America, Jacques Legrand, Longman; USA, 1989.
- ☞ Encyclopedia of Black America, W. A. Low and Virgil A. Clift, (eds.), Mcgraw-Hill; New York, 1981.
- ☞ Ebony, Johnson Publishing; July, 1968, p.94.

783.
C) NEFERTITI
- ☞ The Traveler's Key to Ancient Egypt: A Guide to the Sacred Places of Ancient Egypt. John Anthony West, Alfred A. Knopf; New York, 1985.

Additional Information:
- ☞ The Heretic King, Joy Collier, John Day Co.; New York, 1972.

- ☞ Nile Valley Contributions to Civilization; Exploding the Myths, Volume 1, Anthony T. Browder, Institute of Khamic Guidance; Washington, D.C., 2000, p.94.
- ☞ Black Women in Antiquity, Edited by Ivan Van Sertima, Transaction; 7th Edition, 1992, pp.50, 52, 57, 156.

784.
C) BUFFALO SOLDIERS
- ☞ The Forgotten Heroes: The Story of the Buffalo Soldiers, Clinton Cox, Point Publications; 1996.

Additional Information:
- ☞ Blacks in American Wars, Robert W. Mullen, MONAD Press; New York, 1981.
- ☞ A Pictorial History of Black America. Langston Hughes, Crown; NY, 1983
- ☞ The Voice, The Voice Group Ltd.; London, October 4, 1994, p.16.

785.
A) CAPTAIN
- ☞ The Four Voyages of Christopher Columbus (Penguin Classics), Christopher Columbus, J. M. Cohen, (trans.), Penguin; USA, 1992.

Additional Information:
- ☞ Africa, Mother of Western Civilization, Dr. Yosef A. A Ben Jochannon, Black Classic Press; Baltimore, MD, 1988, p.151.
- ☞ El Diario de Cristóbal Cólon, Christopher Diario Columbus, Marcel Charles Andrade, NTC Publishing Group; 1997.
- ☞ What They Never Told You in History Class, Indus Khamit-Kush, Luxorr Publications; USA, 1983, p.278.

786.
B) FIVE
- ☞ Black Women in Antiquity, Edited by Ivan Van Sertima, Transaction; 7th Edition, 1992, pp.5-6, 31, 128.

Additional Information:
- ☞ Black Athena: The Afroasiatic Roots of Classical Civilsation, Vols. 1 & 2, Martin Bernal, FAB; London, 1991.
- ☞ The Gold of Meroe, Karl-Heinz Priest, Philip Von Zabern Publishers; Mainz, 1993.
- ☞ An Introduction to African Civilisation, Willis Huggins and John G. Jackson, Greenwood Publishing Corporation; Westport, CT, 1969, pp.69-70.

787.
C) LIBERIA
☞ Freedom Ships: The Spectacular Epic of Africa Americans Who Dared to Find Their Freedom Long Before Emancipation, Robert D. Carey and John H, Furbay, Af-Am Links Press; 1999.

Additional Information:
☞ The Cambridge Encyclopedia of Africa. Cambridge University Press; 1981.
☞ Macdonalds Encyclopedia of Africa, Macdonald Educational Ltd.; UK, 1986.
☞ Historical Dictionary of Liberia, D. Elwood Dunn, Amos J. Beyan and Carl Burrowes, Scarecrow Press; 2000.

788.
C) HARRIET TUBMAN
☞ Harriet Tubman: A Guide to Freedom. Sam and Byryl Epstein, Gerrard Publishing Co.; 1968.

Additional Information:
☞ Women, Race and Class, Angela Davis, Women's Press; 1983.
☞ The Essential Black Literature Guide, Published in association with the Schomburg Center for Research in Black Culture, Roger M. Valade II, Visible Ink Press; USA, 1996, pp.364-65.
☞ When and Where I Enter: The Impact of Black Women on Race in America, Paula Giddings, William Morrow; NY, 1984.

789.
B) 640 A.D.
☞ History of the Arabs, Phillip K. Hitti, Macmillan; New York, 1951.

Additional Information:
☞ The Penguin Atlas of World History; From the Beginning to the Eve of the French Revolution. Vol. 1., Herman Kinder and Werner Hilgemann, pp.135-139.
☞ Black Man of the Nile and His Family. Dr. Yosef A. A. Ben Jochannon, Black Classic Press; Baltimore, MD, 1988.
☞ Vanished Cities of Northern Africa, Beatrice Steward Erskine, Hutchinson & Co.; London, 1927.

790.
B) 11th
☞ African History for Beginners. Herb Boyd. Writers & Readers Publishing, Inc.; London, New York, 1994, p.56.

Additional Information:
☞ The Royal Kingdoms of Ghana, Mali and Songhay: Life in Medieval Africa, Pat McKissack Et Al, Henry Holt Books; USA, 1995.
☞ The Destruction of Black Civilization: Great Issues of a Race from 4500 B.C. to 2000 A.D., Chancellor Williams. Third World Press; Chicago, 1976, p.211.
☞ Africa: Its Empires, Nations and People, Mary Penick Motley, Wayne State University Press; Detroit, 1969.

791.
C) POPE CLEMENT VII
☞ Black Women in Antiquity, Edited by Ivan Van Sertima, Transaction; 7th Edition, 1992, p.149.

Additional Information:
☞ The Medici, George Frederick Young, Vols. I and II., E. P. Dutton & Co. Inc.; New York, 1909, pp.493-514.
☞ A Cardinal of the Medici, Mrs. Hicks Beach (Susan Emily Christian), The Macmillan Company; New York, 1937.
☞ Liber Pontificalis (Book of Popes) translated by L. R. Loomis, New York, 1916, pp.17, 40.

792.
B) SOUTH AMERICA
☞ They Came Before Columbus, Ivan Van Sertima, Random House; New York, 1976.

Additional Information:
☞ Nile Valley Contributions to Civilization; Exploding the Myths, Volume 1, Anthony T. Browder, Institute of Khamic Guidance; Washington, D.C., 2000, pp.209-14.
☞ America's First Civilsation: Discovering the Olmec, Michael D. Coe, American Heritage Publishing Co.; New York, 1968.
☞ Nature Knows No Color Line. J. A. Rogers, 3rd Edition, H. M. Rogers Publishers; 1952, p.234.

793.
A) CETEWAYO
☞ World's Great Men of Color, J. A. Rogers, Volume 1, Collier Macmillan Publishers; 1972, pp.286-293.

Additional Information:
☞ Makers of South Africa, B. L. W. Brett, T. Nelson; London, 1944, pp.27-32.
☞ Shaka Zulu, E. R. Ritter, Longmans, Green and Co.; New York, 1955, p.199.
☞ Zululand and Cetewayo, Sir Walter Robert Ludlow, Simpkin, Marshall Company; London, 1882.

794.
A) KHUFU
☞ The Hall of Records: Hidden Secrets of the Pyramid and Sphinx, Jalandris, Holistic Life Travels, San Francisco, CA., 1980.
Additional Information:
☞ Smithsonian Magazine, "Unlocking the Secrets of the Giza Plateau", Dora Jane Hamblin, Washington, D.C., April, 1986.
☞ Great Pyramid: Proof of God. George R. Riffert, Destiny Publishers; Haverhill, Mass., 1944.
☞ Newsweek, "The Pyramids and Sphinx", Desmond Stewart, 1971, USA, p.20,

795.
C) NORTH AMERICA
☞ Atlantic Crossings Before Columbus, Frederick J. Pohl, W. W. Norton & Co.; New York, 1961, p.137.
Additional Information:
☞ The Norse Discoveries of America, "The Windland Sagas", translated by G. M. Snorri Gathorne-Hardy, Clarendon; Oxford, 1970.
☞ The Northmen: Columbus and Cabot, 985-1503, Edited by Julius E. Olson, Charles Scribner's Sons; New York, 1959.
☞ The Voice, The Voice Group Ltd.; London, March 12, 2001, p.53.

796.
C) THE ROCK OF GIBRALTAR
☞ The Legend of Tarik, Walter Dean Myers, The Viking Press; USA, 1981.
Additional Information:
☞ The Golden Age of the Moor. Light of Europe's Dark Age, Ivan Van Sertima, Transaction; New Jersey, 1991.
☞ The Coast of Barbary, Jane Soames, J. Cape; London, 1938.

☞ World's Great Men of Color, J. A. Rogers, Volume II, Collier Macmillan Publishers; 1972, p.541.

797.
A) HYKSOS
☞ Black Man of the Nile and His Family. Dr. Yosef A. A. Ben Jochannon, Black Classic Press; Baltimore, MD, 1988.
Additional Information:
☞ Nile Valley Contributions to Civilization; Exploding the Myths, Volume 1, Anthony T. Browder, Institute of Khamic Guidance; Washington, D.C., 2000, p.66.
☞ Ancient Records of Egypt: Historical Documents From the Earliest Times to the Persian Conquest, Vols. 1-5, James H. Breasted, The University of Chicago Press; Chicago, 1906-1907.
☞ A History of Egypt, James Henry Breasted, Bantam Matrix Books; New York, NY, 1967.

798.
A) KING KENNETH
☞ Black Britannia: A History of Black People in Britain, Edward Scobie, Johnson Publishing Co.; 1972, p.7.
Additional Information:
☞ Ancient and Modern Britons. David MacRitchie, Volume 1, Keegan Paul, Trench & Co.; 1985.
☞ Sex and Race, Volume 1, J. A. Rogers, H. M. Rogers Publishers; USA, 1968, p.198.
☞ African Presence in Early Europe, Edited by Ivan Van Sertima, Transaction; 1986, p256..

799.
B) ABORIGINES
☞ The Aboriginal Peoples of Australia (First Peoples), Anne Bartlett, Lerner Publications Company; 2001.
Additional Information:
☞ The Speaking Land: Myth and Story in Aboriginal Australia, Ronald M. Berndt, Inner Traditions International, 1994.
☞ Aboriginal Cultural Heritage, 18 Kilda Street, Baxter, Victoria, Melbourne, Australia.
☞ The Encyclopedia of Aboriginal Australia, Australian Institute of Aboriginal and Torrest Straight Islander State, Edited by David Horton, Australia, 1994.

800.

C) INDIA

☞ African Presence in Early Asia, Edited by Ivan Van Sertima, Transaction; New Brunswick (USA), Oxford (UK), 1985.

Additional Information:

☞ The Penguin Atlas of World History; From the Beginning to the Eve of the French Revolution. Vol. 1., Herman Kinder and Werner Hilgemann, p.229.

☞ Crash Course in Black History: 150 Important Facts About African Peoples. Zak A. Kondo, Nubia Press; USA, 1988.

☞ Medieval India from the Mohammedan Conquest to the Reign of Akbar the Great, (History of India No. 3), Stanley Lane-Poole, Reprinted Edition Volume 3, AMS Press; 1975.

801.

A) BRITAIN

☞ Black Women in Antiquity, Edited by Ivan Van Sertima, Transaction; 7th Edition, 1992, pp.131-32.

Additional Information:

☞ Black Women for Beginners, Sandra Sharp, Writers and Readers Publishing, Inc.; New York, 1993, p.114.

☞ New African, April 2001, ICP Ltd.; London, pp.6-7.

☞ Women Leaders in African History, David Sweetman, Heinemann International; Oxford, 1984.

802.

A) FLAMANIUS

☞ Nature Knows No Color Line. J. A. Rogers, 3rd Edition, H. M. Rogers Publishers; 1952, p.54.

Additional Information:

☞ Roman History, translated by Cary, Volume VIII, p.419, 423, and Volume IX, p.361.

☞ Decline and Fall of the Roman Empire, Edward Gibbon, Knopf; New York, Vol. 1., 1993, p.200; Vol. 4, 1994, p.273.

☞ La Colonne De Trajane, W. Froehner, Volume II, Plate 88, Paris, 1872.

803.

B) GREECE

☞ Nature Knows No Color Line. J. A. Rogers, 3rd Edition, H. M. Rogers Publishers; 1952, p.111.

Additional Information:

☞ World's Great Men of Color, J. A. Rogers, Volume II, Collier Macmillan Publishers; 1972, p.547.

☞ Un Empéreurs Byzantin, L. Schlumberger, 1911.

☞ The Sea Rovers: Pirates, Privateers, and Buccaneers, Albert Marrin, Atheneum; 1984.

804.

B) FALASHA

☞ Falasha Anthology: The Black Jews of Ethiopia, Wolf Leslau, Schoken Books; 1969.

Additional Information:

☞ From Babylon to Timbuktu; A History of the Ancient Black Races Including the Black Hebrews, Rudolph R. Windsor, Exposition Press; New York, 1969.

☞ The 13th Tribe. Arthur Koestler, Hutchingson & Co.; London, 1976.

☞ The New York Times, March 2, 1984.

805.

C) SWEDEN

☞ Gustave III, R. N. Bain, Volume 1, London. 1894, pp.238-51.

Additional Information:

☞ Nature Knows No Color Line. J. A. Rogers, 3rd Edition, H. M. Rogers Publishers; 1952, p.131.

☞ My Memoirs, Alexandre Dumas, 6 Vols., New York, 1907-1908, Chapter 52.

☞ Sex and Race, Volume 1, J. A. Rogers, 9th Edition, H. M. Rogers Publishers; USA, 1968, p.193.

806.

A) EIGHTEENTH

☞ Black Women in Antiquity, Edited by Ivan Van Sertima, Transaction; 7th Edition, 1992, pp.44-45, 198-99, 207-8, 213-14, 220-21.

Additional Information:

☞ Hatshepsut, Evelyn Wells, Doublday & Company; Garden City, 1969, p.183.

☞ History and Chronology of the Eighteenth Dynasty of Egypt. Donald B. Redford, University of Toronto Press; Toronto, 1967.

☞ The Traveler's Key to Ancient Egypt: A Guide to the Sacred Places of Ancient Egypt. John Anthony West, Alfred A. Knopf; New York, 1985, p. 443.

807.
C) RUSSIA
☞ 100 Amazing Facts About the Negro: With Complete Proof, J. A. Rogers, H. M. Rogers Publishers; USA, 1995, p.37.
Additional Information:
☞ The Ruins of Empire, Count Constantine de Volney, Black Classic Press; Baltimore, MD, 1990.
☞ Sex and Race, Volume 3, J. A. Rogers, 5th Edition, H. M. Rogers Publishers; USA, 1972, p.290.
☞ Histoire Universelle, translated by Abbé Terrasson, Paris, 1758, Book 3, p.341.

808.
B) JAQUES DESSALINES
☞ A History of Pan-African Revolt, C. L. R. James, Drum & Spear Press, Inc.; Washington, D.C., 1969, pp.12-17.
Additional Information:
☞ From Dessalines to Duvalier: Race, Colour, and National Independence in Haiti, David Nicholls, Rutgers University Press; 1995.
☞ The Slave Who Freed Haiti, Katherine Scherman, Random House; New York, 1954.
☞ The Black Jacobins, C. L. R. James, Allison & Busby; 1984.

809.
A) THOMAS JEFFERSON
☞ The President's Daughter, Barbara Chase-Riboud, USA, 1994.
Additional Information:
☞ The Essential Black Literature Guide, Published in association with the Schomburg Center for Research in Black Culture, Roger M. Valade II, Visible Ink Press; USA, 1996, p.74.
☞ 100 Amazing Facts About the Negro: With Complete Proof, J. A. Rogers, H. M. Rogers Publishers; USA, 1995, p.36.
☞ The Racial Attitudes of American Presidents: From Abraham Lincoln to Theodore Roosevelt, George Sinkler, Doubleday; New York, 1971.

810.
B) HADRIAN
☞ Blacks Who Died for Jesus, A History Book, Mark Hyman, Winston-Derek Publishers, Inc.; USA, 1983, p.98.

Additional Information:
☞ Nature Knows No Color Line. J. A. Rogers, 3rd Edition, H. M. Rogers Publishers; 1952, p.71.
☞ The New York Voice, July 2, 1980.
☞ The Voice, The Voice Group Ltd.; London, November 6, 1990, p.14.

811.
C) TAXIDERMY
☞ The Beak and the Finch: The Story of Evolution in Our Time, Jonathon Weiner, Vintage Books; New York, 1995, p.22.
Additional Information:
☞ Notes & Records of the Royal Society of London, Volume 33, "Darwin's Negro Bird Stuffer", R. B. Freeman, London, 1978.
☞ The Autobiography of Charles Darwin, Works of Charles Darwin: Volume 29, England, pp.51-53.
☞ Life and Letters of Charles Darwin: Including an Autobiographical Chapter, Sir Francis Darwin, (ed.), London, 1887, p.40.

812.
A) SEPTIMUS SEVERUS
☞ Septimus Severus: The African Emperor, Anthony Birley, Doubleday and Company; Garden City, 1972.
Additional Information:
☞ The New York Voice, July 2, 1980.
☞ Africa: Mother of Western Civilisation, Dr. Yosef A. A. Ben Jochannon, Black Classic Press; Baltimore, MD, 1988, pp.158-160.
☞ African Glory: The Story of Vanished Negro Civilisation, J. C. De Graft-Johnson, Walker and Company; New York, 1954, p.34.

813.
A) FIRST
☞ The African Origin of Civilization: Myth or Reality, Cheikh Anta Diop, translated by Mercer Cook, Lawrence Hill & Company; 1974.
Additional Information:
☞ Pharaohs of Egypt, Jacquetta Hawkes, American Heritage Publishing Company, Inc.; New York, 1965.
☞ Ancient Records of Egypt: Historical Documents From the Earliest Times to the Persian Conquest, Vols. 1-5, James H. Breasted, The University of Chicago Press; Chicago, 1906-1907.

A History of Egypt, James Henry Breasted, Bantam Matrix Books; New York, NY, 1967.

814.
C) FIRBOLG
☞ Celtic Myth and Legend, Charles Squire, Newcastle Publications; Van Nuys, 1975, p.12.
Additional Information:
☞ Ancient and Modern Britons. David MacRitchie, 4 Vols., Keegan Paul, Trench & Co.; 1985.
☞ The Black Celts, An Ancient African Civilization in Ireland and Britain, Ahmed Ali and Ibriham Ali, Punite Publications; 1993.
☞ Bronze Age America, (C.F. "Celt" Image of Bronze Age Briton), Barry Fell, Frontispiece; 1982.

815.
B) FIVE
☞ Bolivar: Liberator of a Continent, Bill Boyd, Capital Books; 2000.
Additional Information:
☞ Encyclopedia of Latin America, Edited by Helen Delpar, Macgraw-Hill Book Company; 1974.
☞ Hutchingson Encyclopedia, 8th Edition, Hutchingson; UK, 1988.
☞ Sex and Race, Volume 1, J. A. Rogers, 9th Edition, H. M. Rogers Publishers; USA, 1968.

816.
C) BLACK CELTS
☞ Black Britannia: A History of Black People in Britain, Edward Scobie, Johnson Publishing Co.; 1972, p.7.
Additional Information:
☞ Harvard Classics, translated by Thomas Gordon, (Germany, Tacitus) Vol. XXXIII, P. F. Collier & Son; New York, 1938.
☞ Ancient and Modern Britons. David MacRitchie, Volume 1, Keegan Paul, Trench & Co.; 1985, Chapter 3.
☞ Celtic Myth and Legend, Charles Squire, Newcastle Publications; Van Nuys, 1975, p.12. (silures)

817.
B) BELGIUM
☞ Plantagenets, John Harvey, B. T. Batsford Limited; First Edition, London, Chapter 8.

Additional Information:
☞ Plantagenet Encyclopedia: From the Origins of the Angevin Dynasty to the Battle of Bosworth Field-The Essential Guide to the Plantagenets, Elizabeth Hallam, Grove Weidenfeld; 1990.
☞ The Voice, The Voice Group Ltd.; London, March 22, 1999, p.58.
☞ The Four Gothic Kings: The Turbulent History of Medieval England and the Plantagenet Kings (1216-1377 Henry III, Edward I, Edward II, Edward III), Elizabeth Hallam (ed.), Weidenfeld & Nicolson; New York, 1987.

818.
A) HARAPPA
☞ The New York Times, Science Times, p.1, September 24, 1985.
Additional Information:
☞ Philosophies of India, Heinriek Zimmer, Boligen Series XXVI, Princeton University Press; pp.196, 221, 228-29, 291-92.
☞ The African Origin of Civilization: Myth or Reality, Cheikh Anta Diop, translated by Mercer Cook, Lawrence Hill & Company; 1974, p.287.
☞ The Penguin Atlas of World History; From the Beginning to the Eve of the French Revolution. Vol. 1., Herman Kinder and Werner Hilgemann, pp.42-43.

819.
B) THE GRIMALDI
☞ The African Origin of Civilization: Myth or Reality, Cheikh Anta Diop, translated by Mercer Cook, Lawrence Hill & Company; 1974, p.263-64.
Additional Information:
☞ Grimaldi, A. O. Bulleid and H. Gray, The Glastonbury Lake Village, Vol II, London, 1917.
☞ Crisis, "Prehistoric Negroids and their Contribution to Civilization", Dr. Francis Hoggan, N.Y., February, USA, 1920.
☞ African Presence in Early Europe, Edited by Ivan Van Sertima, Transaction; 1986, pp.25-29, 31-32.

820.
B) THE BLACK PRINCE
☞ Plantagenets, John Harvey, B. T. Batsford Limited; First Edition, London, Chapter 8.

Additional Information:
- ☞ Edward, Prince of Wales and Aquitaine: A Biography of the Black Prince, Richard Barber, University of Rochester Press; 1999.
- ☞ The Black Prince, Iris Murdoch, Penguin; 1982.
- ☞ Plantagenet Encyclopedia: From the Origins of the Angevin Dynasty to the Battle of Bosworth Field-The Essential Guide to the Plantagenets, Elizabeth Hallam, Grove Weidenfeld, 1990.

821.
C) PARIS
- ☞ Sex and Race, Volume 1, J. A. Rogers, 9th Edition, H. M. Rogers Publishers; USA, 1968, pp.273-75.

Additional Information:
- ☞ Island of Isis, William Macquitty, Charles Scribner & Sons; New York, 1976.
- ☞ Nile Valley Contributions to Civilization; Exploding the Myths, Volume 1, Anthony T. Browder, Institute of Khamic Guidance; Washington, D.C., 2000, p.190.
- ☞ Les Isiaques de la Gaule, E. Guimet, Paris, 1916.

822.
A) GREENLAND
- ☞ Early Voyages and Northern Approaches 1000-1632, Tryggni J. Oleson, McClelland & Stewart Ltd.; London, 1966, p.44.

Additional Information:
- ☞ American Antiquity, Vol XVIII, No. 3, Part 2, January 1953, pp.32-39.
- ☞ African Presence in Early Europe, Edited by Ivan Van Sertima, Transaction; 1986, pp.14, 245.
- ☞ Ancient and Modern Britons. David MacRitchie, 4 Vols., Keegan Paul, Trench & Co.; 1985.

823.
A) QUEEN ELIZABETH OF ENGLAND
- ☞ The Sunday Times, London, June 6, 1999, p.11.

Additional Information:
- ☞ The Voice, The Voice Group Ltd.; London, February 12, 2001, p.51.
- ☞ Blood Royal: The Illustrious House of Hanover, Christopher Sinclair-Stevenson, 1st American Edition, 1980.

- ☞ Sex and Race, Volume 1, J. A. Rogers, Ninth Edition, H. M. Rogers Publishers; USA, 1968.

824.
C) 1492
- ☞ The Golden Age of the Moor. Light of Europe's Dark Age, Ivan Van Sertima, Transaction; New Jersey, 1991.

Additional Information:
- ☞ Cambridge Encyclopedia, David Crystal, Cambridge University Press; 1990, p.622.
- ☞ The Moors in Spain, Stanley Lane-Pool, T. Fisher Unwin; London, 1887.
- ☞ History of the Mohammedan Dynasties in Spain. Makkari (translated by Pascual De Gayangos), Volume I, London, 1843.

825.
C) AL MAHDI
- ☞ The World and Africa: An Enquiry Into the Part Which Africa Has Played in World History, W. E. B. Du Bois, International Publishers; New York, 1965, p.216.

Additional Information:
- ☞ World's Great Men of Color, J. A. Rogers, Volume 1, Collier Macmillan Publishers; 1972, pp.295-308.
- ☞ Macdonalds Encyclopedia of Africa, Macdonald Educational Ltd.; 1986, UK, p.208.
- ☞ Islam in Africa, Anson P. Atterbury, Negro Universities Press; New York, 1969, pp.104-7.

826.
A) FIFTEENTH
- ☞ Ancient and Modern Britons. David MacRitchie, 4 Vols., Keegan Paul, Trench & Co.; 1985.

Additional Information:
- ☞ Sex and Race, Volume 1, J. A. Rogers, 9th Edition, H. M. Rogers Publishers; USA, 1968, p.114.
- ☞ The Sea Rovers: Pirates, Privateers, and Buccaneers, Albert Marrin, Atheneum; 1984.
- ☞ Les Grands Etapes De L'Histoire Du Maroc, Paris, 1924, pp.50-54.

827.
C) EUROPE'S CARVING UP OF AFRICA
- ☞ The Partitioning and Colonization of Africa, Sir Charles Lucus, UK, 1922.

Additional Information:
- The Partition of Africa, John Scott Keltie, E. Stanford; London, 1893.
- In Darkest Africa, H. M. Stanley, Volume 1-2, New York, C. Scribner & Sons; 1890.
- A History of the Colonization of Africa by Alien Races, Harry H. Johnston, Cambridge University Press; UK, 1899.

828.
B) THE ITALIAN CLEOPATRA
- Black Women for Beginners, Sandra Sharp, Writers and Readers Publishing, Inc.; New York, 1993, p.60.

Additional Information:
- Black Women in Antiquity, Edited by Ivan Van Sertima, Transaction; 7th Edition, 1992, pp.148-49.
- World's Great Men of Color, Volume II, J. A. Rogers, Collier Macmillan Publishers; 1972, pp.24-30.
- The Medici, George Frederick Young, Vols. I, E. P. Dutton & Co.; Inc.; New York, 1909, p.439.

829 A) NORWAY
- A History of the Vikings, Gwyn Jones, Oxford, London, 1969, pp.67-68, 145

Additional Information:
- Heimskringla: The Norse King Saga, Snorri Sturlason, J. M. Dent & Sons Ltd.; London, 1930, p.431.
- African Presence in Early Europe, Edited by Ivan Van Sertima, Transaction; 1986, p.228.
- The Norse Discoverers of America, The Wineland Sagas. G. M. Gathorne-Hardy, Clarendon Press; Oxford, 1970.

830.
C) MAROONS
- The Mother of Us All: A History of Queen Nanny, Leader of the Windward Jamaican Maroons,
Karla Lewis Gottlieb, Africa World Press, Inc.; NJ, 2000.

Additional Information:
- The Maroons of Jamaican, Mavis C. Campbell, Bergin & Garvey; 1988.
- History of Jamaica, Clinton Black, Collins Clear-Type Press; London and Glasgow, 1958, pp.84-87.
- The Iron Thorn: The Defeat of the British by the Jamaican Maroons, Carey Robinson, 1993.

831.
B) PUNIC WARS
- The Penguin Atlas of World History; From the Beginning to the Eve of the French Revolution. Vol. 1., Herman Kinder and Werner Hilgemann, pp.52-54.

Additional Information:
- A History of the Ancient World, 2nd Edition, Chester G.Starr, Oxford University Press; 1974.
- Hannibal: A History of the Art of War Among the Carthagonians and Romans Down to the Battle of Pydna, 168b.c., Theodore Ayrault Dodge, Da Capo Press; New York, 1995.
- The Life and Death of Carthage, Gilbert Charles-Picard, Taplinger; New York, 1968.

832.
B) SONGHAI
- The Royal Kingdoms of Ghana, Mali and Songhay: Life in Medieval Africa, Pat McKissack Et Al, Henry Holt Books; 1995.

Additional Information:
- African Civilizations, Graham Connah, Cambridge University Press; 1989.
- African Kingdoms, Basil Davidson, Time-Life Books; (Nederland), 1980, pp.79-80.
- African History: An Illustrated Handbook, Earl Sweeting and Lez Edmond, London Strategic Policy Unit; 1988, p.16.

833.
B) RAMSES II
- Ramses II: Magnificence of the Nile (Lost Civilisations), By Editors of Time Life Books; Dale M. Brown, (ed.), Time Life, 1994.

Additional Information:
- African Glory: The Story of Vanished Negro Civilisation, J. C. De Graft-Johnson, Walker and Company; New York, 1954, p.12.
- Abu Simbel To Ghizeh: a Guide Book and Manuel, Dr. Yosef A. A. Ben Jochannon, Black Classic Press; Baltimore, MD, 1987.
- Ramesses II: Greatest of the Pharaohs (Discoveries), Bernadette Menu, Harry N. Abrams Publications; 1999.

834.
A) MORANT BAY
☞ The Book of Jamaica, Russell Banks, HarperCollins; 1996.
Additional Information:
☞ Staying Power, Peter Fryer, Pluto Press; UK, 2nd Edition, 1985.
☞ History of Jamaica, Clinton black, Collins Clear-Type Press; London and Glasgow, 1958, pp.84-87.
☞ A-Z of Jamaican Heritage, Oliver Senior, Heinemann Education Books Ltd.; 1985.

835.
C) THUNDER
☞ African History for Beginners, Herb Boyd, Writers & Readers Publishing, Inc.; London, New York, 1994, pp.107-9.
Additional Information:
☞ Archéologie De L'Afrique Noire, D. P. De Pedrals, Payot; Paris, 1950.
☞ African Mythology, Geoffrey Parinda, Paul Hamlyn; London, 1967.
☞ The African Origin of Civilization: Myth or Reality, Cheikh Anta Diop, translated by Mercer Cook, Lawrence Hill & Company; 1974, p.148.

836.
B) AUGUSTUS CAESAR
☞ Black Women in Antiquity, Edited by Ivan Van Sertima, Transaction; 7th Edition, 1992, p.127.
Additional Information:
☞ Newsweek, September 23, 1991, USA, (cover).
☞ Black Athena: The Afroasiatic Roots of Classical Civilsation, Vols. 1 & 2, Martin, Bernal, FAB; London 1991.
☞ Nile Valley Contributions to Civilization; Exploding the Myths, Volume 1, Anthony T. Browder, Institute of Khamic Guidance; Washington, D.C., 2000, pp.143-144, 165.

837.
B) INDIA
☞ Pre-Historic Nations, John Baldwin, Harper & Bros.; New York, 1872.
Additional Information:
☞ Herodotus, Vol. 1., Book 1, Appendix, Essay XI, Section 5.
☞ Your History: From the Beginning of Time to the Present, J. A. Rogers, Black Classic Press; Baltimore, MD, 1983, p.15.

☞ Race Life of the Aryans, J. P. Widney, Vol 11, New York, 1917, pp.238-39.

838.
B) POLAND
☞ Byzantine Portraits, C. Deihl (translated by Harold Bell), New York, 1927, p.215.
Additional Information:
☞ World's Great Men of Color, J. A. Rogers, Volume II, Collier Macmillan Publishers; 1972, p.547.
☞ De Velitatione Bellica Bomini Nicephori Augusti, Leonis Diaconis, (in J. P. Migne, Vol. CXVII, pp.926-1007.
☞ Your History: From the Beginning of Time to the Present, J. A. Rogers, Black Classic Press; Baltimore, MD, 1983, p.69.

839.
C) OSCEOLA
☞ History of the Second Seminole War, 1835-1842, John K. Mahon, University Press of Florida; USA, 1991.
Additional Information:
☞ The Florida War, J. T. Sprague, New York, 1848.
☞ Osceola: Seminole Warrior (Native American Biographies), Joanne F. Oppenheim, Troll Communications; USA, 1979.
☞ 100 Amazing Facts About the Negro: With Complete Proof, J. A. Rogers, H. M. Rogers Publishers; USA, 1995, p.24.

840.
A) HOLLAND
☞ The Negro in Brazil, Arthur Romas, translated by Richard Dattee, The Associated Publishers; Washington, D.C., 1951, pp.161-62.
Additional Information:
☞ Negro History Bulletin; "Henrique Dias: A Brave Soldier", Dorothy J. Willis, Association for the Study of Negro Life and History, Washington, D.C. February, 1941, p.98.
☞ The Middle Passage: Impressions of Five Societies-British, French, and Dutch in the West Indies and South America, V. S. Naipaul, Vintage Books; New York, 2002.
☞ Encyclopedia of Latin America, Edited by Helen Delpar, Macgraw-Hill Book Company; 1974.

History

841.

A) FLORENCE

☞ The Medici, George Frederick Young, Volumes 1 and 2, E. P. Dutton & Co. Inc.; New York, 1909, pp.493-514.

Additional Information:

☞ Black Women in Antiquity, Edited by Ivan Van Sertima, Transaction; 7th Edition, 1992, p.149.

☞ A Cardinal of the Medici, Mrs. Hicks Beach (Susan Emily Christian), The Macmillan Company; New York, 1937.

☞ Sex and Race, Volume 1, J. A. Rogers, 9th Edition, H. M. Rogers Publishers; USA, 1968, p.163.

842.

C) FORTY YEARS

☞ Black Women in Antiquity, Edited by Ivan Van Sertima, Transaction; 7th Edition, 1992, p.129.

Additional Information:

☞ Black Women for Beginners, Sandra Sharp, Writers and Readers Publishing, Inc.; New York, 1993, p.114.

☞ Nzinga: Warrior Queen/King, Roy Arthur Glasgow, Boston Univerity Press;

☞ Women Leaders in African History, David Sweetman, Heinemann International; Oxford, 1984.

843.

C) 185,000

☞ A Grand Army of Black Men: Letter from African-American Soldiers in the Union Army, 1861-1865 (Cambridge Studies in American Literature and Culture), Edwin S. Redkey, (ed.), Cambridge University Press; 1993.

Additional Information:

☞ Blacks in American Wars, Robert W. Mullen, MONAD Press; New York, 1981.

☞ Ebony, Johnson Publishing; Chicago, February, 1997.

☞ Homeward Bound: The Demobilization of the Union & Confederate Armies, 1865-66, William B. Holberton, Stackpole Books; 2001.

844.

C) 189 A.D.

☞ Vatican City, Church of Rome, Archive Records, Circa. July 19, 189a.d.

Additional Information:

☞ Blacks Who Died for Jesus, A History Book, Mark Hyman, Winston-Derek Publishers, Inc.; USA, 1983.

☞ African Origin of the Major Western Religions, Dr. Yosef A. A. Ben Jochannon, Black Classic Press; Baltimore, MD, 1988.

☞ The Ancient Black Christians, Martin De Porres Walsh, Julian Richardson Associates Publishers; San Francisco, 1969.

845.

B) ASHANTI

☞ Topics in West African History, Adu Boahen, Longmans, Green & Company Ltd.; London, 1966, pp.70, 74-76, 78.

☞ *Additional Information:*

☞ Africa, Vol. 22, No. 4, "The Culture of Akan", J. B. Danquah, October 1952, pp.360-66.

☞ Black Kingdoms Black People, Fambamigbe Publishers; Nigeria, 1979.

☞ Cambridge Encyclopedia, David Crystal, Cambridge University Press; 1990, p.76.

846.

A) DENMARK

☞ Ancient and Modern Britons. David MacRitchie, Volume 1, Keegan Paul, Trench & Co.; 1985, pp.113, 121.

Additional Information:

☞ Heimskringla: The Norse King Saga, Snorri Sturlason, Lee M. Hollander, University of Texas Press (For American Scandanavian Foundation); Austin, 1967, p.6.

☞ A History of the Vikings, Gwyn Jones, Oxford, London, 1969, p.67.

☞ Early Voyages and Northern Approaches 1006-1632, Tryggvil J. Oleson, Oxford University Press; London, 1964, Chapter 1.

847.

A) JUDAISM

☞ Black Women in Antiquity, Edited by Ivan Van Sertima, Transaction; 7th Edition, 1992, p.128.

Additional Information:

☞ Black Athena: The Afroasiatic Roots of Classical Civilsation, Vols. 1 & 2, Martin Bernal, FAB; London, 1991.

The Voice, The Voice Group Ltd.; London, February 26, 2001, p.46.

Colonial Histories, Post-Colonial Memories: The Legend of Kahina, A North African Heroine (Studies in African Literature), Abdelmajid Hannoum, Heinemann; 2001.

848.
C) 628

The Struggle of the Nations: Egypt, Syria and Assyria, Gaston Maspero, D. Appleton & Co.; 1987.

Additional Information:

Pharaohs of Egypt, Jacquetta Hawkes, American Heritage Publishing Company, Inc.; New York, 1965, pp.43-44, 53-58, 63-72.

World's Great Men of Color, Volume 1, J. A. Rogers, Collier Macmillan Publishers; 1972, pp.53-56.

A History of Egypt, James Henry Breasted, Bantam Matrix Books; New York, NY, 1967, pp.319-32.

849.
B) MALI

Mansa Musa, Khephra Burns, Harcourt Brace; New York, 2001.

Additional Information:

Mansa Musa, The Golden King of Ancient Mali, Akbarall Thobhani, Kendal/Hunt Publishing Company; 1998.

African Kingdoms, Basil Davidson, Time-Life Books; (Nederland), 1980, pp.83-84, 89.

Macdonalds Encyclopedia of Africa, Macdonald Educational Ltd.; 1986, UK, p.85.

850.
C) 300 YEARS

Black Women in Antiquity, Edited by Ivan Van Sertima, Transaction; 7th Edition, 1992, pp.13, 33.

Additional Information:

Pillars of Ethiopian History, William Leo Hansberry, Edited by Joseph E. Harris, Howard University Press; Washington, D.C., 1974.

Falasha Anthology, The Black Jews of Ethiopia, Wolf Leslau, Schocken Books; New York, 1969.

Your History: From the Beginning of Time to the Present, J. A. Rogers, Black Classic Press; Baltimore, MD, 1983, p.67.

851.
B) ZIMBABWE

African Kingdoms, Basil Davidson, Time-Life Books; (Nederland), 1980, pp.88, 172.

Additional Information:

African History for Beginners, Herb Boyd, Writers & Readers Publishing, Inc.; London, New York, 1994, p.71.

Black Man of the Nile and His Family. Dr. Yosef A. A. Ben Jochannon, Black Classic Press; Baltimore, MD, 1988.

Black Kingdoms Black People, Fambamigbe Publishers; Nigeria, 1979.

852.
A) HAWAII

The Betrayal of Liliuokalani: Last Queen of Hawaii 1838-1917, Helena G. Allen, Mutual Publication Company; USA, 1991.

Additional Information:

Black Women for Beginners, Sandra Sharp, Writers and Readers Publishing, Inc.; New York, 1993, p.116.

To Steal a Kingdom, Michael Dougherty, Island Style Press; 1992.

Kaiulani: The People's Princess, Hawaii, 1889 (The Royal Diaries), Ellen Emerson White, Scholastic Trade, 2001.

853.
C) KEMET

Black Makers of History. The Real McCoy, Frank Forde, Lesnah Hall and Virginia McLean, The Book Place; 1988, p.104.

Additional Information:

The African Origin of Civilization, Myth or Reality, Cheikh Anta Diop, translated by Mercer Cook, Lawrence Hill & Company; 1974.

Nile Valley Contributions to Civilization; Exploding the Myths, Volume 1, Anthony T. Browder, Institute of Khamic Guidance; Washington, D.C., 2000, pp.51-52.

Black Man of the Nile and His Family. Dr. Yosef A. A. Ben Jochannon, Black Classic Press; Baltimore, MD, 1988.

854.
C) TOBACCO

Tobacco and Slaves: The Development of Southern Cultures in the Chesapeake, 1680-1800, Allan Kulikoff, University of North Carolina Press; 1988.

Additional Information:
- ☞ Capitalism and Slavery, Erik Williams, Andre Deutsch Ltd.; London, 1964.
- ☞ The Making of Europe, Christopher H. Dawson, New York, Maridian Books; 1956.
- ☞ Slavery in the United States, Louis Filler, Transaction; New Jersey, 1998.

855.
A) QUEEN TIYE
- ☞ The Traveler's Key to Ancient Egypt: A Guide to the Sacred Places of Ancient Egypt. John Anthony West, Alfred A. Knopf; New York, 1985.

Additional Information:
- ☞ History and Chronology of the Eighteenth Dynasty of Egypt. Donald B. Redford, University of Toronto Press; Toronto, 1967.
- ☞ Black Women in Antiquity, Edited by Ivan Van Sertima, Transaction; 7th Edition, 1992, pp.8, 55-58, 60, 188.
- ☞ Nile Valley Contributions to Civilization; Exploding the Myths, Volume 1, Anthony T. Browder, Institute of Khamic Guidance; Washington, D.C., 2000, p.142.

856.
C) QUEEN MARIE-THERESA OF AUSTRIA
- ☞ Black Women in Antiquity, Edited by Ivan Van Sertima, Transaction; 7th Edition, 1992, pp.142-44.

Additional Information:
- ☞ Sex and Race, Volume 1, J. A. Rogers, 9th Edition, H. M. Rogers Publishers; USA, 1968, pp.252-53.
- ☞ "Documents Concerning the Princess Louise-Marie, Daughter of Louis XIV and Marie-Theresa", The Library of St. Genevieve, France.
- ☞ Black Women for Beginners, Sandra Sharp, Writers and Readers Publishing, Inc.; New York, 1993, p.80.

857.
C) MELBOURNE
- ☞ Aboriginal Melbourne: The Lost Land of the Kulin People, Gary Presland.

Additional Information:
- ☞ The Aboriginal Peoples of Australia (First Peoples), Anne Bartlett, Lerner Publications Company; 2001.
- ☞ But Now We Want the Land Back: A History of the Australian Aboriginal People, Hanna Middleton.

- ☞ The Speaking Land: Myth and Story in Aboriginal Australia, Ronald M. Berndt, Inner Traditions International; 1994.

858.
C) BARCELONA
- ☞ Your History: From the Beginning of Time to the Present, J. A. Rogers, Black Classic Press; Baltimore, MD, 1983, p.30.

Additional Information:
- ☞ The Life and Death of Carthage, Gilbert Charles-Picard, Taplinger, New York, 1968.
- ☞ The Penguin Atlas of World History; From the Beginning to the Eve of the French Revolution. Vol. 1., Herman Kinder and Werner Hilgemann, p.81.
- ☞ Hannibal: A History of the Art of War Among the Carthagonians and Roman Down to the Battle of Pydna, 168b.c., Theodore Ayrault Dodge, Da Capo Press; New York, 1995.

859.
B) NAT TURNER
- ☞ Before the Mayflower: A History of Black America. Lerone Bennett Jr., 5th Edition, Penguin Books; 1984, pp.131-39.

Additional Information:
- ☞ The Nat Turner Slave Insurrection, F. Roy Johnson, Johnson Publication Company; Murfreesboro, N. C., 1966.
- ☞ William Styron's Nat Turner: Ten Black Writers Respond, Edited by John Hendrik Clarke, Beacon Press; Boston, 1968.
- ☞ Nat Turner's Insurrection, Thomas Wentworth Higginson, Boston, Lee & Sheppard Co.; 1889.

860.
A) NAPOLEON I
- ☞ African Presence in Early Europe, Edited by Ivan Van Sertima, Transaction; 1986, p.200.

Additional Information:
- ☞ Nile Valley Contributions to Civilization; Exploding the Myths, Volume1, Anthony T. Browder, Institute of Khamic Guidance; Washington, D.C., 2000, p.180.
- ☞ The Many lives & Secret Sorrows of Josephine B., Sandra Gulland, Scribner; New York, 1999.

☞ Nature Knows No Color Line. J. A. Rogers, 3rd Edition, H. M. Rogers Publishers; 1952, p.121.

861.
B) SEA ROVERS
☞ Staying Power, Peter Fryer, Pluto Press; UK, 2nd Edition, 1985.
Additional Information:
☞ Sex and Race, Volume 1, J. A. Rogers, 9th Edition, H. M. Rogers Publishers; USA, 1968, p.114.
☞ The Voice, The Voice Group Ltd.; London, February 2, 2001, p.55.
☞ Les Grands Etapes De L'Histoire Du Maroc, Paris, 1924, pp.50-54.

862.
A) 1897
☞ Macdonalds Encyclopedia of Africa, Macdonald Educational Ltd.; UK, 1986.
Additional Information:
☞ My Life and Ethiopia's Progress, E. Ullendorff, Oxford University Press; 1976.
☞ Your History: From the Beginning of Time to the Present, J. A. Rogers, Black Classic Press; Baltimore, MD, 1973, p.58.
☞ Haile Selassie I, David Abner Talbot, W. P. Van Stockum, The Hague, 1955.

863.
A) NEOLITHIC AGE
☞ Grzimek Encyclopedia of Ecology, Dr. H. S. Bernard Grzimek (et al), Van-Norstrand, Rienhold, England, 1976.
Additional Information:
☞ Africa, Phyllis Martin and Patrick O'Meara, Indiana University Press; Bloomington, 1986.
☞ Macdonalds Encyclopedia of Africa, Macdonald Educational Ltd.; UK, 1986.
☞ The Encyclopedia of Africa, Franklin Watts, Inc.; New York and London, 1976.

864.
C) SPHINX
☞ The Pyramids and Sphinx, Desmond Stewart, Newsweek, 1971, USA, p.20.
Additional Information:
☞ The Hall of Records: Hidden Secrets of the Pyramid and Sphinx, Jalandris, Holistic Life Travels, San Francisco, CA., 1980.

☞ The Destruction of Black Civilization: Great Issues of a Race from 4500 B.C. to 2000 A.D., Chancellor Williams, Third World Press; Chicago, 1976, pp.73-75.
☞ Smithsonian Magazine, "Unlocking the Secrets of the Giza Plateau", Dora Jane Hamblin, Washington, D.C., April, 1986.

865.
C) 94 YEARS
☞ The Guinness Book of Records 1997, Guinness Publishing Ltd.; UK, 1996, p.210.
Additional Information:
☞ The Destruction of Black Civilization: Great Issues of a Race from 4500 B.C. to 2000 A.D., Chancellor Williams, Third World Press; Chicago, 1976, p.86.
☞ The Struggle of the Nations: Egypt, Syria and Assyria, Gaston Maspero, D. Appleton & Co.; 1987.
☞ Ancient Records of Egypt: Historical Documents From the Earliest Times to the Persian Conquest, Vols. 1-5, James H. Breasted, The University of Chicago Press; Chicago, 1906-1907.

866.
B) THE 25TH
☞ World's Great Men of Color, J. A. Rogers, Volume 1, Collier Macmillan Publishers; 1972, p.539.
Additional Information:
☞ Nile Valley Contributions to Civilization; Exploding the Myths, Volume 1, Anthony T. Browder, Institute of Khamic Guidance; Washington, D.C., 2000, pp.57-58, 64.
☞ The African Origin of Civilization: Myth or Reality, Cheikh Anta Diop, translated by Mercer Cook, Lawrence Hill & Company; 1974.
☞ African Glory: The Story of Vanished Negro Civilisation, J. C. De Graft-Johnson, Walker and Company; New York, 1954.

867.
B) PERSIA
☞ Saite and Persian Demotic Cattle Documents: A Study in Legal Forms and Princilples in Ancient Egypt, (American Studies in Papyrolgy Vol. 26), Eugene Cruz-Uribe, American Society of Papyrologists, USA, 1985.

Additional Information:

☞ Ancient Records of Egypt: Historical Documents From the Earliest Times to the Persian Conquest, Vols. 1-5, James H. Breasted, The University of Chicago Press; Chicago, 1906-1907.

☞ The African Origin of Civilization: Myth or Reality, Cheikh Anta Diop, translated by Mercer Cook, Lawrence Hill & Company; 1974.

☞ The Struggle of the Nations: Egypt, Syria and Assyria, Gaston Maspero, D. Appleton & Co.; 1987.

868.
C) 1630

☞ The Destruction of Black Civilization: Great Issues of a Race from 4500 B.C. to 2000 A.D., Chancellor Williams, Third World Press; Chicago, 1976, pp.235-58.

Additional Information:

☞ Kingdoms of the Savannah, Jan Vansina, Maddison Books; USA, 1964.

☞ Kuba (Heritage Library of African People, Central Africa), Rebecca Leuchak, Rosen Publishing Group; USA, 1997.

☞ Journal of African History, Vol. 1, No. 2, "Recording the Oral History of the Bakuba", Jan Vansina, , 1960.

869.
A) GREEKS

☞ A History of Egypt, James Henry Breasted, Bantam Matrix Books; New York, NY, 1967.

Additional Information:

☞ Greeks in Ptolamaic Egypt: Case Studies in the Social History of the Hellenistic World, Naphtali Lewis, Clarendon Press; 1987.

☞ Black Man of the Nile and His Family. Dr. Yosef A. A. Ben Jochannon, Black Classic Press; Baltimore, MD, 1988.

☞ The African Origin of Civilization: Myth or Reality, Cheikh Anta Diop, translated by Mercer Cook, Lawrence Hill & Company; 1974.

870.
C) A SLAVE REVOLT

☞ Before the Mayflower: A History of Black America. Lerone Bennett Jr., 5th Edition, Penguin Books; 1984, p.457.

Additional Information:

☞ Echo of Lions, Barbara Chase-Riboud, USA, 1989.

☞ Your History: From the Beginning of Time to the Present, J. A. Rogers, Black Classic Press; Baltimore, MD, 1983, p.58.

☞ A Documentary History of the Negro People in the United States, 3 Vols., Edited by Herbert Aptheker, Citadel Press; 1974.

871.
B) ETHIOPIA

☞ The Ancient Black Christians, Martin De Porres Walsh, Julian Richardson Associates, Publishers; San Francisco, 1969.

Additional Information:

☞ African Zion: The Sacred Art of Ethiopia, Yale University Press; UK, 1994.

☞ Blacks Who Died for Jesus, A History Book, Mark Hyman, Winston-Derek Publishers, Inc.; USA, 1983.

☞ African Origin of the Major Western Religions, Dr. Yosef A. A. Ben Jochannon, Black Classic Press; Baltimore, MD, 1988.

872.
A) YAGAN

☞ The Encyclopedia of Aboriginal Australia, Australian Institute of Aboriginal and Torrest Straight Islander State, Edited by David Horton, Australia, 1994.

Additional Information:

☞ The Voice, The Voice Group Limited; May 26, 1997, p.2.

☞ Encyclopedia of Australia, Compiled by Andrew and Nancy Learmonth, Frederick Warne & Co. Ltd.; UK, 1973, p.604.

☞ The New Nation, Western Hemisphere; London, May 26, 1997, p.5.

873.
C) EAST EUROPEANS

☞ Your History:From the Beginning of Time to the Present, J. A. Rogers, Black Classic Press; Baltimore, MD, 1983, p.20.

Additional Information:

☞ The Early Slavs: Eastern Europe from the Initial Settlement to the Kievan Rus, Pavel Markovich Dodlukhanov, Addison-Wesley Publishing Company; 1996.

☞ The Penguin Atlas of Medieval History, Penguin; 1961.
☞ A History of Russia, Nicholas Valentine Riasanovsky, Oxford University Press; 1999.

874.
C) MAMELUKES
☞ The Mamluks 1250-1517 (Men-At-Arms Series, No. 259), David Nicolle and Angus McBride, Martin Windrow (ed.), Osprey Publishing Company; 1993.
Additional Information:
☞ The Mamluks in Egyptian Politics and Society, (Cambridge Studies in Islamic Civilisation), Thomas Philipp and Ulrich Haarmann, (ed.), Cambridge University Press; 1998.
☞ The Destruction of Black Civilization: Great Issues of a Race from 4500 B.C. to 2000 A.D., Chancellor Williams, Third World Press; Chicago, 1976, p.81.
☞ A History of Egypt, James Henry Breasted, Bantam Matrix Books; New York, NY, 1967.

875.
A) ARIZONA
☞ Estenavinico the Black, John Upton Terrell, Westernlore Press; Los Angeles, 1968.
Additional Information:
☞ Chronology of African American History: Significant Events and People from 1619 to the Present, Alton Hornsby, Gale Publishing Group; 1991.
☞ A Short History of the Mississippi Valley, J. K. Hosmer, Houghton, Mifflin and Company; New York, 1901, pp.25-27.
☞ Famous Negro Heroes of America, Langston Hughes, Dodd, Mead; New York. 1958.

876.
A) KING JAJA OF OPOBO
☞ King Jaja of the Niger Delta: His Life and Times 1821-1891, S. J. S. Cookey, Nok Publishers Ltd.; New York-London-Lagos, 1974.
Additional Information:
☞ African Kingdoms, Basil Davidson, Time-Life Books; (Nederland), 1980, p.108.

☞ Rekindling the Ancestral Memory: King Jaja of the Opobo in St. Vincent and Barbados, 1888-1891, Edward L. Cox.
☞ Jaja of Opobo. The Slave Who Became a King, E. J. Alogoa, Longman; 5th Impression, 1982.

877.
B) SHANG DYNASTY
☞ What They Never Told You in History Class, Indus Khamit-Kush, Luxorr Publications; USA, 1983, p.206.
Additional Information:
☞ The Archaeology of Ancient China, Kwang-Chih Chang, Yale University Press; USA.
☞ Your History: From the Beginning of Time to the Present, J. A. Rogers, Black Classic Press; Baltimore, MD, 1983, p.88.
☞ The African Origin of Civilization: Myth or Reality, Cheikh Anta Diop, translated by Mercer Cook, Lawrence Hill & Company; 1974, p.281.

878.
B) POPE NICHOLAS V
☞ Nile Valley Contributions to Civilization; Exploding the Myths, Volume 1, Anthony T. Browder, Institute of Khamic Guidance; Washington, D.C., 2000, p.32.
Additional Information:
☞ Slavery or "Sacred Trust". John H. Harris, Negro University Press; NY, l969.
☞ New African, April 2000, ICP Ltd.; London, p.14.
☞ The Making of Europe, Christopher H. Dawson, New York, Maridian Books; 1956.

879.
A) NINETY
☞ African Encyclopedia, The Oxford University Press; 1974.
Additional Information:
☞ Macdonalds Encyclopedia of Africa, Macdonald Educational Ltd.; UK, 1986.
☞ The Story of Africa and its Explorers, Vols. 1-4, Robert Brown, Cassell & Co. Ltd.; London, 1892-1895.
☞ Makers of South Africa, B. L. W. Brett, T. Nelson; London, 1944.

880.
B) MAHMOUD THE PRAISEWORTHY
☞ 100 Amazing Facts About the Negro: With Complete Proof, J. A. Rogers, H. M. Rogers Publishers; USA, 1995, p.41.
Additional Information:
☞ The Quran, (Chapter 105) Dar Al-Choura, Clemeenceau St. Tajer Bldg., Beirut, 1980.
☞ Understanding Islam, An Introduction to the Muslim World, Thomas W. Lippman, Meridian Books; USA, 1995.
☞ Islam: A Short History, Karen Armstrong, Modern Library Books; 2000.

881.
A) VANDALS
☞ The Africans: A Triple Heritage, Ali A. Mazrui, BBC Publications; 1986.
Additional Information:
☞ Atlas of Ancient Egypt, John Baines and Jaromir Malek, Phaidon Press Ltd.; Oxford, UK, 1986.
☞ The Africans, David Lamb, New York, Vintage Books; New York, 1983.
☞ Africa, Phyllis Martin and Patrick O'Meara, Indiana University Press; Bloomington, 1986.

882.
C) NINE MONTHS
☞ Toussaint L'Overture, Thomas and Dorothy Hoober, Chelsea House; NY, 1990.
Additional Information:
☞ The Slave Who Freed Haiti, Katherine Scherman, Random House; New York, 1954.
☞ A History of Pan-African Revolt, C. L. R. James, Drum & Spear Press, Inc.; Washington, D.C., 1969.
☞ The Black Napoleon: Toussaint L'Overture Liberator of Haiti, James Jess Hannon, First Library Books; 2000.

883.
C) AUNT
☞ African Presence in Early Europe, Edited by Ivan Van Sertima, Transaction; 1986, p.205.
Additional Information:
☞ Black Women in Antiquity, Edited by Ivan Van Sertima, Transaction; 7th Edition, 1992, p.137.

☞ Your History: From the Beginning of Time to the Present, J. A. Rogers, Black Classic Press; Baltimore, MD, 1983, p.9.
☞ Sex and Race, Volume 1, J. A. Rogers, 9th Edition, H. M. Rogers Publishers; USA, 1968.

Politics & Law

Answers and Sources

884.
A) UNITED NATIONS
☞ United Nations Building, Library Department, NY, New York, 10017, USA.
Additional Information:
☞ New African, September 2001, ICP Ltd.; London, pp.33.
☞ USA Today, European Edition, Wednesday June 4, 1997, p.4A.
☞ The New Nation, Western Hemisphere; London, December 23, 1996, p.15.

885.
B) SALIM SALIM
☞ USA Today, European Edition, Wednesday June 4, 1997, p.4A.
Additional Information:
☞ Caribbean Times, Hansib Publishing; London, May 9, 1996, p.12.
☞ New African, September 2001, ICP Ltd.; London, pp.30-31.
☞ West Africa, London, December 28, 1992, - January 10, 1993, p.2240.

886.
B) DR. LOUIS SULLIVAN
☞ From Sharecroppers Daughter to Surgeon General of the United States, Jocelyn Elders MD; USA, 1996.
Additional Information:
☞ Ebony, Johnson Publishing; Chicago, December, 2002, p.140.
☞ Creating Change: Sexuality, Public Policy, and Civil Rights, John D'Emilio (Editor), et al, St.Martin's Press; 2000, p.371.
☞ Tennessean (Nashville), September 8, 1993.

887.
C) JOHNNIE COCHRANE
☞ Journey to Justice, Johnnie L. Cochrane Jr., Ballentine Books; USA, 1996.
Additional Information:
☞ Ebony, Johnson Publishing; Chicago, August, 1995, pp. 60-64.
☞ Vanity Fair, The Condé Nast Publications Ltd.; London, May 1995, pp.50-57.
☞ O. J. Simpson's Legal Pad, Henry Beard and John Boswell, USA, 1995.

888.
B) HOUSE OF LORDS
☞ The House of Lords, London, SW1A 0AA.
Additional Information:
☞ Washington Post, Saturday, August 9th, 2003.
☞ The Observer, Sunday January 20, 2002.
☞ Windrush: The Irresistible Rise of Multiracial Britain. Trevor Phillips, HarperCollins; 1998.

889.
B) U.S. DOLLAR BILLS
☞ Black Women for Beginners, Sandra Sharp, Writers and Readers Publishing, Inc.; New York, 1993, p.158.
Additional Information:
☞ National Association of State Treasurers, Library Archives, North Cap Street, 444 Washington, D.C. 20090.
☞ Who's Who Among Black Americans, 1992-1993, USA, p.1030.
☞ When and Where I Enter: The Impact of Black Women on Race in America, Paula Giddings, William Morrow; NY, 1984.

890.
C) INTERNATIONAL MONETARY FUND
☞ The Weekly Journal, Voice Communications; London, June 2, 1994, p.4.
Additional Information:
☞ International Monetary Fund, Personal Records Department, 19th Street NW, Washington, D.C., USA.
☞ History Dictionary of Cote D'Ivoire, Robert J. Mundt, Scarecrow Press; 1995.
☞ External Finances for Low Income Countries, Papers Presented at the IM☞ and World Bank Conference on External Finanacing for Low-Income Countries.

891.
A) DOMINICA
☞ African and Caribbean Politics: From Kwame Nkruma to the Grenada Revolution, Manning Marable, Verso; London, 1987.

Additional Information:
- Dominican Republic: A Guide to the People, Politics and Culture, David Howard, Interlink Publishing Group; 1999.
- A Future for Small States, Eugenia Charles, (ed.), Stylus Publishing; 1997.
- The Weekly Journal, Voice Communications; London, May 4, 1995, p.9.

892.
B) TRANSPORT AND GENERAL WORKERS UNION
- Black and British, David Bygott, Oxford University Press; 1992, p.5.

Additional Information:
- Windrush: The Irresistible Rise of Multiracial Britain. Trevor Phillips, HarperCollins; 1998.
- Who's Who of Black Achievers, John Hughes, (ed.), Ethnic Media Group; UK, 1999, p.70.
- Black Londoners, 1890-1990, Susan Okokon, Sutton; UK, 1997.

893.
B) NATIONAL SECURITY
- Ebony, Johnson Publishing; Chicago, May, 2001, p.32.

Additional Information:
- The Voice, The Voice Group Ltd.; London, September 17, 2001, p.15.
- Ebony, Johnson Publishing; Chicago, November, 2000, p.136.
- The Voice, The Voice Group Ltd.; January 1, 2001, p.14.

894.
A) JAPAN
- The Measure of a Man; A Spiritual Memoire. Sidney Poitier, HarperCollins; US, 2001.

Additional Information:
- Time, Time Inc.; USA, April 28, 1997, p.75.
- The Voice, The Voice Group Ltd.; London, April 28, 1997, p.23.
- Sidney Poitier: Actor, Carol Bergman, Econo-Clad Books; 1999.

895.
A) CHARLES TAYLOR OF LIBERIA
- HARDtalk, BBC News 24, Tuesday 29 July 2003.

Additional Information:
- The Statesman's Yearbook 2001: The Politics, Cultures, and Economies of the World (Statesman's Yearbook, 2001, Barry Turner (Ed), Palgrave Macmillan; 2000, p.998.
- Deterring Democracy by Noam Chomsky, Hill and Wand, NY, 1992, p.240
- Women, War, Peace: The Independent Experts' Assessment on the Impact of Armed Conflict on Women and Women's Role in Peace-building Progress of the World's Women 2002 Volume One, Elisabeth Rehn and Ellen Johnson Sirleaf, UNIFEM, 2003

896.
C) BATTERSEA
- Roots in Britain, Ziggi Alexander and Audrey Dewjee, Brent Library Service; 2nd Edition, 1981, p.13.

Additional Information:
- Black Londoners, 1890-1990, Susan Okokon, Sutton; UK, 1997.
- Your History: From the Beginning of Time to the Present, J. A. Rogers, Black Classic Press; Baltimore, MD, 1983, p.62.
- History of the Black Presence in London, GLC; London, 1986.

897.
C) 1990
- Ebony, Johnson Publishing; Chicago, March, 1993, p.62.

Additional Information:
- Notable Black American Women, Jessie Carney Smith, (ed.), USA, 1991, pp.278-80.
- Ebony, Johnson Publishing; Chicago, March, 1995, p.116.
- Black Firsts: 2000 Years of Extraordinary Achievement. Jessie Carney Smith, Caspar L. Jordan and Robert L. Johns, Visible Ink Press; USA, 1994, p.217.

898.
C) AMNESTY INTERNATIONAL
- Amnesty Campaign Journal for Amnesty International, UK, Jan/Feb Edition, 1997, Issue No. 81, p.8.

Additional Information:
- Amnesty International, 99 Roseberry Avenue, London, EC1R 4RE

Politics & Law

The Voice, The Voice Group Ltd.; London, March 7, 1995, p.6.

The Weekly Journal, Positive Time and Space Co.; London, December 4, 1996, p.13.

899.
A) OVERTHROWING THE BRITISH GOVERNMENT

History of the Cato Street Conspiracy, G. T. Wilkinson, London, 1820, pp.406-13.

Additional Information:

The Making of the Black Working Class in Great Britain, Ron Ramdin, Gower; 1987, pp.23-24.

Staying Power, Peter Fryer, Pluto Press; 2nd Edition, 1985.

Black Settlers in Britain, 1555-1958, Nigel File and Chris, Power, Heinemann Educational Books; UK, 1981.

900.
C) BLACK PANTHER PARTY

Seize The Time: The Story of the Black Panther Party, Bobby Seale, Arrow Books; London, 1970.

Additional Information:

Rap Attack 2: African Rap to New York Hip Hop, David Toop, Serpents Tail; 1991, p.118.

Blood in My Eye, George L. Jackson, Black Classic Press; Baltimore, MD, 1990.

A Pictorial History of Black America. Langston Hughes, Crown; NY, 1983.

901.
C) LINDA DOBBS

Society of Black Lawyers, Room 9, Winchester House, 11 Cranmer Road, Kennington Park, London, SW9 6 EJ

Additional Information:

Who's Who of Black Achievers, John Hughes, (ed.), Ethnic Media Group; UK, 1999,p.85.

The Weekly Journal, Voice Communications; London, September 15, 1994, p.1.

UK Who's Who, 1997, A & C Black, London.

902.
C) SOCIALISM

The Red Prussian, L. Schwarzchild, 1947, pp.9-25.

Additional Information:

Letter to Friedrich Engels from Karl Marx, March 7, 1856.

Nature Knows No Color Line. J. A. Rogers, 3rd Edition, H. M. Rogers Publishers; 1952, p.130.

Challenge to Karl Marx, J. K. Turner, London, 1941, p.227.

903.
B) RAINBOW COALITION

Jesse Jackson: I am Somebody, Paul Westman and Judith Leo, Dillon Press; 1984.

Additional Information:

Black Americana. Richard A. Long, Admiral; UK, 1985, pp.101, 103-5.

A Pictorial History of Black America. Langston Hughes, Crown; NY, 1983.

A More Perfect Union: Advancing New American Rights, Jessie L. Jackson, Jr., Welcome Rain Books; USA, 2001.

904.
B) STEPHEN LAWRENCE

The Daily Mail, London, February 18, 1997, P.1.

Additional Information:

The Macpherson Report, February 1999, UK.

Stephen and Me: My Friendship with Stephen Lawrence and the Search for Justice, Duwayne Brookes with Simon Hattenstone, UK, 2002.

Caribbean Times, Hansib Publishing; London, May 27, 1997, p.2.

905.
A) MIKE ESPY

Who's Who Among Black Americans, 1992-1993, USA, p.439.

Additional Information:

Ebony, Johnson Publishing; Chicago, July, 1994, p.42.

The Voice, The Voice Group Ltd.; London, October 4, 1994, p.16.

Crisis, USA, March, 1993, p.16.

906.
C) MARK HENDRIK

The Voice, The Voice Group Ltd.; London, March 19, 2001, p.7.

Additional Information:

☞ The Weekly Journal, Voice Communications; London, June 23, 1994, p.2.

☞ The Voice, The Voice Group Ltd.; London, August 9, 1994, pp.17-18.

☞ CE Commission Des Communauties Européene CEE Union Européene, Rue-De La Loi, 200B.

907.
C) SECRETARY OF STATE

☞ Time, Time Inc.; USA, September 10, 2001, (cover).

Additional Information:

☞ Ebony, Johnson Publishing; Chicago, May, 2001, p.32.

☞ New African, April 2001, ICP Ltd.; London, p.23.

☞ Ebony, Johnson Publishing; Chicago, November, 2000, p.84.

908.
B) COMMONWEALTH OF NATIONS

☞ Eye of Fire: A Biography of Chief Emeka Anyaoku Commonwealth Secretary-General, Phyllis Johnson, Africa World Press, Inc.; NJ, 2001.

Additional Information:

☞ The Commonwealth Secretariat, Marlborough House, Pall Mall, London, SW1Y 5HQ.

☞ West Africa, London, June 7-13, 1993, p.956.

☞ The British Empire and Commonwealth: A Short History, Martin Kitchen, Palgrave Publishing; 1996.

909.
C) 1995

☞ Mississippi State Government Senate and Legislature, North State Street, Jackson, 390202-2002, USA.

Additional Information:

☞ Time, Time Inc.; USA, Mar 27, 1995.

☞ The Clarion Ledger, Library Archives, P.O. Box 40, 39205, Jackson, Mississippi.

☞ The Voice, The Voice Group Ltd.; London, February 28, 1995, p.14.

910.
A) 1965

☞ Cambridge Encyclopedia, David Crystal, Cambridge University Press; 1990, p.3.

Additional Information:

☞ The Encyclopedia of Aboriginal Australia, Australian Institute of Aboriginal and Torrest Straight Islander State, Edited by David Horton, Australia, 1994.

☞ Everton Football Club, Goodison Park, Goodison Road, Liverpool, L4 4EL.

☞ Aboriginal Cultural Heritage, 18 Kilda Street, Baxter, Victoria, Melbourne, Australia.

911.
B) ANGLICAN

☞ Black Women for Beginners, Sandra Sharp, Writers and Readers Publishing, Inc.; New York, 1993, p.170.

Additional Information:

☞ Black Firsts: 2000 Years of Extraordinary Achievement. Jessie Carney Smith, Caspar L. Jordan and Robert L. Johns, Visible Ink Press; USA, 1994, pp.324-25.

☞ Black Woman in White America: A Documentary History, Gerda Lerner, (ed.), Vintage Books; New York, 1992.

☞ Chronology of African American History, Alton Hornsby, Jr., USA, p.382.

912.
A) 1999

☞ Electorate Office, 10 Roberts Street, Rozelle, New South Wales, AU, 2039

Additional Information:

☞ Aboriginal Cultural Heritage, 18 Kilda Street, Baxter, Victoria, Melbourne, Australia.

☞ "Newsnight", September 7, 2000, British Broadcasting Corporation, Library Archives, White City, London, W12.

☞ The Encyclopedia of Aboriginal Australia, Australian Institute of Aboriginal and Torrest Straight Islander State, Edited by David Horton, Australia, 1994.

913.
A) JIMMY CARTER

☞ A Pictorial History of Black America. Langston Hughes, Crown; NY, 1983.

Additional Information:

☞ Ebony Pictorial History of Black America: Volume 3. Civil Rights Movement to Black Revolution, Johnson Publishing Company; 1974, p.174.

- The Presidency and Domestic Policies of Jimmy Carter, Herbert D. Rosenbaum and Alexej Ugrinsky, (eds.), Greenwood Publishing Group; 1994.
- When and Where I Enter: The Impact of Black Women on Race in America, Paula Giddings, William Morrow; NY, 1984.

914.
B) VOTING
- Chronicle of America, Jacques Legrand, Longman; 1989.

Additional Information:
- An American Dilemma; The Negro Problem and Modern Democracy, Gunnar Myrdal, Transaction; NJ, 1996.
- Before the Mayflower: A History of Black America. Lerone Bennett Jr., 5th Edition, Penguin Books; 1984.
- African-American Social and Political Thought 1850-1920, Howard Brotz, (ed.), Transaction; NJ, 1991.

915.
B) COLORED MEN'S INSTITUTE
- Staying Power, Peter Fryer, Pluto Press; 2nd Edition, 1985.

Additional Information:
- Black Londoners, 1890-1990, Susan Okokon, Sutton; UK, 1997.
- Your History: From the Beginning of Time to the Present, J. A. Rogers, Black Classic Press; Baltimore, MD, 1983, p.23.
- The Black Press in Britain, Ionie Benjamin, Trentham Books; London, 1995, pp.29-36.

916.
A) DAME MINITA GORDON OF BELIZE
- Thirteen Chapters of a History of Belize, Assad Shoman, The Angelus Press Ltd.; 1994.

Additional Information:
- Nation in the Making: The Junior History of Belize. Jessica Gordon Nembhard, First Edition, Cubola Productions; 1990.
- The Belize High Commission, 22 Harford House, 19 Cavendish Street, London W1.
- The Voice, The Voice Group Ltd.; London, November 20, 2000, p.51.

917.
C) OLAUDAH EQUIANO
- The Interesting Narrative of the Life of Olaudah Equiano or Gustavus Vassa; The African. Written by Himself, Edited by Paul Edwards, Heinemann Educational Books; UK, 1969.

Additional Information:
- The Essential Black Literature Guide, Published in association with the Schomburg Center for Research in Black Culture, Roger M. Valade II, Visible Ink Press; USA, 1996, p.132.
- Black British Literature: An Annotated Bibliography, Prahbu Guptara, Dangaroo Press; London, 1986, pp.79-80.
- African Kingdoms, Basil Davidson, Time-Life Books; (Nederland), 1980, pp.170-71.

918.
A) 1874
- Before the Mayflower: A History of Black America. Lerone Bennett Jr., 5th Edition, Penguin Books; 1984, p.488.

Additional Information:
- Black Firsts: 2000 Years of Extraordinary Achievement. Jessie Carney Smith, Caspar L. Jordan and Robert L. Johns, Visible Ink Press; USA, 1994, p.173.
- Famous First Facts About Negroes, Romeo B. Garrett, Arno Press; USA, 1972.
- America's Black Congressmen, Maurine Christopher, Thomas Y. Crowell; New York, 1971.

919.
C) EDWARD BROOKE
- Ebony, Johnson Publishing; Chicago, August, 2003, pp.78-82.

Additional Information:
- Ebony Pictorial History of Black America: Volume 3. Civil Rights Movement to Black Revolution, Johnson Publishing Company; 1974, pp.77, 198.
- Who's Who Among Black Americans, 1992-1993, USA, p.158.
- Encyclopedia of Black America, W. A. Low and Virgil A. Clift, (eds.), Mcgraw-Hill; New York, 1981.

920.
A) UGANDA
☞ Museveni's Long March: From Frelimo to the National Resistance Movement, Godfrey Ondoga Ori Amaza, Pluto Press; UK, 1997.

Additional Information:
☞ The Weekly Journal, Voice Communications; London, January 19, 1995, p.4.
☞ The Weekly Journal, Voice Communications; London, June 22, 1995, p.4.
☞ What is Aftrica's Problem?, Yoweri K. Museveni and Mwalimu Julius K. Nyerere, Edited by Elizabeth Kanyogonya, University of Minnesota Press; USA, 2000.

921.
A) ALASKA
☞ Ebony, Johnson Publishing; Chicago, March, 1961, p.148.

Additional Information:
☞ When and Where I Enter: The Impact of Black Women on Race in America, Paula Giddings, William Morrow; NY, 1984.
☞ Ebony, Johnson Publishing; Chicago, November, 1969.
☞ Famous First Facts About Negroes, Romeo B. Garrett, Arno Press; USA, 1972, p.186.

922.
C) METROPOLITAN POLICE
☞ Islington Police Station, 2 Tolpuddle Street, London, N1 0YY

Additional Information:
☞ The Job, London, Volume 27, Issue 689, September 30, 1994, p.1.
☞ Hansard Written Answers Text, Published by the House of Commons, June 19, 2000, Column 103W.
☞ The Black Police Association, Room LG11, 105 Regency Street, London SW1P 4AN.

923.
B) MASSACHUSETTS
☞ Before the Mayflower: A History of Black America. Lerone Bennett Jr., 5th Edition, Penguin Books; 1984, p.441.

Additional Information:
☞ From Slavery to Freedom: A History of Negro Americans, John Hope Franklin, Alfred A. Knopf; New York, NY, 1980.
☞ Slavery in the United States, Louis Filler, Transaction; New Jersey, 1998.
☞ Black Firsts: 2000 Years of Extraordinary Achievement. Jessie Carney Smith, Caspar L. Jordan and Robert L. Johns, Visible Ink Press; USA, 1994, p.131.

924.
B) 1833
☞ Black Settlers in Britain, 1555-1958, Nigel File and Chris, Power, Heinemann Educational Books; UK, 1981.

Additional Information:
☞ Staying Power, Peter Fryer, Pluto Press; UK, 2nd Edition, 1985.
☞ Black Britannia: A History of Black People in Britain, Edward Scobie, Johnson Publishing Co.; 1972.
☞ Black and White-The Negro and English Society 1555-1945, James Walvin, Allen Lane, The Penguin Press; 1973.

925.
A) 1987
☞ Black and British, David Bygott, Oxford University Press; 1992, p.3.

Additional Information:
☞ Who's Who of Black Achievers, John Hughes, (ed.), Ethnic Media Group; UK, 1999, p.17.
☞ The Black Press in Britain, Ionie Benjamin, Trentham Books; London, 1995, p.56.
☞ Black Londoners, 1890-1990, Susan Okokon, Sutton; UK, 1997.

926.
B) ATLANTA
☞ Atlanta Police Department, 675 Ponce de Leon Avenue NE, Atlanta, Georgia, 30308.

Additional Information:
☞ Ebony, Johnson Publishing; Chicago, July, 1996, pp.82-84.
☞ Black Noise: Rap Music and Black Culture in Contemporary America, Tricia Rose. Westeyan University Press; 1994.
☞ The Weekly Journal, Voice Communications; London, April 6, 1995, p.10.

Politics & Law

927.

C) CHURCH OF ENGLAND

☞ Chronicle of the Twentieth Century, Jacques Legrand, Longman Books; 1988, p.1251.

Additional Information:

☞ General Synod Enquiries, Church House, Great Smith Street, London, SW1P 3NZ.

☞ Black and British, David Bygott, Oxford University Press; 1992.

☞ Black Londoners, 1890-1990, Susan Okokon, Sutton; UK, 1997, p.87

928.

A) UNITED STATES

☞ Before the Mayflower: A History of Black America. Lerone Bennett Jr., 5th Edition, Penguin Books; 1984, pp.260-61, 483.

Additional Information:

☞ Blacks in American Wars, Robert W. Mullen, MONAD Press; New York, 1981.

☞ Encyclopedia of Black America, W. A. Low and Virgil A. Clift, (eds.), Mcgraw-Hill; New York, 1981.

☞ The Black American Reference Book, Mabel M. Smyth, (ed.), Prentice-Hall Inc.; USA, 1976.

929.

B) CHILDREN'S DEFENCE FUND

☞ Encyclopedia of Black America, W. A. Low and Virgil A. Clift, (eds.), Mcgraw-Hill; New York, 1981, p.331.

Additional Information:

☞ Ebony, Johnson Publishing; Chicago, July, 2000, p.131.

☞ Black Firsts: 2000 Years of Extraordinary Achievement. Jessie Carney Smith, Caspar L. Jordan and Robert L. Johns, Visible Ink Press; USA, 1994, p.83.

☞ Families in Peril: An Agenda for Social Change, Marian Wright Edelman, USA, 1987.

930.

C) FREEDOM AND JUSTICE FOR ALL

☞ Democracy: The God That Failed, Hanns-Hermanne Hoppe, Transaction; New Jersey, 2001.

Additional Information:

☞ Hutchingson Encyclopedia, 8th Edition, Hutchingson; UK, 1988.

☞ New! Encyclopaedia Britannica Print Set, 2002 Edition.

☞ Children's Encyclopedia, Harold Boswell Taylor, (ed.), Treasure Press; 1985, p.107.

931.

A) LOUISIANA

☞ Your History: From the Beginning of Time to the Present, J. A. Rogers, Black Classic Press; Baltimore, MD, 1983, pp.72-73.

Additional Information:

☞ Famous First Facts About Negroes, Romeo B. Garrett, Arno Press; USA, 1972.

☞ The Black American Reference Book, Mabel M. Smyth, (ed.), Prentice-Hall Inc.; USA, 1976.

☞ 1999 Facts About Blacks: A Sourcebook of African American Accomplishment. Raymond M. Corbin, Beckham House Publishers; USA, 1st Edition, 1986, p.19.

932.

A) MARY McCLOUD BETHUNE

☞ Mary McCloud Bethune, Rackman Holt, Doubleday & Co.; New York, 1964.

Additional Information:

☞ Jet, Johnson Publishing; Chicago, July 6, 1992, p.32.

☞ Ebony, Johnson Publishing; Chicago, November, 2000, pp.37A, 37D.

☞ The Black American Reference Book, Mabel M. Smyth, (ed.), Prentice-Hall Inc.; USA, 1976, pp.348, 367, 635, 668.

933.

B) HAMPSTEAD

☞ Who's Who of Black Achievers, John Hughes, (ed.), Ethnic Media Group; UK, 1999, p.974.

Additional Information:

☞ The Black Press in Britain, Ionie Benjamin, Trentham Books; London, 1995, p.38.

☞ West Africa, London, November 25 – December 1, 1991, p.1987.

☞ Black Londoners, 1890-1990, Susan Okokon, Sutton; UK, 1997, p.68.

934.

C) COURT OF APPEALS

☞ Ebony, Johnson Publishing; Chicago, August, 2001, pp.96-100.

Additional Information:
☞ Encyclopedia of Black America, W. A. Low and Virgil A. Clift, (eds.), Mcgraw-Hill; New York, 1981.
☞ Ebony, Johnson Publishing; Chicago, December, 1992, p.110.
☞ The Black American Reference Book, Mabel M. Smyth, (ed.), Prentice-Hall Inc.; USA, 1976.

935.
A) 1909
☞ Dusk of Dawn, W. E. B. Du Bois, Transaction; New Jersey, 1984.
Additional Information:
☞ W. E. B. Du Bois Reader, Edited by Andrew Paschal, The Macmillan Company; New York, 1971.
☞ W. E. B. Du Bois: A Study in Minority Group Leadership, Elliot M. Rudwick, University of Philadelphia Press; Philadelphia, 1960.
☞ Great Negroes: Past and Present. Russell L. Adams, Afro-Am Publishing Company; Chicago, Illinois, 3rd Edition (1981) p.112.

936.
C) PAUL BOATENG
☞ The Guardian, Guardian Newspapers; London, May 8, 1997, p.9.
Additional Information:
☞ Windrush: The Irresistible Rise of Multiracial Britain. Trevor Phillips, HarperCollins; 1998.
☞ Black and British, David Bygott, Oxford University Press; 1992.
☞ The New Nation, Western Hemisphere; London, April 7, 1997, p.29.

937.
B) SHIRLEY CHISHOLM
☞ Unbought and Unbossed. Shirley Chisholm, Houghton Miffling Co.; Boston, 1970.
Additional Information:
☞ The Black American Reference Book, Mabel M. Smyth, (ed.), Prentice-Hall Inc.; USA, 1976 p.584.
☞ The Essential Black Literature Guide, Published in association with the Schomburg Center for Research in Black Culture, Roger M. Valade II, Visible Ink Press; USA, 1996, pp.76-77.

☞ Ebony Pictorial History of Black America: Volume 3. Civil Rights Movement to Black Revolution, Johnson Publishing Company; 1974, pp.171, 200.

938.
A) DAME
☞ Black Londoners, 1890-1990, Susan Okokon, Sutton; UK, 1997, p.112.
Additional Information:
☞ The Black Press in Britain, Ionie Benjamin, Trentham Books; London, 1995, pp.69, 72.
☞ The Weekly Journal, Voice Communications; London, April 6, 1995, p.13.
☞ Windrush: The Irresistible Rise of Multiracial Britain. Trevor Phillips, HarperCollins; 1998.

939.
A) THE STANDING CONFERENCE ON RACIAL EQUALITY IN EUROPE
☞ Black and British, David Bgott, Oxford University Press; 1992.
Additional Information:
☞ The Black Press in Britain, Ionie Benjamin, Trentham Books; London, 1995, p.63.
☞ The Evening Standard, Associated Newspaper Group; London, April 28, 1997, p.7.
☞ The New Nation, Western Hemisphere; London, March 17, 1997, p.23.

940.
C) THIRTEENTH AMENDMENT
☞ Slavery in the United States, Louis Filler, Transaction; New Jersey, 1998.
Additional Information:
☞ An American Dilemma; The Negro Problem and Modern Democracy, Gunnar Myrdal, Transaction; NJ, 1996.
☞ Chronicle of America, Jacques Legrand, Longman; 1989.
☞ History of Black Americans; From Africa to the Emergence of the Cotton Kingdoms. Philip S. Foner, Greenwood Press; 1975.

941.
B) WASHINGTON, D.C.
☞ Who's Who Among Black Americans, 1992-1993, USA, p.77.

Additional Information:

☞ Ebony, Johnson Publishing; Chicago, March, 1996, p.38.

☞ The Guardian, Guardian Newspapers; London, August 9, 1997, p.5.

☞ Ebony, Johnson Publishing; Chicago, May, 1996, p.120.

942.
A) JAMAICA

☞ The Jamaica Daily Gleaner, Kingston, May 28, 2001

Additional Information:

☞ National Democratic Party, St. Catherine, North Western Region, Jamaica, W.I.

☞ The Voice, The Voice Group Ltd.; London, June 11, 2001, p.12.

☞ The Jamaica Daily Gleaner, Kingston, June 23, 2000.

943.
C) SOUL CITY

☞ Black Firsts: 2000 Years of Extraordinary Achievement. Jessie Carney Smith, Caspar L. Jordan and Robert L. Johns, Visible Ink Press; USA, 1994, p.95.

Additional Information:

☞ The Housing Status of Black Americans, Wilhelmina A. Leigh and James B. Stewart, Transaction; New Jersey, 1991.

☞ 1999 Facts About Blacks: A Sourcebook of African American Accomplishment. Raymond M. Corbin, Beckham House Publishers; USA, 1st Edition, 1986, pp.32-33, 61.

☞ The Black American Reference Book, Mabel M. Smyth, (ed.), Prentice-Hall Inc.; USA, 1976.

944.
B) TAILOR

☞ The Making of the Black Working Class in Great Britain, Ron Ramdin, Gower; 1987, pp.23-24.

Additional Information:

☞ Staying Power, Peter Fryer, Pluto Press; 2nd Edition, UK, 1985, pp.334-36.

☞ Black Settlers in Britain, 1555-1958, Nigel File and Chris, Power, Heinemann Educational Books; UK, 1981.

☞ Black Londoners, 1890-1990, Susan Okokon, Sutton; UK, 1997, pp.52, 63.

945.
A) RON BROWN

☞ The Voice, The Voice Group Ltd.; London, September 13, 1994, p.18.

Additional Information:

☞ Ebony, Johnson Publishing; Chicago, July, 1994, p.42.

☞ Crisis, USA, March, 1993, p.16.

☞ Ebony, Johnson Publishing; Chicago, May, 1993, p.62.

946.
B) QUEEN'S COUNSEL

☞ Baroness Scotland of Asthal: Queens Counsel and Politician, Sue Adler, Tamarind Ltd.; UK, 2000.

Additional Information:

☞ Black and British, David Bygott, Oxford University Press; 1992, p.58.

☞ The Voice, The Voice Group Ltd.; 11th August 1997, pp.2, 8.

☞ Windrush: The Irresistible Rise of Multiracial Britain. Trevor Phillips, HarperCollins; 1998.

947.
A) FIFTEENTH

☞ Portuguese Africa, J. Duffy, Cambridge, Mass, 1959.

Additional Information:

☞ Nile Valley Contributions to Civilization; Exploding the Myths, Volume 1, Anthony T. Browder, Institute of Khamic Guidance; Washington, D.C., 2000, p.31-32.

☞ Portuguese in South East Africa 1488-1600, E. V. Axelson, Johannesburg, 1973.

☞ Africa: Mother of Western Civilisation, Dr. Yosef A. A. Ben Jochannon, Black Classic Press; Baltimore, MD, 1988, pp.142-44.

948.
C) VICE PRESIDENT

☞ Nature Knows No Color Line. J. A. Rogers, 3rd Edition, H. M. Rogers Publishers; USA, 1952, p.152.

Additional Information:

☞ Gaston Monnerville: Le Dâemocrate Qui Dâefia De Gaulle, Jean-Paul Brunet, France.

☞ Sex and Race, Volume 2, J. A. Rogers, 7th Edition, H. M. Rogers Publishers; USA, 1980, p.120.

☞ Vingt-Deux Ans De Prâesidence, Gaston Monnerville, France.

949.
B) 1964
☞ Chronicle of America, Jacques Legrand, Longman; 1989.
Additional Information:
☞ Black life and Culture in the United States, Rhoda L. Goldstein, (ed.), Thomas Y. Crowell; New York, 1971.
☞ Black Americana. Richard A. Long, Admiral; UK, 1985.
☞ An American Dilemma; The Negro Problem and Modern Democracy, Gunnar Myrdal, Transaction; NJ, 1996.

950.
C) DICK GREGORY
☞ Dick Gregory's Political Primer. Dick Gregory, Edited by James R. McGraw, Harper & Row; New York, 1972.
Additional Information:
☞ Nigger: An Autobiography. Dick Gregory with Robert Lipsyte, Washington Square Press; New York, 1986.
☞ On the Real Side: A History of African American Comedy. Mel Watkins, Lawrence Hill; USA, 1999, pp.495-503.
☞ The Black Heritage Book of Trivia, Morgan White Jr., Quinlan Press; Boston, 1985, pp.30, 137.

951.
B) 40
☞ Ebony, Johnson Publishing; Chicago, January, 1997, p.64.
Additional Information:
☞ Crisis, USA, March, 1993, p.16.
☞ Ebony, Johnson Publishing; Chicago, February, 1997, p.88.
☞ Ebony, Johnson Publishing; Chicago, May, 1993, p.62.

952.
A) 1910
☞ A Search for Equality: The National Urban League, Jesse Moore, Pennslyvania State University Press; 1981.
Additional Information:
☞ African-American Social and Political Thought 1850-1920, Howard Brotz, (ed.), Transaction; NJ, 1991.

☞ Chronicles of Black Protest, Bradford Chambers, Mentor, NY, 1969.
☞ The Black American Reference Book, Mabel M. Smyth, (ed.), Prentice-Hall Inc.; USA, 1976.

953.
A) 1944
☞ The Essential Black Literature Guide, Published in association with the Schomburg Center for Research in Black Culture, Roger M. Valade II, Visible Ink Press; USA, 1996, p.300.
Additional Information:
☞ The Black American Reference Book, Mabel M. Smyth, (ed.), Prentice-Hall Inc.; USA, 1976.
☞ Pictorial History of Black America. Langston Hughes, Crown; NY, 1983.
☞ Black Manhattan, James Weldon Johnson, Atheneum; New York, 1968.

954.
C) JAMAICA
☞ The Making of the Black Working Class in Great Britain, Ron Ramdin, Gower; 1987, pp.20-23.
Additional Information:
☞ Black and White-The Negro and English Society 1555-1945, James Walvin, Allen Lane, The Penguin Press; 1973.
☞ The Black Press in Britain, Ionie Benjamin, Trentham Books; London, 1995, p.2.
☞ Black Londoners, 1890-1990, Susan Okokon, Sutton; UK, 1997, pp.52, 63, 64.

955.
B) SIR HERMAN OUSELEY
☞ The Commission for Racial Equality: British Bureaucracy and the Multi-ethnic Society, Ray Honeyford, Transaction; New Jersey, 1998.
Additional Information:
☞ Roots of the Future: The Ethnic Diversity in the Making of Britain. CRE; UK, 1996.
☞ Windrush: The Irresistible Rise of Multiracial Britain. Trevor Phillips, HarperCollins; 1998.
☞ The Black Press in Britain, Ionie Benjamin, Trentham Books; London, 1995, pp.61, 639.

Politics & Law

956.
C) DISTRICT COURT
☞ Ebony, Johnson Publishing; Chicago, December, 1992, p.110.
Additional Information:
☞ Black Firsts: 2000 Years of Extraordinary Achievement. Jessie Carney Smith, Caspar L. Jordan and Robert L. Johns, Visible Ink Press; USA, 1994, p.168.
☞ Encyclopedia of Black America, W. A. Low and Virgil A. Clift, (eds.), Mcgraw-Hill; New York, 1981.
☞ The Black American Reference Book, Mabel M. Smyth, (ed.), Prentice-Hall Inc.; USA, 1976.

957.
C) 1966
☞ Ebony, Johnson Publishing; December, 1992, p.116.
Additional Information:
☞ Before the Mayflower: A History of Black America. Lerone Bennett Jr., 5th Edition, Penguin Books; 1984.
☞ Ebony, Johnson Publishing; Chicago, March, 1994, p.44.
☞ Encyclopedia of Black America, W. A. Low and Virgil A. Clift, (eds.), Mcgraw-Hill; New York, 1981.

958.
A) PEOPLE'S NATIONAL PARTY
☞ The Voice, The Voice Group Ltd.; London, August 6, 2001, pp.20-21.
Additional Information:
☞ Caribbean Times, Hansib Publishing; London, Week Ending Saturday October 1, 1994, p.7.
☞ The Weekly Journal, Voice Communications; London, May 25, 1995, p.6.
☞ The New Nation, Western Hemisphere; London, November 18, 1996, p.4.

959.
A) BRENT
☞ Black Londoners, 1890-1990, Susan Okokon, Sutton; UK, 1997, p.70.
Additional Information:
☞ The Voice, The Voice Group Ltd.; London, August 23, 1994, pp.27-28.
☞ Windrush: The Irresistible Rise of Multiracial Britain. Trevor Phillips, HarperCollins; 1998.

☞ Brent Town Hall, (General Enquiries) Fortylane, Wembley, Middlesex, HA9 9HD, England.

960.
B) SECRETARY OF ENERGY
☞ Ebony, Johnson Publishing; Chicago, February, 1995, pp.94-98.
Additional Information:
☞ Ebony, Johnson Publishing; Chicago, July, 1994, p. 42.
☞ Black Firsts: 2000 Years of Extraordinary Achievement. Jessie Carney Smith, Caspar L. Jordan and Robert L. Johns, Visible Ink Press; USA, 1994, p.167.
☞ Ebony, Johnson Publishing; Chicago, May, 1993, p.64.

961.
A) 1972
☞ Barbara Jordan: A Self-Portrait. Barbara Jordan and Shelby Hearon, USA, 1982.
Additional Information:
☞ Barbara Charline Jordan: From the Ghetto to the Capital, D. Armstrong, USA, 1977.
☞ Barbara Jordan, Rose Blue and Corinne Naden, Grolier Books; USA, 2001.
☞ When and Where I Enter: The Impact of Black Women on Race in America, Paula Giddings, William Morrow; NY, 1984.

962.
B) EDUCATION
☞ Hackney Town Hall, Educational Dept., Mare Street, London, E8, 1EA, UK.
Additional Information:
☞ Windrush: The Irresistible Rise of Multiracial Britain. Trevor Phillips, HarperCollins; 1998.
☞ The Voice, The Voice Group Ltd.; London, February 15, 1994, pp.15-16.
☞ The Weekly Journal, Voice Communications; London, February 17, 1994, p.10.

963.
B) PLESSY v. FERGUSON
☞ A Documentary History of the Negro People in the United States, Volume 3, Edited by Herbert Aptheker, Citadel Press; 1974, pp.184-85.

Additional Information:
- ☞ Black Americana. Richard A. Long, Admiral; UK, 1985, p.86.
- ☞ Chronicles of Black Protest, Bradford Chambers, Mentor; NY, 1969.
- ☞ African-American Social and Political Thought 1850-1920, Howard Brotz, (ed.), Transaction; NJ, 1991.

964.
C) LABOR SECRETARY
- ☞ The Voice, The Voice Group Ltd.; London, June 11, 2001, p.12.

Additional Information:
- ☞ Transportation Alternative Magazine, USA, January/February 1999, p.12.
- ☞ Labour Magazine, 76th Year, No. 1998/3, World Confederation of Labour, Rue de Trèves 33, 1040 Brussels.
- ☞ Nomination: Hearing of the Committee on Labor and Human Resources, United States Senate, One Hundred Fith Congress, 'First Session on Alexis M. Herman of Alabama, to be Secretary of Labor, March 18, 1997, USA'.

965.
C) REPUBLICAN PARTY
- ☞ 1999 Facts About Blacks: A Sourcebook of African American Accomplishment. Raymond M. Corbin, Beckham House Publishers; USA, 1st Edition, 1986, p.10.

Additional Information:
- ☞ America's Black Congressmen, Maurine Christopher, Thomas Y. Crowell; New York, 1971.
- ☞ Encyclopedia of Black America, W. A. Low and Virgil A. Clift, (eds.), Mcgraw-Hill; New York, 1981.
- ☞ The Black American Reference Book, Mabel M. Smyth, (ed.), Prentice-Hall Inc.; USA, 1976.

966.
A) ATLANTA
- ☞ Ebony, Johnson Publishing; Chicago, October, 2000, p.134.

Additional Information:
- ☞ Ebony, Johnson Publishing; Chicago, July, 1996, pp.66-72.
- ☞ Who's Who Among Black Americans, 1992-1993, USA, pp.724, 1583.
- ☞ Ebony, Johnson Publishing; Chicago, May, 1994, p.37.

967.
B) VERMONT
- ☞ Before the Mayflower: A History of Black America. Lerone Bennett Jr., 5th Edition, Penguin Books; 1984, p.446.

Additional Information:
- ☞ Slavery in the United States, Louis Filler, Transaction; New Jersey, 1998.
- ☞ 1999 Facts About Blacks: A Sourcebook of African American Accomplishment. Raymond M. Corbin, Beckham House Publishers; USA, 1st Edition, 1986, p.4.
- ☞ From Slavery to Freedom: A History of Negro Americans, John Hope Franklin, Alfred A. Knopf; New York, NY, 1980.

968.
A) COMMUNIST PARTY
- ☞ CE Commission Des Communauties Européene CEE Union Européene, Rue-De La Loi, 200B.

Additional Information:
- ☞ The Weekly Journal, Voice Communications; January 14, 1993 p.4.
- ☞ Andolu Agency, (Turkish News Agency), Hellenic Resources Network, Hellenic Institute, Inc.; January 11, 1999, Paragrath 14, p1.
- ☞ The European Parliament and Supranational Party System: A Study In Institutional Development (Cambridge Studies in Comparative Politics), Amie Kreppel, Cambridge University Press; 2002.

969.
C) APARTHEID
- ☞ Between Anger and Hope: South Africa's Youth and the Truth and Reconcilliation Commission, Witwatersrand, Transaction; USA, 2001.

Additional Information:
- ☞ Apartheid's Rebels, Inside South Africa's Hidden War, Stephen M. Davis, Yale University Press; New Haven, London, 1987.
- ☞ How to Commit Suicide in South Africa, Sue Coe and Holly Metz, Knockabout Comics; 249 Kensal Road, London.
- ☞ Steve Biko, Black Consciousness in South Africa, Millard Arnold, Vintage Books; New York, 1979.

Politics & Law

970.
B) PALESTINIAN LIBERATION ORGANIZATION
☞ 1999 Facts About Blacks: A Sourcebook of African American Accomplishment. Raymond M. Corbin, Beckham House Publishers; USA, 1st Edition, 1986, p.18.
Additional Information:
☞ Black Americana. Richard A. Long, Admiral; UK, 1985.
☞ Chronicle of America, Jacques Legrand, Longman; USA, 1989.
☞ Black Firsts: 2000 Years of Extraordinary Achievement. Jessie Carney Smith, Caspar L. Jordan and Robert L. Johns, Visible Ink Press; USA, 1994, p.181.

971.
A) LOS ANGELES
☞ Taking Back Our Streets: Fighting Crime in America, Willie L. Williams and Bruce B. Henderson, Simon & Schuster; 1996.
Additional Information:
☞ Ebony, Johnson Publishing; Chicago, December, 1992, pp.71-74.
☞ Jet, Johnson Publishing Co.; Chicago, June 20, 1988, p.8.
☞ Ebony Man, Johnson Publishing; March, 1993, pp.18-21.

972.
A) BETHNAL GREEN AND BOW
☞ The Times, London, May 30, 1997, p.18.
Additional Information:
☞ Who's Who of Black Achievers, John Hughes, (ed.), Ethnic Media Group; UK, 1999, p.115.
☞ The Evening Standard, Associated Newspaper Group; London, May 7, 1997.
☞ Windrush: The Irresistible Rise of Multiracial Britain. Trevor Phillips, HarperCollins; 1998.

973.
C) VIRGINIA
☞ Ebony, Johnson Publishing; Chicago, May, 1992, p.26.
Additional Information:
☞ Chronology of African American History: Significant Events and People from 1619 to the Present, Alton Hornsby, Gale Publishing Group; 1991.
☞ Ebony, Johnson Publishing; Chicago, May, 1996, p.90.

☞ Ebony, Johnson Publishing; Chicago, September, 2001, p.170.

974.
B) HOUSE OF LORDS
☞ John Taylor: Lord Taylor of Warwick, Onyekachi Wamba, Tamarind Ltd.; UK, 2000.
Additional Information:
☞ Windrush: The Irresistible Rise of Multiracial Britain. Trevor Phillips, HarperCollins; 1998.
☞ The Voice, The Voice Group Ltd.; London, 26 August, 2002, p.4.
☞ The Evening Standard, Associated Newspaper Group; London, August 22, 1997, pp.25-26.

975.
C) US AIR FORCE
☞ Ebony, Johnson Publishing; Chicago, October, 1995, pp.60-62.
Additional Information:
☞ Who's Who Among Black Americans, 1992-1993, USA, p.610.
☞ Ebony, Johnson Publishing; Chicago, March, 1994, p.46.
☞ Facts on File Encyclopedia of Black Women in America: Business and Professions (Volume 4), Darlene Clark Hine and Kathleen Thompson, (eds.), Facts of File, Inc.; USA, 1997.

976.
A) SHERIFF
☞ Ebony, Johnson Publishing; Chicago, August, 1995, pp.95-98.
Additional Information:
☞ Jet, Johnson Publishing Co.; Chicago, November 23, 1992, pp.58-59.
☞ Ebony, Johnson Publishing; Chicago, July, 1996, p.84.
☞ Ebony, Johnson Publishing; Chicago, September, 1993, p.68.

977.
C) GREATER LONDON ASSEMBLY
☞ The Greater London Assembly, Romney House, 42 Marsham Street, London, SW1P 3PY.
Additional Information:
☞ The Guardian, Guardian Newspapers; London, May 12, 2000.
☞ The Observer, London, April 29, 2001.

A

Windrush: The Irresistible Rise of Multiracial Britain. Trevor Phillips, HarperCollins; 1998.

978.
A) LAWYER
☞ 1999 Facts About Blacks: A Sourcebook of African American Accomplishment. Raymond M. Corbin, Beckham House Publishers; USA, 1st Edition, 1986, p.9.

Additional Information:
☞ Facts on File Encyclopedia of Black Women in America: Law and Government (Volume 8), Darlene Clark Hine and Kathleen Thompson, (eds.), Facts of File, Inc.; USA, 1997.
☞ Encyclopedia of Black America, W. A. Low and Virgil A. Clift, (eds.), Mcgraw-Hill; New York, 1981.
☞ Black Firsts: 2000 Years of Extraordinary Achievement. Jessie Carney Smith, Caspar L. Jordan and Robert L. Johns, Visible Ink Press; USA, 1994, p.153.

979.
C) MICHAEL X
☞ Black Britannia: A History of Black People in Britain, Edward Scobie, Johnson Publishing Co.; 1972, p.273.

Additional Information:
☞ Third World Impact. 8th Edition, Edited by Arif Ali, Hansib Publishing; 1988.
☞ False Messiah: The Story of Michael X, Derek Humphry, UK.
☞ Staying Power, Peter Fryer, Pluto Press; 2nd Edition, 1985.

980.
B) CONGRESS
☞ Time, Time Inc.; USA, November 19, 1990.

Additional Information:
☞ Ebony, Johnson Publishing; Chicago, February, 1995, p.184.
☞ Washington Post, June 16, 1998, USA.
☞ Ebony, Johnson Publishing; Chicago, May, 1996, p.124.

981.
B) SENATE
☞ Who's Who Among Black Americans, 1992-1993, USA, p.1032.

Additional Information:
☞ Ebony, Johnson Publishing; Chicago, March, 1993, p.58.

☞ Jet, Johnson Publishing Co.; Chicago, November 23, 1992, p.8.
☞ Ebony, Johnson Publishing; Chicago, May, 1996, p.126.

982.
B) 1969
☞ Windrush: The Irresistible Rise of Multiracial Britain. Trevor Phillips, HarperCollins; 1998.

Additional Information:
☞ The New Nation, Western Hemisphere; London, January 6, 1997, p.3.
☞ Staying Power, Peter Fryer, Pluto Press; UK, 2nd Edition, 1985.
☞ Black Londoners, 1890-1990, Susan Okokon, Sutton; UK, 1997, p.28.

983.
A) COURT OF DOMESTIC RELATIONS
☞ Ebony, Johnson Publishing; Chicago, March Edition, 1994, p.44.

Additional Information:
☞ Ebony, Johnson Publishing; Chicago, March Edition, 1993, p.56.
☞ Encyclopedia of Black America, W. A. Low and Virgil A. Clift, (eds.), Mcgraw-Hill; New York, 1981, pp.94-95.
☞ The Black American Reference Book, Mabel M. Smyth, (ed.), Prentice-Hall Inc.; USA, 1976.

984.
A) BRAZIL
☞ Benedita Da Silva: An Afro-Brazilian Woman's Story of Politics and Love, By Benedita Da Silva, Medea Benjamin and Maisa Mendonca, Institute for Food Development; 1997.

Additional Information:
☞ Ebony, Johnson Publishing; Chicago, February, 1997, pp.35-36.
☞ Black Women for Beginners, Sandra Sharp, Writers and Readers Publishing, Inc.; New York, 1993, p.138.
☞ The Weekly Journal, Voice Communications; London, March 9, 1995, p.9.

985.
C) KENT
☞ The National Black Police Association, Room LG11, 105 Regency Street, London SW1P 4AN.

Politics & Law

Additional Information:

☞ The Voice, The Voice Group Ltd.; London, 6 October, 2003, p.2.

☞ The Sunday Times, London, September 28, 2003.

☞ The Guardian, Guardian Newspapers; London, 29 September, 2003.

986.
C) THE INKATHA FREEDOM PARTY

☞ Between Anger and Hope: South Africa's Youth and the Truth and Reconcilliation Commission, Witwatersrand, Transaction; USA, 2001.

Additional Information:

☞ West Africa, London, October 12-18, 1992, p.1763.

☞ The Weekly Journal, Voice Communications; London, June 29, 1995, p.10.

☞ The Voice, The Voice Group Ltd.; London, April 26, 1994, pp.10, 12.

987.
B) THREE

☞ The Sheriff of Nottingham's Office, Old Market Square, Nottingham, NG1 2DT.

Additional Information:

☞ Black and British, David Bygott, Oxford University Press; 1992, p.3.

☞ Caribbean Times, Hansib Publishing; London, February 17, 1989.

☞ Hampshire Chronicle, June 6, 2000, UK.

988.
B) GRENADA

☞ Grenada: Isle of Spice, Norma Sinclair, Macmillan Publishers; London, 1987, p.18.

Additional Information:

☞ The Voice, The Voice Group Ltd.; London, November 20, 2000, p.51.

☞ African and Caribbean Politics: From Kwame Nkruma to the Grenada Revolution, Manning Marable, Verso; London, 1987.

☞ Third World Impact. 8th Edition, Edited by Arif Ali, Hansib Publishing; 1988.

989.
A) EUROPEAN UNION OF WOMEN

☞ The Voice, The Voice Group Ltd.; March 30, 1993, pp.13-14.

Additional Information:

☞ The Weekly Journal, Voice Communications; London, October 20, 1994, p.10.

☞ The Voice, The Voice Group Ltd.; London, February 8, 1994, p.13.

☞ The Voice, The Voice Group Ltd.; October 18, 1994, p.5.

990.
B) WORLD COUNCIL OF CHURCHES

☞ African Methodist Episcopal Church, 1134 11th Street NW, Washington, DC., 20001.

Additional Information:

☞ Jet, Johnson Publishing Co.; Chicago, April 1, 1991, p.29.

☞ Black Firsts: 2000 Years of Extraordinary Achievement. Jessie Carney Smith, Caspar L. Jordan and Robert L. Johns, Visible Ink Press; USA, 1994, p.327.

☞ Jet, Johnson Publishing Co.; Chicago, November 18, 1991, p.66.

991.
A) 1878

☞ Black Firsts: 2000 Years of Extraordinary Achievement. Jessie Carney Smith, Caspar L. Jordan and Robert L. Johns, Visible Ink Press; USA, 1994.

Additional Information:

☞ Before the Mayflower: A History of Black America. Lerone Bennett Jr., 5th Edition, Penguin Books; 1984.

☞ America's Black Congressmen, Maurine Christopher, Thomas Y. Crowell; New York, 1971.

☞ Chronology of African American History: Significant Events and People from 1619 to the Present, Alton Hornsby, Gale Publishing Group; 1991.

992.
B) HAITI

☞ Famous First Facts About Negroes, Romeo B. Garrett, Arno Press; USA, 1972, p.46.

Additional Information:

☞ Black Firsts: 2000 Years of Extraordinary Achievement. Jessie Carney Smith, Caspar L. Jordan and Robert L. Johns, Visible Ink Press; USA, 1994, p.154.

☞ Dictionary of American Negro Biography, Rayford W. Logan and Michael R. Winston, W. W. Norton & Co.; New York, 1993.

☞ International Library of Negro Life and Historical Negro Biographies, Robinson, USA, p.132.

993.
A) MICHIGAN
☞ Facts on File Encyclopedia of Black Women in America: Law and Government (Volume 8), Darlene Clark Hine and Kathleen Thompson, (eds.), Facts of File, Inc.; USA, 1997.
Additional Information:
☞ The Negro Politician: His Success and Failure, E. T. Clayton, USA, pp.139-43.
☞ Ebony, Johnson Publishing; Chicago, September, 1967, pp.27-28.
☞ Black Firsts: 2000 Years of Extraordinary Achievement. Jessie Carney Smith, Caspar L. Jordan and Robert L. Johns, Visible Ink Press; USA, 1994.

994.
C) GHANA
☞ Daughters of Africa: An International Anthology of Words and Writings by Women of African Descent from the Ancient Egyptian to the Present. Edited by Margaret Busby, Vintage Books; New York, 1993, p.223.
Additional Information:
☞ The Torn Veil and Other Stories, Mabel Dove Danquah with Phebean Itayemi-Ogundipe, Evans Bros; London, 1976.
☞ Unwinding Threads: Writing by Women in Africa, Charlotte Bruner, (ed.), Heinemann; 1994.
☞ Black Londoners, 1890-1990, Susan Okokon, Sutton; UK, 1997, p.77.

995.
B) THURGOOD MARSHALL
☞ Ebony, Johnson Publishing; Chicago, March, 1993, pp.126-30.
Additional Information:
☞ USA Today, European Edition, December 3, 1996, p.1.
☞ Black Americana. Richard A. Long, Admiral; UK, 1985.
☞ Chronology of African American History: Significant Events and People from 1619 to the Present, Alton Hornsby, Gale Publishing Group; 1991.

996.
A) VETERANS' AFFAIRS
☞ Crisis, USA, March, 1993.
Additional Information:
☞ Ebony, Johnson Publishing; Chicago, April, 1996, p.102.
☞ Ebony, Johnson Publishing; Chicago, May, 1993, p.64.
☞ Ebony, Johnson Publishing; Chicago, May, 1996, p. 120.

997.
B) 1974
☞ A Taste of Power: A Black Woman's Story, Elaine Brown, Anchor Books/Doubleday; USA, 1994.
Additional Information:
☞ 1999 Facts About Blacks: A Sourcebook of African American Accomplishment. Raymond M. Corbin, Beckham House Publishers; USA, 1st Edition, 1986, p.31.
☞ The New York Times, May 5, 1993.
☞ The Black American Reference Book, Mabel M. Smyth, (ed.), Prentice-Hall Inc.; USA, 1976.

998.
B) 1793
☞ A Brief History of the Caribbean, Jan Rogozinskii, Facts on File; 1992, p.214.
Additional Information:
☞ Bleus, Blancs, Náegres: Nantes 1793: Quel Gáenocide?, Jean Danet, France.
☞ Toussaint L'Overture, Thomas and Dorothy Hoober, Chelsea House; NY, 1990.
☞ "There Are No Slaves in France". The Political Culture of Race and Slavery in the Ancient Regime, Sue Peabody, Oxford University Press; 1996.

999.
C) LONDON SCHOOL OF ECONOMICS
☞ LSE, Student's Union, Houghton Street, London WC2A 2AE.
Additional Information:
☞ The New Nation, Ethnic Media Group; London, 3 November, 2003, p.8-9.
☞ The Guardian, Guardian Newspapers; London, December 13, 1999.
☞ A Chronology of Injustice, Legal Action for Winner, Crossroads Women's Centre, P.O. Box 287, London NW6.

1000.

A) LOUISIANA

☞ Race and Democracy: The World Civil Rights Struggle in Louisiana, 1915-1972, Adam Fairclough, University of Georgia Press; Athens, 1995.

Additional Information:

☞ 1999 Facts About Blacks: A Sourcebook of African American Accomplishment. Raymond M. Corbin, Beckham House Publishers; USA, 1st Edition, 1986, p.21.

☞ A Documentary History of the Negro People in the United States, Volume 3, Edited by Herbert Aptheker, Citadel Press; 1974.

☞ David Duke and the Politics of Race in the South, John C. Kuzenski, Charles S. Bullock, Ronald K. Gaddie and Charles S. Bullock III, (eds.), Vanderbilt University Press; 1995.

1001.

B) 28

☞ MP's Biographies: David Lammy, Vacher Dod Publishing Ltd.; London, 2001.

Additional Information:

☞ The Times, London, May 26, 2000.

☞ The Voice, The Voice Group Ltd.; July 2, 2001.

☞ Society Guardian, Guardian Newspapers; London, January 13, 2001.

1002.

B) VIRGIN ISLANDS

☞ Ebony, Johnson Publishing; Chicago, March, 1971, pp.105-8.

Additional Information:

☞ Melvin H. Evans, Roger Hill, USA.

☞ Black Firsts: 2000 Years of Extraordinary Achievement. Jessie Carney Smith, Caspar L. Jordan and Robert L. Johns, Visible Ink Press; USA, 1994, p.150.

☞ Ebony, Johnson Publishing; Chicago, March, 1979, p.26.

1003.

B) FREDERICK MORROW

☞ Civil Rights, The White House, and the Justice Department, 1945-1968: Employment of Blacks by the Federal Government, Michael R. Belknap, (ed.), Garland Publishing; 1991.

Additional Information:

☞ Ebony Pictorial History of Black America: Volume 3. Civil Rights Movement to Black Revolution, Johnson Publishing Company; 1974.

☞ A Pictorial History of Black America. Langston Hughes, Crown; NY, 1983.

☞ 1999 Facts About Blacks: A Sourcebook of African American Accomplishment. Raymond M. Corbin, Beckham House Publishers; USA, 1st Edition, 1986, p.24.

1004.

C) CONGRESSIONAL BLACK CAUCUS

☞ A Pictorial History of Black America. Langston Hughes, Crown; NY, 1983.

Additional Information:

☞ 1999 Facts About Blacks: A Sourcebook of African American Accomplishment. Raymond M. Corbin, Beckham House Publishers; USA, 1st Edition, 1986, p.27.

☞ The Voice, The Voice Group Limited; July16, 2001, p.12.

☞ Ebony, Johnson Publishing; Chicago, September, 2001.

1005.

C) 1967

☞ Promises of Power; A Political Autobiography, Carl Stokes, Simon & Schuster; New York, NY, 1973.

Additional Information:

☞ Ebony Success Library, Vol. 1., Johnson Publishing; USA, p.293.

☞ Who's Who Among Black Americans, 1992-1993, USA, p.198.

☞ Black Firsts: 2000 Years of Extraordinary Achievement. Jessie Carney Smith, Caspar L. Jordan and Robert L. Johns, Visible Ink Press; USA, 1994, pp.210-11.

1006.

B) LOUIS XIV

☞ African Presence in Early Europe, Edited by Ivan Van Sertima, Transaction; 1986, p.199.

Additional Information:

☞ Sex and Race, Volume 1, J. A. Rogers, Ninth Edition, H. M. Rogers Publishers; USA, 1968.

☞ No Green Pasters, Roi Ottley, John Murray Books; London, 1952.

Nouvelles a la Main, Anisson du Perron, Vte. de Grouchy Publ.; Paris, 1898, p.29.

1007.
B) LAMBETH
☞ Who's Who of Black Achievers, John Hughes, (ed.), Ethnic Media Group; UK, 1999, p.83.
Additional Information:
☞ The Voice, The Voice Group Ltd.; London, April 11, 1995, p.3.
☞ Lambeth Town Hall, (General Enquiries) Brixton Hill, London SW2 1RW.
☞ The Voice, The Voice Group Limited; August 8, 1995, p.3.

1008.
A) 1945
☞ 1999 Facts About Blacks: A Sourcebook of African American Accomplishment. Raymond M. Corbin, Beckham House Publishers; USA, 1st Edition, 1986, p.7.
Additional Information:
☞ Famous First Facts About Negroes, Romeo B. Garrett, Arno Press; USA, 1972, p.93.
☞ Dictionary of American Negro Biography, Rayford W. Logan and Michael R. Winston, W. W. Norton & Co.; New York, 1993.
☞ The Black American Reference Book, Mabel M. Smyth, (ed.), Prentice-Hall Inc.; USA, 1976.

1009.
B) THE EQUAL OPPORTUNITIES COMMISSION
☞ Windrush: The Irresistible Rise of Multiracial Britain. Trevor Phillips, HarperCollins; 1998.
Additional Information:
☞ The Voice, The Voice Group Ltd.; August 11, 1997, pp.2, 8.
☞ Black Londoners, 1890-1990, Susan Okokon, Sutton; UK, 1997.
☞ Society of Black Lawyers, Room 9, Winchester House, 11 Cranmer Road, Kennington Park, London, SW9 6 EJ.

1010.
A) AL SHARPTON
☞ The Man Behind the Soundbite: The Real Story of Rev. Al Sharpton, Michael Klein, Costillo International, NY, 1991.

Additional Information:
☞ Ebony, Johnson Publishing; Chicago, July, 2001, p.125.
☞ **Ebony, Johnson Publishing; Chicago, November, 2000, p.88.**

☞ Black Noise: Rap Music and Black Culture in Contemporary America, Tricia Rose. Westeyan University Press; 1994.

1011.
A) 1914
☞ Pan Africanism or Communism, George Padmore, Dennis Dobson, London, 1961, pp.119-23, 134, 197.
Additional Information:
☞ Fêtes du Cinquantenaire du Soudan Français, (Speech by Blaise Diagne), Gouvernement Général d'Afrique Occidentale Français, Gorée, December, 1933, pp.51-53.
☞ World's Great Men of Color, Volume II, J. A. Rogers, Collier Macmillan Publishers; 1972, p.158.
☞ Présence Africaine, "Itinéraire Africain", Lamine Gueye, Paris, 1966, pp.51-63.

1012.
C) LAW ADVICE CENTER
☞ Caribbean Times, Hansib Publishing; London, April 13, 1993, p.2.
Additional Information:
☞ Third World Impact. 8th Edition, Edited by Arif Ali, Hansib Publishing; 1988.
☞ The Black Press in Britain, Ionie Benjamin, Trentham Books; London, 1995, p.47.
☞ Society of Black Lawyers, Room 9, Winchester House, 11 Cranmer Road, Kennington Park, London, SW9 6 EJ.

1013.
A) BERLIN
☞ African Presence in Early Europe, Edited by Ivan Van Sertima, Transaction; 1986, p.199.
Additional Information:
☞ Your History: From the Beginning of Time to the Present, J. A. Rogers, Black Classic Press; Baltimore, MD, 1983, p.50.
☞ Sex and Race, Volume 1, J. A. Rogers, 9th Edition, H. M. Rogers Publishers; USA, 1968, p.178.

- Anton William Amo's Treatise on the Art of Philophising Soberly and Accurately (With Commentaries), T. Uzodinma Nwala.

1014.
B) HARINGEY
- Chronicle of the Twentieth Century, Jacques Legrand, Longman Books; 1988, p.1251.
Additional Information:
- Windrush: The Irresistible Rise of Multiracial Britain. Trevor Phillips, HarperCollins; 1998.
- Third World Impact. 8th Edition, Edited by Arif Ali, Hansib Publishing; 1988.
- The Voice, The Voice Group Ltd.; London, April 14, 1997, p.19.

1015.
C) THE YMCA
- Who's Who Among Black Americans, 1992-1993, USA, p.1099.
Additional Information:
- YMCA of the USA, Association Advancement, 101 North Wacker Drive, Chicago, IL, 60606.
- Black Firsts: 2000 Years of Extraordinary Achievement. Jessie Carney Smith, Caspar L. Jordan and Robert L. Johns, Visible Ink Press; USA, 1994.
- Congressman Donald M. Payne, 2209 Rayburn House Office Building, Washington, DC., 20515-3010.

1016.
A) SENATOR
- The Black American Reference Book, Mabel M. Smyth, (ed.), Prentice-Hall Inc.; USA, 1976, p.627.
Additional Information:
- On the Real Side: A History of African American Comedy. Mel Watkins, Lawrence Hill; USA, 1999, p.122.
- A Pictorial History of Black America. Langston Hughes, Crown; NY, 1983.
- Encyclopedia of Black America, W. A. Low and Virgil A. Clift, (eds.), Mcgraw-Hill; New York, 1981.

1017.
C) PRIME MINISTER
- Imhotep, Jamaison B. Hurry, Oxford University Press; London, 1926.
Additional Information:

- Black Makers of History. The Real McCoy, Frank Forde, Lesnah Hall and Virginia McLean, The Book Place; 1988, p.30.
- Ancient Records of Egypt: Historical Documents From the Earliest Times to the Persian Conquest, Vols. 1-5, James H. Breasted, The University of Chicago Press; Chicago, 1906-1907.
- Herodotus: The Histories. Great Books of the Western World, Encyclopaedia Brittanica; Chicago, 1952.

1018.
C) LION
- Sex and Race, Volume 3, J. A. Rogers, 5th Edition, H. M. Rogers Publishers; 1972, p.137.
Additional Information:
- Your History: From the Beginning of Time to the Present, J. A. Rogers, Black Classic Press; Baltimore, MD, 1983, p.58.
- A Guide of English Coins, Nineteenth and Twentieth centuries, Kenneth E. Bressett, Western Publishing Company; 1968.
- The Signs and Symbols of Primordial Man, Albert Churchward, E. P. Dutton and Co.; New York, 1910.

1019.
B) COLOMBIA
- Colombian Chancery: 2118 Leroy Place NW, Washington, DC 20008
Additional Information:
- Civil Politics of Colombia, The Free Encyclopedia, Wikipedia; http://en.wikipedia.org
- The Economist, 29 December 2003
- El Spectador, Colombia, 30 March 2003

Millennium Dawn

Answers and Sources

1020.
B) GULF WAR
☞ Time, Time Inc.; USA, September 10, 2001, (cover).

Additional Information:
☞ Time, Time Inc.; USA, April 28, 1997, p.57.
☞ Ebony, Johnson Publishing; Chicago, February, 1994, p.138.
☞ The Essential Black Literature Guide, Published in association with the Schomburg Center for Research in Black Culture, Roger M. Valade II, Visible Ink Press; USA, 1996, p.170.

1021.
A) REFUSED TO GIVE UP HER SEAT
☞ Rosa Parks: My Story, Rosa Parks and James Haskins, Puffin Books; USA, 1999.

Additional Information:
☞ Facts on File Encyclopedia of Black Women in America: Social Activism (Volume 10), Darlene Clark Hine and Kathleen Thompson, (eds.), Facts of File, Inc.; USA, 1997.
☞ Chronicle of America, Jacques Legrand, Longman; 1989.
☞ Encyclopedia of Black America, W. A. Low and Virgil A. Clift, (eds.), Mcgraw-Hill; New York, 1981.

1022.
C) NORTH POLE
☞ BBC History Magazine, BBC Worldwide; April 2001, Vol. 2, No. 4, p.10.

Additional Information:
☞ The Daily Mail, February 18, London, 1997, p.7.
☞ They Showed the Way Up, Charlemae Hill Rollins, Thomas Y. Crowell Company; New York, 1964, pp.83-87.
☞ Famous Negro Heroes of America, Langston Hughes, Dodd, Mead; New York. 1958.

1023.
A) 1930
☞ My Life and Ethiopia's Progress, E. Ullendorff, Oxford University Press; 1976.

Additional Information:
☞ Haile Selassie I, David Abner Talbot, W. P. Van Stockum; The Hague, 1955.

☞ Haile Selassie's Government, C. Claphams, London, 1969.
☞ The New Leaders of Africa, Rolf Italiaander (translated by James McGovern), Englewood Cliffs, Prentice-Hall; New Jersey, 1961, pp.55-63.

1024.
A) PHARAOH
☞ Nile Valley Contributions to Civilization; Exploding the Myths, Volume 1, Anthony T. Browder, Institute of Khamic Guidance; Washington, D.C., 2000, p.60.

Additional Information:
☞ Egypt During the Sadat Years, Kirk J. Beattie, Palgrave Publishing; 2000.
☞ Chronicle of the Twentieth Century, Jacques Legrand, Longman Books; 1988.
☞ Macdonalds Encyclopedia of Africa, Macdonald Educational Ltd.; UK, 1986.

1025.
C) WASHINGTON, D.C.
☞ In the Name of Elijah Muhammad: Louis Farrakhan and the Nation of Islam, Mattias Gardell, Duke University Press; 1996.

Additional Information:
☞ Prophet of Rage, Arthur J. Magida, Basic Books, HarperCollins; 1996.
☞ Inside the Nation of Islam: A Historical and Personal Testimony by a Black Muslim, Vibert L. White, University of Florida Press; 2001.
☞ Vibe, Quincy Jones and David Salzman Entertainment, Time Publishing Inc.; February, 1996, p.23.

1026.
A) ISRAEL
☞ Ralph Bunche: UN Peacemaker, Peggy Mann, Coward, McCann & Geoghegan; 1975.

Additional Information:
☞ Ralph J. Bunche: Fighter for Peace. J. Alvin Kugelmass, Messner; 1962.
☞ Chronicle of the Twentieth Century, Jacques Legrand, Longman Books; 1988, pp.679, 683.
☞ The Essential Black Literature Guide, Published in association with the Schomburg Center for Research in Black Culture, Roger M. Valade II, Visible Ink Press; USA, 1996, p.65.

1027.
B) GUANTANAMO BAY
☞ Waging Modern War: Bosnia, Kosovo, and the Future of Combat, General Wesley K, Clark, Public Affairs Books; US, 2002.
Additional Information:
☞ The Guardian, Guardian Newspapers; London, 11 October, 2003, p12.
☞ Silencing Political Dissent: How Post-September 11 Anti-Terrorism. Measures Threaten Our Civil Liberties, Nancy Chang, et al, Seven Stories Press; US, 2002.
☞ Pathologies of Power: Health, Human Rights, and the New War on the Poor, Paul Farmer, University of California Press; 2003, p.52.

1028.
A) 1972
☞ Chronicle of the Twentieth Century, Jacques Legrand, Longman Books; 1988, p.1049.
Additional Information:
☞ New African, April 2000, ICP Ltd.; London, pp.30-31.
☞ The Encyclopedia of Africa, Franklin Watts, Inc.; New York and London, 1976.
☞ African Political Facts Since 1945, Cook & Killingray, Macmillan Press Ltd.; 1983.

1029.
C) GERMANY
☞ Black Women for Beginners, Sandra Sharp, Writers and Readers Publishing, Inc.; New York, 1993, p.114.
Additional Information:
☞ Black Women in Antiquity, Edited by Ivan Van Sertima, Transaction; 7th Edition, 1992, p.132.
☞ New African, September 2001, ICP Ltd.; London, pp.12-13.
☞ Essence, "The Black Woman: A Figure in World History", John Henrik Clarke, May, 1971, p.29.

1030.
B) MEXICO 1968
☞ Chronicles of Black Protest, Bradford Chambers, Mentor; NY, 1969.

Additional Information:
☞ A Hard Road to Glory: A History of the African American Athlete. Volume 3, Arthur Ashe, USA, 1988, pp.190-95.
☞ Chronicle of the Olympics, 1896-1996, Dorling Kindersley Publishing; UK, 1996.
☞ Olympics: Facts and Feats, Stan Greenberry, Guinness Publishing; 1996, p.94.

1031.
A) HAITI
☞ Papa Doc, Baby Doc: Haiti and the Devaliers, James Ferguson, Blackwell Publishers; 1987.
Additional Information:
☞ From Dessalines to Duvalier: Race, Colour, and National Independence in Haiti, David Nicholls, Rutgers University Press; 1995.
☞ Time, Time Inc.; USA, September 26, 1994, pp.18-19.
☞ Chronicle of the Twentieth Century, Jacques Legrand, Longman Books; 1988, p.1265.

1032.
B) PROTECTING THE RAIN FOREST
☞ Fights for the Forest: Chico Mendes in His Own Words, Inland Book Co.; 1990.
Additional Information:
☞ The World is Burning: Murder in the Rain Forest, Alex Shoumatoff, Little, Brown & Company; 1990.
☞ Chico Mendes: Defender of the Rain Forest (A Gateway Green Biography), Joann J. Burch, Milbrook Press; 1994.
☞ The Burning Season: The Murder of Chico Mendes, Andrew Revkin, Books on Tape, Inc.; 1991

1033.
C) GENERAL
☞ Overman Report, United States Senate, 1919.
Additional Information:
☞ US Congress Documents, 66th Congress, Volume 4, 1919, p.115.
☞ Russia and the Negro: Blacks in Russian History and Thought. Allison Blakely, Howard University Press; Washington, 1986.
☞ Nature Knows No Color Line. J. A. Rogers, 3rd Edition, H. M. Rogers Publishers; 1952, p.135.

1034.

C) 1922

☞ Nile Valley Contributions to Civilization; Exploding the Myths, Volume 1, Anthony T. Browder, Institute of Khamic Guidance; Washington, D.C., 2000, p.188.

Additional Information:

☞ Tut'ankhamun's Tomb Series 1: A Handlist to Howard Carter's Catalogue of Objects in Tutankhamun's Tomb, Helen Murray and Mary Nuttall, Oxford University Press; Oxford, 1963.

☞ The Guardian, Guardian Newspapers; London, March 14, 1987.

☞ Chronicle of the Twentieth Century, Jacques Legrand, Longman Books; 1988.

1035.

B) GUYANA

☞ Encyclopedia of Latin America, Edited by Helen Delpar, Macgraw-Hill Book Company; 1974.

Additional Information:

☞ African and Caribbean Politics: From Kwame Nkruma to the Grenada Revolution, Manning Marable, Verso; London, 1987.

☞ Hutchingson Encyclopedia, 8th Edition, Hutchingson; UK, 1988.

☞ Metegee: The History and Culture of Guyana, Ovid Abrams, Eldorado Publications; 1998.

1036.

C) MALCOLM X

☞ The Assassination of Malcolm X, George Breitman, Herman Porter and Baxter Smith, Pathfinder Books; NY, London, Montreal, Sydney, 1991.

Additional Information:

☞ The Autobiography of Malcolm X, Alex Haley, Grove; NY, 1965.

☞ By Any Means Necessary: A Biography, Walter Dean Myers, Scholastic Paperbacks; 1994.

☞ Malcolm X Speaks: Selected Speeches and Statements, Malcom X, George Breitman, (ed.), Grove Press; 1990.

1037.

B) SUDAN

☞ Washington Post, 8 August, 1998, USA, p.1.

Additional Information:

☞ A History of Terrorism, Walter Laqueur, Transaction Books; New Jersey, 2001.

☞ Taliban: Militant Islam, Oil and Fundamentalism in Central Asia, Ahmad Rashid, Yale University Press; USA, 2001.

☞ The New York Times, 12 September, 2001, pp.1-5.

1038.

A) NIGERIA

☞ Identity Transformation and Identity Politics Under Structural Adjustment in Nigeria, Attahiru Jega, Transaction; New Jersey, 2000.

Additional Information:

☞ Africa, Phyllis Martin and Patrick O'Meara, Indiana University Press; Bloomington, 1986.

☞ Macdonalds Encyclopedia of Africa, Macdonald Educational Ltd.; UK, 1986.

☞ African Political Facts Since 1945, Cook & Killingray, Macmillan Press Ltd.; 1983.

1039.

A) SCIENTIST

☞ Great African Thinkers, Volume 1, Edited by Ivan Van Sertima, Transaction; USA, 1987.

Additional Information:

☞ Anthony T. Browder, Institute of Khamic Guidance; Washington, D.C., 2000, pp.19-20, 23, 149, 151.

☞ Black Makers of History. The Real McCoy, Frank Forde, Lesnah Hall and Virginia McLean, The Book Place; 1988.

☞ The Essential Black Literature Guide, Published in association with the Schomburg Center for Research in Black Culture, Roger M. Valade II, Visible Ink Press; USA, 1996, p.111.

1040.

C) BLACK POWER

☞ Ebony Pictorial History of Black America: Volume 3. Civil Rights Movement to Black Revolution, Johnson Publishing Company; 1974.

Additional Information:

☞ The Voice, The Voice Group Ltd.; London, July 7, 1997, p.22.

☞ The Essential Black Literature Guide, Published in association with the Schomburg Center for Research in Black Culture, Roger M. Valade II, Visible Ink Press; USA, 1996, p.70.

☞ Encyclopedia of Black America, W. A. Low and Virgil A. Clift, (eds.), Mcgraw-Hill; New York, 1981.

1041.
B) CUBA

☞ Jesse Jackson: I am Somebody, Paul Westman and Judith Leo, Dillon Press; 1984.

Additional Information:

☞ Chronology of African American History: Significant Events and People from 1619 to the Present, Alton Hornsby, Gale Publishing Group; 1991.

☞ Chronicle of the Twentieth Century, Jacques Legrand, Longman Books; 1988.

☞ Black Americana. Richard A. Long, Admiral; UK, 1985, pp.101, 103-5.

1042.
C) THE CREATION OF THE ATOM BOMB

☞ Blacks in Science: Ancient and Modern, Ivan Van Sertima, (ed.), Transaction; USA, 1985, p.84.

Additional Information:

☞ Ebony, Johnson Publishing; Chicago, February, 1997, p.40.

☞ New African, April 2000, ICP Ltd.; London, p.24.

☞ Black Inventors of America, McKinley Burt, National Book Co; Oregon, 1969.

1043.
B) HUTU

☞ The Key to My Neighbours House: Searching for Justice in Bosnia and Rwanda, Elizabeth Neuffer, Picador; USA, 2001.

Additional Information:

☞ Time, Time Inc.; USA, No. 35, August 29, 1994.

☞ New African, April 2000, ICP Ltd.; London, pp.28-29.

☞ A People Betrayed: The Role of the West in Rawanda's Genocide, Linda Melvern, Zed Books; 2000.

1044.
B) SUDAN

☞ The Guardian, Guardian Newspapers; London, July 22, 2004, P.1

Additional Information:

☞ Amnesty International, 99 Roseberry Avenue, London, EC1R 4RE

☞ New York Times, 30 June, 2004.

☞ Metro, Associated Metro Ltd; July 26, p.4.

1045.
B) MARTIN LUTHER KING

☞ Chronicle of the Twentieth Century, Jacques Legrand, Longman Books; 1988.

Additional Information:

☞ Chronicle of America, Jacques Legrand, Longman; 1989.

☞ Encyclopedia of Black America, W. A. Low and Virgil A. Clift, (eds.), Mcgraw-Hill; New York, 1981.

☞ Black Americana. Richard A. Long, Admiral; UK, 1985.

1046.
A) 1992

☞ The Independent on Sunday, Independent Newspapers; London, October 9, 1996, p.15.

Additional Information:

☞ Ebony Man, Johnson Publishing; March, 1993, p.18.

☞ Black Noise: Rap Music and Black Culture in Contemporary America, Tricia Rose. Westeyan University Press; 1994.

☞ Ebony, Johnson Publishing; Chicago, February, 1994, p.88.

1047.
B) CALIFORNIA

☞ The Times, London, May 11, 1987, p.1.

Additional Information:

☞ The Hot Zone, Richard Preston, Random House; New York, 1994.

☞ A Higher Form of Killing: The Secret Story of Chemical and Biological Warfare. Robert Harris and Jeremy Paxman, Hill & Wang; USA, 1982, p.219.

☞ The Greatest Biological Disaster in the History of Mankind: Aids, The End of Civilization, William Campbell Douglas, A-B Book Publishers; NY, NY, 1992.

1048.
C) SOUTH AFRICA

☞ African Political Facts Since 1945, Cook & Killingray, Macmillan Press Ltd.; 1983.

Additional Information:
☞ The Long Walk to Freedom: The Autobiography of Nelson Mandela. Back Bay Books, Little, Brown; 1995.
☞ The Encyclopedia of Africa, Franklin Watts, Inc.; New York and London, 1976.
☞ Apartheid's Rebels; Inside South Africa's Hidden War, Stephen M. Davis, Yale University Press; New Haven, London, 1987.

1049.
B) EMPIRE WINDRUSH
☞ Windrush: The Irresistible Rise of Multiracial Britain. Trevor Phillips, HarperCollins; 1998.
Additional Information:
☞ With Hope in Their Eyes; Compelling Stories of the Windrush Generation,
☞ Vivian Francis, The X Press; UK, 1998.
☞ The Heart of the Race: Black Women's Lives in Britain, B. Bryan, S. Dudzie, S. Scafe, Virago Press; 1985, p.130.
☞ Black and British, David Bygott, Oxford University Press; 1992.

1050.
B) THE PEOPLE'S TEMPLE, JONESTOWN, 1978
☞ Suicide in Guyana, M. E. Knerr, Belmont Tower Books; New York City, 1978.
Additional Information:
☞ Chronicle of the Twentieth Century, Jacques Legrand, Longman Books; 1988, p.1143.
☞ Suicide Cult: The Inside Story of the Peoples Temple Sect and the Massacre in Guyana, Marshall Kilduff, Ron Javers, Bantum Books; 1978.
☞ Hearing the Voices of Jonestown, Mary McCormick Maaga and Catherine Wessinger, Syracuse University Press; 1998.

1051.
A) KWAME NKRUMAH
☞ Africa Must Unite: Kwame Nkruma, New York, International Publishers; 1972.
Additional Information:
☞ African and Caribbean Politics: From Kwame Nkruma to the Grenada Revolution, Manning Marable, Verso; London, 1987.

☞ African Political Facts Since 1945, Cook & Killingray, Macmillan Press Ltd.; 1983.
☞ New African, IC Publications; London, No. 351, April 1997, pp.10-14.

1052.
A) PUERTO RICO
☞ Puerto Rico Mio: Four Decades of Change, Jack Delano, Smithsonian Institution Press; 1990.
Additional Information:
☞ Chronicle of the Twentieth Century, Jacques Legrand, Longman Books; 1988.
☞ Foreign in a Domestic Sense: Puerto Rico, American Expansion, and the Constitution, Christina Duffy Burnett and Burk Marshall, (eds.), Duke University Press; 2001.
☞ Lonely Planet Puerto Rico (Puerto Rico 2000), Randall S. Peffer, Lonely Planet Books; 1999.

1053.
B) PAUL ROBESON
☞ Paul Robeson, Martin Bauml Duberman, The Bodley Head; London, 1989.
Additional Information:
☞ Paul Robeson: All American, Dorothy Butler Gilliam, New Republic Books; 1976.
☞ Paul Robeson: The Years of Promise and Achievement, Sheila Tully Boyle and Andrew Bunie, University of Massachussetts Press; 2001.
☞ Here I Stand, Paul Robeson and Sterling Stuckey, Beacon Press; 1998.

1054.
C) GEORGE PADMORE
☞ Pan Aficanism or Communism, George Padmore, Doubleday & Co.; NY.
Additional Information:
☞ Macdonalds Encyclopedia of Africa, Macdonald Educational Ltd.; UK, 1986.
☞ African and Caribbean Politics: From Kwame Nkruma to the Grenada Revolution, Manning Marable, Verso; London, 1987.
☞ New African, IC Publications; London, No. 351, April 1997, pp.12-14.

1055.
B) FIRST PRESIDENT OF AFRICA
☞ Black History, Melvin Drimmer, Doubleday and Company; Garden City, New York, 1967, pp.324-510.
Additional Information:
☞ Philosophies and Opinions of Marcus Garvey, Vols. 1-2, 2nd Edition, Cass; London, 1967.
☞ Marcus Garvey: Message to the People, Edited by Tony Martin, Foreword by the Honorary Charles L. James, New Marcus Garvey Library; Book No. 7, 1986.
☞ Garvey and Garveyism, Amy Jacques Garvey, Kingston, Jamaica, 1963, Collier Books; New York, 1970.

1056.
A) SOUTH AFRICA
☞ The Essential Gandhi: His Life, Work, and Ideas; An Anthology, Louis Fischer, Vintage Books; 1983.
Additional Information:
☞ Cambridge Encyclopedia, David Crystal, Cambridge University Press; 1990, p.481.
☞ All Men Are Brothers: Autobiographical Reflections, Mahatma Gandhi, Edited by Krishna Kripalani and Mohandas Karamchand Gandhi, Continuum Publishing Group; 1980.
☞ Gandhi's Passion: The Life and Legacy of Mahatma Gandhi, Stanley A. Wolpert, Oxford University Press; 1980.

1057.
B) LIVE AID
☞ The Weekly Journal, Voice Communications; London, February 9, 1995, p.11.
Additional Information:
☞ Chronicle of the Twentieth Century, Jacques Legrand, Longman Books; 1988.
☞ The Voice, The Voice Group Limited; July 25, 1995, p.7.
☞ Cambridge Encyclopedia, David Crystal, Cambridge University Press; 1990, p.486.

1058.
B) DECOLONIZATION OF AFRICA
☞ Pan Africanism or Communism, George Padmore, Dennis Dobson; London, 1961.

Additional Information:
☞ Staying Power, Peter Fryer, Pluto Press; UK, 2nd Edition, 1985.
☞ History of the Black Presence in London, GLC; London, 1986.
☞ Black Londoners, 1890-1990, Susan Okokon, Sutton; UK, 1997, p.76.

1059.
B) SOCIAL WORKER
☞ Winnie Mandela. Mother of a Nation, Nancy Harrison, Grafton Books; London, 1986.
Additional Information:
☞ Winnie Mandela. Part of My Soul Went With Him, Edited by Anne Benjamin, W. W. Norton & Co.; New York and London, 1984.
☞ Between Anger and Hope: South Africa's Youth and the Truth and Reconciliation Commission. Karin Chubb and Lutz van Dijk, Transaction; New Jersey, 2001.
☞ Time, Time Inc.; USA, May 1, 1995, p. 19.

1060.
C) W. D. FARD
☞ The Nation of Islam: An American Millenarian Movement, Martha F. Lee, Syracuse University Press; 1996.
Additional Information:
☞ Inside the Nation of Islam: A Historical and Personal Testimony by a Black Muslim, Vibert L. White, University of Florida Press; 2001.
☞ In the Name of Elijah Muhammad: Louis Farrakhan and the Nation of Islam, Mattias Gardell, Duke University Press; 1996.
☞ Ebony Pictorial History of Black America: Volume 3. Civil Rights Movement to Black Revolution, Johnson Publishing Company; 1974, pp.50, 233.

1061.
A) ZIMBABWE
☞ A Short History of Africa, Roland Oliver (and J. D. Fage) Penguin Books; 1990.
Additional Information:
☞ African Political Facts Since 1945, Cook & Killingray, Macmillan Press Ltd.; 1983.
☞ Zimbabwe: A Rhodesian Mystery. Roger Summers, Nelson; South Africa, 1963.

☞ Africa, Phyllis Martin and Patrick O'Meara, Indiana University Press; Bloomington, 1986.

1062.
B) BELINDA AND KIMBERLEY
☞ The New York Times, January 30, 2001.
Additional Information:
☞ The Times, London, January 18, 2001.
☞ The Voice, The Voice Group Ltd.; London, March 19, 2001, p.7.
☞ Harpo Productions Archive Dept., P.O. Box 9097115, Chicago, Illinois, USA, 60690.

1063.
C) HAILE SELASSIE
☞ My Life and Ethiopia's Progress, E. Ullendorff, Oxford University Press; 1976.
Additional Information:
☞ Haile Selassie I, David Abner Talbot, W. P. Van Stockum; The Hague, 1955.
☞ The New Leaders of Africa, Rolf Italiaander (translated by James McGovern), Englewood Cliffs, Prentice-Hall; New Jersey, 1961, pp.55-63.
☞ Chronicle of the Twentieth Century, Jacques Legrand, Longman Books; 1988, p.398.

1064.
B) CLAUDIA JONES
☞ I Think of my Mother, Claudia Jones, Buzz Johnson, Karia Press; 1985.
Additional Information:
☞ The Black Press in Britain, Ionie Benjamin, Trentham Books; London, 1995, pp.4, 43.
☞ Women, Race and Class, Angela Davis, Women's Press;
☞ The Heart of the Race: Black Women's Lives in Britain, B. Bryan, S. Dudzie, S. Scafe, Virago Press; 1985.

1065.
C) DESMOND TUTU
☞ No Future Without Forgiveness, Desmond Mpilo Tutu, Doubleday; 2000.
Additional Information:
☞ Tutu, Voice of the Voiceless, Shirley Du Boulay, Hodder & Stoughton; 1988.
☞ Between Anger and Hope: South Africa's Youth and the Truth and Reconciliation Commission. Karin Chubb and Lutz van Dijk, Transaction; New Jersey, 2001.

☞ Chronicle of the Twentieth Century, Jacques Legrand, Longman Books; 1988.

1066.
A) THE BOMBING OF PEARL HARBOUR
☞ Day of Infamy: The Classic Account of the Bombing of Pearl Harbor, Walter Lord, Henry Holt & Company, Inc.; 2001.
Additional Information:
☞ Chronology of African American History: Significant Events and People from 1619 to the Present, Alton Hornsby, Gale Publishing Group; 1991.
☞ The Black American Reference Book, Mabel M. Smyth, (ed.), Prentice-Hall Inc.; USA, 1976.
☞ 1999 Facts About Blacks: A Sourcebook of African American Accomplishment. Raymond M. Corbin, Beckham House Publishers; USA, 1st Edition, 1986, p.49.

1067.
A) 1915
☞ Negro; An Anthology, Nancy Cunard, Frederick Ungar Publishing Co.; NY, 1970.
Additional Information:
☞ 1999 Facts About Blacks: A Sourcebook of African American Accomplishment. Raymond M. Corbin, Beckham House Publishers; USA, 1st Edition, 1986, p.11.
☞ Chronicle of America, Jacques Legrand, Longman; USA, 1989.
☞ Ebony, Johnson Publishing; Chicago, February, 2001, p.122.

1068.
A) CHIEF ABIOLA
☞ Reparations-Papers on the African International Conference, Lagos, Nigeria, December 1990.
Additional Information:
☞ Caribbean Times, Hansib Publishing; London, No. 719, Week Ending 4th March 1995, p.13.
☞ The Weekly Gleaner, London, May 31, 1994, p. 8.
☞ The Black Press in Britain, Ionie Benjamin, Trentham Books; London, 1995, pp.84, 115.

1069.
C) SURINAM
☞ Suriname (Major World Nations Series), Noelle Blackmer Beatty, Chelsea House Publishers; 1997.
Additional Information:
☞ Encyclopedia of Latin America, Edited by Helen Delpar, Macgraw-Hill Book Company; 1974.
☞ Hutchingson Encyclopedia, 8th Edition, Hutchingson; UK, 1988.
☞ The Javanese in Suriname: Ethnicity in an Ethnically Plural Society, Parsudi Suparlan, Arizona State University Press; 1995.

1070.
C) MOBUTU SESE SEKO OF ZAIRE
☞ The Rise and Decline of the Zairian State, Crawford Young and Thomas Turner, University of Wisconsin Press; 1985.
Additional Information:
☞ The Times, London, March 25, 1997, p. 13.
☞ In the Footsteps of Mr. Kurtz: Living on the Brink of Disaster in Mobutu's Congo, Michael Wong, HarperCollins; 2001.
☞ The Independent, Independent Newspapers; London, May 8, 1997, p.15.

1071.
A) PRIME MINISTER
☞ The Assassination of Lumumba, Ludo De Witte, Translated by Renee Fenby and Ann Wright, Verso Books; 2001.
Additional Information:
☞ New African, April 2000, ICP Ltd.; London, pp.26-27.
☞ African and Caribbean Politics: From Kwame Nkruma to the Grenada Revolution. Manning Marable, Verso; London, 1987.
☞ Rise and Fall of Patrice Lumumba, Thomas Kanza, Schenkman Books; 1979.

1072.
A) SUEZ CANNEL
☞ Suez, 1956 (International Crisis and the Role of Law), Robert R. Bowie, Oxford University Press; 1974.

Additional Information:
☞ Nasser, Anthony Nutting, E. P. Dutton Publ.; New York, 1972.
☞ Chronicle of the Twentieth Century, Jacques Legrand, Longman Books; 1988.
☞ The Cairo Documents; The inside Story of Nasser and His Relationship with World Leaders, Rebels, and Statesmen, Muòhammad Òhasanayn Haykal, Doubleday; 1973.

1073.
B) KWANZAA
☞ A Plentiful Harvest: Creating Balance and Harmony Through the Seven Living Virtues, Terrie Williams, Warner Books; 2003.
Additional Information:
☞ Kwanzaa: A Progressive and Uplifting African-American Holiday. Institute of Positive Education, Third World Press; Chicago.
☞ African American Holidays, James C. Anyike, Volume 1, Popular Truth, Inc.; Chicago, IL, 1991.
☞ Ebony, Johnson Publishing; Chicago, December, 2000, pp.42,45.

1074.
B) 1969
☞ Libya Since Independence: Oil and State-Building, Dirk Vandewalle, Cornell University Press; 1998.
Additional Information:
☞ Chronicle of the Twentieth Century, Jacques Legrand, Longman Books; 1988.
☞ Hutchingson Encyclopedia, 8th Edition, Hutchingson; UK, 1988.
☞ Libya's Qaddafi: The Politics of Contradiction, Mansour O. El-Kikhia, University Press of Florida, 1998.

1075.
C) PEACE KEEPING FORCE
☞ Time, Time Inc.; USA, December 4, 1995.
Additional Information:
☞ West Africa, London, August 31–September 6, 1992, pp.1470-71.
☞ West Africa, London, June 1-7, 1992, p.934.
☞ New African, IC Publications; London, November 1993.

1076.
B) ENROLLING AT A HIGH SCHOOL IN LITTLE ROCK, ARKANSAS
☞ A Life is More Than a Moment: The Desegregation of Little Rock's Central High, Will Counts, Indiana University Press; USA, 1999.
Additional Information:
☞ Ebony, Johnson Publishing; Chicago, February, 2001.
☞ Black Americana. Richard A. Long, Admiral; UK, 1985.
☞ Ebony Pictorial History of Black America: Volume 3. Civil Rights Movement to Black Revolution, Johnson Publishing Company; 1974.

1077.
A) TANZANIA
☞ The Lake Regions of Central Africa: From Zanzibar to Lake Tanganyika, Sir Richard Francis Burton, Narrative Press; 2001.
Additional Information:
☞ African Political Facts Since 1945, Cook & Killingray, Macmillan Press Ltd.; 1983.
☞ Hutchingson Encyclopedia, 8th Edition, Hutchingson; UK, 1988.
☞ Lonely Planet Tanzania, Zanzibar and Pemba, Mary Fitzpatrick, Lonely Planet Books; 1999.

1078.
C) BURNING SPEAR
☞ Kenyatta and the Politics of Kenya, G. Arnold, London, 1974.
Additional Information:
☞ Facing Mount Kenya; Jomo Kenyatta, Vintage Books; New York, 1962.
☞ The Cambridge Encyclopedia of Africa, Cambridge University Press; 1981, p.211.
☞ African and Caribbean Politics: From Kwame Nkruma to the Grenada Revolution, Manning Marable, Verso; London, 1987.

1079.
A) 1979
☞ The New York Times, March 1, 1979, p.1.
Additional Information:
☞ Nile Valley Contributions to Civilization; Exploding the Myths, Volume 1, Anthony T. Browder, Institute of Khamic Guidance; Washington, D.C., 2000, p.53.

☞ Archaeology Monthly, Volume 33, No. 5, September-October Edition, 1980.
☞ Blacks in Science: Ancient and Modern, Ivan Van Sertima, (ed.), Transaction; USA, 1985, pp.24, 206.

1080.
C) JOURNALIST
☞ In Defence of Mumia, Edited by S. E. Anderson and Tony Madina, Writers & Readers Publication Inc.; 1996.
Additional Information:
☞ All Things Considered, Mumia Abu-Jamal, Noelle Hanrahan, (ed.), Seven Stories Press; USA, 2000.
☞ Ebony, Johnson Publishing; Chicago, November, 2000, p.55.
☞ The New Nation, Western Hemisphere; London, September 8, 1997, p.11.

1081.
A) 2300 YEARS
☞ Nile Valley Contributions to Civilization; Exploding the Myths, Volume 1, Anthony T. Browder, Institute of Khamic Guidance; Washington, D.C., 2000, p.60.
Additional Information:
☞ Egypt from Monarchy to Republic: A Reassessment of Revolution and Change, Shimon Shamir, (ed).
☞ African Political Facts Since 1945, Cook & Killingray, Macmillan Press Ltd.; 1983.
☞ The Cairo Documents; The inside Story of Nasser and His Relationship with World Leaders, Rebels, and Statesmen, Muòhammad Òhasanayn Haykal, Doubleday; 1973.

1082.
C) ENGAGING THE FASCIST BLOC IN NORTH AFRICA
☞ The New York Times, August 29, 1940.
Additional Information:
☞ The New York Times, May 18, 1944.
☞ Distinguished Negroes Abroad, B. J. Flemming and M. J. Pryde, The Associated Publishers; Washington, D.C., 1946, pp.95-104.
☞ Negro History Bulletin, "Félix Eboué: First Negro Governor of French Equatorial Africa",
J. Alvarez-Pereyre, Association for the Study of Negro Life and History, Washington, D.C., November, 1941, pp.27-30

1083.
B) ELIJAH MUHAMMED
☞ In the Name of Elijah Muhammad: Louis Farrakhan and the Nation of Islam, Mattias Gardell, Duke University Press; 1996.
Additional Information:
☞ Ebony Pictorial History of Black America: Volume 3. Civil Rights Movement to Black Revolution, Johnson Publishing Company; 1974, pp.25, 50, 80, 83, 105-6, 225, 233, 271.
☞ A Pictorial History of Black America. Langston Hughes, Crown; NY, 1983.
☞ The Nation of Islam: An American Millenarian Movement, Martha F. Lee, Syracuse University Press; 1996.

1084.
A) FRANTZ FANON
☞ Frantz Fanon: A Critical Study. Irene L. Gendzier, Pantheon; 1973.
Additional Information:
☞ The Wretched of the Earth, translated by Constance Farrington, Penguin Books; 1985.
☞ The Essential Black Literature Guide, Published in association with the Schomburg Center for Research in Black Culture, Roger M. Valade II, Visible Ink Press; USA, 1996, p.136.
☞ Black Skin White Masks, Frantz Fanon (translated by Charles Lam Markmann), Paladin; London, 1970.

1085.
A) SIX
☞ Time, Time Inc.; USA, January 17, 2000, pp.58-67
Additional Information:
☞ Time, Time Inc.; USA, April 17, 2000, (cover).
☞ Time, Time Inc.; May 1, 2000, (cover).
☞ The Voice, The Voice Group Ltd.; London, December 11, 2000, p.11.

1086.
A) THE ATLANTIC CHARTER
☞ African and O.A.U. Diplomacy on Dual Paradigms of Self-Determination 1945-1985: A Study of African Foreign Policy co-ordination on Decolonisation, and the Subsequent Maze of Ethno-nationalism, Legala Tita-Ghebdinga;

Additional Information:
☞ Chronicle of the Twentieth Century, Jacques Legrand, Longman Books; 1988, pp.679, 683.
☞ The Black Press in Britain, Ionie Benjamin, Trentham Books; London, 1995, p.19.
☞ The Atlantic Charter, Douglas Brinkley and David Facey-Crowther, (ed.), 1994.

1087.
B) FIGHTER AIRCRAFT PILOTS
☞ Tuskegee Airman: The Biography of Charles E. McGee, Air Force Fighter Combat Record Holder, Charlene E. McGee Smith (et al), Branden Publishing Co.; USA, 1999.
Additional Information:
☞ Ebony, Johnson Publishing; Chicago, November, 1994, pp.62-66.
☞ Ebony, Johnson Publishing; Chicago, February, 1994, p.120.
☞ Ebony, Johnson Publishing; Chicago, November, 2000, p.36D.

1088.
C) OGONI
☞ Amnesty Campaign Journal (For Amnesty International), UK, Jan/Feb Edition, 1997, Issue No. 81, p.8.
Additional Information:
☞ West Africa, London, January 11-17, 1993, p.10.
☞ The Weekly Journal, Voice Communications; London, January 19, 1995, p.4.
☞ The New Nation, Western Hemisphere; London, November 18, 1996, p.14.

1089.
B) AL QAEDA
☞ Why America Slept: The Failure to Prevent 9/11, Gerald L. Posner, Random House; 2003.
Additional Information:
☞ The Guardian, Guardian Newspapers; London, 11 October, 2003, p.12.
☞ A History of Terrorism, Walter Laqueur, Transaction Books; New Jersey, 2001.
☞ New York September 11, Magnum Photographers, David Halberstam, PowerHouse Books; 2001.

1090.
B) OPERATION SOLOMON
☞ The Sunday Times, London, May 26, 1991.
Additional Information:
☞ The Voice, The Voice Group Ltd.; London, June 4, 2001, p.11.
☞ Time, Time Inc.; June 3, 1991.
☞ Rescue: The Exodus of the Ethiopian Jews, Ruth Gruber, Atheneum; New York, 1987.

1091.
B) NAGASAKI
☞ Hiroshima, Marion Mass, Wayland Publishers; 2nd Edition, UK, 1987.
Additional Information:
☞ "White Paper on Statements Relating to the Atom Bomb", August 12, 1945, USA.
☞ Chronicle of the Twentieth Century, Jacques Legrand, Longman Books; 1988.
☞ Cambridge Encyclopedia, David Crystal, Cambridge University Press; 1990, p.828.

1092.
A) ZIMBABWE
☞ The Times, London, September 10, 2001, p.11.
Additional Information:
☞ Foreign Aid; Debt and Growth in Zambia. Research Report No. 112. Per-Åke Andersson, Arne Bigsten and Håkan Persson, Transaction; New Jersey, 2001.
☞ The Times, London, March 6, 2001, p.1.
☞ New African, April 2001, ICP Ltd.; London, pp.12-13.

1093.
A) UNITA
☞ Chronicle of the Twentieth Century, Jacques Legrand, Longman Books; 1988, p.1103.
Additional Information:
☞ African Political Facts Since 1945, Cook & Killingray, Macmillan Press Ltd.; 1983.
☞ The Weekly Journal, Voice Communications; London, April 28, 1994, p.5.
☞ The Voice, The Voice Group Limited; July 25, 1995, p.15.

1094.
C) ANGELA DAVIS
☞ Angela Davis. An Autobiography, Women's Press; UK, 1990.
Additional Information:
☞ Black Women for Beginners, Sandra Sharp, Writers and Readers Publishing, Inc.; New York, 1993.
☞ The Essential Black Literature Guide, Published in association with the Schomburg Center for Research in Black Culture, Roger M. Valade II, Visible Ink Press; USA, 1996, p.103.
☞ When and Where I Enter: The Impact of Black Women on Race in America, Paula Giddings, William Morrow; NY, 1984.

1095.
A) THE DERG
☞ Chronicle of the Twentieth Century, Jacques Legrand, Longman Books; 1988.
Additional Information:
☞ The Voice, The Voice Group Ltd.; London, January 3, 1995, p.3.
☞ Macdonalds Encyclopedia of Africa, Macdonald Educational Ltd.; UK, 1986.
☞ The Weekly Journal, Voice Communications; London, December 22, 1994, p.4.

1096.
C) SYPHILIS
☞ Bad Blood: The Tuskegee Syphilis Experiment, James H. Jones, New York, The Free Press; 1982.
Additional Information:
☞ The Voice, The Voice Group Limited; May 26, 1997, p.11.
☞ The Isis Papers, Dr. Frances Cress Welsing, Third World Press; Chicago, 1991.
☞ The Voice, The Voice Group Ltd.; London, January 24, 1995, pp.18-20.

1097.
B) NEGRITUDE
☞ On African Socialism, Leopold Senghor, Praeger; New York, 1964.
Additional Information:
Cambridge Encyclopedia, David Crystal, Cambridge University Press; 1990, p.1089.
☞ African Political Facts Since 1945, Cook & Killingray, Macmillan Press Ltd.; 1983, p.151.

☞ The Essential Black Literature Guide, Published in association with the Schomburg Center for Research in Black Culture, Roger M. Valade II, Visible Ink Press; USA, 1996, p.330.

1098.
C) 1975
☞ Amilcar Cabral: Revolutionary Leadership and People's War, Patrick Chabal, Cambridge University Press; 1983.
Additional Information:
☞ Macdonalds Encyclopedia of Africa, Macdonald Educational Ltd.; UK, 1986, p.202.
☞ The Africans, David Lamb, New York, Vintage Books; New York, 1983.
☞ Africa, Phyllis Martin and Patrick O'Meara, Indiana University Press; Bloomington, 1986.

1099.
C) MALCOLM X
☞ The Assassination of Malcolm X, George Breitman, Herman Porter and Baxter Smith, Pathfinder Books; NY, London, Montreal, Sydney, 1991.
Additional Information:
☞ The Autobiography of Malcolm X, Alex Haley, Grove, NY, 1965.
☞ A Pictorial History of Black America. Langston Hughes, Crown; NY, 1983.
☞ Death and Life of Malcom X, Peter Louis Goldman, University of Illinois Press; 1979.

1100.
B) ALABAMA
☞ Negro: An Anthology. Nancy Cunard, Frederick Ungar Publishing Co.; NY, 1970, pp.155-74.
Additional Information:
☞ The Essential Black Literature Guide, Published in association with the Schomburg Center for Research in Black Culture, Roger M. Valade II, Visible Ink Press; USA, 1996, p.249.
☞ Encyclopedia of Black America, W. A. Low and Virgil A. Clift, (eds.), Mcgraw-Hill; New York, 1981.
☞ Sex and Race, Volume 2, J. A. Rogers, 7th Edition, H. M. Rogers Publishers; USA, 1980, p.269.

1101.
B) NIGERIA
☞ My Odyssey: An Autobiography, Nnamdi Azikiwe, 1970.
Additional Information:
☞ African Political Facts Since 1945, Cook & Killingray, Macmillan Press Ltd.; 1983.
☞ Macdonalds Encyclopedia of Africa, Macdonald Educational Ltd.; UK, 1986.
☞ The Black Press in Britain, Ionie Benjamin, Trentham Books; London, 1995, p.85.

1102.
A) REVEREND
☞ Decolonisation in Africa, J. D. Hargreaves, Longman; UK, 1988, p.206.
Additional Information:
☞ Africa for the Africans, Edward W. Crosby and Linus A. Hoskins, Institute for African American Affairs, Kent, OH, 1991.
☞ The Cambridge Encyclopedia of Africa, Cambridge University Press; 1981.
☞ Africa, Phyllis Martin and Patrick O'Meara, Indiana University Press; Bloomington, 1986.

1103.
A) ST. PAUL'S CATHEDRAL
☞ Coretta Scott King: Keeper of the Dream. Sondra Henry and Emily Taitz, Enslow Pubs., 1992.
Additional Information:
☞ The Voice, The Voice Group Ltd.; June 29, 1993, p.9.
☞ Black Firsts: 2000 Years of Extraordinary Achievement. Jessie Carney Smith, Caspar L. Jordan and Robert L. Johns, Visible Ink Press; USA, 1994, p.319.
☞ Coretta Scott King, Diane Patrick, Watts, 1991.

1104.
A) ENGLAND
☞ Bob Marley: An Intimate Portrait by his Mother. Cedella Booker and Anthony Winkler, UK, 1996.
Additional Information:
☞ Third World Impact. 8th Edition, Edited by Arif Ali, Hansib Publishing; 1988, pp.411-12.
☞ Bob Marley, Conquering Lion of Reggae, Stephen Davis, Plexus; London, 1990.

Millenium Down

Bob Marley: Spirit Dancer, Bruce W. Talamon, W. W. Norton & Co.; 1994.

1105.
B) 1981
The Heart of the Race: Black Women's Lives in Britain. B. Bryan, S. Dudzie, S. Scafe, Virago Press; 1985, pp.201, 239.
Additional Information:
Black Londoners, 1890-1990, Susan Okokon, Sutton; UK, 1997, pp.114-15.
The Black Press in Britain, Ionie Benjamin, Trentham Books; London, 1995, p.69.
The New Nation, Western Hemisphere; London, May 12, 1997, p.2.

1106.
A) JAMAICA
A-Z of Jamaican Heritage, Oliver Senior, Heinemann Educational Books; 2nd Edition, 1988, p.28.
Additional Information:
African and Caribbean Politics: From Kwame Nkruma to the Grenada Revolution, Manning Marable, Verso; London, 1987.
Hutchingson Encyclopedia, 8th Edition, Hutchingson; UK, 1988.
The Book of Jamaica, Russell Banks, HarperCollins; 1996.

1107.
B) MUHAMMAD ALI
King of the World: Muhammad Ali and the Rise of An American Hero, David Remnick, Vintage Books; New York, 1999.
Additional Information:
Muhammad Ali: His Life and Times, Thomas Hauser, Touchstone Books; 1992.
More Than a Hero: Muhammad Ali's Life Lessons Presented Through His Daughter's Eyes, Muhammad Ali and Hana Ali, Pocket Books; 2000.
Ghosts of Manila: The Fateful Blood Feud Between Muhammad Ali and Joe Frazier, Mark Kram, HarperCollins; 2001.

1108.
B) ROBBEN ISLAND
The Long Walk to Freedom: The Autobiography of Nelson Mandela, Back Bay Books, Little, Brown; 1995.

Additional Information:
Nelson Mandela. The Man and the Movement, Mary Benson, W. W. Norton & Co.; New York and London, 1986.
Robben Island, (Mayibuye History & Literature Series, No. 76.), Charlene Smith, BHB International, 1998.
Higher than Hope: Nelson Mandela, Fatimox Meer, Hamish Hamilton Limited; 1989.

1109.
C) MISSISSIPPI
Remembering Medgar Evers...For a New Generation, A Commemoration Developed by the Civil Rights Research and Documentation Project, Afro-American Studies Program, The University of Mississippi, Heritage Publications; 1988.
Additional Information:
Ebony, Johnson Publishing; Chicago, June, 2003, p.84.
Encyclopedia of Black America, W. A. Low and Virgil A. Clift, (eds.), Mcgraw-Hill; New York, 1981.
Ebony, Johnson Publishing; Chicago, September, 2001, p.166.

1110.
A) WOMEN'S ARMY AUXIALIARY CORPS.
Ebony, Johnson Publishing; Chicago, March, 1994, p.130.
Additional Information:
The Heart of the Race: Black Women's Lives in Britain, B. Bryan, S. Dudzie, S. Scafe, Virago Press; 1985, p.129.
The Weekly Journal, Voice Communications; London, May 4, 1995, p.10.
Staying Power, Peter Fryer, Pluto Press; UK, 2nd Edition, 1985.

1111.
B) SIXTY-SEVEN
Chronicle of the Twentieth Century, Jacques Legrand, Longman Books; 1988.
Additional Information:
Steve Biko: Black Consciousness in South Africa, Millard Arnold, Vintage Books; New York, 1979.
Macdonalds Encyclopedia of Africa, Macdonald Educational Ltd.; UK, 1986.

African and Caribbean Politics: From Kwame Nkruma to the Grenada Revolution, Manning Marable, Verso; London, 1983.

1112.
B) IVORY COAST
☞ African Success Story: The Ivory Coast, Marc Bernheim, Harcourt Brace; 1970.
Additional Information:
☞ African Political Facts Since 1945, Cook & Killingray, Macmillan Press Ltd.; 1983, pp.59, 102.
☞ Macdonalds Encyclopedia of Africa, Macdonald Educational Ltd.; 1986, UK, p.200.
☞ The Ivory Coast, John Allan Carpenter, Children's Press; 1977.

1113.
B) TRANSPORT MINISTER
☞ Chronicle of the Twentieth Century, Jacques Legrand, Longman Books; 1988, pp.1237, 1249.
Additional Information:
☞ Diplomatic Baggage: MOSSAD and Nigeria, The Dikko Story. By Kayode Soyinka.
☞ This House Has Fallen: Midnight in Nigeria, Karl Maier, Public Affairs Publ.; 2000.
☞ Time (Europe), September 9, 1985.

1114.
C) CAPETOWN
☞ Tutu: Voice of the Voiceless. Shirley Du Boulay, Hodder & Stoughton; 1988.
Additional Information:
☞ No Future Without Forgiveness, Desmond Mpilo Tutu, Doubleday; 2000.
☞ Chronicle of the Twentieth Century, Jacques Legrand, Longman Books; 1988. p.1273.
☞ The Essential Black Literature Guide, Published in association with the Schomburg Center for Research in Black Culture, Roger M. Valade II, Visible Ink Press; USA, 1996, pp.362-63.

1115.
C) EAST TEMOR
☞ The Guardian, Guardian Newspapers; London, May 20, 2000, p.16

Additional Information:
☞ Time (Pacific), No.51, Time Inc.; December 25, 2000.
☞ The Guardian, Guardian Newspapers; London, September 6, 2001.
☞ Represented Communities: Fiji and World Decolonization, Martha Kaplan and John Dunham Kelly, University of Chicago Press; 2001.

1116.
A) THIRTY FIVE YEARS
☞ Time, Time Inc.; USA, August 21, 1995, pp.18-19.
Additional Information:
☞ Instant Empire: Saddam Hussein's Ambition for Iraq, Simon Henderson, Mercury House; 1991.
☞ Chronicle of the Twentieth Century, Jacques Legrand, Longman Books; 1988.
☞ Out of the Ashes: The Resurrection of Saddam Hussein, Andrew and Patrick Cockburn, HarperPerennial Library; 2000.

1117.
C) 1976
☞ Lessons of Struggle: South African Internal Opposition, 1960-1990, Anthony W. Marx, Oxford University Press; 1992.
Additional Information:
☞ Steve Biko: Black Consciousness in South Africa. Millard Arnold, Vintage Books; New York, 1979.
☞ Nelson and Winnie Mandela, John Vail, Chelsea House Publishers; NY, 1989.
☞ Whirlwind Before the Storm: The Origins and Development of the Uprising in Soweto and the Rest of South Africa from June to December 1976, By Alan Brooks.

1118.
A) 1900
☞ Black Londoners, 1890-1990, Susan Okokon, Sutton; UK, 1997, pp.7, 101, 109.
Additional Information:
☞ Staying Power, Peter Fryer, Pluto Press; UK, 2nd Edition, 1985.
☞ The Black Press in Britain, Ionie Benjamin, Trentham Books; London, 1995, pp.11-12, 17.

☞ History of the Black Presence in London, GLC; London, 1986.

1119.
C) TAMIL TIGERS
☞ States, Nations, Sovereignty: Sri Lanka, India, and the Tamil Eelam Movement, Sumantra Bose, Sage Publications; 1994.
Additional Information:
☞ Chronicle of the Twentieth Century, Jacques Legrand, Longman Books; 1988, p.1221.
☞ The Tamil Tigers: Armed Struggle for Identity, By Dagmar Hellmann-Rajanayagam.
☞ Cambridge Encyclopedia, David Crystal, Cambridge University Press; 1990, p.1184.

1120.
B) YUGOSLAVIA
☞ The Guardian, Education Section, Guardian Newspapers; London, Tuesday July 1, 1997, pp.10-11.
Additional Information:
☞ United Nations Building, Library Archives, NY, New York, 10017, USA.
☞ Enemies: The Clash of Races, Haki R. Madhubuti, Third World Press; Chicago, 1978.
☞ Yuruga: An African-Centered Critique of European Cultural Thought and Behaviour, Marimba Ani, Africa World Press, Inc.; NJ, 1994.

1121.
B) BHOPAL
☞ Shared Vulnerability: The Media and American Perceptions of the Bhopal Disaster, Lee Wilkins, Greenwood Publishing Group; 1987.
Additional Information:
☞ The Guardian, Guardian Newspapers; London, December 7, 1996, p.5.
☞ Advocacy After Bhopal: Environmentalism, Disaster, New Global Orders, Kim Fortun, University of Chicago Press; 2001
☞ The Uncertain Promise of Law: Lessons from Bhopal, Jamie Cassels, University of Toronto Press; 1993.

1122.
A) PORTUGAL
☞ African Political Facts Since 1945, Cook & Killingray, Macmillan Press Ltd.; 1983.

Additional Information:
☞ Macdonalds Encyclopedia of Africa, Macdonald Educational Ltd.; UK, 1986.
☞ African and Caribbean Politics: From Kwame Nkruma to the Grenada Revolution, Manning Marable, Verso; London, 1987.
☞ Africa, Phyllis Martin and Patrick O'Meara, Indiana University Press; Bloomington, 1986.

1123.
B) FBI
☞ Memo to Field Officers, August 23, 1967.
Additional Information:
☞ Memo to Albany Office, March 4, 1968.
☞ J. Edgar Hoover's FBI Wired the Nation, Dempsey J. Travis, Urban Research Press; USA, 2000.
☞ Ebony Pictorial History of Black America: Volume 3. Civil Rights Movement to Black Revolution, Johnson Publishing Company; 1974, pp.171, 98.

1124.
B) LENIN PEACE PRIZE
☞ Sekou Ture's Guinea, L. Adakan, London, 1976.
Additional Information:
☞ Macdonalds Encyclopedia of Africa, Macdonald Educational Ltd.; UK, 1986.
☞ African Political Facts Since 1945, Cook & Killingray, Macmillan Press Ltd.; 1983.
☞ Guinea Bissau: From Liberation Struggle to Independent Statehood, By Carlos Lopes.

1125.
A) GRENADA
☞ Chronicle of the Twentieth Century, Jacques Legrand, Longman Books; 1988, p.1226.
Additional Information:
☞ Forward Forever! Three Years of the Grenadan Revolution, Maurice Bishop, Sydney, Pathfinder Press; 1982.
☞ African and Caribbean Politics: From Kwame Nkruma to the Grenada Revolution, Manning Marable, Verso; London, 1987.
☞ Grenada: Isle of Spice, Norma Sinclair, Macmillan Publishers; London, 1987.

1126.
A) PSYCHIATRIST
☞ The Isis Papers, Dr. Frances Cress Welsing, Third World Press; Chicago, 1991.
Additional Information:
☞ The Nubian Times, Volume 3, Issue 2, USA, February 2001.
☞ Dr. Frances Cress Welsing, M.D., General Enquiries Office: 7603 Georgia Avenue, NW, No. 402, Washington, D.C., 20012.
☞ Village Voice, October 24, 1995.

1127.
C) CHE GUEVERA
☞ Che Guevara: A Revolutionary Life, Jon Lee Anderson, Grove Press; 1998.
Additional Information:
☞ The Cambridge Encyclopedia of Latin America and the Caribbean, Cambridge University Press; 1989, pp.273, 278-79, 304-5, 330.
☞ Guerrilla Warfare: Che Guevara, Ernesto Guevara and Marc Becker, Bison Books Corporation; 1998.
☞ Che: Images of a Revolutionary, Fernando Diego Garcia and Oscar Sola, Pluto Press; 2000.

1128.
C) STEVE BIKO
☞ Steve Biko: Black Consciousness in South Africa. Millard Arnold, Vintage Books; New York, 1979.
Additional Information:
☞ The Testimony of Steve Biko, Edited by Millard Arnold, Panther, Granada Publishing; London, 1979.
☞ New African, IC Publications; London, No. 351, April 1997, pp.40-41.
☞ African Political Facts Since 1945, Cook & Killingray, Macmillan Press Ltd.; 1983, p.235.

1129.
A) NAMIBIA
☞ The Voice, The Voice Group Ltd.; London, December 13, 1994, p.15.
Additional Information:
☞ To Be Born a Nation. The Liberation Struggle for Namibia, Department of Information and Publicity, SWAPO of Namibia, Zed Press; London, 1981.
☞ Namibia, Chris McIntyre, Bradt Publications; 1999.

☞ The Colonising Camara: Photographs in the Making of Namibian History, Wolfram Hartmann, Jeremy Silvester and Patricia Hayes, (eds.), Ohio University Press; 1999.

1130.
B) KOFI ANNAN AND THE UNITED NATIONS
☞ Norwegian Nobel Committee, Drammensveien 19, N/0255, Oslow, Norway.
Additional Information:
☞ The Evening Standard, Associated Newspaper Group; London, October 12, 2001, p.22.
☞ New African, September 2001, ICP Ltd.; London, pp.33.
☞ Kofi Annan: The Peacekeeper, John Tessitore, Franklin Watts Incorporated; USA, 2001.

Index

I

NAME INDEX

H

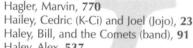

N

O

P

U

V

W

X

Index

SUBJECT INDEX

C

D

Index

Heartbreak Hotel (song), *191*
Hebrews, **833**
Heisman Trophy, **666**
HeLa Cells, **308**
Helen of Troy (Greek classical), **457**
Hello (song), **208**
Heptathlon, **705**
Herero Women, **1029**
Hero's Fountain, **312**
Hiawatha's Wedding Feast (classical composition), **199**
Hibiscus Flower, **341**
Hieroglyphs, **499**
High Jump, **664, 711**
Higher Learning (film), **120**
Hindu Language, **550**
Hip Hop, **6, 79, 222**
Hippopotamus, **363**
Hiroshima Bomb, *1066, 1091*
History and Description of Africa (book), **608**
Hit the Road Jack (song), *94*
Hollywood Shuffle (film), **118**
Holograms, **283**
Hot Hot Hot (song), **197**
Hound Dog (song), *191*
House of Lords (U.K.), **888, 982, 974**
House of Representatives (U.S.), **918**
Houston Rockets, **684**
How Many Ways (song), **142**
Howard University, **593**
Human Insulin, **255**
Human Rights, **1080**
Human rights Commission, *1009*
Hunchback of Notre Dame, the (film), **14**
Husia (religious book), *516*
Hutu (ethnic group), **1043**
Hyksos (Shepherd kings), **797**
Hypotenuse, **247**

I

IBM, **227**
I believe I can fly (song), *124*
I Can See Clearly Now (song), **211**
I Can't Get No Satisfaction (song), *24*
I Can't Stop Loving You (song), *94*
I Feel For You (song), **223**
I Know Why the Cage Bird Sings (autobiography), **555**
I'll Be Missing You (song), **204**
ISA Systems, **227**
I Shot the Sheriff (song), **11**
I Spy (TV), **189**

I Want You Back (song), **3**
I Will Always Love You (song), **154**
I'll Be Missing You (song), **204**
I'm Every Woman (song), **223**
I'm Gonna Get You Sucka (film), **134**
IBM Computers, **301**
Ice Cream, **337**
Iced (novel), *535*
If We Must Die (poem), **510**
Igbo (ethnic group), **531**
Il Trovatore (opera), **57**
Iliad, the (Greek classical), **560**
In Living Color (TV), **140**
In the Ditch (novel), **519**
In Too Deep (film), **135**
Independence Day (film), **143**
Independent Woman (song), **27**
Indomitable Lions (Cameroon's national soccer team), **649**
Induction Railway Telegraph, **326**
Influenza, **317**
Inherit the Wind (song), *578*
Inkatha Freedom Party, **986**
International Amateur Athletics Federation, **681**
International Cricket Council, **708**
International Monetary Fund, **890**
International Red Cross, **317**
International Reparations Group, **1068**
Internet, **226**
Internet Twins (Belinda and Kimberley), **1062**
Invisible Man (novel), **524**
Ipet Isut Library, **601**
Ironing Board, **281**
Ironside (TV), **93**
Ishango Bone, **239**
Islam, **349, 532**
Island, (record label), **224**
Israelites, the (song), **62**
It's Real (song), **23**

J

Jackie Brown (film), **190**
Jah Shaka (sound system), *59*
Jamaica Labour Party, *958*
Jamaica Gleaner, the (newspaper), **580**
Jamestown, (Virginia), **778**
Janjiweed (Arab militia), **1044**
Jazz, **4, 39, 158, 215**
Jazz Soul, **214**
Jerry McGuire (film), **175**
Jesus Christ, the (ship), *339*

N

Picture Sources

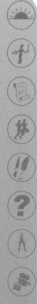

PICTURE SOURCES

I have taken every effort to determine the source of photographic material used in this publication, but where I have been unable to establish the original source, I have stated the source from which it has come. I would like to specially thank again all of those whose pictures are included in this work.

Entertainment

1. **Beethoven** (Sketch from life by Letronne, engraved by Hofel) Courtesy of Paul Bekker's Beethoven, Part 2, p.80, Berlin, 1911

2. **Michael Jackson** Courtesy of The Voice Newspaper : - *Also Front Cover*

3. **Lauryn Hill** (Picture: Colin Patterson) Courtesy of The Voice Newspaper: - *Also Front Cover*

4. **Kirk Franklin** *Courtesy of The Voice Newspaper*

5. **Bob Marley** 'Rebel Music' Courtesy of Island Def Jam Music Group: - *Also Front Cover*

6. **James Brown** (Picture: Colin Patterson) Courtesy of The Voice Newspaper

7. **Angela Bassett** (Unable to determine original source at time of publication) Courtesy of adorocinema.cidadeinternet.com.

8. **Dennis Emmanuel Brown** Courtesy of The Voice Newspaper

9. **Lester Young** (Unable to determine original source at time of publication) Courtesy of Jazz Greats Seminar Flyer, BHM, Willesden Green Library, October 2003: - *Also Front Cover*

10. **Spike Lee** (Picture: Corey Ross) Courtesy of The Voice Newspaper: - *Also Front Cover*

11. **Craig David** (Picture: Colin Patterson) Courtesy of The Voice Newspaper

12. **R. Kelly** (Picture: Colin Patterson) Courtesy of The Voice Newspaper

13. **Will Smith** (Picture: Colin Patterson) Courtesy of The Voice Newspaper

14. **Samantha Mumba** Courtesy of The Voice Newspaper

15. **Omar** Courtesy of Kongo Music: - *Also Front Cover*

16. **Gladys Knight** (Picture: Colin Patterson) Courtesy of The Voice Newspaper

17. **Shaggy** (Picture: Colin Patterson) Courtesy of The Voice Newspaper: - *Also Front Cover*

Science & Engineering

18. **George Carruthers with *Ultra-Violet Spectrograph*** Courtesy of Hattie Carwell

19. **Imhotep** Courtesy of The British Museum: - *Also Front Cover*

20. **Dr. Mae Jemison,** (Unable to determine original source at time of publication) Courtesy of Beverly Hawkins Hall and Sandra Sharp, Black Women for Beginners, Writers & Readers, 1993, p.169.

21. **Ernest Just** Courtesy of Hattie Carwell

22. **Charles Turner** Courtesy of Hattie Carwell

23. **Mary Seacole** Courtesy of Silver Graphic Ink

24. **George Washington** Courtesy of Hattie Carwell: - *Also Front Cover*

25. **Traffic Light** (Picture: GAM Designs) Courtesy of Glynis Minors: - *Also Front Cover*

26. **Granville T. Woods** Courtesy of Hattie Carwell

27. **Meredith Gourdine** Courtesy of Hattie Carwell

28. **Benjamin Banneker** (Picture: GAM Designs) Courtesy of Glynis Minors

General Knowledge

29. **Notting Hill Carnival** (Picture: Kevin Small) Courtesy of The Voice Newspaper

30. **Isis and Horus** Courtesy of The British Museum

31. **Nubian Jak Board Game** Courtesy of Jak Bubeula-Dodd

32. **Iman** (Picture: Colin Patterson) Courtesy of The Voice Newspaper

33. **Madame C. J. Walker** Courtesy of Hattie Carwell

34. **Sean Jean "P Diddy" Combs** (Picture: Ken Passley) Courtesy of The Voice Newspaper

35. **Oprah Winfrey,** (Unable to determine original source at time of publication) Courtesy of The Voice Newspaper "The Richest Most Influential Black People in the World 2001, Part 2"

36. **Kente cloth and Kwanzaa celebration** Courtesy of The Voice Newspaper

Literature & Art

37. **Hieroglyphs** Courtesy of the reading room in The British Museum

38. **The Rosetta Stone** Courtesy of The British Museum

39. **Terry McMillan** Courtesy of The Voice Newspaper

40. **Alexander Pushkin** Courtesy of the Revue de Moscou, January 1, 1937

41. **Toni Morrison** (Picture: Sharon Wallace) Courtesy of The Voice Newspaper

42. **Buchi Emecheta** Courtesy of The Voice Newspaper

43. **Benin Art** Courtesy of The Black Cultural Archives

44. **Maya Angelou,** Courtesy of Kinlock Communications Ltd

45. **Derek Walcott** Courtesy of The Voice Newspaper

46. **Venus of Willendorf** Courtesy of the Museum of Natural History, Vienna, Department of Prehistory: - *Also Front Cover*

47. **Henry Louis Gates, Jr.** (Picture: Corey Ross) Courtesy of The Voice Newspaper

Sport

48. **Jerry Rice** (Unable to determine original source at time of publication) Courtesy of The Voice Newspaper

49. **Tiger Woods,** (Picture: Colin Patterson) Courtesy of The Voice Newspaper: - *Also Front Cover*

50. **Venus and Serena Williams** Courtesy of The Voice Newspaper: - *Also Front Cover*

51. **Hank Aaron,** (Unable to determine original source at time of publication) Black Firsts: 2000 Years of Extraordinary Achievement. Jessie Carney Smith, Caspar L. Jordan and Robert L. Johns, Visible Ink Press, USA, 1994, p.372.

52. **Brian Lara,** (Picture: Ken Passley) Courtesy of The Voice Newspaper: - *Also Front Cover*

53. **Mike Tyson** Courtesy of The Voice Newspaper

54. **Marion Jones** Courtesy of The Voice Newspaper

55. **Don King and Howard Eastman** (Picture: Ken Passley) Courtesy of The Voice Newspaper

56. **Frazier, Foreman and Ali** (Picture: Sharon Wallace) Courtesy of The Voice Newspaper: - *Ali Also Front Cover*

57. **Linford Christie** Courtesy of The Voice Newspaper

58. **Debi Thomas** (Unable to determine original source at time of publication) Black Firsts: 2000 Years of Extraordinary Achievement. Jessie Carney Smith, Caspar L. Jordan and Robert L. Johns, Visible Ink Press, USA, 1994, p.395.

59. **Micheal Jordan** (Unable to determine original source at time of publication) Courtesy of The Voice Newspaper "The Richest Most Influential Black People in the World 2001, Part 2"

History

60. **The Sphinx** Courtesy of Joseph Jules

61. **Zulu King Shaka** (Picture: GAM Designs) Courtesy of Glynis Minors: - *Also Front Cover*

62. **Sojourner Truth,** (Unable to determine original source at time of publication) Courtesy of Beverly Hawkins Hall and Sandra Sharp, Black Women for Beginners, Writers & Readers, 1993, p.165.

63. **Harriet Tubman** Courtesy of http://www.lysistrataproject.org/assets/harriet _tubman.jpg: - *Also Front Cover*

64. **Olmec Stone Head** (Unable to determine original source at time of publication)

65. **Gizah Pyramid** Courtesy of Joseph Jules

67. **Queen Hatshepsut** Courtesy of the reading room in The British Museum

68. **Queen Nefertiti** Courtesy of the reading room in The British Museum:- Also Front Cover

69. **Transatlantic Slave ship** Courtesy of the Black Cultural Archives

70. **Toussaint L'Overture** (Picture: GAM Designs) Courtesy of Glynis Minors

71. **Queen Makeda of Sheba** (Picture: GAM Designs) Courtesy of Glynis Minors

72. **Hannibal of Carthage.** Painting by Qiana Minors-Dodd age 13 years

73. **Queen Charlotte of England** Courtesy of Queen Charlotte Hospital: - *Also Front Cover*

Politics & Law

74. **Reverend Jesse Jackson and Baroness Patricia Scotland** Courtesy of Kinlock Communications Ltd

75. **Olaudah Equiano** Courtesy of Black Cultural Archives: - *Also Front Cover*

76. **Kofi Annan** (Unable to determine original source at time of publication) Courtesy of The Voice Newspaper

77. **Johnnie Cochrane** (Picture: C. Max) Courtesy of The Voice Newspaper

78. **Mary Eugenia Charles** (Picture: Colin Patterson) Courtesy of The Voice Newspaper

79. **Condoleezza Rice,** (Unable to determine original source at time of publication) Courtesy of The Voice Newspaper "The Richest Most Influential Black People in the World 2001, Part 2"

80. **Neville and Doreen Lawrence at the Stephen Lawrence enquiry** (Picture: Colin Patterson) Courtesy of The Voice Newspaper

81. **Colin Powell** (Unable to determine original source at time of publication) Courtesy of The Voice Newspaper "The Richest Most Influential Black People in the World 2001, Part 2": - *Also Front Cover*

82. **Specioze Wandira Kazibwe** Courtesy of The Ugandan High Commission (UK)

83. **P. J. Patterson** (Unable to determine original source at time of publication) Courtesy of The Gleaner (UK)

84. **Bernie Grant, Oona King and Diane Abbott**
(Picture: Colin Patterson) Courtesy of The
Voice Newspaper

85. **Carol Mosely Braun** (Unable to determine
original source at time of publication) Black
Firsts: 2000 Years of Extraordinary
Achievement. Jessie Carney Smith, Caspar L.
Jordan and Robert L. Johns, Visible Ink Press,
USA, 1994, p.185

86. **Lord David Pitt of Hamstead** Courtesy of The
Voice Newspaper

Millennium Dawn

87. **Marcus Garvey** Courtesy of Karia Press

88. **Winnie Mandela** (Unable to determine
original source at time of publication) Courtesy
of The Voice Newspaper

89. **El Hajj Malik El-Shabazz (Malcolm X)**
(Unable to determine original source at time of
publication) Courtesy of The Voice
Newspaper: - *Also Front Cover*

90. **Nelson Mandela** (Unable to determine
original source at time of publication) Courtesy
of The Voice Newspaper: - *Also Front Cover*

91. **Kwame Nkrumah** Courtesy of Information
services, Photo Library, PO Box 745, Accra,
Ghana

92. **Haile Selassie I** Courtesy of
www.library.okstate.edu/about/awards/winners/
selassie.htm

93. **Martin Luther King** (Picture: Dan Weiner)
Courtesy of Sandra Weiner for The Voice
Newspaper

Other front cover photo's not included in book

Halle Berry (Unable to determine original source
at time of publication) Courtesy of www.halle-
berry-pictures.com/
Kelly Holmes Courtesy of Reuters News Agency
Martin Luther King (Unable to determine original
source at time of publication) Courtesy of The
Metro, 6 September, 2004, p.13.